APPROACHES TO MARVELL

THE YORK TERCENTENARY LECTURES

APPROACHES TO MARVELL

THE YORK TERCENTENARY LECTURES

by

Philip Brockbank · John Carey · Robert Ellrodt
Donald M. Friedman · S. K. Heninger, Jr · Christopher Hill
John Dixon Hunt · Barbara Kiefer Lewalski · Louis L. Martz
C. A. Patrides · Balachandra Rajan · Christopher Ricks
A. J. Smith · Frank J. Warnke · Joseph Anthony Wittreich, Jr

edited by

C. A. PATRIDES

ROUTLEDGE & KEGAN PAUL

LONDON, HENLEY AND BOSTON

First published in 1978
by Routledge & Kegan Paul Ltd
39 Store Street, London WC1E 7DD,
Broadway House, Newtown Road,
Henley-on-Thames, Oxon RG9 1EN and
9 Park Street, Boston, Mass. 02108, USA
and printed in Great Britain by
Lowe & Brydone Printers Ltd
Thetford, Norfolk
Plates printed by
Headley Brothers Ltd, Ashford, Kent

British Library Cataloguing in Publication Data

Approaches to Marvell.

1. Marvell, Andrew – Criticism and interpretation
I. Patrides, Constantinos A
821'.4 PR3546 78–40727

ISBN 0 7100 8818 3

To
the students
of the University of York

Contents

Illustrations

(between pages 334 and 335)

The Contributors

PHILIP BROCKBANK, Professor of English and Related Literature, University of York

JOHN CAREY, Merton Professor of English Literature, University of Oxford

ROBERT ELLRODT, Professor of English, University of the Sorbonne Nouvelle

DONALD M. FRIEDMAN, Professor of English, University of California at Berkeley

S. K. HENINGER, Jr, Professor of English, University of British Columbia

CHRISTOPHER HILL, Master of Balliol College, Oxford

JOHN DIXON HUNT, Reader in English, Bedford College, London

BARBARA KIEFER LEWALSKI, Alumni-Alumnae University Professor of English, Brown University

LOUIS L. MARTZ, Sterling Professor of English, Yale University

C. A. PATRIDES, Professor of English and Related Literature, University of York

BALACHANDRA RAJAN, Senior Professor of English, University of Western Ontario

CHRISTOPHER RICKS, Professor of English, University of Cambridge

A. J. SMITH, Professor of English, University of Southampton

FRANK J. WARNKE, Professor of English, Queens College, and Professor of Comparative Literature and Germanics, The Graduate Center, in the City University of New York

JOSEPH ANTHONY WITTREICH, Jr, Professor of English, University of Maryland

Preface

Let Marvel, house of Marvel rejoice . . .
Christopher Smart

The lectures published here were delivered at the University of York in 1977 and 1978 to mark the occasion of the 300th anniversary of the death of Andrew Marvell in 1678.

With two exceptions – the lecture by Dr Hill and the special contribution by Dr Hunt – all the lectures are published in the order in which they were delivered. The general pattern is not unlike that of our series on Milton.[1] Now, as before, the order of the lectures was not premeditated, and neither was the nature of the series. Our lecturers were simply invited to speak on Marvell, their particular approach subject only to their interests.

Dr Hill's lecture, delivered second in the series, is here published first in recognition of its particular argument. Dr Hunt's special contribution, not delivered as a lecture but commissioned expressly for this collection, is published last, in line with the parallel endeavour by Mr J. B. Trapp on the iconography of the Fall in the former series.

The celebration of Marvell at York differs from the previous occasion on Milton in that he may be claimed to be Yorkshire's foremost poet. Born at Winestead in Holderness nearly fifty miles from York, Marvell remained throughout his career fully committed to Yorkshire, not least as Member of Parliament for Kingston upon Hull from 1659 until his death. His second longest poem was composed not far from York, at Nun Appleton, where he resided for some two years.

Two of the lectures were, *honoris causa,* delivered at Appleton

House, where we enjoyed the warm hospitality of its present owner, Miss Joan Dawson.

My own contribution was first delivered as my Inaugural Lecture at York.

Acknowledgment is gratefully made to the following publishers who have given permission to quote the poems discussed by Professor Ricks (below, pp. 124 ff.): Faber and Faber Ltd for the poems of Messrs Seamus Heaney, Ted Hughes, and Paul Muldoon; Victor Gollancz Ltd for the poems by Mr Michael Longley; Harper & Row Inc. for the poem by Mr Ted Hughes (copyright 1971 by Ted Hughes); Longman Group Ltd for the poem by Mr Harold Massingham; Oxford University Press in New York for the poems by Mr Seamus Heaney; Oxford University Press in Oxford for the poems by Mr Derek Mahon; and Wesleyan University Press for the poem 'The Soldier' by Mr David Ferry, quoted in its entirety (copyright 1957 by David Ferry).

Acknowledgment is also gratefully made to the institutions which have given permission to reproduce the illustrations whose sources are as follows. For the emblem on p. 97: the Henry E. Huntington Library; for the plates relating to chapter 9: the Galleria Borghese in Rome (no. 9.1, photo: The Mansell Collection), Santa Felicità in Florence (no. 9.2, photo: The Mansell Collection), the Trustees of the National Gallery in London (nos 9.3, 9.4, 9.5, 9.7, 9.8), and the Uffizi Gallery in Florence (no. 9.6, photo: The Mansell Collection); and for the plates relating to chapter 15: the Bodleian Library (no. 15.1), the Royal Institute of British Architects (no. 15.3, photo: Freeman), the Trustees of the Chatsworth Settlement (no. 15.4, photo: The Courtauld Institute), the Trustees of the British Library (nos 15.2, 15.5, 15.6, 15.19, 15.22), the Warburg Institute (no. 15.7), the Biblioteca Hertziana in Rome (nos 15.8, 15.9, 15.12, 15.23, 15.24), the National Gallery in Prague (no. 15.10), the Collection of Sir Harold Acton (no. 15.11, photo: German Institute, Florence), the Louvre (no. 15.17), the Museo Storico in Florence (no. 15.18, photo: Gabinetto Fotografico, Uffizi), the Albertina in Vienna (no. 15.20), the National Portrait Gallery in London (no. 15.21), and the Walters Art Gallery in Baltimore (no. 15.25).

Unless otherwise indicated quotations from Marvell's poetry

and prose are from *The Poems and Letters of Andrew Marvell*, edited by H. M. Margoliouth and revised by Pierre Legouis and E. E. Duncan-Jones, and *The Rehearsal Transpros'd*, edited by D. I. B. Smith, alike published by Oxford University Press in 1971.

The King's Manor
York *C.A.P.*

Note

1 *Approaches to 'Paradise Lost': The York Tercentenary Lectures*, ed. C. A. Patrides, London, Edward Arnold, and Toronto, University of Toronto Press, 1968.

I

Milton and Marvell

Christopher Hill

Fifty years ago I sat at school in York working for School Certificate, the then equivalent of O-levels. My English literature texts included the poems by Milton, Marvell and Dryden in *The Golden Treasury*. Those who drafted the School Certificate syllabus had good precedent for linking Milton, Marvell and Dryden. On 7 September 1658 the three of them walked, as employees of the Protectorate, in the procession at Oliver Cromwell's funeral.[1] Dryden soon abandoned the convictions – or interests – which led him, like Marvell, to write celebratory poems to Cromwell: but Milton and Marvell remained true to the beliefs which had united them in the 1650s and which, I shall argue, continued to unite them until Milton's death in 1674.

At first sight Marvell and Milton seem far apart – the metaphysical, lightly-elegant wit, and the organ-voiced inspired bard. On closer examination we find greater similarities of theme and treatment. Marvell was more serious than some of the books suggest; Milton – thank God! – a great deal less serious than the image. In their political outlook, in their dislikes, they had much in common.

I hope I need not apologize for dealing with Milton and Marvell mainly as political figures. Others in this series of lectures will deal with Marvell as poet; such expertise as I have is not literary. Politics was an essential part of the experience of both poets. Throughout the eighteenth century Marvell was renowned primarily as a courageous partisan of liberty, though his poems were never as neglected as we used to think. Milton's politics as well as his poetry inspired

Thompson, Blake, Wordsworth, Shelley, the Chartists and countless others. I have no sympathy for the gentlemanly aestheticism which mars even so good a book as Leishman's *The Art of Marvell's Poetry*. Leishman contrasts writing for cultivated gentlemen with Marvell's 'rather philistine and ill-informed . . . post-restoration activities', devoting 'a disproportionate attention to matters which wisdom would dismiss with, at the most, a weary smile'.[2] Such a view suggests a lack of imagination horrifying in one who sets up to be a critic of poetry. If it is impossible for this sort of critic to conceive the cultural consequences of living under a tyranny, there are many parts of the world today to which he could turn for education. Marvell's activities which Leishman's 'wisdom would dismiss with a weary smile' included keeping Milton alive and free to write *Paradise Lost*, *Paradise Regained* and *Samson Agonistes*, as well as trying to shield dissenters from persecution and his country from becoming a French puppet state.

I sympathize much more with those critics who see even Marvell's apparently unpolitical verse as shot through with consciousness of living at a great historical turning-point – such as informs 'An Horatian Ode' and 'The First Anniversary of the Government under O. C.': even 'To his Coy Mistress' is full of witty allusions to political and religious happenings of Marvell's day which are missed by many critics.[3] The conversion of the Jews, for instance, was a subject of current controversy in the 1640s and 1650s. It was agreed to be a necessary antecedent of the overthrow of Antichrist, the Pope. One favoured date for this event, based on the careful calculations of the best mathematicians of the time, was 1656. Since Noah's Flood took place in the year 1656 from the Creation, the next cataclysmic event might be expected in AD 1656. So in

I would
Love you ten years before the Flood:
And you should if you please refuse
Till the Conversion of the *Jews*
(ll. 7–10)

the two periods follow logically from one another. If the lady continues to refuse 'Till the Conversion of the *Jews*' she may find that the time is shorter than she thinks.[4]

There remains the interesting problem of why all Marvell's best poetry seems to date from the early 1650s, as though it relates to the tensions of his politically undecided period, and could not be recovered once Marvell was politically committed. But there may be optical illusions here, since few of Marvell's poems can be confidently dated. I shall quote from time to time from pieces doubtfully attributed to Marvell, like 'Britannia and Rawleigh' and the 'Dialogue between the Two Horses'. I do not wish to argue for their authenticity; but since some contemporaries believed them to be by Marvell it is reasonable to suppose that they express views not very dissimilar to his.[5]

We do not know when Milton and Marvell first became acquainted. The record starts in February 1653 with a letter from Milton to John Bradshaw, president of the court which had condemned Charles I in 1649, and in 1653 President of the Council of State. Milton (aged 45) had recently gone completely blind, which clearly hampered his efficiency as the republic's Secretary for Foreign Tongues. In this letter Milton pushed the 32-year-old Marvell as a possible assistant to him, and praised him in generous terms as 'a man whom both by report and the converse I have had with him is of singular desert for the state to make use of; who also offers himself, if there be any employment for him'. ('The forward youth that would appear / Must now forsake his Muses dear / Nor in the shadows sing / His numbers languishing'.) Milton referred to Marvell's father, lately the Puritan minister of Hull – one of those who had swung Hull to support Parliament in the Civil War, Bishop Hacket thought.[6] Milton also referred in 1653 to the fact that Marvell had spent four years abroad in Holland, France, Italy and Spain, 'to very good purpose as I believe, and the gaining of those four languages; besides he is a scholar and well-read in Latin and Greek authors'. As an added recommendation Milton reminded Bradshaw that Marvell 'comes now lately out of the house of the Lord Fairfax who was General', where he was language tutor to Mary Fairfax. Marvell's French was good enough for him to act as interpreter at French-speaking courts when he was secretary to the embassy of the Earl of Carlisle in 1663–4, as well as translate speeches into Latin. Like Milton, Marvell wrote Latin poems.[7] 'It would be hard to find a man so fit every way', Milton concluded in 1653, hinting that Marvell had the makings of a man who might rise to ambassadorial rank.[8]

This letter gives us some information about Marvell's early career which we should not otherwise have; and it poses some interesting problems. Why should Milton push this young man so hard? He was not prima facie Milton's type. Marvell as a Cambridge undergraduate had had a brief connection with the Jesuits, though it did not lead to lasting conversion as in the case of that other son of a Yorkshire Puritan minister, Richard Crashaw. The fact that Marvell was sent down from Trinity may charitably be attributed to nonresidence following the death of his father when Marvell was 19: Milton we recall had himself been rusticated. Marvell's four years abroad had been between 1642 and 1646: so he appears to have opted out of the Civil War which had meant so much to Milton. Marvell's connections in the 1640s seem to have been royal rather than parliamentarian. Biographers have perhaps made too much of Marvell's alleged royalism: the only poem which Margoliouth calls 'unequivocally royalist' is, he agrees, of doubtful attribution. Marvell's poem to Lovelace no more commits him to Lovelace's royalist politics than Milton's help to the imprisoned Davenant in 1652 (if he did help him) committed Milton to Davenant's.[9]

The opening stanza of the 'Horatian Ode', although of course ironical, suggests an uncommitted person consciously moving towards commitment, rather than a change of allegiance.[10] The poem distinguishes between Charles I's personal virtues and the historic force which Oliver Cromwell personifies. I find it difficult to believe that 'Tom May's Death', with its sneers at May as a turncoat from courtier to propagandist for Parliament, was written when May died only a few months after the 'Horatian Ode' was composed. There are in fact many echoes of May in the Ode.[11] It seems to me more likely that at any rate the final version of the poem on May was written after the Restoration; lines 85–90 appear to refer to the exhumation of May's body from Westminster Abbey in September 1661. It may well be that Marvell had some personal grudge against May, who like Marvell seems to have had connections both with Hull and with Fairfax;[12] but a post-Restoration date makes it a less unpleasant poem than if it was written immediately after May's death in November 1650, and opens up the possibility of all sorts of ironical overtones. Post-1660 turncoats included ex-parliamentarians whose enthusiastic new-found royalism could not be openly attacked. ('Coward churchmen', for instance.)

In 1653 or early 1654 Mrs Anne Sadleir told Roger Williams that Marvell had helped Milton in writing *Eikonoklastes*, his demolition of *Eikon Basilike*. *Eikonoklastes* was published in October 1649, so if Mrs Sadleir was right, Marvell must have got to know Milton not later than the summer of 1649. French and Parker assumed that she was mistaken, and that if Marvell did help Milton with anything it should be the *Defensio* (February 1651) or John Phillips's *Responsio* of December 1651. But it is always rash to be wiser than a contemporary; Mrs Sadleir was the aunt of Cyriack Skinner, the mutual friend of Milton and Marvell; Marvell's father dedicated a sermon to her; and her reference to 'that most accursed libel' sounds more like *Eikonoklastes* than either of the other two tracts.[13] Mrs Sadleir's remark that Milton 'had two or three wives living' when he wrote his divorce tracts is inaccurate; but it may well be a distortion of correct information. Milton believed polygamy to be lawful, and during his first wife's absence he had a 'design of marrying one of Dr Davis's daughters'. He was 'in treaty' for this marriage when his wife returned, we are told by the anonymous biographer whom Parker believed to be Cyriack Skinner.[14]

There are other possible links between the two poets. Marvell was born fifteen miles outside Hull, and all his life he was associated with the town of which his father had been minister; in 1658 and from 1659 to his death he was its MP. Cyriack Skinner, Milton's pupil in the mid-1640s and his very special friend, came from Barrow-on-Humber. Marvell mentioned him in a letter to Milton of 2 June 1654.[15] The Skinners were close friends of the Marvell family. Andrew's father had been drowned in 1640 whilst crossing the Humber with 'Madam Skinner', probably Cyriack's sister.[16] Margoliouth plausibly suggested that Marvell's poem 'The Picture of little T.C. in a Prospect of Flowers' was written about Theophila Cornewall, Cyriack's niece. Margoliouth indeed supposed that Marvell's foreign travels might have been undertaken as tutor to Edward Skinner, Cyriack's brother, and conjectured that Cyriack introduced Marvell to Milton.[17] Aubrey, in listing Milton's 'familiar learned acquaintance', named Andrew Marvell first and Skinner second. Wood called Marvell 'some time one of John Milton's companions'.[18]

Now from 1648 to 1655, and again in 1659–60, the governor of Hull was Robert Overton, himself born at Easington in Holderness, just outside Hull. Milton in 1654 referred to Overton as an intimate friend over many years, and Marvell in a letter to Milton of the same year spoke with 'an affectionate curiosity' about 'Colonel Overton's business', his arrest for republican activities.[19] Overton's chaplain at Hull in the 1650s was John Canne, who must have been known to Milton since they were both propagandists for the republic and Canne often echoes Milton in his writings. Skinner, Overton or Canne might have introduced Marvell to Milton.

Another possible link is Fairfax, in whose household Marvell lived, probably from the beginning of 1651 until just before Milton's letter to Bradshaw of February 1653. Milton wrote a sonnet to Fairfax in 1648, must have known him as a member of the Council of State until Fairfax retired in 1650, and still praised him warmly in 1654.[20] This still leaves the problem of how Marvell came to be employed by Fairfax. Apart from the possibility that Milton had a hand in it, there were traditional links between the West Riding and Hull, which had been strengthened during the Civil War when these were the two main parliamentarian areas in Yorkshire. Fairfax was often in Hull.

Milton failed to get Marvell a job in the government service in 1653; instead the younger poet went to Eton as tutor to Cromwell's ward, William Dutton, no doubt on Milton's recommendation. At Eton Marvell lived in the house of John Oxenbridge. Milton knew Oxenbridge well enough to send him a copy of the *Defensio Secunda* in 1654.[21] Oxenbridge is believed to have been the source of Marvell's knowledge of Bermuda, whither Oxenbridge had fled as a religious refugee under Laud. It would be nice to know more of Oxenbridge's influence on Marvell. The sour Antony Wood described him as 'a person noted to be of no good principles'. In 1634 he was deprived of his tutorship by Laud, Chancellor of Oxford University. Oxenbridge's offence was organizing student participation in moves to democratize the government of Magdalen Hall. He sought refuge in Bermuda, 'safe from the storms and prelates' rage', as Marvell put it, 'an isle far kinder than our own'. In 1641 or 1642, he returned, when 'liberty of conscience had returned'. I quote from Marvell's epitaph on Jane Oxenbridge. Oxenbridge preached 'very enthusiastically', apparently for some years as an itinerant. After the Battle of Marston Moor he settled at Beverley, very near Hull, where he remained until the early 1650s. His second wife was the daughter of Hezekiah Woodward, whose name was often associated with Milton's in the 1640s. In 1660 Oxenbridge emigrated again, this time to Surinam, then to Barbados, ending up in Boston, New England. At Magdalen Hall, Oxenbridge had been tutor to John Bidle, the main exponent of anti-Trinitarianism in England in the 1640s and 1650s. Milton was an anti-Trinitarian: Marvell was accused of the same heresy. If he held it, he was as careful as Milton was never to proclaim it publicly; like Milton, Marvell defended Arians.[22]

Masson suggested, plausibly enough, that the Latin poems which Marvell wrote in 1653–4 may have been intended to keep himself and his literary skills before the eyes of officialdom. The first was 'A Letter to Doctor Ingelo', a Fellow of Eton who had accompanied Bulstrode Whitelocke as chaplain on his embassy to Sweden. This is in effect 'a political poem celebrating the Protector's alliance with Sweden'; it was followed by two epigrams on Cromwell's portrait given to Queen Christina.[23] The eulogy on Christina in 'A Letter to Doctor Ingelo' recalls Milton's extravagant praise of her in his *Second Defence* of 1654.

Not later than January 1656 Marvell took William Dutton to France. He may have circulated Milton's *Pro Se Defensio* at Saumur.[24] In September 1657 Marvell at last became Latin Secretary to the Commonwealth – through Milton's influence, Samuel Parker alleged.[25] We catch glimpses of Marvell in August 1658 trailing ambassadors around.[26] In July 1659, under the restored Rump of the Long Parliament, he occupied lodgings in Whitehall.[27] We recall that Milton had lost his lodgings there in 1651. If, as would appear, Marvell was promoted by the restored Rump, this throws a light on his political attitudes which deserves emphasis. The deposition of Protector Richard Cromwell and the restoration of the republic were moves to the left, short-lived though they proved to be. Colonel Overton returned from jail to political influence; Marvell's conservative superior John Thurloe disappeared from the scene. The radical John Canne for a short time replaced Marchamont Nedham as editor of *Mercurius Politicus*. Milton, who had gradually withdrawn from political activity with the growing conservatism of the Protectorate, returned hopefully to the fray in 1659 with a series of pamphlets in which he tried (vainly) to reunite the radicals in face of the return to monarchy which above all things he abhorred. If

Marvell was promoted by the Rump, it looks as though they thought he too supported them. Early in 1653 (almost certainly) Marvell had in 'The Character of Holland' lauded the English Commonwealth as the 'darling of heaven, and of men the care'.[28]

This is important evidence for our assessment of Marvell's attitude towards Oliver Cromwell. Some biographers, including Professor Wallace, have seen 'The First Anniversary' as a plea for Cromwell to accept the crown. Others, like Professors Zwicker and Patterson in this century, and Marvell's opponent Bishop Samuel Parker in the seventeenth century, saw it as an *attack* on kingship, and a warning to Oliver not to accept the crown, similar to those which Milton uttered in the *Second Defence*.[29] Although I cannot argue the case here, the latter view seems to me correct: re-read lines 15–16, 22–4, 103–30, 249–58, 387–94 (and Margoliouth's note on line 106) with an open mind, a nodding acquaintance with the Bible, and an awareness of the historical situation. Marvell promised kings that, if he was given time, he would 'with graver accents shake / Your royal sloth, and your long slumbers wake'. For Marvell, as for Milton in the first *Defence*, and again in *Samson Agonistes*, 'matchless Gideon' was an example of a great leader who refused the crown.[30] In 1659 Marvell was associated with James Harrington's republican Rota Club, whose president was Cyriack Skinner. There are many traces of Harringtonian ideas in Marvell's writings, some of them dating from before Harrington published.[31]

Yet Marvell never committed himself publicly to hostility to the Stuarts with the venom that Milton had shown in *Eikonoklastes* and the *Ready and Easy Way*. In consequence he was in a position to help Milton at the Restoration, when by some miracle, still not fully explained, the latter was saved from the hanging, disembowelling and quartering which befell so many of his friends and associates. Sir William Davenant and the Boyles no doubt helped; but Marvell had Fairfax's ear, and Fairfax was an important man in 1660. Not only was Milton saved from execution, he was released from prison and received an official pardon. Marvell even had the audacity to raise in the House of Commons (December 1660) the fact that Milton had been charged excessive fees by his jailer. Marvell's motion was seconded by Colonel Edward King, whose wife was the daughter of Bridget Skinner, Cyriack's niece.[32]

After 1660 Milton was silenced. A marked man, it was for long impossible for him to publish. He turned from pamphleteering to perfecting his radically heretical theological treatise, the *De Doctrina Christiana*, and to those intensely political poems *Paradise Lost, Paradise Regained* and *Samson Agonistes*. Not until 1673 was there enough of a political thaw for him to risk pamphleteering again, and then he returned to battle with a series of tracts which I shall discuss later.

We know little about the political activities of either Milton or Marvell in the 1660s. Milton lay very low. Some young men, including Samuel Parker, 'haunted his house day by day', taking part in seditious discussions. Marvell first met Parker there; the latter was then discussing how long the restored monarchy would last.[33] We have traces of Marvell's activities in the House of Commons in 1667 in Milward's *Diary*. He defended the old parliamentarian civil servant Phineas Pett against attempts to make him the scapegoat for the disasters of the second Dutch war.[34] He even came to the rescue of Clarendon when MPs tried to saddle him with responsibility for the war (which in fact he had opposed), though Marvell did not miss the opportunity to stress Clarendon's alleged remark that 'the King was an unactive person and indisposed for government'. In 1668, though in a minority, Marvell spoke up courageously against the Conventicles Act.[35] He accused the government of truckling to France, and was 'most sharp' against Arlington and some of the Council. He is alleged to have said that the Duke of Lauderdale deserved a halter rather than a garter. Defoe tells us that Marvell invented the nickname 'Cabal' to describe the government of Clifford, Arlington, Buckingham, Ashley-Cooper and Lauderdale, which has stuck.[36]

The famous republican conspirator, Colonel Blood the crown-stealer, in 1670 mentioned Marvell as one of his associates.[37] Marvell described Blood admiringly as 'a most bold and yet sober fellow', who 'astonished the King and the court with the generosity and wisdom of his answers'.[38] Professor Haley has produced evidence to suggest that Marvell shared in the clandestine plotting organized by Peter du Moulin in the 1670s, in contact with the Dutch government. In 1662–3 Marvell had been in the Netherlands for nearly a year on unidentified 'business'. He was reported there again early in 1674, at a time when there is a gap in his correspondence. These visits may have been entirely innocent; but the Netherlands was the natural refuge of English republican exiles, and Marvell was a close friend of at least one Dutch agent. A list of conspirators' code names in 1674 includes Marvell's, and he was denounced more than once to the authorities by informers.[39] Marvell may have been writing pamphlets for this group, and perhaps helping with others; the ironical style of its most significant tract, du Moulin's *England's Appeal* (1673), seems to me strongly reminiscent of Marvell.[40] Marvell's own major pamphlet, *An Account of the Growth of Popery and Arbitrary Government in England* (1677), is an elaboration of *England's Appeal*.

Professor Haley was interested mainly in the connection with the Dutch republic, the natural ally of the English opposition. But for our purposes even more interesting is Marvell's association with what in 1671 was referred to as 'Marchamond . . . and Milton with their junto'.[41] Marchamont Nedham was a professional journalist who in the 1640s wrote first for Parliament, then for the king. In his first parliamentary phase, Nedham seems to have shared many of Milton's views – his insistence on religious liberty, his Erastian rejection of clerical domination, his dislike for Dr Featley.[42] After Nedham's arrest in 1649 Milton (it seems) persuaded him to revert to the parliamentarian allegiance. So thorough was the transformation that in May 1650 Nedham published a book, *The Case of the Commonwealth*, defending the republic in terms which endeared him to eighteenth-century republicans; and in June Nedham was appointed editor of a semi-official weekly newspaper, *Mercurius Politicus*, under Milton's supervision. At the Restoration Nedham fled to the Netherlands until the Act of Oblivion was passed. Despite republishing some of his earlier pro-royalist writing in 1661, Nedham remained, in Antony Wood's words, 'a great crony of Milton's, the latter's disciple'.[43]

They were closely linked in the public mind. In 1662 the Leveller John Lilburne joined Nedham and Milton in praise. Three years later the arch-regicide, John Bradshaw, a month before his death, altered his will so as to leave a legacy of £10 each to Milton and Nedham. In 1660 the royalist propagandist Roger L'Estrange associated Milton and his 'brother' Nedham as possible authors of a pamphlet which 'runs foul, tends to tumult'.[44] Edward Phillips referred to Nedham as one of Milton's 'particular friends', along with Andrew Marvell, 'young Lawrence' and Cyriack Skinner. So the friendship between

Milton and Nedham lasted for twenty years. But the reference in 1671 to the 'junto' of Milton and Nedham suggests that they had resumed active political co-operation as opposition to Charles II's government grew.

Pamphlets arising from Marvell's controversy with Samuel Parker frequently associate the former with Nedham and Milton. In his posthumous *History of his own Time* (1728) Parker refers to 'that vile fellow Marvell' as 'one of the cabal of 1660, a remnant of the rebellion, who had bound themselves by oath from the beginning to embarrass the King. If he was not the conspirators' secretary, yet he was admitted to all their seditious consultations on account of the old friendship between them'; and Milton was Marvell's patron. Richard Leigh said Milton and Nedham served as models for Marvell, who was Milton's 'fellow journeyman' and lickspittle. L'Estrange and several other pamphleteers suggested that Milton guided Marvell's pen. Echard associated Marvell and Nedham as 'both pestilent wits and noted incendiaries'. The attacks of Parker and his satellites so incensed Milton that he proposed to reply himself. But his friends dissuaded him, his nephew tells us. Those friends must certainly have included Marvell, whose dignified defence of Milton appeared in the second part of *The Rehearsal Transpros'd*.[45]

We can see two tactics pursued by this junto. The first was that of *The Rehearsal Transpros'd* (1672), to try to isolate the high Tories and high-flying Anglicans like Samuel Parker, and to persuade Charles II to act as heir to Oliver Cromwell, building up his own tolerationist party in opposition to the persecutors who dominated the House of Commons. This tactic succeeded at least to the extent that the king, who issued his Declaration of Indulgence in 1673, was amused by Marvell's book and protected its author – thanks to the mediation of Milton's old friend the Earl of Anglesey. It is probably to this period that we should relate the stories that both Milton and Marvell were approached by government agents who invited them to sell their pens to the government – as Nedham in fact did after 1675: Milton and Marvell refused. Or they may refer to the period in 1670 when efforts were being made to persuade Charles II to divorce his childless and papist queen in order to marry a Protestant. The divorce case of Lord Roos, in which the king was very interested, offered a possible precedent; Milton may have been consulted as a well-known expert on divorce. Marvell also took note of the Roos case, drawing his nephew William Popple's attention to the fact that all but three of the bishops voted in the Lords with the Duke of York and 'all the papist lords' against the Roos divorce.[46]

When this failed, the second tactic was that of Marvell's *Growth of Popery and Arbitrary Government in England.* Here perhaps Milton can help us to understand Marvell. In 1673 Milton found it possible to resume pamphleteering, which would earlier have been dangerous for a marked man like him. Charles II's Declaration of Indulgence had opened up possibilities of liberty for Protestant dissenters, whilst at the same time exciting fears that the king's main aim was to secure toleration for Roman Catholics, for sinister political purposes. Until this date Milton had not spent much energy on attacking popery: he did not like it, but he had more immediate enemies. But by the 1670s it seemed quite possible that the king might declare himself a papist – for political purposes which Milton understood. Charles had close relations with Louis XIV, the personification of the union of popery with absolutism. Here was an international Catholic/absolutist menace, analogous to the regime of Laud and Henrietta Maria, the object of Milton's first political assaults. He saw an issue on which it was possible for him to appear in print again.

In 1673 he published *Of True Religion, Heresy, Schism, Toleration; and what means may be used against the Growth of Popery.* 'The increase of popery is at this day no small trouble and offence to [the] greatest part of the nation', declared the opening sentence. Milton's stated object was to unite 'all true protestants' against the national enemy. He even quoted the 39 Articles in an attempt to embrace Anglicans as well as dissenters in this alliance. How right was his assessment of the possibilities of uniting Protestants is shown by the fact that when in April 1675 Danby's friends in the House of Commons wanted to head off a motion of censure against the minister, they decided (rightly) that the best diversion would be to encourage a wide discussion of the dangers of popery. What was different about *Of True Religion* was Milton's daring attempt to use conventionally accepted anti-popery as a lever to win a remarkably wide tolerance. The poet assumed that 'Anabaptists, Arians, Arminians and Socinians' were all Protestants, who should be tolerated equally with Lutherans and Calvinists. He devoted more space to Arians and Socinians than to any other sect.[47]

Milton was not alone in using anti-popery for political purposes.

William Dell had tried in 1667 to break a similar long silence by publishing a pamphlet entitled *The Increase of Popery in England*, but it was 'seized in the press', and did not appear until the greater liberty of 1681. Marvell, as I have already suggested, may have had a hand in Peter du Moulin's *England's Appeal*, which also appeared in 1673. William Penn's *One Project for the Good of England* (1679) had the same aim of uniting English Protestants.

Marvell shared Milton's dislike of absolute monarchy, and like Milton attacked the absolutist tendencies, as he saw them, of Charles II's government, under cover of attacking popery. 'There has now for divers years a design been carried on to change the lawful government of England into an absolute tyranny, and to convert the established protestant religion into downright popery': so the opening sentence of *An Account of the Growth of Popery and Arbitrary Government in England* makes explicit the theme of Milton's *Of True Religion, Heresy, Schism* of 1673. Marvell virtually quoted Milton when he wrote 'Popery is such a thing as cannot, but for the want of a word to express it, be called a religion'. Marvell, like Milton, referred to the papal agent Rinuccini 'assuming the temporal as well as spiritual power in Ireland' at the head of the rebels in the 1640s: 'all which ended in the ruin of his Majesty's [Charles I's] reputation, government and person'.[48] Marvell had hinted to the mayor of Hull that papists were responsible for the Fire of London. He reported in February 1671 on the House of Commons' concern about 'the dangerous growth of popery'. In his private letters to William Popple he is much more concerned with the dangers of absolutism; popery is not mentioned.[49] 'The Statue in Stocks-Market', uncertainly attributed to Marvell, mocks the statue which had originally been designed for John Sobieski but was adapted for Charles II, who was incongruously depicted trampling on a Turk. It recalls Milton's translation of *Letters Patents* for the election of John Sobieski as King of Poland in 1674. The point about Sobieski was that he was an *elected* and patriotic monarch, who was to pursue a forceful foreign policy with great success.[50]

The Growth of Popery was something very different from *The Rehearsal Transpros'd*. Apart from its greater seriousness, there is a difference in attitude towards Charles II, whose personal policy Marvell was in fact attacking, though the pretence of respect for the king is kept up. The government offered £100 – a sizeable sum in those days – as a reward for the discovery of the author of *The Growth of Popery*. No more royal protection! The very elaborate precautions which Marvell took to prevent his authorship becoming known remind us of the serious risks which those who publicly attacked the government took. The printer of the unlicensed *Mr. Smirke* was imprisoned in 1676.[51] Sir John Coventry had his nose slit for a light-hearted reference to Charles II and actresses, and Dryden was cudgelled at the orders of a duke. The blind Milton feared assassination in the 1660s. Marvell was threatened with assassination in the next decade. His remark, recorded by Aubrey, that he would not drink in any man's company to whom he would not entrust his life, may have been grim rather than facetious.[52]

It is essential to bear the censorship in mind when considering the literature of this period: otherwise we fall into non-sequiturs like the argument that because anti-Trinitarianism is not overtly mentioned in *Paradise Lost* therefore we can reject the plain evidence of anti-Trinitarian views in the *De Doctrina Christiana*, on which Milton was working at the same time as *Paradise Lost*, but which he recognized he could not publish.[53] Even Marvell's letters to his constituents have to be read with this in mind. In October 1675 he wrote to the mayor of Hull: 'I desire that what I write down to you may not easily or unnecessarily return to a third hand at London.' Next month 'it seems . . . that there is some sentinel set both upon you and me'; he repeated the warning not to 'do, say or write anything but what we care not though it be public'. If we compare Marvell's private letters to his nephew with his official letters to Hull we get an interesting gloss on the deadpan style of the latter.[54]

Literary historians I fear do not always bear sufficiently in mind the subterfuges which writers necessarily had to adopt in order not to expose themselves to danger. Marvell's urbane flattery of Charles II in *The Rehearsal Transpros'd* is not 'naive', as Professor Wallace suggests; nor is it merely 'opportunist' or 'insincere', the only alternatives he is prepared to consider.[55] It is part of the accepted discourse of the time, deriving partly from the censorship but also from agreed conventions of this post-revolutionary society. If you wanted to put forward a serious political argument which would be listened to by your opponents – as opposed to writing a libellous lampoon – you had to assume, or pretend to assume, that the king could do no wrong, that if wrong was done it was the ministers' fault,

and that the only problem was getting information through to the king.[56]

Outspoken anti-monarchism like that of 'Britannia and Rawleigh' and the 'Dialogue between the Two Horses' – whether or not they are Marvell's – was possible only in satires which circulated privately and illegally. The technique of attributing perfection to the king and all errors to his ministers is demonstrated in *An Account of the Growth of Popery*.[57] In his official correspondence with Hull Marvell always treated the king with respect. But in private letters to his nephew Marvell does not keep up the pretence that the king is never to blame. The very funny mock 'royal speech' of 13 April 1675 shows that Marvell did not fail to hold Charles personally responsible for his actions. In *Last Instructions to a Painter* he uses the fate of Charles I as a warning to his son.[58] 'As none will deny that to alter our monarchy into a Commonwealth were treason, so by the same fundamental rule, the crime is no less to make that monarchy absolute.' 'For one man's weakness a whole nation bleeds' – words which recall those for which the Long Parliament sent Henry Marten to the Tower in 1643.[59]

During the last years of his life Marvell had business-political relations with a couple of relatives both of himself and his Hull friends the Thompsons. One at least of these was a dissenter, probably an Independent; both were allies of Shaftesbury. They were fierce opponents of the ruling clique in the City, and when they were bankrupted Marvell may have been convinced 'that they were the victims of a persecution provoked by their stand for the religious and civil liberties of the City'. At all events, he sheltered them in his house when they had to go to ground, as Milton had been sheltered in 1660. The political associations of the group extend backwards to Agitators of the New Model Army and forward to Rye House plotters.[60]

Marvell was continually trying to unite the opponents of absolutism. Milton had tried to unite all other Protestants against bishops in 1641–2, all opponents of censorship in 1644, opponents of monarchy in 1649 and 1659–60; in 1673, as we saw, he quoted the 39 Articles in an attempt to bring together as many Protestants as possible against the danger of popery and absolutism. This no more meant Milton's conversion to Anglicanism than Marvell's praise of the independent royalist gentry meant that he idealized them or shared all their views: in each case a short-term alliance seemed possible.

Marvell's famous remark about the Good Old Cause in *The Rehearsal Transpros'd* must be read in this light. Marvell was anxious by this book to unite the broadest possible opposition to the high-flyers; and so, though Part I of the pamphlet is unsigned, he wants not to be provocative. But the words 'the cause was too good to have been fought for. Men ought to have trusted God; they ought and might have trusted the King with the whole matter' cannot be interpreted as a rejection of the Good Old Cause.[61] If the cause was too good to have been fought *for*, *a fortiori* it was too good to fight *against* – as Charles I had done. Samuel Parker saw this point clearly enough: so did the author of *A Common-Place Book out of the Rehearsal Transpros'd*.[62] 'In this world a good cause signifies little, unless it be as well defended', Marvell wrote in 1671.[63] His famous phrase meant that the war *should* not have been fought because it *need* not have been fought, because the victory of Parliament was inevitable, war or no war. In *The Rehearsal Transpros'd* Marvell continued, with considerable irony,

> The King himself, being of so accurate and piercing a judgment, would soon have felt where it stuck. For men may spare their pains when nature is at work, and the world will not go the faster for our driving. Even as our present Majesty's happy restoration did itself come, all things else happen in their best and proper time, without any need of our officiousness.[64]

Here Marvell was following the historical and political theory of his friend James Harrington. Worshippers of the Royal Martyr would again note Marvell's implied criticism of Charles I's intransigence.

In the 1650s Marvell had been very sharp against the Levellers, the radical democrats, whom like Oliver Cromwell he probably deliberately confused with the communist Diggers:

> this naked equal Flat,
> Which *Levellers* take Pattern at. . . .
> The World when first created sure
> Was such a Table rase and pure.
> Or rather such is the *Toril*
> Ere the Bulls enter at Madril.[65]

This seems a reference to Hobbes: the egalitarian state of nature necessarily leads to the state of war until political authority is established to tame the many-headed monster. Milton was much less hostile to the Levellers. In 1649 he ignored the Council of State's instructions to attack them, though he acted immediately on an order to attack the Irish royalists. Levellers continued to speak sympathetically of Milton as late as 1657. But Marvell, though opposed to Cromwell's acceptance of the crown, seems never to have committed himself against monarchy as an institution with the virulence of Milton in 1649 and 1660 – unless 'Britannia and Rawleigh' is by Marvell.

So perhaps we can put the relation between the two poets in perspective. Marvell was originally pushed forward by Milton, and almost certainly got his position in government service through Milton; he retained – as Masson stressed – a deference for Milton which was almost servile. He was a member of Milton's circle in the 1660s of his 'junto' in the 1670s. Both retained their convictions of the 1650s: neither was to be bought, though overtures were apparently made to both on behalf of the government. Both died poor. So Marvell's dignified defence of Milton in *The Rehearsal Transpros'd*, and his poem before the second edition of *Paradise Lost*, are the culmination of over twenty years of discipleship and friendship.

There are, it seems to me, continuing parallels between the political attitudes of the two men, from their first co-operation in 1649 or the early 1650s till Milton's death in 1674. Both hated bishops, for instance, and the whole hierarchy of the church. Like Milton, Marvell saw Constantine as the villain of the early history of Christianity, who endowed the church with property and confirmed the political power of bishops. Marvel speaks of 'the ambition of bishops', and – in the decent obscurity of a Latin poem – asks if a prelate can be innocent ('insons'). In 1678 he even opposed a bill 'for securing the protestant religion' because it gave too much power to bishops. He more than once hinted at the desirability of secularizing the property of the hierarchy. At least the incomes of the lesser clergy should be augmented at the expense of rich pluralists.[66]

Both Milton and Marvell believed that priests 'from the time of the Apostles onwards' had been responsible for persecution. Both resented the distinction between clergy and laity. Marvell even likened some clerics to the devil:

> there have never been wanting among such as would set the magistrate upon the pinnacle of the temple, and showing him all the power, wealth and glory of the kingdoms of the earth have proffered the prince all, so he would be tempted to fall down and worship them.[67]

(We recall *Paradise Regained.*) We must not be deceived by the apparent mildness of Marvell's irony, as when he advised the bishops that 'it were not amiss' if parsons were to be asked to give 'some account of their Christianity: for the world has always hitherto been so uncivil as to expect something of that from the clergy'.[68] Marvell's adversaries had no doubt where he stood. Nonconformists have mightily bought up the original *Rehearsal*, declared Henry Stubbe. 'If at any time the fanatics had occasion for [Marvell's] help', Samuel Parker agreed, 'he presently issues forth of his cave like a gladiator or wild beast.'[69] Like Milton, Marvell declared firmly against religious intolerance – from 'Bermudas', where the exiles were escaping from 'the prelates' rage', to *Mr. Smirke* in 1676. 'One that is a Christian in good earnest', Marvell wrote, 'when a creed is imposed, will sooner eat fire than take it against his judgment.'[70] We recall Milton on being a heretic in the truth.

Scholars are just beginning to realize how much millenarianism there is in Marvell. Here too he links up with Milton, for whom Christ was 'shortly-expected King' in 1641, whose return would remove all earthly tyrannies, he declared in 1649. Milton saw the sentence on Charles I as an anticipation of the Last Judgment, and continued to the end to look forward to the reign on earth of Christ in his saints.[71]

It is I hope superfluous to explain that there were many millenarians in the 1640s and early 1650s, expecting the coming of Christ in the near future, who had nothing to do with the small Fifth Monarchist party of the years after 1653, which strove to expedite that coming by military violence. Marvel illustrates the distinction in 'The First Anniversary', which is a millenarian poem whose author attacks Fifth Monarchists.[72] Like Milton's, Marvell's millenarianism does not call for immediate political action to establish the rule of the saints; on the contrary, the magistrates themselves must become godly. Marvell's praise of Cromwell in millenarian terms – 'if these the times, then this must be the man' – uses the Protector's virtues to suggest that the millennium may be approaching. It has nothing to do with advocating kingship for Oliver. Marvell (like Milton) sees the monarchy as a later and less satisfactory period of Jewish history than the rule of the judges, though superior to the rule of the priests.[73]

Marvell also shared a millenarian internationalism with Milton and his friends, Lady Ranelagh, Henry Oldenburg and John Dury, and with Lady Ranelagh's brother Robert Boyle. Cromwell 'to all states not free / Shall climacteric be'.[74] Like Milton, Marvell held that human actions are directed by Providence. Milton carried this to the extent of believing that his muse was divinely inspired; Marvell said, apropos of *The Rehearsal Transpros'd*: 'I am (if I may say it with reverence) drawn in, I hope by a good providence, to intermeddle in a noble and high argument which therefore by how much it is above my capacity I shall use the more industry not to disparage it.'[75]

A problem which Marvell encountered earlier than Milton was that of coming to terms with history. After the failure of the Revolution to which he had sacrificed twenty years of his life, and his eyesight, Milton faced the task of justifying to men the ways of a God who appeared to have spat in the faces of his most devoted servants. *Paradise Lost, Paradise Regained* and *Samson Agonistes* were the result. Marvell's problem was less tragic; but he too in 'An Horatian Ode' records the impact of an impersonal historical force, apparently transcending good and evil, 'The force of angry Heavens flame', which led Cromwell

> To ruine the great Work of Time
> And cast the Kingdome old
> Into another Mold.
> Though Justice against Fate complain,
> And plead the antient Rights in vain:
> But those do hold or break
> As Men are strong or weak.
> (ll. 34–40)

Charles I died with dignity; but Cromwell was the instrument of Providence: the Revolution cannot be wished away. The poet comes to terms with history, as Adam did in the last two books of *Paradise Lost*, and as Samson did in *Samson Agonistes*. This was perhaps less of an effort for Marvell than acceptance of the Restoration was to be for Milton. 'The world will not go the faster for our driving', but neither will it go the slower for our regrets. It would have been useless for Charles I to call 'the *Gods* with vulgar spight / To vindicate his helpless Right'. Like it or not, history had to be accepted.[76] Wisdom is 'to make their *Destiny* their *Choice*'. 'We must nevertheless be content with such bodies', Marvell wrote, 'and to inhabit such an earth, as it hath pleased God to allot us.' That was the lesson which Adam had learnt by the end of *Paradise Lost*.[77]

But Marvell's sense of historic destiny is part of a wider outlook, which informs his poetry as well as his prose. Earl Miner has suggested that the underlying theme of 'The Nymph complaining for the death of her Faun' is the loss of innocence in the face of historical violence, a loss which is regrettable but inevitable.[78] We recall the many poems in which 'Fate does Iron wedges drive, / And alwaies crouds it self betwixt'; 'her Decrees of Steel / Us as the distant Poles have plac'd'. 'Necessity', Marvell wrote in 1672, 'drove the great iron nail through the axle-tree of nature.'[79] Marvell had Milton's sense – a conception surely born of the agonies and triumphs and sufferings of the Revolution? – of good attained through evil, of the impossibility of good without evil, of the pointlessness of rejecting good because of concomitant evil. It was from the rind of one apple tasted in a garden that knowledge of good and evil came into the world. Tearing our pleasures 'with rough strife, / Thorough the Iron gates of Life' makes them greater, not less. The highest praise of Cromwell was that he

as the *Angel* of our Commonweal,
Troubling the Waters, yearly mak'st them Heal.

Or as Endymion, who wanted the moon, said to Cynthia:

Though I so high may not pretend,
It is the same so you descend.

In a lengthy simile in 'The First Anniversary' primitive man, terrified by the setting of the sun and the shadows, continues to look for light in the west, and is beginning to despair –

When streight the Sun behind him he descry'd,
Smiling serenely from the further side.[80]

It is impossible not to be struck by the recurrence in Marvell of the linked themes of liberty and necessity, of innocence crushed or by learning from external violence (the Mower Poems, 'The Nymph'), of the pressures of time or passion, of love and beauty inevitably giving rise to tyranny and war once the garden state of childhood innocence has passed. Love is defined as begotten upon impossibility by 'Magnanimous Despair': the conjunction of the mind faces the opposition of the stars; lovers kept apart by Fate's 'Decrees of Steel' can never come together 'Unless the giddy Heaven fall, / And Earth some new Convulsion tear'. In the 'Dialogue between the Soul and Body', the soul is 'Shipwrackt into Health again'. In 'The Match' a self-immolating explosion is the answer to time.[81] There are various ways in which time can be outwitted – 'Thus, though we cannot make our Sun / Stand still, yet we will make him run', in the 'Coy Mistress'; by a contemplative withdrawal or philosophic ecstasy ('The Garden'), or by the power of an heroic historical agent like Cromwell, who – unlike 'heavy Monarchs' – 'the force of scatter'd Time contracts, / And in one Year the work of Ages acts'.[82]

Milton wrestled with similar paradoxes: absolute freedom was essential, but so was self-discipline and co-operation with God's purposes; the Son of God in *Paradise Regained* rejected violence, but Samson slaughtered God's enemies later in the same volume. Adam chose death with Eve rather than life alone in Paradise in one of the finest passages of romantic love in the English language: a few lines later he was dismissed as 'fondly overcome by female charm'. True glory is rejection of glory: this conclusion of *Samson Agonistes* repeats a theme of Marvell's 'The Coronet' and 'A Dialogue between The Resolved Soul, and Created Pleasure'. The man whom his contemporaries called 'learned Mr Milton' in *Paradise Regained* rejected learning as a Satanic temptation, in words which recall Marvell's 'Dialogue' again:

> None thither mounts by the degree
> Of Knowledge, but Humility.
>
> (ll. 73–4)

So – very different though they seem at first sight – the two poets are in fact closely linked. Marvell owed his career to Milton, and remained very deferential. 'I shall now study it even to the getting of it by heart', he wrote of Milton's *Second Defence of the People of England*. The words sound exaggerated; but Marvell's 'The First

Anniversary' has been described as almost a versification of the *Second Defence*.[83] Thirteen references to Milton's 1645 *Poems* have been noted by Marvell's editors, and many more to Milton's prose, in *Last Instructions to a Painter* as well as in 'The First Anniversary' – and in 'Britannia and Rawleigh'. In 1660 and in 1672 the patronage worked the other way. In 1674 Marvell's 'On Mr. Milton's *Paradise lost*' was designed to sell the second edition of the epic to the London public.

A curious thing about 'On Mr. Milton's *Paradise lost*' is its reference to Samson. On first reading the epic Marvell was worried lest Milton would ruin

> The sacred Truths to Fable and old Song,
> (So *Sampson* groap'd the Temples Posts in spight)
> The World o'rewhelming to revenge his Sight.
> (ll. 8–10)

But Milton's Samson in *Samson Agonistes* did not 'grope the temple's posts in spite'. The notion that personal revenge is a main motive is present in the Book of Judges, but not in Milton's poem.[84] Marvell must have known this, must have read *Samson Agonistes*, and was better fitted to understand *Paradise Lost* than most. What is he up to? Marvell's 'misdoubts' about the theme of *Paradise Lost* remind me of what Milton's old friend and fellow-translator, Theodore Haak,[85] told his compatriot Benthem about *Paradise Lost*. When Milton's friends heard the poem's title, they feared that it would be a lament for the loss of England's happiness with the downfall of the revolutionary regime. But when they read it, they saw that Milton had dealt only with the fall of Adam; reassured, they withdrew their objections to publication. But, Benthem says, 'so far as I understand from what Haak told me and what I read for myself', although at first sight the epic's subject was indeed the fall of our first parents, in fact 'this very wily politician [dieser sehr schlau Politicus] concealed under this disguise exactly the sort of lament that his friends had originally suspected'.[86] Haak was likely to know about Milton's intentions: Marvell even more so.

Marvell may have been afraid that Milton would give the game away too easily; or he may – as he expressly says – have feared that Milton would trivialize his theme, 'to show it in a lay'. (We recall the 'memorable Scene' of the '*Royal Actor*' on 'the *Tragic Scaffold*', and

Milton's 'masking scene' on the same occasion.) Charles had not called on 'the *Gods* with vulgar spight', as Samson 'groaped the Temples Posts'. Marvell's Samson is not after all the Samson of Judges but of *Samson Agonistes*. Marvell's anxiety

> Through that wide Field how he his way should find
> O're which lame Faith leads Understanding blind
> (ll. 13–14)

proved to be unjustified. Marvell accepted Milton's own belief that heaven rewarded with prophecy 'thy loss of Sight' – as it rewarded Samson.

Mr Wilding I think is right to argue that many of Milton's allusions to himself in *Paradise Lost* are intended to remind his readers of his political past, and to stress that he is 'unchanged . . . though fallen on evil days . . . and evil tongues'. In particular his claim to exalted status as the blind bard is a defiant riposte to royalist propagandists who suggested that God had so afflicted him as a punishment for his defence of regicide. On the contrary, Milton and Marvell implicitly claim: Milton had been rewarded for deliberately sacrificing his eyes in the service of God's cause.[87] God led the blind Samson on to successful political action, victory won after coming to terms with defeat.

Milton and Marvell have in common profound political convictions, shared for twenty-five years, and the belief that – like Abdiel, like Samson, like Marvell and Milton themselves – it is impossible to cease to struggle for what one believes to be right. Both poets were confident that in the long run the world can be changed by human effort.[88] But they also have in common a sense of humour. There is no space to illustrate Marvell's gay and Milton's sarcastic wit, but Marvell makes the point in 'On *Paradise Lost*' by aligning himself with Milton against the 'tinkling Rhime' of 'the *Town-Bays*', who 'tires without his Bells'; and then recalls that his own condemnation of rhyme is made in rhymed couplets.

Rhyme in drama and long poems was a political issue: favoured by Charles II and the court, rhyme was attacked by Buckingham in the Epilogue to *The Rehearsal* which Marvell 'transprosed'. Milton claimed to have liberated his compatriots from the bondage of rhyme. Did the two poets remember the 1658 procession in which Dryden took part? Milton must have smiled with grim appreciation when in 'On *Paradise Lost*' his political ally praised England's most notorious defender of regicide not only as a prophet but in terms appropriate to a king – 'That majesty, which through thy work doth reign'. It was rather a good joke, if you think about it, especially if we take it as coming from one republican to another. But of course the majesty is not inherent in John Milton personally. What reigns in him is the will of God, the God of Milton and Marvell who is also history, fate, which – as even the blind Samson came to recognize – ''Tis Madness to resist or blame'.

Notes

1 *Calendar of State Papers, Domestic, 1658–9*, London, Longmans Green, 1860, p. 131.

2 J. B. Leishman, *The Art of Marvell's Poetry*, London, Hutchinson, 1972, pp. 20–2. First published 1966.

3 In my 'Society and Andrew Marvell' (*Puritanism and Revolution*, London, Panther ed., 1968, pp. 324–50) I may have over-argued the case; but I remain convinced that there is a case to argue.

4 I have made this point at greater length, and documented it, in *Antichrist in Seventeenth-Century England,* Oxford University Press, p. 181. Contrast John Crowe Ransom, in *Andrew Marvell*, ed. J. Carey, Penguin Books, 1969, p. 213 – a classic case in which a little historical knowledge would have saved a critic from writing nonsense and grossly misleading his readers about the skills of a great poet. Even less historical knowledge would have been necessary to prevent him objecting to 'the tide of Humber' as periphrastic poetic diction. Marvell's father was drowned in these tidal waters.

5 Contrast J. M. Wallace, *Destiny His Choice: The Loyalism of Andrew Marvell*, Cambridge University Press, 1968, pp. 146, 185–6. Having attributed 'loyalist' monarchist views to Marvell, Professor Wallace uses these views as a yardstick for rejecting some anti-monarchical poems from the canon. Whether or not they are to be rejected, these arguments seem to me inadequate.

6 J. Hacket, *Scrinia Reserata*, London, 1693, II, p. 186.

7 G. Miège, *A Relation of Three Embassies*, London, 1669, pp. 361, 415, 451. Carlisle, whom Marvell had known as Charles Howard, Cromwellian major-general, courtier and peer, 'hath no language, and so must wholly trust his secretary'. The comment is that of George Downing, another Cromwellian civil servant who survived the restoration (S. Konovalov, 'The English in Russia: Three Embassies, 1662–5', *Oxford Slavonic Papers*, X (1962), especially pp. 65–7).
8 Milton, *Complete Prose Works*, New Haven, Conn., Yale University Press, 1953– , IV, pp. 859–60.
9 Andrew Marvell, *Poems and Letters*, ed. H. M. Margoliouth, Oxford University Press, 1971, I, pp. 429–36.
10 Contrast Elsie Duncan-Jones, 'Marvell: A Great Master of Words', *Proceedings of the British Academy*, LXI (1975), p. 284.
11 Cleanth Brooks, 'Marvell's Horatian Ode', in Carey, as above (note 4).
12 Contrast E. Duncan-Jones, as above (note 10), pp. 282–3, who favours the earlier dating; and p. 285 for Hull and Fairfax.
13 J. M. French, *Life Records of John Milton*, New Brunswick, NJ, Rutgers University Press, 1949–58, III, p. 396; W. R. Parker, *Milton: A Biography*, Oxford University Press, 1968, II, pp. 964, 1022. Professor Le Comte thought that 'An Horatian Ode' quoted Milton's *Defence of the People of England*, and suggested that Marvell must have seen the manuscript before publication (E. Le Comte, *Poet's Riddles*, Port Washington, NY, 1975, p. 158).
14 Parker, as above (note 13), II, p. 926. Cf. Mrs Duncan-Jones's suggestion that Marvell may have helped Milton with the Latin version of the *Declaration of the Parliament of England* of March 1649 (E. Duncan-Jones, as above (note 10), p. 287).
15 Parker, above (note 13), I, pp. xiv-xv, 248; Milton, *Complete Prose Works*, IV, p. 864.
16 Parker, as above (note 13), II, p. 1022; D. Masson, *Life of Milton*, London, Macmillan, 1859–80, IV, p. 623.
17 Leishman, as above (note 2), p. 182; Margoliouth, as above (note 9), I, p. 293, II, p. 377.
18 H. Darbishire, *Early Lives of Milton*, London, Constable, 1932, p. 7; A. Wood, *Athenae Oxonienses*, ed. P. Bliss, Oxford University Press, 1813–20, IV, p. 230.
19 Parker, as above (note 13), I, p. 452, II, p. 837; Milton, *Complete Prose Works*, IV, pp. 670, 864.
20 Milton, *Complete Prose Works*, IV, pp. 669–70.
21 Parker, as above (note 13), I, p. 451; cf. II, p. 861.
22 Wood, as above (note 18), III, pp. 593, 1026–8; Marvell, *Mr. Smirke*, in *Complete Works*, ed. A. B. Grosart, Fuller Worthies' Library, for

private circulation, 1872–5, IV, pp. 65–6. Katherine Philips, the Matchless Orinda, was Oxinden's niece.

23 Masson, as above (note 16), IV, pp. 623–5; Margoliouth, as above (note 9), I, pp. 104–8, 314–19.

24 P. Legouis, *Andrew Marvell*, The Clarendon Press, 1965, p. 106.

25 Parker, as above (note 13), II, p. 1062.

26 *Thurloe State Papers*, London, 1742, VII, pp. 298, 373.

27 G. Davies, *The Restoration of Charles II, 1658–1660*, Oxford University Press, 1955, p. 104.

28 A letter from Marvell to George Downing, English ambassador in the Netherlands, dated February 1659, in which Marvell speaks disparagingly of the republicans, and of the partisans of Richard Cromwell as 'our side', was of course written in Marvell's official capacity, and need not necessarily represent his personal feelings (Margoliouth, as above (note 9), II, p. 294).

29 Wallace, as above (note 5), pp. 108–14, 122–3; S. Parker, *History of his own Time*, London, 1728, p. 215; S. N. Zwicker, 'Models of Government in Marvell's "The First Anniversary" ', *Criticism*, XVI (1974), pp. 1–12; Annabel Patterson, 'Against Polarization: Literature and Politics in Marvell's Cromwell Poems', *English Literary Renaissance*, V (1975), pp. 264–8.

30 Ll. 249–58; cf. 'On the Victory obtained by Blake', ll. 6–8; contrast ll. 139–40.

31 For Marvell's friendship with Harrington, see p. 16.

32 W. R. Parker, as above (note 13), I. p. 576, II, p. 1088.

33 Ibid., I, p. 631.

34 *The Diary of John Milward*, ed. C. Robbins, Cambridge University Press, 1938, p. 108. Cf. the famous lines on Pett in *Last Instructions to a Painter* (ll. 165–90).

35 Robbins, as above (note 34), p. 86, 116, 328, 185, 225, 238.

36 D. Defoe, *A Tour through England and Wales*, London, Everyman Library, J. M. Dent, 1928, I, p. 51.

37 *Calendar of State Papers, Domestic, 1671*, p. 496.

38 Margoliouth, as above (note 9), II, p. 326.

39 K. H. D. Haley, *William of Orange and the English Opposition, 1672–4*, Oxford University Press, 1953, pp. 57–9, 63, 97–8, 166, 196; D. Davison, 'Marvell and Politics', *Notes and Queries*, CC (1955), p. 202; L. N. Wall, 'Marvell and the Third Dutch War', ibid., CCII (1957), pp. 296–7.

40 Cf. especially the passages quoted in Haley, as above (note 39), p. 103; and cf. p. 222.

41 *The Correspondence of Henry Oldenburg*, ed. A. R. and M. B. Hall,

Wisconsin University Press, VII, 1970, pp. 439–41. Oldenburg was a friend both of Milton and of Cyriack Skinner (W. R. Parker, as above (note 13), II, p. 1047).

42 I owe these points to Mr Ian McCalman, who is completing a thesis on Marchamont Nedham.

43 A. Wood, *Fasti Oxonienses*, ed. P. Bliss, Oxford University Press, 1815–20, I, p. 484; Darbishire, as above (note 18), pp. 44, 74.

44 See my *Milton and the English Revolution*, London, Faber & Faber, 1977, pp. 225–6. Others who linked Milton and Nedham in 1659–62 include William Prynne, *A True and Perfect Narrative*, London, 1659, p. 50; [Richard Watson,] *The Panegyricke and the Storme*, n.p., 1659; Colonel Baker, *The Blazing Star*, London, 1660, p. 5; [Anon.,] *A Third Conference between Oliver Cromwell and Hugh Peters*, London, 1660; [Anon.,] *The London Printers Lamentation*, London, 1660; Henry Foulis, *The History of the Wicked Plots*, London, 1662, p. 24. I owe all these references to the kindness of Mr McCalman.

45 S. Parker, *A Reproof to the Rehearsal Transpros'd*, London, 1673, p. 212 and *passim*; S. Parker, *A History of his own Time*, pp. 214–25; [Anon.,] *S'Too him, Bayes*, Oxford, 1673; [Anon.,] *A Common-Place Book out of the Rehearsal Transpros'd*, London, 1673; [Richard Leigh,] *The Transproser Rehears'd*, Oxford, 1673, pp. 32, 52, 131–2, 135–7, 146–7; cf. pp. 9, 30, 41–3, 55–6, 72, 98, 110, 113, 126–9; *Works of Andrew Marvell*, ed. Capt. Edward Thompson, London, 1776, II, p. 486; W. R. Parker, as above (note 13), I, p. 630. Cf. *Calendar of State Papers, Domestic, 1677–8*, pp. 121–2 – which sounds to me like a forgery or a provocation; and *Calendar of State Papers, Domestic, 1678*, p. 373.

46 Margoliouth, as above (note 9), II, p. 315; cf. Marvell, *The Rehearsal Transpros'd*, ed. D. I. B. Smith, Oxford University Press, 1971, pp. 137–8, and my *Milton and the English Revolution* (as above, note 44), p. 223.

47 *The Diaries and Papers of Sir Edward Dering, Second Baronet, 1644 to 1684*, ed. M. F. Bond, London, HMSO, 1976, pp. 61–3; see my *Milton and the English Revolution*, pp. 218–19.

48 Grosart, as above (note 22), IV, p. 248; cf. pp. 250, 259–60.

49 Margoliouth, as above (note 9), II, pp. 53, 132, 315–17; cf. I, p. 402.

50 A poem dubiously ascribed to Rochester was similarly facetious about this statue. Margoliouth, as above (note 9), I, p. 395; my *Milton and the English Revolution*, pp. 219–20.

51 Legouis, as above (note 24), p. 205.

52 J. Aubrey, *Brief Lives*, ed. A. Clark, Oxford University Press, 1898, II, pp. 53–4.

53 Cf. A. C. Dobbins, *Milton and the Book of Revelation*, Alabama University Press, 1975, p. 133.
54 Margoliouth, as above (note 9), II, pp. 92–3, 166, 169–70, 313–18, 321–2, 341–3, 346–8.
55 Wallace, as above (note 5), p. 207.
56 Contrast Donal Smith, 'The Political Beliefs of Andrew Marvell', *University of Toronto Quarterly*, XXXVI (1966–7), pp. 55–67, who takes Marvell's profession of respect for Charles I seriously and rejects the evidence of the satires – partly because of uncertainties of attribution, partly because there is 'a high degree of convention in the court lampoons'.
57 Grosart, as above (note 22), IV, 249; cf. pp. 307–8.
58 Ibid., II, p. 431; Margoliouth, as above (note 9), II, pp. 267, 286; cf. II, p. 269, I, pp. 170–1.
59 Grosart, as above (note 22), IV, p. 261; 'An Historical Poem', l. 133 (Margoliouth, as above (note 9), I, p. 221).
60 F. S. Tupper, 'Mary Palmer alias Mary Marvell', *Proceedings of the Modern Language Association*, LIII (1938), pp. 368–92; L. N. Wall, 'Marvell's Friends in the City', *Notes and Queries*, CCIV (1969), pp. 204–7.
61 *The Rehearsal Transpros'd*, p. 135.
62 [S. Parker,] *A Reproof to the Rehearsal Transpros'd*, p. 443; *A Common-Place Book*, pp. 51–2; Edmund Hickeringhill, *Gregory Father Grey-Beard, With his Vizard off*, London, 1673, pp. 135–6.
63 Margoliouth, as above (note 9), II, p. 324.
64 *The Rehearsal Transpros'd*, p. 135. Cf. Isaac Barrow's suggestion that 'letting the world move on its own hinges' ensures stability both in the natural world and in politics (quoted in Margaret C. Jacob's *The Newtonians and the English Revolution, 1689–1720*, Cornell University Press, 1976, p. 62).
65 *Upon Appleton House*, ll. 449–50, 445–8 (Margoliouth, as above (note 9), I, p. 76; cf. pp. 21, 115).
66 *The Rehearsal Transpros'd*, pp. 237, 380; *Mr. Smirke*, in Grosart, as above (note 22), IV, pp. 41, 105; II, pp. xxix–xxx; cf. Margoliouth, as above (note 9), I, pp. 388, 404.
67 Grosart, as above (note 22), IV, pp. 94–8, 129–30, 152; *The Rehearsal Transpros'd*, pp. 44, 94, 135–42.
68 Grosart, as above (note 22), IV, p. 9.
69 [H. Stubbe,] *Rosemary and Bayes*, London, 1672, pp. 12–13, 18–19 (attributed to Stubbe in the Bodleian copy); S. Parker, *A History of his own Time*, p. 214.
70 Grosart, as above (note 22), IV, p. 126.

71 Cf. my *Milton and the English Revolution*, ch. XXII.
72 Margoliouth, as above (note 9), I, p. 116, ll. 297–320. I would not wish to associate Marvell – as Professor Wallace does – exclusively with millenarian nihilists like Anthony Ascham. For the distinction between millenarianism and Fifth Monarchism see the unpublished Cambridge Ph.D. thesis of J. P. Laydon, 'The Kingdom of Christ and the Powers of the Earth: The Political Uses of Apocalyptic and Millenarian Ideas in England, 1648–1653', 1976, *passim*.
73 That Marvell (like Milton) thought monarchy antichristian was one of the charges brought against him by Richard Leigh (*The Transproser Rehears'd*, pp. 95–6).
74 See J. R. Jacob, 'Boyle's Circle in the Protectorate: Revelation, Politics and the Millennium', *Journal of the History of Ideas*, XXXVIII (1977), p. 136. A similar revolutionary internationalism is preached in 'Britannia and Rawleigh'.
75 Margoliouth, as above (note 9), II, p. 328. This is the traditional Puritan position: we must keep our powder dry *because* we are fighting God's battles (cf. my *God's Englishman*, Harmondsworth, Penguin ed., 1972, ch. IX).
76 See my *Puritanism and Revolution*, pp. 344–5.
77 *The Rehearsal Transpros'd*, p. 231.
78 Earl Miner, 'The Death of Innocence in Marvell's "Nymph Complaining for the Death of her Faun" ', *Modern Philology*, LXV (1967); *The Metaphysical Mode from Donne to Cowley*, Princeton University Press, 1969, pp. 246–71.
79 *The Rehearsal Transpros'd*, p. 230.
80 L. 341–2 (Margoliouth, as above (note 9), I, pp. 28, 119, 126, 117).
81 Cf. Ann E. Berthoff, *The Resolved Soul: A Study of Marvell's Major Poems*, Princeton University Press, 1970, pp. 77–9, 87, 100, 125, 132–3, 143.
82 Ruth Nevo, *The Dial of Virtue: A Study of Poems on Affairs of State in the Seventeenth Century*, Princeton University Press, 1963, pp. 91, 98, 109, 178; Isabel Rivers, *The Poetry of Conservatism: A Study of Poets and Public Affairs from Jonson to Pope*, Cambridge, Rivers Press, 1973, pp. 78–83, 113; A. E. Berthoff, as above (note 81), pp. 152–3; cf. pp. 106, 114, 122–3; M. McKeon, *Politics and Poetry in Restoration England*, Cambridge, Mass., Harvard University Press, 1975, pp. 184–5.
83 Patterson, as above (note 29), p. 266. There are possible reminiscences of *Eikonoklastes* in 'An Horatian Ode' and 'The First Anniversary' (ll. 99–158) as well as in 'The Statue in Stocks-Market'; the *Last Instructions to a Painter* also recalls Milton's *Defence* (A. Patterson,

p. 264; R. Nevo, as above (note 82), p. 182; cf. p. 5 above). Margoliouth heard echoes of Milton's first *Defence* in 'Britannia and Rawleigh' (ll. 149–52), and of *Paradise Lost* in *Last Instructions* (ll. 142–6, 788). Cf. 'An Historical Poem', ll. 101–2.

84 Cf. S. Fish, 'Question and Answer in *Samson Agonistes*', *Critical Quarterly*, IX (1969), p. 256.

85 W. R. Parker, as above (note 13), I, pp. 250, 295; II, pp. 972, 1186; P. R. Barnett, *Theodore Haak, F.R.S. (1605–1690)*, 'S Gravenhage, 1962, *passim*, especially pp. 156, 162–3.

86 H. L. Benthem, *Engelaendischer Kirch- und Schulen-Statt*, Lüneburg, 1694, p. 58.

87 Michael Wilding, 'Regaining the Radical Milton', in *The Radical Reader*, ed. S. Knight and M. Wilding, Sydney, Wild & Woolley, 1977, pp. 126–7, 143.

88 See the penetrating analysis of *Paradise Regained* in Irene Samuel's 'The Regaining of Paradise', in *The Prison and the Pinnacle*, ed. B. Rajan, London, Routledge & Kegan Paul, 1973, pp. 123–4, 132–4.

2

'Till prepared for longer flight': The sublunar poetry of Andrew Marvell

C. A. Patrides

I

That agreeable gossip, John Aubrey, had a theory about Marvell's inspiration. Marvell, he reported, 'kept bottles of wine at his lodgeing, and many times he would drinke liberally by himselfe to refresh his spirits, and exalt his Muse'.[1]

Aubrey is of course describing not so much Marvell as Aubrey. The transposition is perfectly understandable, however, since Marvell's poetry habitually elicits rather personal confessions than aesthetic responses: we ascribe to him, that is to say, assumptions characteristic of ourselves. The persuasion of Gerard Manley Hopkins that Marvell is 'a rich and nervous poet'[2] was after all professed by a poet equally as rich, and no less nervous.

Judgments on Marvell should be ventured within the framework suggested. True, we have grown much in perception of late, for we look with some hesitation on the opinion of Victoria Sackville-West that Marvell wrote, as she elegantly maintained, 'preposterous rubbish'.[3] To our further credit, we also regard Samuel Parker with some suspicion because, having been pursued by Marvell 'thorow thick and thin, hill or dale, over hedge and ditch',[4] he extracted ample revenge in the portrait of Marvell he sketched later ('A vagabond, ragged, hungry Poetaster, being beaten at every tavern, he daily receiv'd the rewards of his sawciness in kicks and blows').[5] But other opinions, elevated into doctrines just as readily, are admitted without even a minimum of reflection. We endorse, for example, T. S. Eliot's vast generalizations on Marvell (1921), apprehensive though we should have been that in his second essay (1923) Marvell was proclaimed a lesser talent than the distinctly minor poet Henry King.[6] Eliot's pronouncements are nevertheless permitted to pandiculate, even to the extent that his considered vision of Marvell's 'alliance of levity and seriousness' has become yet another dogma, what one critic unhappily calls Marvell's 'joco-serious approach'.[7] There is finally the view, also inspired by Eliot and rather too casually articulated by others, that 'Marvell may have written a few great poems, but he was not a great poet'.[8] Applied prodigally, the measure of greatness here proffered would presently affect other major poets as well, among them Mallarmé.

Embarrassing questions are also raised by the several claims on the diverse influences said to have been exerted on Marvell. Such claims, indispensable if we are to appreciate Marvell's remarkable powers of assimilation, are nevertheless so often ventured in absolute terms that they yield not clarity but confusion. Where cautiously phrased claims illumine – that 'Clorinda and Damon' is a 'predominantly Spenserian poem', that 'The Coronet' intimates the presence of Herbert, and that several poems suggest 'certain resemblances' with Herrick[9] – categorically stated opinions merely obscure. T. S. Eliot, for example, imposed on Marvell 'the vast and penetrating influence of Ben Jonson'; but another critic asserts that Marvell's 'master' was in fact Donne, even as a third denies the same premise altogether ('Marvell has no connection with Donne').[10] Judgments on individual poems vex equally. 'On a Drop of Dew', for instance, is said to have affinities with Herbert on the one hand, and Crashaw on the other;[11] while 'Eyes and Tears' is alleged to have been 'derived' from Crashaw's 'The Weeper' when it patently manifests the entwined influences of Marino, Góngora, and Cleveland, as much as that of Donne.[12]

Details do matter; but we are also in need of the larger picture. We may remind ourselves that a great poet exposes himself to a diversity of particular influences in order promptly to transcend them, annihilating all that's made to his given sensibility, else adjusting tradition to his individual talent. Once properly considered, the larger context in Marvell's case should provide us with his characteristic achievement, the intricate balance between his personal predilections and the aggregate of literary precedents: the embroidered luxuriance of Spenser, the temperate umbrage of Jonson, the intellectual foliations of Donne, the daedalian animation of Herrick, the expansive lushness of Crashaw, the indesinent fecundity of Herbert.

Marvell did not draw solely on these poets, however. His affinities demonstrably lie elsewhere as well, with Shakespeare and Milton within English literature, and the Greek and Roman poets without. To appreciate this range of reference, as I propose to do in part here, is to confirm that Marvell's poems are all-inclusive yet utterly unique, and in consequence passionately committed to realism.

II

It will I know seem odd that I impute realism to a poet who on the face of it is full of sounds and sweet airs that give delight and hurt not. Is there not in Marvell 'a strong tinge of escape'?[13] Was he not happiest when conferring with birds and trees in the grounds of Nun Appleton, and happier still when he dwelt in the solitariness of his garden? He even confronted a coy but panic-stricken mistress with his 'vegetable love' – a sort of lecherous cabbage, solemnly said by a critic to be 'an ironic version of dendro-eroticism'.[14]

Marvell's pastoral poems will engage us presently. But I should initially prefer to consider his expressly political poems, not only because in them realism is necessarily an omnipresent dimension but because they display most lucidly Marvell's adjustment of literary precedents to his sensibility. The best example in this respect is also the most predictable one, 'An Horatian Ode upon Cromwell's Return from Ireland'.

The Ode is in the first instance Horatian because of its external demeanour: it deploys the four-line structure also used by Marvell's friend Milton on three occasions.[15] But the Ode is especially Horatian in that it accommodates within its circumference elements internal to Horace's poems. It may indeed be said of Marvell what has been asserted of Horace, that

> he is extremely clever at disposing his novelties so that they are not obtrusive and the style appears uniform. Stylistic tact and appropriateness are Horace's outstanding qualities, but for this to

> be appreciated the reader's ear needs to be constantly attuned to the tone of the poet's voice, for it is in such small-scale works as the *Odes* that significant tonal effects, often dependent on but a single word, are possible. This splendid movement and complexity of tone is an exact counterpart to the complexity of ideas, and together they make an adequate reading of the *Odes* a rich (and varied) poetic experience.[16]

Marvell likewise has that within which passes show. The apparent uniformity of his verses constantly belies their actual agitation as the tone veers suddenly if imperceptibly to oblige reconsideration of 'but a single word'. The innocuous monosyllables are particularly suspect, as in the lines on Cromwell's likely progress after the execution of Charles:

> Nor yet grown stiffer with Command,
> But still in the *Republick's* hand:
> (ll. 81–2)

where the second word in each line, if stressed in accordance with the regular iambic rhythm, will suggest the least attractive of the possible alternatives:

> Nor *yet* grown stiffer with Command,
> But *still* in the Republick's hand.

Marvell's espousal of more than a single point of view echoes the similar predilection in Horace, who could celebrate martial endeavours (III, 2) even as he reproached Iccius for pursuing them (I, 29), or joy at the prospect of the death of Cleopatra, the 'wild Queen' who opposed the designs of Rome, even as he admired the nobility of her final gesture:

> Yet she preferred a finer style of dying:
> She did not, like a woman, shirk the dagger
> Or seek by speed at sea
> To change her Egypt for obscurer shores,
>
> But, gazing on her desolated palace
> With a calm smile, unflinchingly bid hands on
> The angry asps until
> Her veins had drunk the deadly poison deep. . . .[17]

Marvell did not merely echo the Horatian patterns, however. He also amended them slyly, thereby promoting an irony that informs every line of his Ode. Horace lauded Octavius without qualification ('While Caesar stands guard, peace is assured, the peace / No power can break' (IV, 15)), but Marvell praised Charles as well as Cromwell, even as he modulated his judgments on both. In similar fashion, Horace acclaimed the imperial arts of war, but Marvell transferred that praise from the sovereign to the usurper, even as he chillingly warned of the potential consequences. A passage from Lucan, whose *Pharsalia* includes a hostile portrait of Caesar (I, 143–55) and an encomiastic one of Pompey (IX, 192–200), best illumines Marvell's intricate balance. Lucan's Caesar is poised to wield

> His forward Sword; confident of successe,
> And bold the favour of the gods to presse:
> Overthrowing all that his ambition stay,
> And loves that ruine should enforce his way:
> As lightning by the wind forc'd from a cloud
> Breakes through the wounded aire with thunder loud,
> Disturbes the Day, the people terrifyies,
> And by a light oblique dazels our eyes. . . .[18]

Marvell's Ode similarly begins with the analogy to the 'forward' youth, and advances on Cromwell who

> through adventrous War
> Urged his active Star.
> And, like the three-fork'd Lightning, first
> Breaking the Clouds where it was nurst,
> Did thorough his own Side
> His fiery way divide . . .
> Then burning through the Air he went,
> And Pallaces and Temples rent. . . .
> (ll. 11–16, 21–2)

Granted the evident affinities between Lucan's Caesar and Marvell's Cromwell, it is I believe no less imperative to discern their fundamental differences. The lightning in Lucan provides a naturalistic context; but the *three*-forked lightning in Marvell endows that context with a further dimension, palpably supernatural and fraught with apocalyptic implications. Should we care to regard Cromwell's cyclonic activities as divinely sanctioned, we are likely to invoke the poet's express admonition:

'Tis Madness to resist or blame
The force of angry Heavens flame:
(ll. 25–6)

If on the other hand we regard the lightning as a merely earth-bound phenomenon, Cromwell's self-urged 'active Star' is abruptly transformed into a blasphemous presumption and the poet's admonition is qualified with shattering irony:

'Tis Madness to resist or blame
The force of angry Heavens flame:
And, if we would speak true,
Much to the Man is due. . . .

Lucan afforded Marvell a framework, much as Horace did; but the final structure is entirely Marvell's own.

The Horatian dimension of the 'Horatian Ode' must then be understood in a particular sense, much qualified as it was by pressures exerted on Marvell from other directions. The Ode's *color romanus*, in fact, need not be sought solely in Rome when it was readily accessible in London as well, in an obvious yet so far neglected place: Shakespeare's *Julius Caesar*. The emphases in the Ode as in the play run at times along lines sufficiently parallel to raise expectations that they will eventually meet. Yet barring the obvious concern in both works with political assassination and its consequences, how far may one venture in pursuit of closer affinities? Is Marvell's three-forked lightning related to the symbolic testimony of Cassius that 'the cross blue lightning seem'd to open / The breast of heaven' (I, iii, 50)? Is there a connection between the advent of Marvell's fiery Cromwell and Calphurnia's forebodings ('Fierce fiery warriors fight upon the clouds . . .' (II, ii, 19)), or between Marvell's 'Royal Actor' (l. 59) and Brutus' exhortation to his fellow-conspirators to act 'as our Roman actors do' (II, i, 226)? The actor changing roles on the stage of history is basic to the 'Horatian Ode' and frequent enough in Marvell's other poems. We may wonder, too, if the spectators' response to the king's performance in the Ode ('the armed Bands / Did clap their bloody hands') is connected in any way with the emphasis in *Julius Caesar* on hands, from the instant that the conspirators seal their pact by joining hands (II, i, 112) to the moment that Mark Antony with a similar gesture pretends – 'as our Roman actors do' – to endorse the murder (III, i, 184–90 and 218). After the assassination Brutus' blasphemous invitation to the other assassins is followed by ominous prophecies that the 'scene', acted once in Rome, would be re-enacted thereafter:

> *Brutus.* Stoop, Romans, stoop,
> And let us bathe our hands in Caesar's blood
> Up to the elbows, and besmear our swords:
> Then walk we forth, even to the market-place,
> And waving our red weapons o'er our heads,
> Let's all cry, 'Peace, freedom, and liberty!'
> *Cassius.* Stoop, then, and wash. How many ages hence
> Shall this our lofty scene be acted over,
> In states unborn, and accents yet unknown!
> *Brutus.* How many times shall Caesar bleed in sport,
> That now on Pompey's basis lies along,
> No worthier than the dust!
>
> (III, i, 105–16)

One marks that the 'memorable Scene' in Marvell's Ode terminates in the vision of Cromwell holding aloft a sword only recently besmeared with Irish blood. It is done for 'effect' (l. 116).

Marvell's vision of history is veritably Aeschylean in the way crime is seen to link with crime, and blood shed to merge with blood shed. It is also Shakespearean, at least to the extent that it vibrates in response to John of Gaunt's celebrated paean to England as the happy and dear isle, a 'fortress', a latter-day garden of Eden bound in with the triumphant sea, yet self-conquered and expiring in shame (*Richard II*, II, i, 40 ff.). The narrator in *Upon Appleton House* gathers up the echoes and moulds them within the Fall of Man:

> Oh Thou, that dear and happy Isle
> The Garden of the World ere while,
> Thou *Paradise* of four Seas,
> Which *Heaven* planted us to please,
> But, to exclude the World, did guard

With watry if not flaming Sword;
What luckless Apple did we tast,
To make us Mortal, and The Wast?
(st. 41)

Judged against this background, the execution of Charles is not endorsed. Neither is it deplored. It is accepted. Realistic in the extreme, Marvell was not in the least concerned with what might or should have been; and temperamentally disinclined to indulge in utopian speculations, he would have agreed with Milton's sentiment in *Areopagitica*:

> To sequester out of the world into *Atlantick* or *Eutopian* polities, which never can be drawn into use, will not mend our condition; but to ordain wisely as in this world of evill, in the midd'st whereof God hath plac't us unavoidably.[19]

If Marvell is concerned with the past, it is only because he wishes to understand how that past has shaped the present, and how both could – but *need* not – affect the future. Cromwell and Charles are therefore observed in the Ode as they ride different assumptions on the way to their historic confrontation. The terrain is marked by the poem's well-attested ironies which suggest that we may honour the qualities inherent in exalted ideals yet dread their enactment, and that we may admire the nobility of soaring visions yet fear the fanaticism that so often attends them. Like the visionaries in Yeats's poem, Cromwell and Charles embody 'a terrible beauty'.

The confrontation of Marvell's protagonists changes both radically. Charles, who is but a shadow until his great performance on the scaffold, unexpectedly seizes the opportunity to create subsequent history to his image; and becomes, in death, a more palpable presence than he ever was in life. Cromwell, who believed that he could direct history at will, discovers that he has inadvertently helped his opponent to greatness; and the more he seeks to resume his role as director, the more he finds himself obliged to 'act' (in both senses of the word). At this moment in time, as Marvell pauses to suggest the options still open, the poem once more bristles with ambiguities. As already noted, monosyllabic words are crucial:

Nor *yet* grown stiffer with Command,
But *still* in the Republick's hand.

The warning sounded here ranges across the analogy introduced within a few lines to elucidate the relations between Cromwell and the state:

> So when the Falcon high
> Falls heavy from the Sky,
> She, having kill'd, no more does search,
> But on the next green Bow to pearch;
> Where, when he first does lure,
> The Falckner has her sure.
>
> (ll. 91–6)

We are often enough assured that the falcon is Cromwell, and the falconer the State.[20] Might not the reverse be equally true, however? Cromwell 'kill'd', in Ireland; but so did the state in condemning Charles to the scaffold. The word 'lure', it may be added, appertains as much to the state as to Cromwell's increasingly brilliant performance.

The implications of the Ode are frequently proclaimed with some abandon. We have been told, for instance, that Marvell endorsed a necessitarian view of history ('freedom is the knowledge of necessity'), and that therefore he urged 'the subordination of self to political purposes'.[21] With respect, however, I cannot credit that Marvell was, even by anticipatory osmosis, a marxist. History is not determined by impersonal forces latent within it. History is determined solely by individuals; and though individuals may be destroyers or redeemers or (most likely) both, they are nevertheless free to pursue the course of their choice. The subordination of self is indeed advocated by Marvell, but it is a subordination to moral not to political purposes. Hence the Ode's Roman parallels and mounting ambiguities. The Roman parallels are not deployed in order ironically to concatenate two political experiences: they are especially meant to remind us of a moral order whose violation in time past remains a constant threat to times future. The ambiguities, similarly, are not only intended to celebrate Marvell's retrospective political insights: they are especially designed to admonish that individuals who accept that past events could be acted over in states unborn and accents yet unknown, have already predetermined the occurrence of those events and are self-ordained to relive them. The past belongs to the past, unalterably so; but its cumulative experiences forcefully warn us that the luckless apple will be tasted yet again unless opportunities in the present are used to 'mend our condition' in the future. Freedom is the knowledge, and the exercise, of moral option.

III

Marvell wrote two other poems on Cromwell, one on the first anniversary of Cromwell's accession to absolute power (1655), the other on his death (1658). They are not universally admired as poems, nor widely respected as profound analyses of the strained years under the Protectorate. Each is indeed singular, in that the sublunar Cromwell of the 'Horatian Ode' has now yielded to 'Angelique *Cromwell*', '*Heavens Favorite*', a cosmic figure 'nearer to the Skyes', 'like a Star', and ever-impelled by 'A secret Cause', 'an higher Force'.[22] The changed emphasis in the argument coincides with the displacement of the Horatian four-line structure by the heroic couplet. Our response is qualified accordingly; for here, certainly, the heroic couplet is for Marvell largely what blank verse was for Milton. It celebrates. It is acclamatory, ceremonial, ritualistic, even sacramental. It is consequently dedicated to idealistic issues consciously articulated in sublime terms. The still centre is not time but eternity, not the historical Cromwell but a transcendent authority of impeccably moral credentials. The demanding vision disturbs; and we protest, suspicious as we are of those who gaze as if admonished from another world. We therefore dismiss the vision as artificial, until we summon up remembrance of Sir Thomas Browne: 'all things are artificiall, for nature is the Art of God' (*Religio Medici*, I, 17).

The cosmic morality that sustains the two poems on the Lord Protector illumines the varieties of human imperfection delineated elsewhere: implicitly in the tactful measures of the Ode as we have seen, explicitly in the tellingly ludicrous rhythms of 'Clarindon's

House-Warming', in the crushing satire of the three 'painter poems' – especially the stunning *Last Instructions to a Painter* – and in the merciless prosecution of the demented Mr Bayes, alias Samuel Parker, in *The Rehearsal Transpros'd* (e.g. 'the Church of *England* is much obliged to Mr. *Bayes* for having proved that Nonconformity is the Sin against the Holy Ghost').[23] But the same cosmic morality also informs the rest of Marvell's poems, equally concerned as they all are with the reality of imperfection within the created order.

The reality so designated is, in theological terms, the fact of the Fall. As a datable historical event, the Fall is nowhere expressly formulated in Marvell's poetry; but as an ever-present human experience, it is never absent from his consciousness. Its configurations are manifold. 'Bermudas', for instance, implies that perfection 'in this world of evill' (to quote Milton again) is beyond the realm of possibility. True, such is the enchantment of the isles that they hardly appear to warrant their traditional appellation as 'still-vexed'; and we are prone rightly to regard them as partaking of the isle of Prospero, and indeed the prelapsarian world. However, just as Shakespeare and Milton introduced discordant elements into their respective visions, so Marvell suggests the distant threat of the huge sea-monsters and of the roaring waves – and may even have meant us to recall not so much Spenser's Garden of Adonis as his ominous Bower of Bliss.[24] The threat presses even harder upon the precarious domain of 'The Picture of little T.C. in a Prospect of Flowers', where an idealized young girl is invited to reform 'the errours of the Spring' introduced by the Fall, yet is warned that she is no less mortal than the flowers and buds she gathers. Death brought into the world by the luckless apple tasted, casts its maleficent shadow over any number of other poems as well: 'Young Love' and 'The Match', 'The unfortunate Lover' and 'The Nymph complaining for the death of her Faun' – and of course 'To his Coy Mistress', where an initially light-hearted variation on a common enough theme (*carpe diem*, in short, seduction) advances expeditiously along unforeseen tracts to an alarming apprehension of the ravenous nature of time and death. Such emphases are brilliantly hypostasized in 'The Coronet' which, read as it must be in the light of Herbert's aspiration to dedicate poetry to religious uses, pleads for Christ's intercession because mere man – fallen man – is prevented by other interests from consecrating the flowers of poetry to the Creator:

Alas I find the Serpent old
That, twining in his speckled breast,
About the flow'rs disguis'd does fold,
With wreaths of Fame and Interest.
(ll. 13–16)

It is a measure of Marvell's ambidextrous art, however, that a poem which confesses its inability to praise Christ is nevertheless a poem in praise of Christ.

Mortality intimated in the midst of life is also the common theme of the four mower poems. These displant the benevolent shepherd of traditional pastoral poetry by the destructive mower who in his indiscriminate decimation of the natural order is expressly said to resemble death ('Death thou art a Mower too').[25] The four poems are essentially dramatic, beginning with 'The Mower against Gardens' where the narrator ferociously denounces 'luxurious man' for having imposed art on nature, and the formal garden on the wilderness:

He first enclos'd within the Gardens square
  A dead and standing pool of Air:
And a more luscious Earth for them did knead,
  Which stupifi'd them while it fed.
(ll. 5–8)

The burden of the actual argument is carried in the first instance by the word 'luxurious', which is to say lecherous or lascivious (one recalls the contours of *The Revenger's Tragedy* inclusive of the aptly named Lussurioso). But as the word also meant outrageous or excessive, we are invited to observe that it applies most ineluctably to the strident tone of the narrator himself. His language, indeed, is obsessively possessed of sexual references – 'seduce', 'luscious', 'eunuchs', and the like – so that the effect is not dissimilar to that of the central panel of Bosch's *Garden of Delights* where the frantic sexuality of the ravelled figures disarranges the natural order. In this respect 'The Mower against Gardens' is best annotated by the three poems appended to it: 'Damon the Mower', in which Damon suffers 'hot desires' under Juliana's 'scorching beams'; 'The Mower to the Glo-Worms', in which the narrator's mind is 'displac'd' by his sexual passion; and 'The Mower's Song', in which the mind so affected considers wreaking 'revenge' on the innocent flowers and grass –

'Depopulating all the Ground', as Damon had earlier remarked with savage lucidity ('Damon the Mower', l. 74). Thus introduced, the mower appears yet again in the very different context of *Upon Appleton House*.

The difference resides in that poem's apparent affinities with the tradition-bound celebrations of country houses. Nun Appleton in Yorkshire, the seat of the Lord General Fairfax and his home after his resignation as commander of the parliamentary army (1650), was intimately known to Marvell who lived there for two years as tutor to young Mary Fairfax. Sustained by an adequate history, the house could also claim that its present master was a poet responsible for several verses – to be exact, 'one hundred and twenty five couplets and thirty five quatrains' – collectively entitled *Honny dropps*. Here is one drop:

> A good man questionless was never hee
> That strives nott allways better for to be

Or to quote from the ambitious 'Songe of Prayse' to the providence of God:

> The East the West tast of his Care
> Hott Affrick nor the freezinge Beare
> From his al seeinge eye is hidd[26]

Upon Appleton House discreetly avoids any reference to Fairfax's extraordinary muse, but extols his considerable talents in architectonic horticulture. Marvell's Fairfax is rather like Sir Thomas Browne's Cyrus, 'Not only a Lord of Gardens, but a manuall planter thereof: disposing his trees like his armies in regular ordination'.[27] The retired general is said to have laid out his garden 'in sport / In the just Figure of a Fort'; and the respectful flowers

> as at *Parade*,
> Under their *Colours* stand displaid:
> Each *Regiment* in order grows,
> That of the Tulip Pinke and Rose.
> (ll. 285–6, 309–12)

The house itself, moreover, responds to its master in no uncertain terms:

the laden House does sweat,
And scarce indures the *Master* great:
But where he comes the swelling Hall
Stirs, and the *Square* grows *Spherical*.
(ll. 49–52)

T. S. Eliot was not amused. The image, he declared, 'is more absurd than it was intended to be'.[28] But the poem should perhaps be judged in the light of Browne's whimsical *Garden of Cyrus*; for we might then discern that absurdity in the one, like whimsicality in the other, is pressed to the service of a larger design. This design suggests that *Upon Appleton House* praises Fairfax to the same extent that the 'Horatian Ode' praises Cromwell, and that consequently both poems are involved in the reality of the Fall 'in this world of evill'.

Upon Appleton House may not be regarded as 'an extended jest'.[29] True, it has moments of playfulness and even light-heartedness, deployed with great tact and even greater goodwill; but it remains a most earnest examination of profound issues profoundly affirmed. Consider the crucial stanza (71) at the end of the narrator's sombre reflections on the 'Traitor-Worm' which ravages 'the tallest Oak' from within:

Thus I, *easie Philosopher*,
Among the *Birds* and *Trees* confer:
And little now to make me, wants
Or of the *Fowles*, or of the *Plants*.
Give me but Wings as they, and I
Streight floting on the Air shall fly:
Or turn me but, and you shall see
I was but an inverted Tree.

'Easie', we are informed, means 'at ease, detached from care, free from pain, annoyance, or burden, free from pressure or hurry';[30] and we are mildly amused, I will suppose, by the narrator's evident effort at self-reproach. But 'easie' could also mean on the one hand credulous, which considerably strengthens the self-reproach, and on the other gentle, which considerably weakens it. By the same token, the apparently amusing vision of the narrator turned upside down to resemble an inverted tree – itself no less comic – should be placed within the context of the time-honoured idea that 'man may be compared to an inverted tree: for he has his roots, or his hair, in the air, while other trees have their hairs, or their roots, in the earth'.[31] Should these examples not suffice to deflect us from precipitous responses, we ought certainly not to disregard the narrator's own admonition:

> Thrice happy he who, not mistook,
> Hath read in *Natures mystick Book*.
> (ll. 583–4)

'Not mistook' carries, if any single phrase can be said to carry, the burden of Marvell's impressive realism.

The Fall is diversely delineated in *Upon Appleton House*. It confronts us first in the unlikely episode of 'the Suttle Nunns', residents of Nun Appleton when it was still a monastic retreat. Extreme in length, the episode is also extreme in tone, but forewarned by its forceful exposition of the nature of retreat and its consequences, we are better able to evaluate two later manifestations of retreat in the same grounds: Fairfax's retirement into his artificial fort (st. 44), and shortly thereafter the experiences of the narrator himself (sts 47 ff.). The word 'artificial' should not be misconstrued: it intimates here as before (p. 40) the natural order, 'the Art of God', now extended by Fairfax with agreeably good humour ('in sport'). On the other hand, Fairfax's actual retreat sets off reverberations emanating largely from the statement that he 'might' have made 'our Gardens spring / Fresh as his own' (ll. 347–8). His retirement from the affairs of England – 'The Garden of the World ere while' (as above, p. 37) – is perilously analogous to his retirement from the meadow within reach of the House proper, 'the Abbyss' whose 'unfathomable Grass' is abandoned to the mercy of a particular breed of men, the mowers:

> With whistling Sithe, and Elbow strong,
> These Massacre the Grass along:
> While one, unknowing, carves the *Rail*,
> Whose yet unfeather'd Quils her fail.
> (ll. 393–6)

The natural order, wearing man's smudge, is reduced to its original chaos; and with the mowers in command of the field, the narrator eventually takes 'sanctuary' in the wood. But the nightmare continues as the natural order in turn duplicates the destructiveness of man, and incarnadines all making the green one red. The peril now is an internal one. It is enclosed within 'the tallest Oak':

the Tree . . .
A *Traitor-Worm*, within it bred.
(As first our *Flesh* corrupt within
Tempts impotent and bashful *Sin*.)
And yet that *Worm* triumphs not long,
But serves to feed the *Hewels young*.
While the Oake seems to fall content,
Viewing the Treason's Punishment
(st. 70)

The innocuous monosyllable 'seems' speaks for itself.

The narrator is understandably alarmed. He therefore leaves the wood, only to descend into the ultimate retreat of self-deception. After assuming the cloak of the 'easie Philosopher', he meets young Maria and explodes in hyperbolic praise to the point of incredulity (ll. 651 ff.).

Maria has been welcomed with immense enthusiasm, and evident relief, by a battalion of critics. She has been described as 'a true representative of purity and innocence', as the embodiment of 'the ideal union of active and contemplative virtues', as 'the epitome of beauty, law, and harmony', and even as the conjunction of the wisdom of Pallas Athena ('the virgin of virgins') and Sophia ('the graver and more potent daughter of Jehovah').[32] With respect, however, I am not certain I understand how a poem which advances from a cry of despair over the luckless apple tasted to a harrowing vision of fallen man's rampant destruction of nature, can abruptly introduce an idealized figure and expect us to assent without protest. The evidence on the contrary points to a figure which the poet – but not the narrator – qualifies substantially. Elaborate praise, after all, was not a habit Marvell indulged in aimlessly; nor was he prepared to abscind from his general view of fallen humanity an individual however young and innocent. In associating Maria with a comet (l. 683), the poet intends us to regard not only the 'flame which purifies because it is heavenly'[33] but the menacing overtones which the passing of comets through Renaissance literature invariably suggests. Our suspicions once aroused, we perceive that Marvell's Maria is removed from Donne's Elizabeth Drury thrice as far as is the centre from the utmost pole:

> Hence *She* with Graces more divine
> Supplies beyond her *Sex* the *Line;*
> And, like a *sprig of Misleto,*
> On the *Fairfacian Oak* does grow;
> Whence, for some universal good,
> The *Priest* shall cut the sacred Bud;
> While her *glad Parents* most rejoice,
> And make their *Destiny* their *Choice.*
> (st. 93)

Such are the echoes that inhabit a major poem that we cannot dispart 'the Fairfacian Oak' from the account earlier given of 'the tallest Oak' enclosing a traitor-worm. Moreover, be the associations attendant upon the mistletoe what they may, we cannot ignore that it is also parasitic – 'baleful Misseltoe', in Shakespeare's common phrase (*Titus Andronicus*, II, iii, 95). In other words, even as Maria amasses praise rightly lavished, Marvell's realism interposes a reminder that as a member of the postlapsarian world she is, potentially at least, a threat. To deem otherwise is to credit that Marvell sequestered 'out of the world into *Atlantick* and *Eutopian* polities, which never can be drawn into use'.

Maria is therefore not the 'resolution' of *Upon Appleton House*. Just as Milton's *Comus* transcends the Lady and her brothers as much as Comus and his crew to acclaim the joyous dance of life, so Marvell's poem courses beyond Maria and her family as much as the mowers to celebrate the delightfully light-hearted prospect of the last stanza:

> But now the *Salmon-Fishers* moist
> Their *Leathern Boats* begin to hoist;
> And, like *Antipodes* in Shoes,
> Have shod their *Heads* in their *Canoos.*
> How *Tortoise like*, but not so slow,
> These rational *Amphibii* go?
> Let's in: for the dark *Hemisphere*
> Does now like one of them appear.

Except for the two poems on the cosmic figure of the Lord Protector, Marvell circumscribed mere idealism by the circle of reality. But his ambidextrous art also suggests, as it does here, that sublunar reality must on the one hand induce disquiet because the dark hemisphere remains dark, yet on the other instil confidence because the same hemisphere could 'appear' like the protective shell of the amiable tortoise within the natural order.

IV

Marvell's art, comprised in part of elements selectively drawn from a variety of poets as noted earlier (pp. 32 ff.), depends in the final analysis on the practice of his Greek and Roman predecessors. The poet whom Milton described as 'a scholar and well read in the Latin and Greek authors'[34] – spectacular praise considering the source! – applied his direct knowledge of classical poetry partly to his Latin poems and consistently to his English. The qualities harvested are well-attested: respect for form, restraint in the use of language, economy in phraseology, and discretion in the display of emotions.

So much for appearances. For Marvell also evinces a Donne-like theatricality, especially when he wishes pointedly to call attention to a deviation from the titular norms. The nominal serenity of the verse is not thereby negated; it is confirmed, not in spite but because of the currents that seethe beneath the surface in controlled turbulence. The effect is oddly reminiscent of the stylized Racine who could as in *Bajazet* abruptly lash out with incredible savagery. It puzzles readers, inviting questions raised with mounting irritation. What is the issue debated in 'A Dialogue between the Soul and Body'? Is the poem a dialogue at all? Are its two protagonists 'a comic duo' perhaps?[35] By the same token, is 'The Definition of Love' a proper definition, or indeed about love? Was its title 'attached to the poem by mistake'?[36] Equally, is 'The Nymph complaining for the death of her Faun' fraught with religious overtones, or is it strictly pagan, what a German critic ever so impressively calls 'eine bacchantisch-erotische Szene zwischen Nymphen und Faunen'?[37]

But no poem has forced critical hairs to stand on end more than 'The Garden'. Its background has been said to be Platonic in general or Plotinian in particular, and Hermetic as well as Epicurean or even Cartesian, while the narrator in the foreground has been conflated with any number of mythological figures inclusive of the androgynous Adam.[38] Marvell's vexatious garden scarcely confirms Bacon's view that a garden is 'the purest of human pleasures, . . . the greatest refreshment to the spirits of man'.[39]

'The Garden' may be described best after the fashion of the *theologia negativa*, i.e. not what it is but what it is not. Marvell's theology is after all like Shakespeare's, not dogmatic but suggestive, entirely subordinate to the demands of an art which is nevertheless founded upon a given order of theological premises. Thus the poem's fifth stanza – the evocation of the garden's sensuous fruits like the 'curious Peach' – terminates in the narrator's 'fall on Grass' and thereby might be said to intimate the Fall. It is on the other hand rather odd that such an intensely emotional experience should occur *after* the exorcism of 'Passions heat' mentioned in the previous stanza, and indeed *after* the indication ventured even earlier that the garden encloses not uncessant labour but repose, not toil but quiet, not action but contemplation. The chronology of the poem, I am suggesting, does not accord with the sequence of events in the 'historical' Fall; and because it does not, we are cautioned against a precipitous identification of the narrator with Adam, androgynous or not. As if to admonish us further, Marvell deploys throughout the poem a cluster of irksome adjectives, and in this stanza one in particular: 'curious', presented in improbable modification of the peach. Could 'curious' mean only delicate or dainty? But there are any number of other meanings, all relevant, and alike dementing: anxious, attentive, careful, cautious, concerned, eager, ingenious, recondite, skilful, solicitous, studious – and the like.

The Fall may of course be present in the fifth stanza not 'historically' but mythically, as the recurrent experience that it is. If so, what is its connection with the concurrent movement described in the next stanza?

> Mean while the Mind, from pleasure less,
> Withdraws into its happiness:
> The Mind, that Ocean where each kind

Does streight its own resemblance find;
Yet it creates, transcending these,
Far other Worlds, and other Seas;
Annihilating all that's made
To a green Thought in a green Shade.

The monosyllabic 'less' of the first line, initially obscured by the outward serenity of the verse, distracts by its excess of clarity. Does the phrase 'from pleasure less' mean that the mind withdraws 'from a pleasure that is inferior', or 'from the lessening of pleasure' (in the sense that it is 'made less by pleasure')[40] – or indeed 'from the lessening of pleasure induced by its incapacity to feel pleasure'? Moreover, does 'annihilating' mean reducing, possibly even obliterating, or – in diametric contrast – transcending? Our answers will in each instance determine the reading immediately of the import of 'a green Thought in a green Shade', and mediately of the entire poem. The greenness should in any case not be stressed to the exclusion of other elements,[41] lest we elevate a transient detail to Armado's generalization in *Love's Labour's Lost* ('Green indeed is the colour of lovers' (I, ii, 87)), or reduce it to Gonzalo's perception in *The Tempest*:

Gonzalo. How lush and lusty the grass looks! how green!
Antonio. The ground indeed is tawny.
Gonzalo. With an eye of green in 't.
Antonio. He misses not much.

(II, i, 52–5)

The tenor of 'The Garden' to the end of the sixth stanza conditions our response to what ensues. In the seventh stanza we run into the soul. It has glided into the boughs where, 'like' a bird, it is self-consciously engaged in an uncessant labour:

it sits, and sings,
Then whets, and combs its silver Wings;
And, till prepar'd for longer flight,
Waves in its Plumes the various Light.

The hyperbole is assessed best if the soul's pastime here is referred to the echoes it collects from wisdom's activities in *Comus*:

Wisdoms self
Oft seeks to sweet retired Solitude,
Where with her best nurse Contemplation
She plumes her feathers, and lets grow her wings
That in the various bussle of resort
Were all to ruffl'd, and sometimes impair'd.
(ll. 375–80)

The soul in Marvell's poem is also 'ruffl'd', and perhaps even 'impair'd'; but its predicament is largely the result of its own 'bussle'. In consequence, I am not persuaded that the soul 'rises towards divine beauty'. [42] Strictly intent upon itself, the soul is only vaguely considering the possibility ('till') that it might eventually be 'prepar'd' for longer flight. Earth-bound for the foreseeable future, it is oddly similar to the garden's other sublunar representatives of 'mortal Beauty' – Daphne and Syrinx among them – who also ended into the boughs, in their case literally (ll. 27–32).

The transmuted Daphne and Syrinx are not the only members of the fair sex who inhibit Marvell's garden. There are two more: Quiet and her 'sister dear' Innocence (ll. 9–10). The narrator therefore deludes himself when in the penultimate stanza he compares his circumstances to 'that happy Garden-state, / While Man there walk'd without a Mate'. Having retreated into self-deception – much as his counterpart in *Upon Appleton House* does – he can now only revert to the natural order which alone (as Milton said) 'can be drawn into use'. Hence the last stanza:

How well the skilful Gardner drew
Of flow'rs and herbes this Dial new;
Where from above the milder Sun
Does through a fragrant Zodiack run;
And, as it works, th' industrious Bee
Computes its time as well as we.
How could such sweet and wholsome Hours
Be reckon'd but with herbs and flow'rs!

The 'Dial new' is not in fact new at all. The natural order of the poem's outset – the order of palms and oaks and bays (l. 2) – is of the self-same universe which the Creator endowed upon its inception with extraordinary beauty and perfection. The change is solely in the narrator's recognition that the natural order is indeed perfect, indeed beautiful. For a while the sun appeared to be less mild, and the zodiac less fragrant, because several experiences intervened to suggest so: the narrator's own extreme responses, or the mutilation of the garden of the world by the mower-like 'cruel' lovers (ll. 19–20). The man-induced horrors of 'this world of evill', it is clear, are not bypassed. Acknowledged as a fact of existence, they are concurrently placed within the larger context of the time-bound universe of 'sweet and wholsome Hours' under the supervision of 'the skilful Gardner'.

Marvell's theology, here as elsewhere, trembles on the brink of non-existence. Yet it is vital to his poetry all the same, in measure equal to his agreement with Sir Thomas Browne that 'the greatest mystery of Religion is expressed by adumbration'.[43] The adumbration in Marvell's case involves a sustained vision not of the supernatural order, however, as of the pendant world. He seems always prepared for longer flight, it is true; but he'd much rather sit and sing, then whet and comb his silver wings.

Notes

1 *Brief Lives*, ed. Oliver L. Dick, 3rd ed., London, Secker & Warburg, 1960, p. 196. Two abbreviations used hereafter should be noted: Carey (i.e. John Carey, ed., *Andrew Marvell*, Penguin Critical Anthologies, Harmondsworth, Penguin Books, 1969) and Wilding (i.e. Michael Wilding, ed., *Marvell*, 'Modern Judgements', London, Macmillan, 1969).

2 27 February 1879; in *Correspondence of Gerard Manley Hopkins and Richard Watson Dixon*, ed. C. C. Abbott, London, Oxford University Press, 1935, II, p. 23.

3 In her biography of the poet (1929); in Carey, p. 33.

4 *The Rehearsal Transpros'd*, ed. D. I. B. Smith, London, Oxford University Press, 1971, p. 187.

5 Samuel Parker, *A History of his own Time*, trans. Thomas Newlin, London, 1727, p. 332.

6 The first essay was published in the *Times Literary Supplement* on 31 March 1921; the second, in the *Nation and the Athenaeum* on 29 September 1923. Both are available in Carey, pp. 46–60, and Wilding, pp. 45–59.

7 Eliot, in Carey, p. 50, and in Wilding, p. 49. The critic quoted is Maren-Sofie Røstvig, 'Andrew Marvell and the Caroline Poets', in *English Poetry and Prose, 1540–1674*, ed. Christopher Ricks, London, Sphere Books, 1970, p. 223.

8 A. Alvarez, *The School of Donne*, London, Chatto & Windus, 1961, p. 104; also in Wilding, p. 182.

9 Seriatim: J. B. Leishman, *The Art of Marvell's Poetry*, London, Hutchinson, 1966, p. 119; Joseph H. Summers, 'Marvell's "Nature" ', *Journal of English Literary History*, X (1953), p. 135 (also in Carey, p. 150); and Kitty Scoular, *Natural Magic*, Oxford, The Clarendon Press, 1965, p. 176 (also in Carey, p. 312).

10 Seriatim: Eliot, in Carey, p. 55; Pierre Legouis, *Andrew Marvell*, 2nd ed., Oxford, The Clarendon Press, 1968, pp. 42, 62, etc.; and J. B. Broadbent, *Poetic Love*, London, Chatto & Windus, 1964, p. 252 (also in Carey, p. 158).

11 J. H. Summers, in Carey, p. 140, and J. B. Leishman, as above (note 9), p. 202, respectively.

12 The case for 'The Weeper' was proposed by P. Legouis, as above (note 10), p. 35. The sane judgment involving Marino *et al.* is by Donald M. Friedman, *Marvell's Pastoral Art*, London, Routledge & Kegan Paul, 1970, p. 46.

13 Patrick Cruttwell, *The Shakespearean Moment*, New York, Random House, 1960, p. 199 (also in Carey, p. 118).

14 Harold E. Toliver, *Marvell's Ironic Vision*, New Haven, Conn., Yale University Press, 1965, p. 159.

15 Twice in Latin (the elegies on the Bishop of Ely and the Vice-Chancellor at Cambridge), and once in English (the translation of Horace's *Ode*, I, 5):

> What slender youth, bedewed with liquid odours,
> Courts thee on roses in some pleasant cave,
> Pyrrha? For whom bind'st thou
> In wreaths thy golden hair . . . ?
> (etc.)

16 Gordon Williams, *The Nature of Roman Poetry*, London, Oxford University Press, 1970, p. 174.

17 *The Odes of Horace*, I, 37; trans. James Michie, Harmondsworth, Penguin Books, 1967.

18 From Thomas May's translation of Lucan (1626); quoted and discussed by R. H. Syfret in *Review of English Studies*, n.s., XII (1961), pp. 160–72. Syfret also remarks perceptively on Marvell's affinities with Horace.
19 *Selected Prose*, ed. C. A. Patrides, Harmondsworth, Penguin Books, 1974, p. 219.
20 E.g. M. C. Bradbrook and M. G. Lloyd Thomas, *Andrew Marvell*, Cambridge University Press, 1940, repr. 1961, p. 75; *et al.*
21 Christopher Hill, *Puritanism and Revolution*, London, Secker & Warburg, 1958, pp. 362, 364. The Ode has also been reduced to a document in support of Cromwell, else a treatise in censure of his Machiavellianism. The first theory is by John M. Wallace, *Destiny his Choice: The Loyalism of Andrew Marvell*, Cambridge University Press, 1968, ch. II; the second, by Joseph A. Mazzeo, *Renaissance and Seventeenth-Century Studies*, New York, Pantheon Books, 1964, ch. VIII (initially published in the *Journal of the History of Ideas*, XXI (1960), pp. 1–17, where it was severely criticized by Hans Baron (ibid., pp. 450–1)).
22 'The First Anniversary of the Government under O.C.', ll. 46, 101, 126, 239; and 'A Poem upon the Death of O.C.', ll. 101, 157.
23 As above (note 4), p. 91.
24 As R. M. Cummings argues in 'The Difficulty of Marvell's "Bermudas"', *Modern Philology*, LXVII (1969–70), p. 338.
25 'Damon the Mower': the concluding line.
26 *The Poems of Thomas Third Lord of Fairfax*, ed. Edward B. Reed, *Transactions of the Connecticut Academy of Arts and Sciences*, XIV (1909), pp. 261 and 262.
27 *The Garden of Cyrus*, in *The Major Works*, ed. C. A. Patrides, Harmondsworth, Penguin Books, 1977, p. 327.
28 In Carey, p. 51, and Wilding, p. 50.
29 Robin Grove, in Carey, p. 296.
30 Louis L. Martz, *The Wit of Love*, Notre Dame (Ind.) University Press, 1969, p. 186.
31 From *The Hermetic Museum* (1677), quoted together with other references by A. B. Chambers, ' "I was but an inverted Tree": Notes toward the History of an Idea', *Studies in the Renaissance*, VIII (1961), pp. 291–9. The idea harks back to Plutarch's view of man 'inverted to point to heaven' (*De exilio*, V (600F)).
32 Seriatim: Maren-Sofie Røstvig, in *English Studies*, XLII (1961), p. 350; Frederic H. Roth, Jr, in *Texas Studies in Literature and Language*, XIV (1972), p. 281; Barbara K. Lewalski, *Donne's 'Anniversaries' and the Poetry of Praise*, Princeton University Press, 1973, p. 359; and Don

Cameron Allen, *Image and Meaning*, Baltimore, Johns Hopkins University, 1960, pp. 149 ff. Only one critic has shrewdly observed that Maria's portrait is sketched with 'affectionate gaiety', 'a distinct jocularity' (Frank J. Warnke, *Versions of Baroque*, New Haven, Conn., Yale University Press, 1972, pp. 121–2).

33 Kitty Scoular, op. cit. (note 9), p. 178.

34 From Milton's recommendation of Marvell for employment by the republican government, February 1653.

35 Peter Berek, 'The Voices of Marvell's Lyrics', *Modern Language Quarterly*, XXXII (1971), p. 144.

36 Frank Kermode, 'Definitions of Love', *Review of English Studies*, n.s., VII (1956), p. 184.

37 Werner Vordtriede in his translation of the poem in *Die Neue Rundschau*, LXXII (1961), p. 869.

38 On the latter, see Lawrence W. Hyman in *Journal of English Literary History*, XXV (1958), pp. 13–22. Plotinus is invoked by Milton Klonsky in *Sewanee Review*, LVIII (1950), pp. 16–35; the Hermetic tradition, by Maren-Sofie Røstvig in *English Studies*, XL (1959), pp. 65–76; Epicureanism, by John M. Potter in *Studies in English Literature*, XI (1971), pp. 137–51; and Cartesianism, by Daniel Stempel in *Journal of the History of Ideas*, XXVIII (1967), pp. 99–114. The Platonic dimension is averred with various emphases, depending on the thesis argued.

39 'Of Gardens', in *Essays* (1625), XLVI; in *Works*, ed. James Spedding *et al.*, London, 1861, VI, pp. 485–92.

40 The first alternative was espoused by Legouis (in Carey, p. 267), who is followed by Leishman and Summers; and the second, by William Empson (in Carey, p. 239). See also Kermode (in Carey, p. 260) and Warnke, op. cit. (note 32), pp. 117 f.

41 Cf. Stanley Stewart: 'greenness in itself does not present the final statement of value in the poem' (*The Enclosed Garden*, Madison, University of Wisconsin Press, 1966, p. 162).

42 Frank Kermode, 'The Argument of Marvell's "Garden" ', *Essays in Criticism*, II (1952), p. 241 (also in Carey, p. 265).

43 Thomas Browne, as above (note 27), p. 376.

3

Marvell's metaphysical wit

A. J. Smith

Anyone who seeks a shaping spirit in Marvell's best poetry risks being mocked for a solemn ass by the ironic many-sidedness of the poems themselves. So be it then, if this is the price of interrogating that urbane poise whose elegance is yet so far removed from the manners of a Dorimant or a Mirabell. Marvell's wit can be dry, even droll, and he is adept at evading our attempts to pin down the poet in the poetry. I am concerned with a quality which I think is truly there in the writing, and gives Marvell's poetry its peculiar power; but to the extent that I have to be categorical about it I feel uneasy when I go back to the poems themselves. Marvell scarcely strikes one as a committed poet, a Vaughan or a Milton or a Herbert, or a Donne either. He is a rare kind of artist who will touch the profoundest concerns of his day in the course of weaving an elegant compliment, or animating a graceful fiction, or simply striking a bold poetic attitude. You cannot induce a metaphysic from the poems; but I doubt if you can account for the way they work, and for much that is in them, unless you allow that for him as for some other seventeenth-century poets wit was a means to final truth. If I can bring out that point for him I shall have fewer qualms about hacking my way single-mindedly through those subtle imaginative textures.

The poetry which concerns me now was written in the few years from the mid-1640s to the early 1650s when Marvell was aged between 24 and 32 or so. It almost exactly coincides with the climax in

Vaughan's inner life which caused that abrupt turn from fashionable love verse to the search for regeneration in rural Brecon, and issued in the two parts of *Silex Scintillans* – 1650 and 1655. In all I say, then, I am implicitly interested in the way Marvell's poetry relates to other seventeenth-century poetry, especially metaphysical poetry, and in what it tells us of the issues which were running in England in the wake of the Civil Wars. It seems obvious enough that Marvell's lyric poetry is engaged in some way with the great moral and metaphysical questions that preoccupied some of the best English minds in the early 1650s. But it makes its own terms with those issues when it transforms them into graceful wit, entertaining them speculatively and often with amused self-mockery rather than urgently seeking to bring them into intellectual coherence, or to find through their poetic resolution a means of spiritual renewal. When we ask ourselves what Marvell's wit is doing, what kind of apprehension it embodies, we are already taking up that particularly subtle engagement with the life of those times.

The poise of Marvell's lyric poetry is partly an effect of the way that things continually confront their opposites in it, without heat. I mean not only that Marvell likes the form of poetic debate but that his poems get some of their power from a kind of inner dialectic as attitudes set each other off, or a developing argument implicitly supposes its opposite case, or seemingly opposite qualities are brought into unexpected relation:

> To make a final conquest of all me,
> Love did compose so sweet an Enemy,
> In whom both Beauties to my death agree,
> Joyning themselves in fatal Harmony;
> That while she with her Eyes my Heart does bind,
> She with her Voice might captivate my Mind.
> ('The Fair Singer', ll. 1–6)

This is the dialectical manner that the Caroline poets picked up from Donne; but even in his modish pieces Marvell's witty movements have a substance which you will not find in the chop logic of a Stanley or a Cleveland. He will bring opposed forces to a tense equipoise, balancing a woman's beauties which might repair the whole world's shortcomings against her lover's passions which can ignite all nature:

So we alone the happy rest,
Whilst all the World is poor,
And have within our Selves possest
All Love's and Nature's store.
('The Match', ll. 37–40)

Or he will coolly leave the conflicting possibilities unresolved in the interest of a more wisely perceived equivocalness; as when he brushes aside people's cynically ingenious explanations of Clora's tears over Strephon's body with a refusal to add his own conjecture:

How wide they dream! The *Indian* Slaves
That sink for Pearl through Seas profound,
Would find her Tears yet deeper Waves
And not of one the bottom sound.
('Mourning', ll. 29–32)

The curious and beautiful equating of physical action with metaphysical speculation, so simply done in the play on 'profound', shows how even this playing wit assumes a metaphysic. Or the final voice in a debate may seem less than conclusive in the circumstances because the issues remain in tension, or a deciding choice between two opposite possibilities is at best tentative and hopeful. Which of the pictures in a gallery most fitly represents Clora? Shall we best see her as inhuman murderess, or a soft Aurora? as a ghoulish enchantress, or a shell-wafted Venus? The lover turns away from the teasing alternatives in favour of the picture of her that took him when he first entered the gallery, which shows her just as

A tender Shepherdess, whose Hair
Hangs loosely playing in the Air,
Transplanting Flow'rs from the green Hill,
To crown her Head, and Bosome fill.
('The Gallery', ll. 53–6)

The poem will not let us decide whether she is demon, goddess, or simple shepherdess, and plainly the chances are that she has a bit of all three in her. Or still more telling, the poet shows us attitudes abruptly turning into their opposites as occasions shift, not in a spirit of sceptical relativism but with an amused sense of how circumstances may alter our most confirmed postures and professions, how little in our affairs is unambiguously stable. Chloe earnestly repels Daphnis just until she thinks she can prevent his departure by yielding:

> But, with this sad News surpriz'd,
> Soon she let that Niceness fall;
> And would gladly yield to all,
> So it had his stay compriz'd.
> ('Daphnis and Chloe', ll. 9–12)

Daphnis is hot in his importunity just until Chloe yields, when he at once refuses the offered fruition because it would pollute the pure grief of parting and heighten the anguish of loss. Not only that but the valediction itself is a fake. In the very last stanzas the poet comes back jauntily on his own device –

> But hence Virgins all beware.
> Last night he with *Phlogis* slept;
> This night for *Dorinda* kept;
> And but rid to take the Air.

And then he manages yet another dialectical twist to finish love off:

> Yet he does himself excuse;
> Nor indeed without a Cause.
> For, according to the Lawes,
> Why did *Chloe* once refuse?

The poem has already made it clear that the laws which condemn coyness and denial cannot themselves be received unambiguously, for Nature needs both innocence and coupling:

> Nature so her self does use
> To lay by her wonted State,
> Lest the World should separate;
> Sudden Parting closer glews.
> (ll. 13–16)

That may be all very well for Nature; whereas our dilemma is that innocence and fruition are now contradictory states.

In these neo-Caroline love lyrics Marvell toys elegantly and amusingly enough with a premise which he elsewhere sets out with some force, playing upon the assumption that our impulses are hopelessly at odds with the intractable nature of things. It is not so much the vagaries of a cruel mistress his lovers decry as the contradictoriness of circumstance itself, when love stands in hopeless opposition to Fate and has for its only fit emblem a lover who is

by the Malignant Starrs,
Forced to live in Storms and Warrs:
('The unfortunate Lover', ll. 59–60)

The drama of the elements that breaks around Marvell's unfortunate lover is simply mature love itself, by which we seek 'To make impression upon Time'. The reward of love is an eternal doom of tears, sighs, hopes, despairs, which assail the lover as elemental forces such as he may not hope to overcome but can only defy:

The Sea him lent these bitter Tears
Which at his Eyes he alwaies bears.
And from the Winds the Sighs he bore,
Which through his surging Breast do roar. . . .

Whilst he, betwixt the Flames and Waves,
Like *Ajax*, the mad Tempest braves.
(ll. 17–20, 47–8)

You can see what Marvell is doing here if you put this beside Petrarch's bold figure of the lover as a vessel assailed and astray in a projection of his own spiritual turbulence, 'Passa la nave mia'. In Marvell's poem it is not so much the lady as the universe itself which denies him a fruition of his love:

No Day he saw but that which breaks,
Through frighted Clouds in forked streaks.
While round the ratling Thunder hurl'd,
As at the Fun'ral of the World. . . .

See how he nak'd and fierce does stand,
Cuffing the Thunder with one hand;
(ll. 21–4, 49–50)

Indeed the ironic title of the poem called 'The Definition of Love' simply points up the universal irony of a condition in which a perfect love is begotten by despair and defined precisely by the impossibility of its fruition. To consummate such a love would be to deny or abolish altogether the present state of things:

> For Fate with jealous Eye does see
> Two perfect Loves; nor lets them close:
> Their union would her ruine be,
> And her Tyrannick pow'r depose.
> (ll. 13–16)

Marvell's cool impersonal irony plays off against the assurance of Donne's 'The Exstasie', the more pointedly in the way Marvell brings in hard images from current sciences – iron wedges, planisphere and all – to define a precisely opposite condition of right love from Donne's:

> And therefore her Decrees of Steel
> Us as the distant Poles have plac'd,
> (Through Loves whole World on us doth wheel)
> Not by themselves to be embrac'd.
> (ll. 17–20)

That parenthesis so nicely takes off the Donne mode as to be all but tongue in cheek. It comes as a particularly ironic glance at the old hyperbole of fulfilled lovers when the point it serves is that this love is perfect and enduring just because it can have no consummation, being enviously debarred from its natural course by Fate, and kept to nothing more satisfying than a 'Conjunction of the Mind, / And Opposition of the Stars'. These lovers stand beyond the reach of time and the world's changes not because they 'dye and rise the same, and prove / Mysterious' by their love but because their passion is eternally frustrated of its end. Marvell laments the brevity of desire in his own ironic way; but no less than the love poetry of Suckling and Rochester his poem turns on a disillusioned acknowledgment that our commitments must be frail when their fruition brings instant change.

The common outcry of seventeenth-century love poets was that love is self-contradictory because beauty and innocence are threatened by the very passions they kindle, and passion itself is destroyed by the consummation it seeks. Poets who turn from the woman-hunt to argue against fruition have at least the logic of despair, for if passion dies with its fulfilment then the best state of love must be that in which love is not consummated, or innocence does not arouse desire:

> Common Beauties stay fifteen;
> Such as yours should swifter move;
> Whose fair Blossoms are too green
> Yet for Lust, but not for Love.
> ('Young Love', ll. 9–12)

Marvell's invitation to a mutual love which might crown the lovers joint monarchs of love's empire is pointedly addressed to a young girl not yet nubile, and nicely mingles the yearning for a love that endures with the trappings of amorous intrigue, and a wistful awareness of the way love destroys young innocence and itself. Deceiving her father with their snatched illicit sport they defeat time also:

> Pretty surely 'twere to see
> By young Love old Time beguil'd:
> (ll. 5–6)

The one way the poet can be sure of having her to himself is to seize her in infancy when he need fear no rivals. Indeed the entire peremptory invitation to love is made urgent by a haunted sense of the inevitable momentariness of our commitments, the general uncertainty of our state:

> Now then love me: time may take
> Thee before thy time away:
> Of this Need wee'l Virtue make,
> And learn Love before we may.
>
> So we win of doubtful Fate; . . .
> (ll. 17–21)

Opposite possibilities persistently confront each other in these love poems as the poet's mind beats about for ingenious ways of outfacing or evading the hard facts of love's case. On the one hand Arcadian lovers rise above the brief joys of their amorous sport in a choral hymn of praise to the author of enduring joy, great Pan ('Clorinda and Damon'); or they turn their yearning spirits from the shortcomings of their present state to the perfected idyll of Elizium, where

sheep are full
Of sweetest grass, and softest wooll;
('A Dialogue between Thyrsis and Dorinda', ll. 31–2)

On the other hand an amorous haymaker brusquely settles the question whether women better assure love by denial or by exchanging love for love, breaking off the nice emblematic debate with an invitation to seize the moment that offers –

Then let's both lay by our Rope,
And go kiss within the Hay.
('Ametas and Thestylis making Hay-Ropes', ll. 15–16)

These Arcadian dialogues draw their strange wistful beauty from a sense of the way love's delights, and our lives altogether, are threatened by the brevity of things and by time. They offer us pastoral lovers who feel themselves menaced from within by the frailty of passion, the shortness of desire, and a sense of the fatal contradiction between the pleasures of sense and the joys of spirit:

C. I have a grassy Scutcheon spy'd,
Where *Flora* blazons all her pride.
The Grass I aim to feast thy Sheep:
The Flow'rs I for thy Temples keep.
D. Grass withers; and the Flow'rs too fade.
C. Seize the short Joyes then, ere they vade. . . .
Near this, a Fountaines liquid Bell
Tinkles within the concave Shell.
D. Might a Soul bath there and be clean,
Or slake its Drought?
('Clorinda and Damon', ll. 3–8, 13–16)

This is surely very beautiful, not least in that sudden shudder into metaphysical sentience which is possible only to poets who feel in nice equipoise an imaginative commitment to two distinct orders of being at once. It is part of the strange effect these little Arcadian poems have that in them the delights of sense lie so close to the anticipated delights of spirit from which they are irredeemably divided.

'Had we but World enough, and Time'. The tone of 'To his Coy Mistress' marvellously catches a complex human attitude – a very diverting one too – so that it seems crude to speak of the piece as a formal argument at all. Like Donne's 'The Exstasie' Marvell's poem gives another dimension to the persuasion to love, which I am tempted to call a metaphysical dimension if only because of the way the writing continually holds unlike possibilities of being in one imaginative order. Marvell's dialectical attitude itself implies a metaphysic. 'Had we . . .' – 'But . . .' – 'Now therefore . . .'. An imagined timeless idyll is coolly confronted with the bleak realities of our existence and the human response proposed. What really counts here of course is the ironic urbanity with which the issues are pushed through to their universal consequences. The wit, so precise in its hold on the complexities of our being, is no less precisely pitched to catch the human attitude to them. There is the humorous indulging of her coyness – and her vanity too – in hyperbolic conceits:

An hundred years should go to praise
Thine Eyes, and on thy Forehead Gaze.
Two hundred to adore each Breast:
But thirty thousand to the rest.
(ll. 13–16)

Always we have that sense of the mind wholly in control, knowing just what it is about and how far to go, coolly and speculatively weighing our condition rather than passionately flying out against it or being overwhelmed by it. With what exquisite delicacy of ironic understatement Marvell raises the bleak prospect of death, corruption, and an empty eternity!

Thy Beauty shall no more be found;
Nor, in thy marble Vault, shall sound
My ecchoing Song: then Worms shall try
That long preserv'd Virginity:
And your quaint Honour turn to dust;
And into ashes all my Lust.
The Grave's a fine and private place,
But none I think do there embrace.
(ll. 25–32)

Those haunted, and haunting, emblems and quibbles and conceits would be simply macabre if they were less elegantly or less self-mockingly rendered.

The lover's invitation to act is put in conceited images whose sensuous freshness itself beautifully catches the momentariness of things:

> Now therefore, while the youthful hew
> Sits on thy skin like morning dew,
> And while thy willing Soul transpires
> At every pore with instant Fires,
> Now let us sport us while we may;
> (ll. 33–7)

Here the writing finely hovers between sense and spirit, or tacitly calls our crude categories in question; and the bland persuasive reasonableness of the tone contrasts ironically with the images of force which put the one action open to lovers who dare evade time so far, that human assault upon the iron impediments of our condition, and seizing of fate.

The implicit concern of the poem is our lives in the world as we have it, love at the mercy of place, time, chance, the momentary offers of fortune. Much of its power comes from the concreteness with which universal issues are realized, or imaginatively experienced in a particular sensuous being, and from the supple grace with which the allowed limitations of our state are entertained and urbanely mastered. It is a brave mastery when he achieves it so resourcefully, and without dismay. The human return upon our intractable circumstances is to accept and use them, to triumph not in spite of time, death, and mere fortuity, but because of them.

'To his Coy Mistress', as Donne's love poems, puts love in pawn to time. But for Donne right love lifts the lovers uniquely beyond time and change while Marvell allows only the possibility of a brief defeat of time by a brave opportunism. The lovers must seize their moment, exploit such accidents as offer. The finely judged irony of Marvell's poem is the stance of a mind which sees little else to hold on to in our commitments of passion than the suppleness of its own wit, the exquisite assurance of its poise.

Innocence, a very different state from coyness, might be one point of stability while it lasts. Marvell delicately plays on the great myth of an original innocence lost, striking resonances from it within the acceptable terms of pastoral love or celebratory garland. His concern with innocence is at once tender and subtle; he can be warm in imaginative sympathy with young minds while wholly allowing that innocence itself is a radically equivocal quality in our world. The delicate ambiguities and complexities of 'The Picture of little T.C. in a Prospect of Flowers' make it both a subtly graceful and a searching celebration of childhood. T.C.'s innocence is a sacred power, so much at one with the natural life around it that she may sustain nature and even amend its defects:

> Mean time, whilst every verdant thing
> It self does at thy Beauty charm,
> Reform the errours of the Spring;
> Make that the Tulips may have share
> Of sweetness, seeing they are fair;
> And Roses of their thorns disarm:
> But most procure
> That Violets may a longer Age endure.
> (ll. 25–32)

But this very involvement of innocence with the processes of organic life makes it especially vulnerable to the common hazards of frail nature, and the forces that work against us in our universe and ourselves:

> But O young beauty of the Woods,
> Whom Nature courts with fruits and flow'rs,
> Gather the Flow'rs, but spare the Buds;
> Lest *Flora* angry at thy crime,
> To kill her Infants in their prime,
> Do quickly make th'Example Yours;
> And, ere we see,
> Nip in the blossome all our hopes and Thee.
> (ll. 33–40)

In a neat witty quibble Marvell reminds us that innocence itself will mature into dangerous sexuality and become cruel, even self-corrupting:

> O then let me in time compound,
> And parly with those conquering Eyes;

Ere they have try'd their force to wound,
Ere, with their glancing wheels, they drive
In Triumph over Hearts that strive,
And them that yield but more despise.
(ll. 17–22)

Then in what a delicate figure he conflates his fine praise of her innocent infancy as a beauty in shadow with a prayer to be shielded from the deadly force of her splendours when they emerge!

Let me be laid,
Where I may see thy Glories from some shade.

But in these poems the real threat to retired innocence comes from the world beyond the garden and preys upon the humane impulses. The qualities which make innocence most vulnerable in the world are gentle inoffensiveness and tender fellow-feeling:

The wanton Troopers riding by
Have shot my Faun and it will dye.
Ungentle men! They cannot thrive
To kill thee. Thou neer didst alive
Them any harm: alas nor cou'd
Thy death yet do them any good.
I'me sure I never wisht them ill;
Nor to I for all this; not will:

'The Nymph complaining for the death of her Faun' is a pastoral lament of tender beauty which in nuance of phrase and image continually plays off an idyll of ardent innocence against the harsh realities of betrayal and destruction. Pitching the situation so nicely between pastoral fiction and human actuality Marvell distances, without dimming, the guilt of blood and of such wanton violations of the simple bond of fellow-feeling as the little girl bemoans. The painful lesson the poem urges upon us is that innocent compassion itself can survive in the world only as cold marble or alabaster, violable by nothing but its own tears:

First my unhappy Statue shall
Be cut in Marble; and withal,
Let it be weeping too: but there
Th'Engraver sure his Art may spare;

For I so truly thee bemoane,
That I shall weep though I be Stone:
Until my Tears, still dropping, wear
My breast, themselves engraving there.
(ll. 111–18)

The clean weight of word and cadence is exactly placed to bring up the ironic grace of the conceit. The ironies of this beautiful poem are far from urbane but there is nothing in the least sentimental about it either; on the contrary, its mental life of allusion and ingenious conceit is steel-hard, and precisely to the point in its witty complexity.

Marvell's poetry continually offers such fresh ways of considering how we stand towards the life of nature now. That equivocal figure of the amorous mower is a marvellously imaginative device. In quaintly comic yet luminous conceits the mower laments the effect of love upon his labours, and upon his bond with nature:

Ye living Lamps, by whose dear light
The Nightingale does sit so late,
And studying all the Summer-night,
Her matchless Songs does meditate;
('The Mower to the Glo-Worms', ll. 1–4)

In taking up so divertingly the idea that sexual passion only distracts us from our natural offices Marvell gives fresh force and naturalness to the old conceit that the heats of love scorch the meadows as well as the lover. Here such ingenious pleasantries express the way the mower's labours put him at one with nature:

On me the Morn her dew destills
Before her darling Daffadils.
And, if at Noon my toil me heat,
The Sun himself licks off my Sweat.
While, going home, the Ev'ning sweet
In cowslip-water bathes my feet.
('Damon the Mower', ll. 43–8)

Distracted by love the mower mows himself; yet he can heal his scythe's wound with the natural virtues of herbs and plants, whereas death alone will cure the wound of love. He reminds himself not only of his own mortality but of what makes him mortal; for nature renews and heals itself, while our unnatural and infected wounds have no healing in the world. We had better not get too solemn about such diverting conceits, but they are not all ingenuity for ingenuity's sake either.

A conventional paradox of these Mower Poems is that their outcry against the tyranny of love makes a graceful compliment to the lady whose beauties cause such disturbances. But then the mower himself is a thoroughly ambiguous figure, being at once the accomplice of nature and a death-dealing leveller; and the deeper ambiguity of his lovelorn state is that his distraction from his task lets the meadows flourish:

> But these, while I with Sorrow pine,
> Grew more luxuriant still and fine;
> That not one Blade of Grass you spy'd,
> But had a Flower on either side;
> When *Juliana* came, and She
> What I do to the Grass, does to my Thoughts and Me.
> ('The Mower's Song', ll. 7–12)

Landscape gardening becomes a moral issue, and something more. We assume a right to bring wild chaotic nature into order by the destruction and levelling of grass, but what justifies our imposing an order upon nature? Or what order are we to impose?

> Luxurious Man, to bring his Vice in use,
> Did after him the World seduce:
> And from the fields the Flow'rs and Plants allure,
> Where Nature was most plain and pure. . . .
> With strange perfumes he did the Roses taint.
> And Flow'rs themselves were taught to paint.
> The Tulip, white, did for complexion seek;
> And learn'd to interline its cheek:
> ('The Mower against Gardens', ll. 1–14)

The mower's quaintly laboured conceits raise an issue which is not just quaint, or simply moral. May we see a garden as a necessary correcting of errant nature, a step back towards the first garden? Or must we take it as an imposing of man's corrupted vanity and doubleness upon a nature which didn't fall of itself? There is a felt tension in those Mower Poems, which invite us all the time to hold our present state of things against another possible order and imaginatively experience the disparity between the two. For all his detached grace Marvell's concern with gardens and pastoral life has a Shakespearean urgency, and a like metaphysical scope.

In his pastoral poems Marvell explores in imagination such states of nature as may still be partly exempt from the disturbing forces of the world and our own passions. What might in another age be mere Arcadian day-dream becomes in the 1650s the entertainment of a possible recourse, a search for a real moral innocence and refreshment beyond the pain and guilt of history. Marvell's one unequivocal expression of a supposed return to Eden is the hymn he gives to the English Protestants whose boat providence itself has guided to a new world altogether:

> He hangs in shades the Orange bright,
> Like golden Lamps in a green Night.
> And does in the Pomgranates close,
> Jewels more rich than *Ormus* show's.
> ('Bermudas', ll. 17–20)

Here the conceits, like Milton's in Book IV of *Paradise Lost*, simply define a right order of nature and distinguish it from our own familiar order. The hopeful voyagers celebrate a haven of purely organic riches and amenities where there is no fatal apple, the very trees recall the holy land, night is not black but green, the pearls are gospels, and the living rocks make a natural temple. Yet this is no mere fantasy of a place where the life of sense can be one with the life of spirit. For although this unspoiled second Eden stands quite apart from the blighted society we take for the world it actually exists; and its discovery is offered to us here as an authentic return of those whom providence has deemed fit to a bit of the original creation which still survives in our world. Even so unambiguous a poem plays off this uncorrupted real place against the rest of the world.

Another tension of 'Bermudas' is that a place so soon to be peopled may yet offer ironic testimony of the tenet that quiet and innocence are sacred plants, to be found here only among the plants. Marvell elevates old Isaac Walton's epigraph, study to be quiet, into a spiritual imperative. Like Walton he thinks of quiet contentment in rural surroundings as a retreat from the conflicts, social ambitions, passions, which blight the world beyond. Yet Marvell's garden poetry never lets us forget the world outside the garden, or our own incapacity to sustain such a paradisal life for more than a moment. 'The Garden' itself marvellously catches the sense of resolved quiet of mind in a real garden which is the theme of that complex meditation upon retreat:

> How vainly men themselves amaze
> To win the Palm, the Oke, or Bayes;
> And their uncessant Labours see
> Crown'd from some single Herb or Tree.
> (ll. 1–4)

Yet no one could take such witty writing for mere nature poetry. The equivocalities of the situation are so elegantly played on in a tautly graceful performance whose poise depends upon its detachment, that ironic amused alertness with which the poet holds unlike possibilities in play. The wit is always inviting us to hold the activities of 'the world' against these briefly enjoyed natural pleasures, or humorously reminding us of the natural divinity which plants have kept and we have forfeited, or implicitly prompting us to compare our state in this garden with our fallen condition, and our falls:

> Stumbling on Melons, as I pass,
> Insnar'd with Flow'rs, I fall on Grass.
> (ll. 39–40)

So perfectly is the tone of mellow rumination caught and pitched, so gracefully civil the flow, that we may well take for no more than witty humours the conceits which with quiet persistence hold in balance before us those nice moral alternatives, the pressing choices of the day. Why should we value incessant public activity before inner repose? society before solitude? sexual passion before calm self-content? mechanically ordered time before the natural rhythms of organic life? common wealth before private wisdom? Then there is a still more inward consideration for us when such a life of innocent sense is put against the life of mind, and of soul, and both possibilities are tried against our very first state:

> Mean while the Mind, from pleasure less,
> Withdraws into its happiness: . . .

Here at the Fountains sliding foot,
Or at some Fruit-trees mossy root,
Casting the Bodies Vest aside,
My Soul into the boughs does glide:
There like a Bird it sits, and sings,
Then whets, and combs its silver Wings;
And, till prepar'd for longer flight,
Waves in its Plumes the various Light.

Such was that happy Garden-state,
While Man there walk'd without a Mate:
(ll. 41–2, 49–58)

Behind even so graciously portrayed a natural self-transcendence from sense to mind, mind to soul, we come upon the strong reminder of a state in which the life of sense was one with the life of spirit, a life of spirit inherent in a life of sense. There is also the quite unMiltonic suggestion that Eve's arrival in the Garden was our first loss of bliss, no doubt as much because her coming made a society out of a solitude as because she brought in sexual passion.

The particular point of Marvell's choice of real, known country domains for types of his natural state is that he celebrates an achieved and not a merely wished-for retreat towards that first bliss. Complimentary description, moral emblem, and metaphysical meditation develop together and as one by the coadunative power of wit, as though the wit is simply a means of bringing out the harmonious wholeness of its object:

See how the arched Earth does here
Rise in a perfect Hemisphere! . . .
It seems as for a model laid,
And that the World by it was made.
('Upon the Hill and Grove at Bill-borow', ll. 1–2, 7–8)

The terrain of Fairfax's estate at Bilborrow becomes the outward style of a moral character, which has formed upon a model of order and divinity beyond nature; though it would more exactly catch the force of the conceit to say that the physical and the metaphysical orders are one here because the estate embodies the qualities of its master:

Here learn ye Mountains more unjust,
Which to abrupter greatness thrust,
That do with your hook-shoulder'd height
The Earth deform and Heaven fright, . . .
Learn here those humble steps to tread,
Which to securer Glory lead.

(ll. 9–16)

Marvell's conceits define a public eminence which is set off by retired meditation; as though worldly action grows just only when it is undertaken as a sacred calling and sustained by communion with the virtue of the natural state.

Upon Appleton House is the communion itself. Marvell presents the poem to us as just such a regenerative meditation, showing us how a man may become wise by pondering the history, design, regimen of a country house. The poem enacts a progress through the day, and the year, and a retreat back through Old Testament times to a type of innocent virtue in the garden; before the darkening prospect itself gently reminds us of the realities of our condition.

The controlling sense of this elaborate conceit is given us in the opening laud of the dynasty of the Fairfaxes, which tells how that new sacred order replaces with a better truth the old formal regimen of the nuns who previously held the house as their convent. The nuns represent a life of retired insulation from the world, which is admirable enough in its way but self-debilitating and hence frail before the onslaught of the ancestral Fairfax:

Some to the Breach against their Foes
Their *Wooden Saints* in vain oppose.
Another bolder stands at push
With their old *Holy-Water Brush*.
While the disjointed *Abbess* threads
The gingling Chain-shot of her *Beads*.
But their lowd'st Cannon were their Lungs;
And sharpest Weapons were their Tongues.

(ll. 249–56)

This time the disruptive force from outside has justice with it, and shows as fate supervening upon old order and time-hallowed growth to make a better state:

Yet, against Fate, his Spouse they kept;
And the great Race would intercept.
(ll. 247–8)

That better state, of marriage and offspring, undeniably presents itself as fate if only because it has already happened so – the offspring are there.

A new religious house is founded then, that of the Fairfaxes, which embodies a sounder understanding of active life and our relation to the world because it grows straight out of a wise reciprocity between the moral order of a man's inner being and the order of nature:

For he did, with his utmost Skill,
Ambition weed, but *Conscience* till.
Conscience, that Heaven-nursed Plant,
Which most our Earthly Gardens want.
A prickling leaf it bears, and such
As that which shrinks at ev'ry touch;
But Flowers eternal, and divine,
That in the Crowns of Saints do shine.
(ll. 353–60)

Such a right relationship even helps nature, so that the man may partly restore the order of the lapsed creation, as it were imposing his own inner harmony upon it. Marvell has the garden itself peacefully enacting the ceremonial order of the man's life, as if to right or repel the ruin which attends such military operations beyond, and always reminding us that it is itself only an inevitably imperfect semblance of the larger order which the world once presented, an elect island where by grace and wise virtue something of the primal order has been better preserved:

See how the Flow'rs, as at *Parade*,
Under their *Colours* stand displaid:
Each *Regiment* in order grows,
That of the Tulip Pinke and Rose.
(ll. 309–12)

From an elect nation to an elect, and embattled, country estate – there is the imaginative dwindling down of English sacramental history as the seventeenth century wore on, and the Civil Wars dealt their own fatal backhander to the idea of a providence at work to restore Britain to the state of Eden:

> Oh Thou, that dear and happy Isle
> The Garden of the World ere while,
> Thou *Paradise* of four Seas,
> Which *Heaven* planted us to please,
> But, to exclude the World, did guard
> With watry if not flaming Sword;
> What luckless Apple did we tast,
> To make us Mortal, and The Wast?
>
> Unhappy! shall we never more
> That sweet *Militia* restore,
> When Gardens only had their Towrs,
> And all the Garrisons were Flowrs,
> When Roses only Arms might bear,
> And Men did rosie Garlands wear?
> (ll. 321–34)

Britain, wrecked from within, by what apple tasted? what new Fall? These are the questions which made urgent the search for an order nearer the first state in the early 1650s.

Yet it is a search which Marvell's poem conducts in quiet, ingenious geniality even as it celebrates the changing life of the Fairfax estate. In the tall grass the grasshoppers become giants and mock the men who walk beneath them:

> They, in their squeking Laugh, contemn
> Us as we walk more low then them:
> (ll. 373–4)

Dew and slaughtered quails rain down together, as manna upon the Israelites of old. The very cattle now appear scaled down as in a painting, now as spots on faces, now fleas, and now as the heavenly constellations:

> They seem within the polisht Grass
> A Landskip drawen in Looking-Glass.
> And shrunk in the huge Pasture show
> As Spots, so shap'd, on Faces do.

Such Fleas, ere they approach the Eye,
In Multiplying Glasses lye.
They feed so wide, so slowly move,
As *Constellations* do above.
(ll. 457–64)

Such extraordinary conceits enact the brilliant transformation scenes by which the estate becomes a world and cosmos in itself, at the same time as they suggest a return through Old Testament times towards primal innocence:

This *Scene* again withdrawing brings
A new and empty Face of things; . . .
The World when first created sure
Was such a Table rase and pure.
(ll. 441–6)

A necessary condition of wisdom seems to be the unsettling of our present certitudes. So humanity is dispossessed of its supposed pre-eminence in nature as the perspective shifts; and an Ovidean metamorphosis of species and functions disturbs our assumption of a stable order with the Swift-like suggestion that everything is relative to point of view and circumstance:

Let others tell the *Paradox*,
How Eels now bellow in the Ox;
How Horses at their Tails do kick,
Turn'd as they hang to Leeches quick;
How Boats can over Bridges sail;
And Fishes do the Stables scale.
How *Salmons* trespassing are found;
And Pikes are taken in the Pound.
(ll. 473–80)

The instability of what we take for knowledge is caught in bizarre images of total relativeness, which are the more telling because they present the world suddenly changed, as it is when we see it through the optical instruments just then invented.

The estate which enacts this hieroglyphic of relativism for us also provides the purifying Flood, and the saving Ark, the Ark being simply the green wood itself in which the poet takes refuge on equal terms with all other created life:

Where the first Carpenter might best
Fit Timber for his Keel have Prest.
And where all Creatures might have shares,
Although in Armies, not in Paires.
(ll. 485–8)

We are carried back through relativeness, chaos, and Flood, to a better state, that of the *prischi teologi* who shared the language and wisdom of the original creatures. The conceits divertingly show the poet moving towards that wise oneness with plants and animals in which he can understand nature's mystic book:

Thus I, *easie Philosopher*,
Among the *Birds* and *Trees* confer:
And little now to make me, wants
Or of the *Fowles*, or of the *Plants*.
Give me but Wings as they, and I
Streight floting on the Air shall fly:
Or turn me but, and you shall see
I was but an inverted Tree.
(ll. 561–8)

Such ironically outlandish wit half-mocks while it enacts the search for return to the natural state and the primal language, yet it keeps a sharp hold on the paradox that what the world takes for unnaturalness may be simple truth. So his better state as creature of vegetable being is pointedly played off against mere worldly wisdom, passion, rank. The seeming oddity of the conceit that transforms a man into a natural prelate may be only an index of the falsity of our understanding of priesthood:

And see how Chance's better Wit
Could with a Mask my studies hit!
The Oak-Leaves me embroyder all,
Between which Caterpillars crawl:
And Ivy, with familiar trails,
Me licks, and clasps, and curles, and hales.
Under this *antick Cope* I move
Like some great *Prelate of the Grove*,
(ll. 585–92)

Certainly the brilliant playing fancy is there to be savoured; but the play of wit shows a consistent sense, a coherent strength, and – I think – a fundamental sanity of concern.

For one thing, the wit never allows us to forget that we are still in the world, and that natural life itself is no longer an Arcadian idyll. The extraordinary conceits in which Marvell puts his self-struggle between the wish to remain in the garden, and need to return to the world, forcefully express the price he conceives that he must pay for such a natural restraint there, which is to bear gladly in himself those living nails and thorns instead of inflicting his sins upon Christ in the world:

Bind me ye *Woodbines* in your 'twines,
Curle me about ye gadding *Vines*,
And Oh so close your Circles lace,
That I may never leave this place:
But, lest your Fetters prove too weak,
Ere I your Silken Bondage break,
Do you, O *Brambles*, chain me too,
And courteous *Briars* nail me through.
(ll. 609–16)

Then the estate is all the time being played off against the lapsed world, which it cannot opt out of even while it offers a model of a better, less corrupted state. What emerges in the garden after the flood is a world as if born again without malice and without deceitful distortions, a prospect momentarily – but only momentarily – rendering back the first state of Eden:

No *Serpent* new nor *Crocodile*
Remains behind our little *Nile*;
Unless it self you will mistake,
Among these Meads the only Snake.

See in what wanton harmless folds
It ev'ry where the Meadow holds;
And its yet muddy back doth lick,
Till as a *Chrystal Mirrour* slick;
Where all things gaze themselves, and doubt
If they be in it or without.

And for his shade which therein shines,
Narcissus like, the *Sun* too pines.
(ll. 629–40)

Mary Fairfax's appearance in the garden even suspends the course of nature for a moment before darkness returns, the *bizarrie* of the conceits catching – defining as it were – the untowardness of a situation which ought to be as natural as Eve's first ministrations in Eden:

So when the Shadows laid asleep
From underneath these Banks do creep, . . .
The modest *Halcyon* comes in sight,
Flying be twixt the Day and Night;
And such an horror calm and dumb,
Admiring Nature does benum.

The viscous Air, wheres'ere She fly,
Follows and sucks her Azure dy;
The gellying Stream compacts below,
If it might fix her shadow so;
The stupid Fishes hang, as plain
As *Flies* in *Chrystal* overt'ane;
(ll. 665–78)

In her innocent virtue the little girl converses with nature, bestows her own pure beauty upon it, puts aside love's wars and snares:

She streightness on the Woods bestows;
To *Her* the Meadow sweetness owes;
Nothing could make the River be
So Chrystal-pure but only *She*; . . .

Hence *She* with Graces more divine
Supplies beyond her *Sex* the *Line*;
And, like a *sprig of Misleto*,
On the *Fairfacian Oak* does grow;
Whence, for some universal good,
The *Priest* shall cut the sacred Bud;
While her *glad Parents* most rejoice,
And make their *Destiny* their *Choice*.
(ll. 691–4, 737–44)

The poet's personal tribute to the nurture, station, prospects of his young pupil is wittily at one with the vast metaphysical conceit of regeneration; which also takes in the moral idea that as far as we can make ourselves one with regenerated nature we restore some part of the original order, and our own nature.

Yet Mary's innocence itself cannot altogether keep back night or chaos in the world. Marvell draws the poem together with a final curious reminder of the world's presence, and its return even upon this garden:

> 'Tis not, what once it was, the *World*;
> But a rude heap together hurl'd;
> All negligently overthrown,
> Gulfes, Deserts, Precipices, Stone.
> Your lesser *World* contains the same.
> But in more decent Order tame;
> *You Heaven's Center, Nature's Lap.*
> *And Paradice's only Map.*
>
> (ll. 761–8)

The conceit presents the general ruin of an order which has been revived, by particular grace, just in this one household. At Nun Appleton alone the materials have their proper places, so that the house shares with the girl the mighty hyperboles of those lines which speak of 'Your lesser *World*' as heaven's centre and sole map of paradise. The notorious – yet oddly beautiful – conceits of the final stanza follow straight on from this picture of the disorders beyond the garden:

> But now the *Salmon-Fishers* moist
> Their *Leathern Boats* begin to hoist;
> And, like *Antipodes* in Shoes,
> Have shod their *Heads* in their *Canoos*.
> How *Tortoise like*, but not so slow,
> These rational *Amphibii* go?
>
> (ll. 769–74)

Must we take these brave ingenuities just as observed fact fantastically transformed, Dylan Thomas fashion? I think not. Marvell's wit is far from comic fantasy; and the lines divertingly show the common order reasserting itself even here. There is no disorder in the garden, but no escaping time there either, as returning darkness brings back the ambiguities, reversals, topsy-turvydom of things. Light passes to the other side:

> Let's in: for the dark *Hemisphere*
> Does now like one of them appear.

A nice observant drollery is also the fit close to a meditation upon the right order of nature, bringing sensible face and metaphysical idea into one.

Such an emblematic oneness of thing and idea is more than just ingenious device, a mere yoking of heterogeneous elements by force. It would be horribly solemn to describe it as an apprehending of a metaphysical reality in the physical event, yet it brings up precisely that relation of sensible order to intelligible or spiritual order which is central in Marvell's lyrics. The two metaphysical dialogues, for example, do not simply pit soul against body or spiritual life against sensual indulgence. They show us powerfully that the relation between the two orders of our being is more agonizingly complex than that. What those powerful conceits precisely define (and they are as penetrating as they are strange) is the agony of embodied spirit, the dilemma of spiritualized sense. The soul is bolted, fettered, manacled in the body by bones and limbs; deafened and blinded with the senses; hung upright

> in Chains
> Of Nerves, and Arteries, and Veins.
> Tortur'd, besides each other part,
> In a vain Head, and double Heart.
> ('A Dialogue between the Soul and Body', ll. 7–10)

The body is goaded by the fierce demands of spirit and intellect, demon-ridden by moral awareness:

> What but a Soul could have the wit
> To build me up for Sin so fit?
> (ll. 41–2)

The debate starkly shows up the disaccord between soul and sense in our nature as it is, when these elements are interinvolved with one another yet oppress and torment each other instead of being at one. The pleasure the resolved soul contests is not at first any old hedonistic self-indulgence but created pleasure, the delight of sense in its organic oneness with the natural life around it:

Lay aside that Warlike Crest,
And of Nature's banquet share:
Where the Souls of fruits and flow'rs
Stand prepar'd to heighten yours.
('A Dialogue between The Resolved Soul, and
Created Pleasure', ll. 13–16)

But then these poems are not so much moral debates as attempts to define our nature, whose complexities and contradictions Marvell vividly comprehends in this stark opposition of ends.

'Eyes and Tears' raises the division between sense and spirit in a still more equivocal case, that in which the two contrary impulses come together in the same organ:

How wisely Nature did decree,
With the same Eyes to weep and see!
That, having view'd the object vain,
They might be ready to complain.
(ll. 1–4)

The conceits define the peculiar anguish of existence in a double state, when our sense draws us one way, our spirit another, and we know the world at all only at the cost of our innocence. To be human is to be pleased with the corrupted world and yet grieve at our corruption, a condition which cannot be eased until sense and spirit are again at one:

Thus let your Streams o'reflow your Springs,
Till Eyes and Tears be the same things:
And each the other's difference bears;
These weeping Eyes, those seeing Tears.
(ll. 53–6)

Just such a witty fusing of sensuous and emblematic properties in sharp spiritual self-awareness animates that beautiful flight of sustained poetic thinking, 'The Coronet':

When for the Thorns with which I long, too long,
With many a piercing wound,

My Saviours head have crown'd,
I seek with Garlands to redress that Wrong:
Through every Garden, every Mead,
I gather flow'rs (my fruits are only flow'rs)
Dismantling all the fragrant Towers
That once adorn'd my Shepherdesses head.
(ll. 1 ff.)

The flowing development of the dialectic enacts a growing moral awareness, carrying the poet from sin to piety and then from simple piety to a better sense of the world and his own involvement in it. With the flowers which he culls and wreathes into pious art comes the disguised serpent also, the flowers inevitably intertwined with the hidden evil, the poetry folded about 'With wreaths of Fame and Interest'. If the very attempt to repair his sins with garlands for Christ corrupts itself then Christ alone may disentangle the good impulses from the bad; or he may choose to destroy both garland and serpent together:

But thou who only could'st the Serpent tame,
Either his slipp'ry knots at once untie,
And disintangle all his winding Snare:
Or shatter too with him my curious frame:
And let these wither, so that he may die,
Though set with Skill and chosen out with Care.
That they, while Thou on both their Spoils dost tread,
May crown thy Feet, that could not crown thy Head.
(ll. 19–26)

Flowers, poems, and the 'curious frame' of the poet's own corrupted nature may alike need to be shattered to adorn Christ, who will be adorned in any case one way or another. The argument goes forward in several terms at once, coupling the blight of flowers with the poet's tainted motive for writing verses to Christ as if flowers and motive are one, being subject to the same forces of corruption and saving power which oppose each other in nature. To separate out the elements of the conceit is to see how marvellously the rhetoric sweeps the growing thought to its perfecting close, which is simply the gathering of all these elements into single apprehension. The witty vision is possible only because the elements are seen as already interinvolved – because, for this poet, thorns and flowers in themselves display the moral and metaphysical conditions of which they are emblems, and in this are one with all other organic life. The poet is caught up with them in the one complex order which intertwines organic being with spiritual being.

'On a Drop of Dew' puts the quarrel between body and soul in a formal analogue which is much more than mere figure. The morning dew in the rose really is in a sense the pure nature in the fleshly nature, the spiritual in the sensible; and it expresses its own distaste for sense, and yearning towards its sacred element:

> Yet careless of its Mansion new;
> For the clear Region where 'twas born
> Round in its self incloses:
> And in its little Globes Extent,
> Frames as it can its native Element.
> How it the purple flow'r does slight,
> Scarce touching where it lyes,
> But gazing back upon the Skies,
> Shines with a mournful Light;
> Like its own Tear,
> Because so long divided from the Sphear.
> (ll. 4–14)

But no less, the body is the rose, with a vital beauty of its own and its own involvement in organic nature. What this poem shows us very finely is that the issue between sense and spirit cannot be resolved; for the life of the body has a worth and richness of being quite distinct from the pure essence of the soul. If the fleshly element is transitory the spiritual element simply loses itself in eternity, dissolved from its white cold purity into 'the Glories of th' Almighty Sun'. The poem expresses the metaphysical dilemma of creatures of a double nature who find themselves caught irresolvably between the opposite qualities and allegiances of the two elements of their being, unable to reconcile the life of nature with the life of grace.

To judge by 'An Horatian Ode', that most civilized of political poems, Marvell's powerful vision in these years is that such nice counterposing of opposite elements is a universal principle. The Ode is a poem of 1650, which we must take for a historical document in the precise sense that it belongs to its time and place, seizes the particular public moment; but it invests the circumstances of the moment with a meaning unconfined by time and place. The metaphysical force which the poet finds at work in current history transforms Cromwell from country gardener into a power beyond nature and pits him against the king in a clash of universal opposites. Divinely sanctioned power opposes ancient rights, the order of necessity challenges the order of time:

Though Justice against Fate complain,
And plead the antient Rights in vain:
  But those do hold or break
  As Men are strong or weak.
Nature that hateth emptiness,
Allows of penetration less:
  And therefore must make room
  Where greater Spirits come.
(ll. 37–44)

In thus raising the events of his own day to a consequence beyond time, assimilating the order of history to the order of final things, Marvell shows us universal forces brought into historical confrontation. But the strength of the poem is that they are human impulses also, which are not to be judged by their outcome alone. The humane complexity of Marvell's vision, that civilized figuring of the equivocalness of our affairs, and fine celebration of a human comportment which outbraves belittling necessity, follows out his sense of our ambiguous condition altogether.

You know it was there when it stops. 'An Horatian Ode' gets some of its power from its very boldness of conceit, from the way that a seemingly unpropitious political occasion unexpectedly reveals timeless truth. Cromwell's death just eight years later offered more obvious scope for a metaphysical hyperbole, especially to a student of Donne who had already drawn heavily on the conceits of the great funeral *Anniversaries* for his poem on the first anniversary of Cromwell's rule. So it is striking that 'A Poem upon the Death of O.C.' turns out to be a wholly secular funeral elegy without any such power of witty vision. Cromwell now figures just as a moral and political force, a dead leader who has gone to heaven leaving only his exemplary fame behind him. On the evidence of this piece Marvell has already moved away from the vision which made him, for a few years, a metaphysical poet. He marches indefatigably on to his career as politician and political satirist; and a half century of metaphysical sentience begins to give place to the manners of the Town.

What makes Marvell a metaphysical poet then? We might generally and approximately speak of him so in virtue of his imaginative concerns. He puts the big questions before us, prompting us to ponder the kind of universe we inhabit, the constitution of our nature, our standing in time and eternity, the reason that life falls ever further short of the natural bliss it might be and once was. But he is a seventeenth-century English metaphysical poet in a closer way than this, with a vision that required his wit. There is his sense of the relativeness of things, which impels him to present contrary cases wittily in a dialectical tension or a conflict of opposites, as if they are both strong from their own point of view, or even to find universal contrarieties in human events. There is that subtle awareness of our double nature and allegiance, expressed with urbane irony or anguish as may be. There is the radical impulse to entertain issues wittily in conceited arguments, emblems, images, nice nuances of tone, which themselves have a distinctive metaphysical life in the way they hold unlike orders of being together in the one apprehension. Marvell's metaphysical wit amounts to something more than his speculative interests or bizarre trappings. I think of the way his poetry wittily embodies tensions which we can only call metaphysical, gets its special power and quality from a distinctive apprehension, a kind of double or multiple vision realized in the wit. It is a manner of metaphysical wit which has little to do with the clever game Johnson so brilliantly characterized in his essay on Cowley.

4

Marvell's 'Geometrick yeer': A topos for occasional poetry

S. K. Heninger, Jr

When we look at the Marvell canon, we find a fair number of poems prompted by some particular occasion. At the very beginning, we have a commendatory poem upon the publication of Lovelace's *Lucasta* and an elegy upon the death of Lord Hastings. Somewhat later we have odes in response to *public* events, such as the colonization of the Bermudas and a naval victory over the Spanish at Teneriffe, and more *personal* odes, such as 'The Picture of little T. C. in a Prospect of Flowers'. During the Cromwell government, Marvell was so diligent in noting important occasions and so politic in speculating upon their significance that he has been called Cromwell's unofficial laureate. His career in this role is clearly marked by 'An Horatian Ode upon Cromwell's Return from Ireland', 'The First Anniversary of the Government under O. C.', and 'A Poem upon the Death of O. C.' While these may not be Marvell's best poems, they none the less comprise a considerable body of work. And while we need not proclaim them unmitigated successes, we may use them to throw light upon how Marvell conceived the function of the poet and the methods of his art.

First, perhaps, we should think a bit about what 'occasional poetry' implies. To begin, we may say that it deals with an occasion, with an historical occurrence, with something that the poet has himself experienced – usually directly, though sometimes vicariously. Of course, every poem must deal with something the poet has experienced either directly or vicariously, and so every poem is in some sense occasional. We usually think of art as some sort of individual experience which is made public and permanent. The artist, whatever medium he might work in, begins with his personal experience – perhaps even, as Yeats confesses, 'in the foul rag and bone shop of the heart'; but by his artistry, he transmutes what is private and transient into something which is – well, if not universal, at least he would have us believe it so; and if not eternal, at least he egotistically hopes it will be around for a long while. So all art is occasional in this general sense. It records the experience of the artist.

But I am using the phrase as an instrument of definition, and by 'occasional poetry' I mean only those poems that have the overt intention of commemorating a particular occurrence in human affairs. Actually, the practice of such poetry, if not the phrase itself, goes far back in our cultural history. In the classical period the urge to commemorate in poetry is well attested by victory odes and political panegyrics and epithalamia and funeral elegies; and this practice has continued, though somewhat abated in recent years, to our own day. So an occasional poem records a particular event and endows it with significance.

This intention may be achieved in a variety of ways, and certainly we have a variety of occasional poems, ranging in English from Spenser's 'Epithalamion', a private event made public, to Yeats's 'Easter 1916', a public event made private. But I think we may roughly reduce the rich variety of occasional poems to two categories, defined basically by which of the two classical concepts of time each poem implies. Very early in our intellectual history there were two opposing concepts of time put forward by the giants of Greek philosophy, Plato and Aristotle. Both these explanations of time were widely known in the Renaissance, were regularly expounded, and frequently contrasted.

Plato argued, most concisely in the *Timaeus*, that time as we know it began only at that instant when the godhead gave physical extension to an archetypal idea in his mind and created the time–space continuum that we call our universe. Before that moment, time existed in the mind of the deity, but only as an idea without physical demonstration. Time as an idea in the divine mind cannot be differentiated into portions, of course; it is homogeneous and unending, what we in our efforts to understand the ineffable call 'eternity'.

But that time which we *can* comprehend – the measurable time that we perceive with our senses through changes in the physical items of our natural world – that durational time began when the godhead set our time–space continuum apart from his own being and endowed it with a recognizable degree of autonomy. And at that instant, he placed the heavenly bodies in the sky, especially the sun and moon, to mark the passage of time. The opening chapter of the Book of Genesis gives much the same account of how earthly time began.

Both Plato and the Book of Genesis are using creation as a metaphor for time in order to explain the paradox of time. When referred to the changeable items of our sense-perceptible world, time is always passing; when referred to the everlasting deity, time is static. The paradox lies in the fact that man exists within both these co-ordinates for time. And creation reveals the relationship between them. Creation explains how the eternal becomes ephemeral, how the timeless becomes timely, and therefore creation is a metaphor for the paradox of time. Just as our universe, though definable by its physicalness, still paradoxically consists in the non-physical being of the deity, so our time, though portionable into minutes, days, months, and years, consists paradoxically in the undiscriminated continuum of eternity. Indeed *our* time, as Timaeus suggests, is 'a moving image of eternity'.

Occasional poetry written in accordance with this Platonic concept of time will see the poem as a comparable image of its idea. Just as creation is a metaphor for time, bringing that concept into the sphere of our mortal senses, so the poem is a metaphor for the value that the occasion signifies. The poem is an effort to render palpable some idea that the event exemplifies. To use a somewhat technical term, the particular event is interpreted as a 'type', representing all those events with a similar significance. Spenser's 'Epithalamion', I believe, is an occasional poem of this sort. Spenser views his own wedding day as a 'type' for all nuptials, and thereby he reveals to us the principles and purposes of marriage in the most fundamental, yet farthest reaching, ways. The particular is a key-hole through which we view the universal, and that's what we are invited to do at the end of the 'Epithalamion'.

Although Aristotle, man and boy, spent twenty years in Plato's Academy, he had a quite different view of time. He was a materialist, whereas Plato was an idealist; and Aristotle thought that ultimate reality resides among the objects of physical nature, not among ideas in a remote divine mind. Therefore to him – as to Heraclitus, the most eminent of his materialistic predecessors – time consists in a series of passing moments, each of which is characterized by the qualities of the constituent physical items at that particular moment. Aristotle developed a concept of time as the *nunc*, to use the Latin term, as 'the now' – perhaps even 'the here-and-now', to use one of our own tags and include the factor of space as well as of time in this definition. Time is the *nunc*, the 'now', the 'here-and-now'. It is localized both temporally and spatially.

In this tradition, any broader thinking about time conceives it as a series of moments, a succession of nows. This is a linear concept of time, and can be readily counterposed against the Platonic concept of time, which is circular. According to the Platonists, the movement of time is determined by the heavenly bodies as they roll in their courses; and therefore, after a fixed period, time returns to a starting-point, when the heavenly bodies return to their initial positions at the instant of creation. This fixed period was the Platonic Great Year, figured variously at 26,000 or 36,000 or 49,000 of our earthly years.[1] In any case, time according to Plato returns upon itself, and therefore is circular and unified. Henry Vaughan makes the point at the beginning of one of his best known poems:

> I saw Eternity the other night
> Like a great *Ring* of pure and endless light.
> ('The World', ll. 1–2)

In contrast to this endless ring of eternity, time according to Aristotle is linear and fragmentable. It emerges from an unfathomable past, proceeds by discrete portions, and heads forward into a boundless future.

Donne was familiar with both these concepts of time and effectively plays one off against the other at the beginning of one of his many occasional poems of a highly personal sort. 'The Anniversarie' opens with:

> All Kings, and all their favorites,
> All glory' of honors, beauties, wits,
> The Sun it selfe, which makes times, as they passe,
> Is elder by a yeare, now, then it was

When thou and I first one another saw:
All other things, to their destruction draw,
  Only our love hath no decay;
This, no tomorrow hath, nor yesterday,
Running it never runs from us away,
But truly keeps his first, last, everlasting day.

Donne draws a clear distinction between his circumstance and that of everything else. Through their love, he and his mistress inhabit a Platonic world which 'no tomorrow hath, nor yesterday'; but everything else is relegated to an Aristotelian world of passing time. Donne sneers somewhat contemptuously at 'all other things, [which] to their destruction draw'. They are mutable and therefore decay towards annihilation. But he and his mistress, having (like time) returned to their original status at the end of the year and having thereby renewed their vigour, are constant and immortal. Their love 'keeps his first, last, everlasting day'.

But others have written occasional poetry without reference to the transcendent world of Plato's absolute being, and they have sought import for the event within the confines of our observable, phenomenal world. Let's speculate briefly about an occasional poem written in accordance with Aristotle's concept of time. In this system, since time is a series of passing moments, the significance of an event does not lie in its being typical, but rather in its being unusual, special, out of the ordinary. The occasional poem commemorating an event in this fashion will attempt to show how it stands out from all the other moments in passing time. It is a juncture or a climax or some other prominent node along the linear movement of time. Naturally, such a poem will be more concerned to record the distinctive details of the event than to suggest its universal or everlasting significance. It is directed to the contemporary rather than to the eternal.

The occasional poet who adheres to Aristotle's concept of time does have recourse to one method of endowing the particular event with a more than ephemeral significance. If he writes within the Judaeo-Christian tradition, he can view the particular event as part of God's omniscient plan. He may seek to enhance the import of an historical occurrence by relating it to what has gone before and to what may reasonably follow. The present is then seen as a sequential link in the chain of cause and effect that makes up human history, which unfolds according to the divine plan. The event is interpreted optimistically as evidence of providential order.[2]

Marvell's occasional poems about Oliver Cromwell for the most part take this tack. In 'An Horatian Ode upon Cromwell's Return from Ireland', Cromwell has struck England like lightning, the deity's traditional instrument of wrath. As the poem says, Cromwell acts with 'the force of angry Heavens flame' (l. 26); and at the end, with providence on his side, he 'march[es] indefatigably on' (l. 114). In the poem on 'The First Anniversary of the Government under O. C.', Cromwell is still 'indefatigable' (l. 45), and his actions are seen as efforts to establish the millennium of the Fifth Monarchy in accordance with the Book of Revelation, thereby realizing the Biblical prophecy of a holy community on earth (especially ll. 99–158). In the last lines of that poem, Cromwell is 'the *Angel* of our Commonweal' (l. 401), the agent entrusted with the divine plan for England. The much more personal elegy when Cromwell died, 'A Poem upon the Death of O. C.', opens with recognition of 'that Providence which had so long the care / Of *Cromwell's* head' (ll. 1–2), and closes by noting the omens that designate Richard Cromwell a heaven-sent successor to his father.

We have little difficulty dealing with occasional poetry of this kind. We are familiar with it, and even expect it. Such poetry accords with our own largely unexamined assumptions about time. But Marvell attempted also the other sort of occasional poetry, the more distinctively Renaissance occasional poem written in accordance with Platonic postulates. And since this other sort of poetry is farther from our usual ways of thinking, we need greater care in dealing with it.

An example of occasional poetry based upon time as a recurring cycle comes very early in Marvell's career, at a stage when he was most strongly influenced by the Spenserian tradition. In 1649 Marvell wrote and published a funeral elegy 'Upon the Death of Lord Hastings'; and while this is not a great poem, it is interesting for several reasons. At the least, it provides a *terminus a quo* for Marvell's poetic development. And for our purposes it has the additional attraction that no one else in this series of lectures is likely to say much about it.

This elegy appeared in a small memorial volume with the fashionable title *Lachrymae musarum*. When Henry Lord Hastings died of smallpox on 24 June 1649, he was 19 years old. At the time, he was engaged and soon to be married to the daughter of Sir Theodore Turquet de Mayerne, physician to the king. Mayerne enters the poem at line 48, where he is gently chided for not using his medical competence to save the life of his intended son-in-law – rather in the way that Milton chides the Nymphs for not saving the life of Lycidas. I do not know how familiar Marvell may have been with Lord Hastings, nor what his relationship might have been with the young nobleman's family.

The first two verse paragraphs of the elegy place it firmly within the co-ordinates of Platonic time, and therefore I should like to read these eighteen lines with you:

> Go, intercept some Fountain in the Vein,
> Whose Virgin-Source yet never steept the Plain.
> *Hastings* is dead, and we must finde a Store
> Of Tears untoucht, and never wept before.
> Go, stand betwixt the *Morning* and the *Flowers*;
> And, ere they fall, arrest the early *Showers*.
> *Hastings* is dead; and we, disconsolate,
> With early *Tears* must mourn his early *Fate*.
>   Alas, his *Vertues* did his *Death* presage:
> Needs must he die, that doth out-run his *Age*.
> The Phlegmatick and Slowe prolongs his day,
> And on Times Wheel sticks like a *Remora*.
> What man is he, that hath not *Heaven* beguil'd,
> And is not thence mistaken for a *Childe*?
> While those of growth more sudden, and more bold,
> Are hurried hence, as if already old.
> For, there above, They number not as here,
> But weigh to Man the *Geometrick* yeer.

The first verse paragraph is straightforward enough. We are told to mourn because '*Hastings* is dead'. And there is compliance with the conventions of elegy, especially pastoral elegy. '*Hastings* is dead' is repeated, rather in the manner of Milton, though less gracefully; '*Lycidas* is dead, dead ere his prime, / Young *Lycidas*'.

The second verse paragraph is more complex, or at least more cryptic. But when analysed, it proves to be a pastiche of familiar motifs. Hastings was too good to live, so 'his *Vertues* did his *Death* presage'. The good die young.[3] Furthermore, he had lived his allotted time, perhaps even was ahead of his time; and 'needs must he die, that doth out-run his *Age*'. There is a sad joke that some prolong their lives by holding back 'Times Wheel' like a remora holding back a ship, a bit of unnatural natural history about a sucking-fish that attaches itself to a ship's hull. But only 'the Phlegmatick and Slowe' resort to this delaying tactic, and Hastings's manliness removed him from this category. At this point, we should look again at line 9 and pick up the literal meaning of 'virtue'. The word comes, of course, from the Latin *vir*, 'man', and 'virtue' therefore means 'manliness', 'vigour'. Hastings's virtues in this sense sped him along in life, and consequently his virtues presage his death. He lived at such a pace that he went through life quickly and death came early.

The next couplet depends upon a sublimated pun and opens out from the double meaning of the italicized word '*Childe*' in line 14. 'Child' has of course its original meaning of 'infant'; the couplet implies that everyone attempts to delay death by misleading the gods into thinking he is still young, a mere child. But 'child' also has a secondary meaning, already archaic in the seventeenth century but none the less viable. 'Child' more particularly meant a youth of noble birth (*OED*, 5); and from its use as a title of honour in medieval romances, it became almost synonymous with 'knight'. In Spenser's *Faerie Queene*, for example, it appears in this sense. In Marvell's poem, 'child' as 'knight' picks up the verbal play begun by the italicized word 'virtues' in line 9, and made pointed by the word 'man' at the beginning of this couplet, line 13:

> What man is he, that hath not *Heaven* beguil'd,
> And is not thence mistaken for a *Childe*?

By intention, every man wishes to appear young in the eyes of heaven, with the hope of being regarded as a 'child' in the first sense, a youngster. But instead, he may be mistaken for a 'child' in the second sense, as a bold adventurer. And this possibility leads into the next couplet. He may be mistaken as one of 'those of growth more sudden, and more bold'; and this would thwart his intent of slowing down Time's wheel, because the adventurous, hastening through the experiences that comprise life, 'are hurried hence, as if already old'.

But then, by way of excusing this error on heaven's part, Marvell concludes the second verse paragraph with this couplet:

> For, there above, They number not as here,
> But weigh to Man the *Geometrick* yeer.

The meaning of this passage is less than apparent because of the phrase 'the *Geometrick* yeer', which has proved an interpretative crux. Many commentators have attempted to explain it, but no one is more helpful than Professor Margoliouth. In the notes on the poem in his edition of Marvell, Margoliouth observes with blunt (though admirable) honesty: '*Geometrick yeer*: an obscure phrase for which I can find no other authority.' Here I should like to venture a suggestion, which will necessarily take us far afield. But I shall begin with the lines immediately before us, and I promise in the not-so-long run to return to them.

The 'They' in line 17 who do the numbering must be the gods, because they reside 'there above'. A distinction is made between 'them' and 'us', who reside 'here' below. Furthermore, a distinction is made between the manner in which they 'number' and the manner in which we 'number'. They number by 'weigh[ing] to Man the *Geometrick* year'. But what might '*Geometrick* yeer' mean? Obviously it has to do with geometry. Perhaps it is the year conceived as some sort of geometric figure. But what?

The direction our query should take is indicated by Marvell's choice of words in this passage. In the couplet appear the words 'number' and 'weigh'; and in the very next line ('Had he but at this Measure still increast') appears the word 'Measure'. This is an unmistakable reference to a well-known dictum attributed to King Solomon: 'God created the universe according to number, weight, and measure' – a dictum by the way, echoed again by Marvell late in his career in the final line of his poem on *Paradise Lost*. Even though 'number, weight, and measure' comes from the sacred writings of the Judaeo-Christian tradition – to be exact, the Book of Wisdom, chapter 21, verse 11 – it had been early assimilated by the Platonic tradition, especially as the *Timaeus* transmits that tradition. There also, as Plutarch later confirmed,[4] the deity is a geometer who creates the cosmos according to mathematical principles. That we are right in looking to the Platonic tradition for our explanation is supported by the reference to 'Times Wheel' in line 12. Time is a wheel, a circle determined by the heavenly bodies as they roll about in their courses. This is the concept of time as eternity, a system of recurrent cycles. This is the way the gods view time, *sub specie aeternitatis*. 'They number not as here'; for we, confined within our mortal limitations, see time as a series of passing moments, a succession of changing states, *sub specie vicissitudinis*. Incarcerated within the Aristotelian *nunc*, each of us sees time from our narrow human perspective.

None the less, there is no cause for despair, or even alarm. The whole point of cosmos is that man may understand the world and his place in it by observing the beautiful order of nature. Just as God created according to number, weight, and measure, so we may arrive at knowledge of the divine intention by discovering the natural mathematics of our universe, especially the patterns prescribed by the heavenly bodies. The pattern of day and night, for example, interprets the universe as a binary system. Day and night is the daily unit of time, and the sun and the moon in their succession of one another can be used from our mortal point of view as a glimpse of eternity. Milton makes the point explicitly:

> light and darkness in perpetual round
> Lodge and dislodge by turns, which makes through Heav'n
> Grateful vicissitude, like Day and Night.
>
> (*Paradise Lost*, VI, 6–8)

By their endless repetition of the daily unit of time, by their 'perpetual round', the sun and moon extrapolate to eternity. Moreover, the succession of day and night, though evidence of mutability, is '*grateful* vicissitude' because only through this patterned sequence, this orderly change, can eternity from our vantage-point, *sub specie vicissitudinis*, be achieved.

Similarly, in addition to the *daily* unit of time, which is a binary system, there are more elaborate patterns for the *annual* unit of time. There are the four seasons, which is a quaternary system, and the twelve months or the twelve signs of the zodiac, which are twelve-part systems. In the thinking of the Renaissance, our world was frequently depicted in these forms, and here, I believe, we find a precise and concrete meaning for the phrase '*Geometrick* yeer'.

One example (Figure 5.1), which to me is a conclusive gloss on Marvell's lines, appears in a mid-sixteenth-century emblem book

AETERNA HOMINVM NATVRA.

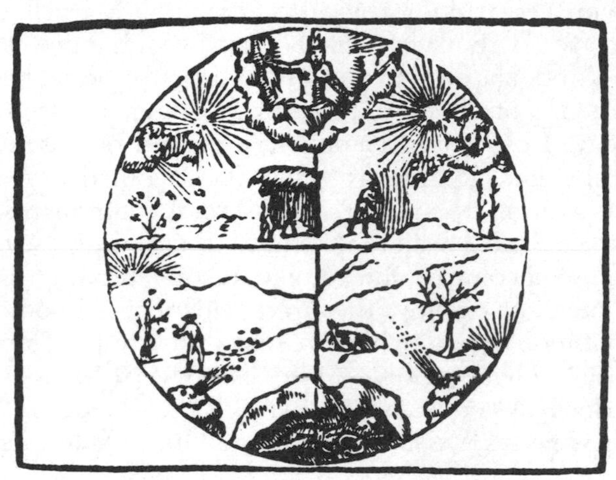

VER, Aestas, Autumnus, Hyems, Hæ quattuor annis
Sunt tempestates, orbe volubilibus
QVATTVOR ætates homo sic habet integer æui.
Qui puer, hinc iuuenis, mox vir, & inde senex:
Aeterno vt similis mundo reuolutio vitæ
Nos itidem æternos arguat eße homines.

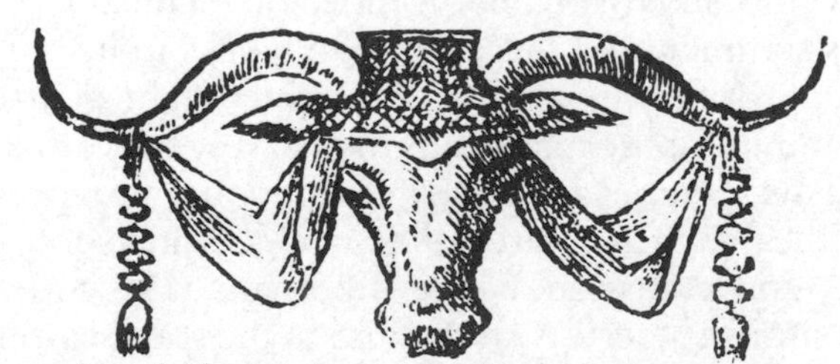

5.1 From Barthélemy Aneau, *Picta Poesis*, Lyons, 1552.

compiled by Barthélemy Aneau, printed at Lyons in 1552 and entitled *Picta poesis*, a title that we may translate as 'poetry rendered into visual images'. I do not wish to argue that Marvell knew this volume; in fact, I think it unlikely that he did, since it was not reprinted. Nor did he need to know this particular book, because the concept was one of the most common of commonplaces well past Marvell's day. I use Aneau's emblem, however, because it explains so graphically and completely what the 'geometric year' really means. It is a complex concept, with several components and far-reaching effects; and Aneau felt the need to draw upon several sorts of discourse to encompass and convey its total meaning. Like most emblem-writers, he employs the *direct* statement of gnomic saying, *Aeterna hominum natura*, which we may translate as, 'The nature of man is eternal'. He also employs the discourse of *poetic* statement, and a hexastich of verses appears beneath the woodcut. When we translate these verses, we see their applicability to Marvell's poem:

> Spring, summer autumn, winter – these are the four seasons as the years roll by in a circle. Likewise man in his lifetime has four ages: he is first a child, then a youth, next an adult, and finally an old man – so that the cycle of human life, like the undying world, reveals to us that men are undying.[5]

Finally, and most cogent for our purposes, Aneau employs the discourse of *visual image*. The woodcut depicting this emblem is rich with meaning.

To begin with the obvious, this is manifestly a representation of the year as a geometric form. We have a four-sided figure enclosing a circle, which in turn is divided into four quarters. And each quarter is devoted to one of the four seasons. The lower left quarter represents spring, and there we see a 'type' of man beside a burgeoning tree while the sun rises on the horizon. The upper left quarter represents summer, and there the man works in his fields beneath a sun that approaches its zenith. The upper right quarter represents autumn, and there the man reaps his harvest beneath a sun that has already passed overhead. The lower right quarter represents winter, and there the man waves farewell to a lifeless and soon-to-be sunless landscape, and enters a cave to hibernate. The four quarters, of course, comprise a perfect circle, just as the four seasons comprise a complete unit of time, the year.

But there is more to this woodcut than simply a diagram of the year. At the bottom of the figure, the man is entombed to demonstrate his mortality. We have traced his linear path through time as a series of moments; and at the end of his allotted time, he dies. But symmetrically placed at the top of the figure, immediately opposite along the up-down axis, sits a refulgent deity within a shrine of clouds representing heaven. This Jove-like Jehovah, holding his thunderbolt and rod and wearing his crown and robe, presides over all that takes place below. Most importantly, he serves as agent for eternity and provides an inclusive context for the multifarious scenes beneath him. Paradoxically, although there are four seasons and they change continually one into the other, by this 'grateful vicissitude' they complete the annual pattern of time and thereby inhere in eternity. As Donne concludes in his elegy on 'Change', 'Change' is the nursery / Of musicke, joy, life, and eternity' (ll. 35–6).

So the woodcut is a metaphor to explain the paradox of time that we have already noted; it shows how time is both mutable yet static – as T. S. Eliot has put it, how the wheel may turn, and still be forever still. Furthermore, since the type of man entombed at the bottom has gone through the four seasons of his life, he also has completed the basic pattern of time and similarly inheres in eternity. In Christian terms, he will be raised from the tomb to sit in attendance upon the Most High in a perfect state of bliss. The woodcut is then seen rightly as a metaphor to explain also the paradox of man; it shows how man is both mortal yet immortal. We may view him *sub specie vicissitudinis*, in which case his end is in the grave; but also we may view him *sub specie aeternitatis*, in which case his end is his beginning.

And this, I propose, is Marvell's '*Geometrick* yeer'. And now, I believe, the meaning of our troublesome couplet becomes evident. From our vantage-point we see a man in his physical state, and we measure his age by the number of his passing years. We say that he is 'this many' years old. But there above, they number not as here. The gods allot to each man a geometric year, a prototypical pattern for time which comprises all the components of time, such as the four seasons, and therefore the full range of possible experience. When a man has completed this pattern, regardless of how many earthly years have passed, he has fulfilled the period that the gods allow. 'Those of growth more sudden, and more bold' complete the pattern more quickly than the 'Phlegmatick and Slowe', and therefore they 'are hurried hence' – whatever their age in passing years may be, 'as if already old'. Their virtues do indeed their death presage.[6]

The tradition of Aneau's motif is long and much revered, and I won't go into it here, especially since I have explored it at length elsewhere.[7] However, I should like to bring the geometric year into the mainstream of our literary history at another point – at a point somewhat before Marvell, but not so long before that it would have been dissipated by the contending currents of literary practice. This motif of man's life compared to the four seasons is one of the underlying patterns of Spenser's *Shepheardes Calender*, as E. K. brings inescapably to our attention in the argument to the 'December' eclogue:

> [Colin Clout] proportioneth his life to the foure seasons of the yeare, comparing hys youthe to the spring time, when he was fresh and free from loves follye. His manhoode to the sommer, which he sayth was consumed with greate heate . . . by which hee meaneth love . . . His riper yeares he resembleth to an unseasonable harveste wherein the fruites fall ere they be rype. His latter age to winters chyll and frostie season, now drawing near to his last ende.

The Shepheardes Calender is prototypical of occasional poetry as the Renaissance practised it in the Platonic mode. The poem grew directly out of Spenser's personal circumstance in 1579 and out of his view of political events, especially Elizabeth's apparent determination to marry a prince of France. It is topical in almost every line. And yet the poem transcends the limitations of its ephemeral allusions, so that generations who never heard of the Duc d'Alençon have praised the work, and even today most readers are satisfied to leave Hobbinol as Colin's 'very speciall and most familiar freend', in E. K.'s words, without metamorphosing him into the historical personage, Gabriel Harvey. Spenser has so transmuted the actual facts of 1579 that they succeed as an artistic abstraction.

Now the point of Spenser's poem – a point made by a succession of admired poets from Horace forward – is simply that *man* as mortal creature necessarily conforms to the linear pattern for time, while idealized *nature*, exemplified by the Arcadian setting, consists in circular time. Nature continues unendingly through a seamless sequence of four seasons. At the end of winter, spring begins anew. But man, transient that he is, proceeds through the pattern only once. No one states the proposition more succinctly than Chapman in *Byron's Tragedy*:

> Summer succeeds the Spring; Autumn the Summer;
> The frosts of Winter the fall'n leaves of Autumn:
> All these and all fruits in them yearly fade,
> And every year return: but cursed man
> Shall never more renew his vanish'd face.
>
> (V, iv, 248–52)

This is the pessimistic view of man: his life is limited, brief. As Marvell says, the gods 'weigh to Man the *Geometrick* yeer' – no more, no less. But in this very finality lies the seed of optimism. When a man has completed the total pattern of time, he has exhausted the possibilities of experience. He has perfected the plan, the basic unit of which eternity is composed. He has realized in microcosm the full potential of the macrocosm. Thereby he has fulfilled the message of the Book of Genesis that man culminates creation; indeed, he is made in God's image. This is cause for joy, a recognition that we, though mortal, inhere in a larger being that knows no such limitation. And this is the comfort that the topos of the geometric year brings with it.[8]

In this tradition, our universe and the time that measures it are thought of as a projection from deity which in the end returns to deity. Our temporal world is an ephemeral aberration, God's perfection temporarily rendered physical, which streams out from the deity in a circular course. But this circular course, a vestige of divine perfection, insures that all will return to its godly origin.

Perhaps the most popular image of time as a circular construct – certainly, the least esoteric – compared time to the extensive water system that flows through the universe. According to the popular natural history of the period, water was carried from the sea by subterranean passages which underlay the surface of our earth. This water rose at certain places to form lakes, and from these lakes the same water returned by rivers to the sea. Eternity was likened to the vast sea, and passing time was likened to the streams of water which flow from it and which, no matter how deviously, return to it as their source. John Swan, a fellow-student with Milton at Cambridge, published a commentary on Genesis in 1635 which opens with a definition of time in just these terms:

> *Time*, by whose revolutions we measure houres, dayes, weeks, moneths and yeares, is nothing else but (as it were) a certain space borrowed or set apart from eternitie; which shall at the last return to eternitie again: like the rivers, which have their first course from the seas; and by running on, there they arrive, and have their last.[9]

With this principle and this image of time in mind, we can now turn again to the opening of Marvell's poem on the death of Lord Hastings and, I hope, read it with a larger dimension of meaning. Our instruction from Marvell is precise:

> Go, intercept some Fountain in the Vein,
> Whose Virgin-Source yet never steept the Plain.
> *Hastings* is dead, and we must finde a Store
> Of Tears untoucht, and never wept before.

In order to perform properly as mourners, we must seek out some subterranean stream before it surfaces as a river, because presumably there the water will be more pure. Translating this passage into a metaphor for time, we must dip into the temporal cycle at an early stage – at a stage appropriate to the youth of the loved one whose early death we mourn.

The image of time as a system of waterways which derive from and return to the sea brings to Marvell's mind another system which involved the element of water. The atmospheric cycle similarly depends upon drawing water from the sea. Water in the form of vapours rises from the sea and ascends through the region of air. These vapours are congealed into clouds by the cold of night, and eventually, condensed into dew or rain, they fall upon our earth.[10] At this point, they join the rivers and wend their way back into the sea. As a corollary to the first quatrain, then, with line 5 Marvell echoes his opening by means of a parallel construction:

> Go, stand betwixt the *Morning* and the *Flowers*;
> And, ere they fall, arrest the early *Showers*.
> *Hastings* is dead; and we, disconsolate,
> With early *Tears* must mourn his early *Fate*.

Once more, to reinforce his previous command, Marvell tells us to draw our tears from the dew before it falls upon the flowers. And the time of day is '*Morning*', early in the daily cycle of time, correspondent with spring in the annual cycle of time, as the emphasis on '*Flowers*' and '*Showers*' suggests. The repetition of the word 'early' three times in this quatrain again stresses the urgency of the situation and the need for haste.

There is one strand of verbal imagery in the first eight lines that might bear closer scrutiny. To many readers, the word 'fall' in line 6 suggests the Fall of Man, and I am willing at least to countenance the possibility. The context supports such a reading. We are told to intercede in the atmospheric process and catch the morning dews 'ere they fall'. Some readers would extend the image and add: 'ere they fall, and become sullied by contact with the ground', a notion that informs another of Marvell's poems, 'On a Drop of Dew'. This notion has been prepared for in the first quatrain when we are told to fetch our tears from a 'Virgin-Source' because our store of tears should be 'untoucht'. It is implied that the early stages of a process enjoy a state of innocence, but the later stages degenerate into corruption, even sin. And that, of course, is the pattern of man's fall in Eden, a motif that becomes explicit in our poem with line 20 ('And on *The Tree of Life* once made a Feast, / As that of *Knowledge*'). But I don't want to make this reading too heavy, because the tone here is set by rhetorical device and poetic convention. These lines are artificial, and there is no profundity of either thought or emotion in them.

Another strand of verbal imagery is perhaps more interesting, though not so evident or precise. In these first eight lines it is notable how forceful the verbs are. Marvell uses the imperative mood: 'Go' is twice placed in strong positions, at the beginning of lines 1 and 5, to mark the rhetorical structure of the passage. And other imperatives are sprinkled liberally throughout the passage: again line 1, 'intercept'; in line 5, 'stand betwixt'; in Line 6, 'arrest'. What strikes me about these verbs is their energy, almost their violence. 'Go' is not a particularly active word; but placed at the beginning of a line of poetry, as here, and set off by a comma, it acquires an unwonted force. Furthermore, 'go' in this position within the poetic line violates the metrical pattern. Marvell is writing in rhymed iambic pentameter couplets, what soon was to become the staple of staid

Augustan verse; and the first syllable of the line should be unaccented. But 'Go' refuses to be repressed: and backed up by the comma that follows, it demands emphasis. 'Go, intercept some Fountain in the Vein'. It launches the poem with a lurch and imposes a trochaic rhythm on its first foot, so that the iambic rhythm, the true metre of the poem when it settles down, is not discernible until the end of the line. Metrical violence of a similar sort recurs in line 3, though somewhat subdued, with the blunt announcement, '*Hastings* is dead'. The first syllable of the line, unexpectedly accented, disrupts the established rhythm. In the second quatrain, rhetorically co-ordinate with the first, the metrics are wrenched in identical ways, repeating and confirming the evidence of dislocation. Line 5 begins with the same explosive 'Go,' and line 7 with the same disruptive '*Hastings*', so that the initial vehemence echoes and reverberates. The reader is forced to recognize that in this opening verse paragraph the metrics are under constant assault.

The other imperative verbs are equally strenuous. We are to 'intercept' a stream, 'stand betwixt' the dew and the flowers, and 'arrest' the dew before it falls. The force of our grief, presumably, justifies such frenzied action. But something more subtle, though none the less efficacious, is going on, I think, and we might do well to return to our topos of the geometric year to understand it.

According to the concept of time which underpins this topos, time is an orderly cycle marked by the heavenly bodies, and it is rendered evident by a number of palpable patterns: the diurnal pattern of day and night, the annual pattern of the four seasons, the annual pattern of twelve months, and perhaps others. Man, being a creature in nature, shares in these patterns; and, in fact, his life may be emblematized as any one of them. In the normal course of events, each man completes an entire cycle. In that way, he experiences the whole pattern and thereby participates in eternity. But what about the man who is *not* allowed to complete the geometric year normally allotted to each of us? What about premature death? According to John Dryden in his elegy on the death of Hastings in the same volume,

> But hasty Winter, with one blast, hath brought
> The hopes of Autumn, Summer, Spring, to nought.[11]

What about this aberration from the providential plan? In premature death lies horror. And this horror, I suggest, is conveyed through the violent verbs that Marvell chooses in the introductory verse paragraph of this elegy. In response to Hastings's death we should feel not only grief, but also frenzy, and even an active repulsion.

The horror attendant upon early death may define a genre of tragedy quite different from either the classical or the medieval concept of tragedy. When based upon Aristotle, tragedy requires a self-conscious hero who commits one prideful act that brings about a justifiable punishment. The medieval concept of tragedy traces a fall from high place as a result of Fortune's turning her wheel. The third sort of tragedy that I conceive, however, results from the turning of 'Times Wheel', to pick up Marvell's phrase. What controls in this tragedy is not the hazardry of Fortune's wheel, which in its irrationality provides no source of consolation, but rather the predictable turning of Time's wheel with its intimations of immortality. Tragedy of this kind derives from the fact that man's geometric year may be interrupted, and thereby his potential for perfection may be thwarted. A man may be cut off in the morning of his life, or in his springtime – to use an archaic term in its literal sense, in his 'prime'. Lycidas, for example, is 'dead ere his prime'.

An excellent example of this sort of tragedy is *Romeo and Juliet*, which has eluded analysis in terms of either classical or medieval tragedy. The tragedy of Romeo and Juliet, of course, is simply that the young lovers are cut down in their prime. The circumstances surrounding their death are hardly their doing, so they can't be Aristotelian tragic heroes. Neither could Chaucer's Monk include them on his list of exempla, because they are hardly hapless victims of fickle Fortune who fall from high place to a despicable lowliness. Rather, the fate of Romeo and Juliet hangs in their stars. As the heavens turn and generate time, some cosmic anomaly unfolds to terminate their earthly existence. Beautiful though they are – indeed, for the very reason that they *are* beautiful – they are vulnerable, like Herrick's daffodil and Keats's globed peony, to destruction. And much of their beauty as well as much of the tragedy of their demise is expressed in the seasonal imagery of the geometric year. When old Capulet finds Juliet apparently lifeless, for example, he says:

> Death lies on her like an untimely frost
> Upon the sweetest flower of the field.
> (IV, v, 28–9)

Winter has closed the life of Juliet just as she began to flower in what appeared to us to be her springtime.

In a markedly similar vein, in the final stanza of his poem on 'The Picture of little T. C. in a Prospect of Flowers', Marvell imprecates against an early death for the young girl. He has seen the child taming the wilder flowers and giving them names, and has fantasized about how her beauty will charm the young men who come to woo her. But he warns against imperiousness, and especially against tampering with nature's course as she brings her verdant creatures to maturity in the spring. In the final stanza of the poem Marvell addresses the little girl directly, for the first time, and he warns against plucking the flowers before they open:

> But O young beauty of the Woods,
> Whom Nature courts with fruits and flow'rs,
> Gather the Flow'rs, but spare the Buds;
> Lest *Flora* angry at thy crime,
> To kill her Infants in their prime,
> Do quickly make th'Example Yours;
> And, ere we see,
> Nip in the blossome all our hopes and Thee.

Marvell fears that the child, unusually well endowed with virtues, may offend against the due course of time, and in consequence may be struck down by the angry gods, an infant killed in her prime. The death of Hastings, Marvell would have us believe, is a tragedy of the same sort. He has been nipped in the bud. His geometric year has been interrupted. Our topos can provide definition for a certain kind of tragedy as well as for occasional poetry.

After the first two verse paragraphs, 'Upon the Death of Lord Hastings' goes on at considerable length. To my mind, however, the tautness of its opening is soon dissipated in awkwardness and obscurity. Marvell meanders recklessly through the conventions of funeral elegy and maunders disconnectedly about the blasted hopes of the mourners. None the less, the poem deserves more attention than it has received. For one thing, it connects Marvell with the Elizabethan tradition and links his name with Spenser and Donne and Shakespeare. Even more important, it displays in its opening a vitality of thought and a facility with language that Marvell put to better use in his later work. For though this elegy in its total effect is clumsy and shallow, a minor poem, it bears the mark of a major poet.

Notes

1 Marvell gives direct evidence of familiarity with this theory: cf. 'The First Anniversary of the Government under O. C.', ll. 13–18.
2 See C. A. Patrides, *'The Grand Design of God': The Literary Form of the Christian View of History*, London, Routledge & Kegan Paul, 1972.
3 As Westmoreland puts it in his elegy, 'The best and precious things are soonest gone' (*Lachrymae musarum*, ed. Richard Brome, London, 1649, sig. A4).
4 See 'How Plato is to be understood, when he saith: that God continually is exercised in Geometry' ('Of Symposiaques', VIII, 2), in *The Morals*, trans. Philemon Holland, London, 1603, pp. 767–8.
5 *Picta poesis*, Lyons, 1552, p. 26. Cf. *The Shepheards Calender*, London, 1618, sigs A6v–B1.
6 For the same reasoning, see Marvell's 'Young Love', especially ll. 9–10 and 17–18.
7 See *Touches of Sweet Harmony*, San Marino, Calif., Huntington Library, 1974, pp. 223–5.
8 Cf. Ben Jonson, 'To the immortall memorie and friendship of that noble paire, Sir Lucius Cary, and Sir H. Morison', especially ll. 43–52.
9 *Speculum mundi*, Cambridge, 1635, p. 45.
10 Cf. Marvell, 'Eyes and Tears', ll. 21–4; also George Herbert, 'Vertue', ll. 1–4.
11 *Lachrymae musarum*, p. 91.

5

'Its own resemblance'

Christopher Ricks

I

The Mind, that Ocean where each kind
Does streight its own resemblance find.
('The Garden', ll. 43–4)

characteristic figure of speech in Marvell is that which goes beyond saying of something that it *finds* its own resemblance, and says instead, more wittily and mysteriously, that something *is* its own resemblance. When William Empson remarked such a figure in Shelley –

So came a chariot in the silent storm
Of its own rushing splendour. . . .

And others mournfully within the gloom
Of their own shadow walked, and called it death.
('The Triumph of Life')

– Empson called it a self-inwoven simile or a short-circuited comparison.[1] Others have since called it reflexive imagery. Often it signs itself with the word 'self' or the word 'own'. It is at home to the acknowledged characteristics of Marvell's poetry: balance and yet conflict; inclusion and yet exclusion; withdrawal and yet emergence; microcosm and yet macrocosm; self and yet all else. It is at home with, and accommodates too, both the phases of seventeenth-century wit:

> Contradiction is at the centre of poetic wit in the seventeenth century. In its pure form it becomes paradox in the first half of the century, and antithesis in the second; that is, contraries are reconciled in the one, and opposed in the other.[2]

For the self-inwoven simile is a figure which both reconciles and opposes, in that it describes something both as itself and as something external to it which it could not possibly be. In one of its most teasing forms, something finds itself compared to both of the terms within a comparison.

With a range of mood, intent, and form, Marvell uses it in every important kind of poem that he writes; and showing so is the first half of what I want to do here. In his political-religious poetry, for instance, it figures the largest knowledge – of all past, present, and future – which we must try to imagine and which we must also acknowledge as unimaginable. Marvell sets the terms for his own poetic providence in the opening of 'A Poem upon the Death of O.C.':

> That Providence which had so long the care
> Of *Cromwell's* head, and numbered ev'ry hair,
> Now in its self (the Glass where all appears)
> Had seen the period of his golden Years.

Here the turn witnesses to the wonder of a religious paradox; Providence is seen as (and yet can scarcely by visualized as) that which sees, that which is seen, and that wherein is seen. Abraham Cowley speaks of this same paradox in his *Davideis,* Book II: 'Shap'd in the *glass* of the divine *Foresight*'; but Cowley, unlike Marvell, found no shape for the paradox such as would express it rather than speak of it, for there is no greater mystery in his line of verse than in the equable prose with which he glosses the glass: 'It is rightly termed a *Glass* or *Mirror*, for God foresees all things by looking only on himself, in whom all things always are.' Marvell's lines inspire awe at Providence as the seer, the seen, and the seen in. As so often with reflexive imagery, literal reflections also catch the light, with their paradoxes of identity and difference, transposition, unreal reality, and substantial insubstantiality. Rosalie Colie remarked, apropos of Marvell's 'On a Drop of Dew', that 'the mirror image is taken as both thinking (reflection, speculation), and the instrument to stimulate thinking'.[3]

Marvell inaugurates his poem on the death of Cromwell with this mystery set before us with the greatest lucidity; the wit is subdued, and time is suspended in the high unimaginability of Providence's relation to time. The obvious contrast, one that here is to Marvell's honour, is with Milton's time-ridden elaboration of Providence's paradox in Book III of *Paradise Lost,* of which J. B. Broadbent remarked with imaginative pertinence: 'He leads us into a corridor of verbal mirrors in which unbodied concepts are defined by their antitheses so all we can do is mark time with our lips.'[4] And if we ask why Marvell succeeds where Milton fails, the answer is not only that Marvell does not subdue his momentaneous insight to the doled-out world of discourse, but that Marvell seizes upon a simply literal fact which incarnates the metaphysical paradox, the fact that the eye is itself a mirror, and can be the seer, the seen, and the seen in.[5] 'Looking babies' is one form of this teasing reality, as the lover gazes into the loved one's eyes; another is the military proximity, eyeball to eyeball, which is accorded the highest honours in 'An Elegy upon the Death of my Lord Francis Villiers':

Lovely and admirable as he was,
Yet was his Sword or Armour all his Glasse.
Nor in his Mistris eyes that joy he tooke,
As in an Enemies himselfe to looke.
(ll. 51–54)

'By Andrew Marvell', wrote the honest and excellently informed George Clarke in his copy of the poem about 250 years ago; and there is something characteristic of Marvell, though not unique to him, in the turn with 'himselfe': 'As in an Enemies himselfe to looke', where there is both 'he himselfe' and the reflexive verb 'looke himselfe':

And for a Glass the limpid Brook,
Where *She* may all *her* Beautyes look.
(*Upon Appleton House*, ll. 701–2)

Within one kind of religious poetry, then, the vast outward vistas of Providence are glimpsed through this telescopic figure. Within another kind, the meditative poem, the same turn is used microscopically for a no less characteristic miniature miracle of inward vistas:

> How it the purple flow'r does slight,
> Scarce touching where it lyes,
> But gazing back upon the Skies,
> Shines with a mournful Light;
> Like its own Tear,
> Because so long divided from the Sphear.
> ('On a Drop of Dew', ll. 9–14)

The assonantal rhyme-sequence – slight/lyes/Skies/Light – is given a further delicate weightiness by the mourning head-words too:

> But gazing back upon the *Skies*,
> *Shines* with a mournful *Light*;
> *Like* its own Tear;

– at which the self-infolded comparison is at its most succinct. 'Like its own Tear': this invites us to see the dew drop as a tear wept by itself; to see it therefore both as eye and tear, a vision which is unimaginable and yet is more than clear, is plausible, because of that shared liquidity of shape which Proust observed with saddened grotesquerie:

> He slipped his other hand upwards along Odette's cheek; she fixed her eyes on him with that languishing and solemn air which marks the women of the old Florentine's paintings, in whose faces he had found the type of hers; swimming at the brink of her fringed lids, her brilliant eyes, large and finely drawn as theirs, seemed on the verge of breaking from her face and rolling down her cheeks like two great tears.

(How strange is the metamorphosis there from 'she fixed her eyes on him' – *elle le regarda fixement* – to the image of her weeping her eyes out.)

> She looked back at him with eyes welling with affection, ready to detach themselves like tears and to fall upon his face.
> (*Swann in Love*)[6]

The author of 'Eyes and Tears' might have appreciated Proust's repeated fancy, at once painful and comic; yet the poignancy of Marvell's vistas of regression and involution comes from a sense of division – 'Because so long divided from the Sphear' – not *within* but *from*. There is a chastened tone in Marvell's figure, 'Like its own Tear', that is animated by a fear of the rounded yet ephemeral sufficiencies of self, with this form of reciprocity – that of the eye and the tear – itself too self-infolded; so that the effect is that Marvell's line shares something with Wilfred Owen's Virgilian feeling for

> Whatever shares
> The eternal reciprocity of tears.
> ('Insensibility')

What is missing from the lines of Richard Crashaw which Marvell probably knew –

> Each Ruby there,
> Or Pearle that dare appeare,
> Be its owne blush, be its owne Teare.
> ('Wishes. To his (supposed) Mistresse')

– is such a sense of awed transposition; for there is no haunting interminability, such as exists when we try to imagine a drop of water wept by itself, between a pearl and 'its owne Teare'; instead of Marvell's fluid windows, we are handed something which crystallizes as cleverness.

In another poetic kind, the love poem, Marvell contemplates very different tears but again under the aspect of this same figure of speech.

> And, while vain Pomp does her restrain
> Within her solitary Bowr,
> She courts her self in am'rous Rain;
> Her self both *Danae* and the Showr.
> ('Mourning', ll. 17–20)

Whereas the dew drop's tear was chastened, this turn is chastening. For it puts the sardonic, though thrillingly musical, point of view of those ('Yet some affirm . . .') who are sceptical of her tears and believe them to be a self-indulgence. She loves her love and her self, her grief and her tears. Dead Strephon once courted her, now she courts herself. And the ancient ingenuity of Zeus' rape-seduction of Danae, ensconced by her father in her tower but not safe from a golden shower of amorous rain, is matched by the modern ingenuity of this turn. The effect of 'Her self both *Danae* and the Showr' is to give to the previous line, 'She courts her self in am'rous Rain', a taunting quality of understatement or – looked at from the other end – of overstated courtesy. Can Zeus fairly be said finally to have *courted* Danae? The lady is fancied to be both of the partners in a rape-seduction story. The air of the lines is wonderfully easy, yet, in such a story, ease is cause of wonder. (The tone altogether precludes the fevers and chills endemic in the sort of word which Harold Toliver uses about all such moments in Marvell: 'homo-erotic', 'auto-erotic', and 'mono-virginal'.)[7] The psychological acumen and delicacy of the insight into the gratification of grief must rank with those manifested in *Twelfth Night*'s capacious understanding of Olivia; Marvell's lyrical succinctness compacts the reflexive verb and the reflexive image –

She courts her self in am'rous Rain;
Her self both *Danae* and the Showr.

– in an acknowledgment of one strange yet natural form which self-infolded self-division may take.

Self-division is the animation of another of Marvell's notable kinds, the debate poem. The Soul has the first word in 'A Dialogue between the Soul and Body':

O who shall, from this Dungeon, raise
A Soul inslav'd so many wayes?
With bolts of Bones, that fetter'd stands
In Feet; and manacled in Hands.
Here blinded with an Eye; and there
Deaf with the drumming of an Ear.

The very faculties of the body incapacitate, and they preclude what they seem to promise, since they offer travesties of true and incorporeal faculties. Yet how various and unpriggish are the forms which Marvell gives to this age-old spiritual or soulish grievance.[8] 'Here blinded with an Eye' is something other than a mere easy reversal, since it arms itself with a love-cliché to compound its disapproval of the Body. Lovers are always being blinded by eyes (and the Body is to blame for this), but lovers – indeed all of us – are mistaken to think that it is the eyes of others which most blind us: it is our own eyes. 'Deaf with the drumming of an Ear' finds its persuasive power elsewhere (again, though, vigilant not to offer a mere reversal): in the simple fact of the ear-drum, which is used to press the spiritual claim that, far from being made to hear by the ear-drum, we are permanently deafened by the drumming of the ear. Even the strictures which seem most bald have their play of variety; 'that fetter'd stands / In Feet' rises above the jingle of polemic, since 'fetter'd' is etymologically cognate with 'Feet'; and 'manacled in Hands' repeats and yet does not repeat this, since 'manacled' is not etymologically cognate with 'Hands' and yet Latin beckons. . . . (The sheer resourcefulness of the Soul's recriminations can be felt if you simply substitute 'handcuffed in hands'.) But with only the spectral tacit etymology of 'manacled', and with no physical counterpart such as lends colour to the accusation against the ear-drum, there remains to hand another cliché to be retorted with. For though, if there is one thing you can't be manacled with, it is your own hands, the Soul's turn of speech inspiredly or perversely seizes upon something which was often said, and something which is again apt to the Soul's indictment of the Body: that other people's hands manacle you. As when Robert Herrick warned that women's

> Armes, and hands, and all parts else,
> Are but Toiles, or Manicles
> Set on purpose to enthrall
> Men, but Slothfulls most of all.
> ('Disswasions from Idlenesse')

'And manacled in Hands': for something of the same teasing knot of clarity and inconceivability, we might go to Steinberg's fantastical – or Escher's realistic – drawing of a hand drawing a hand. E. H. Gombrich has said of Escher: 'What all these prints have in common is that they compel us to adopt an initial assumption that cannot be sustained as we try to follow it through';[9] and it is this challenging tension – to visualize the unvisualizable – which Dr Leavis pinned down as just the quality which cannot be pinned down in a poem like 'A Dialogue between the Soul and Body': 'Of its very nature it eludes, defies and transcends visualization. . . . That undoubted force . . . is not in the least a matter of their compelling us to *visualize* anything; it is that they are paradoxes the essence of which is to elude or defy visualization.'[10]

Compel, no; challenge, yes, as is implied by the word 'defy'. And with perfect equipollence or evenhandedness, the figure with which the Soul challenged the Body is then retorted by the Body against the Soul:

> O who shall me deliver whole,
> From bonds of this Tyrannic Soul?
> Which, stretcht upright, impales me so,
> That mine own Precipice I go;

The Body is both what falls and what it falls down, by a night-mare of self-division such as induces a vertigo in the mere thought (the mere unthinkable thought); and 'impales' even adds some fear that the Body, 'stretcht upright', is not only that which falls and that which it falls down, but also that which it falls upon: 'impales me so'.

> O the mind, mind has mountains; cliffs of fall
> Frightful, sheer, no-man-fathomed.
> (Hopkins, 'No worst, there is none')

Marvell's lines are to me more frightening, less melodramatic, than Hopkins's, and than William Golding's fierce stroke in *Pincher Martin* when the rock to which the man clings is felt to be the tooth within his own head. There is in Marvell a resilience and a vibrancy of anger such as intimate a nobler fear.

Within Marvell's pastoral poetry, fear is called up but to be fended off. The flooding of the meadows need cause no perturbation, but it causes the astonishment which Marvell's figure delights to recognize:

> The River in it self is drown'd,
> And Isl's th' astonish'd Cattle round.
> (*Upon Appleton House*, ll. 471–2)

By enlarging so that it becomes more than itself, the river loses its self; but fortunately it is lost only to be found again later. Yet even so, when the flooding has gone and the river is restored, at this moment too Marvell must have recourse to his reflexive paradox:

> No *Serpent* new nor *Crocodile*
> Remains behind our little *Nile*;
> Unless it self you will mistake,
> Among these Meads the only Snake.
> (ibid., ll. 629–32)

The miraculous abiogenesis of the great Nile, breeding snakes from its mud, is outdone by the humble English counterpart, 'our little *Nile*', since this river breeds, inconceivably, the snake of itself. The good-natured reproof to such credulity –

> Unless it self you will mistake,
> Among these Meads the only Snake –

itself evolves into a mistake, since the next lines take the fancy as having an established life:

> See in what wanton harmless folds
> It ev'ry where the Meadow holds. . . .

How gently, with what paradisal innocence, this snake holds something in its folds.

But such implications, famous as they rightly are in the appreciation of Marvell, are not what I want to follow. For it is the variety and ubiquitousness of the self-infolded simile in Marvell which I have wished first of all to establish. And it is grist to my mill – indeed, is itself both grist and mill – that T. S. Eliot, when he wished to deplore the related (though not strictly reflexive) images which finally close up *Upon Appleton House* within their Chinese boxes or their Russian dolls:

> But now the *Salmon-Fishers* moist
> Their *Leathern Boats* begin to hoist;
> And, like *Antipodes* in Shoes,
> Have shod their *Heads* in their *Canoos.*
> How *Tortoise like,* but not so slow,
> These rational *Amphibii* go?

Let 's in: for the dark *Hemisphere*
Does now like one of them appear.

– that Eliot, deploring these lines, should himself have succumbed to this very Marvellian image: 'images . . . which support nothing but their own misshapen bodies'.[11] For it may be said of many of Marvell's reflexive images that, as Empson said in paraphrasing one of Shelley's, 'it sustains itself by supporting itself'. Marvell's lines here, characteristically, at once expand and contract, in a double perspective which calmly blinks; I am reminded of a newspaper advertisement I once saw which began 'expanding contracting industry requires draughtsmen . . .'.

The political-religious poem, the meditative poem, the love poem, the debate poem, the pastoral poem – there remains certainly one kind of poem which mattered greatly to Marvell: satire. So let me round off this first half of my round-up by quoting four lines from *The Last Instructions to a Painter.* The attribution of the poem to Marvell seems to me to gain some weight from the masterly turn within – and not just the presence of – such a reflexive image as this:

But when he came the odious Clause to Pen,
That summons up the *Parliament* agen;
His Writing-Master many a time he bann'd,
And wish'd himself the Gout, to seize his hand.
(ll. 469–72)

Wished himself to be his own gout? Wished for himself gout? Either way – or, if Marvell, both ways – it has for me the ring of an authentic Marvellian reflexive image. And like all such images, it has clear affinities with much else in Marvell, particularly his recourse to balance and to mirroring. For, like those, the reflexive image is at once two and one – and is all the more crucial then to such metaphysical poetry as is genuinely metaphysical in its preoccupation (as James Smith argued in *Scrutiny*, 1933) with the metaphysical problem of the One and the Many.

Nature that hateth emptiness,
Allows of penetration less.
('An Horatian Ode', ll. 41–2)

But art delights to outdo nature, and to make two things occupy the one space; and Marvell's is famously, and in both senses, an art of penetration.

II

The self-inwoven simile burgeoned in the poems of Marvell and his contemporaries as never before. (And as never since? Not altogether so, since I shall claim that it is at the heart of the achievement of a recent group of poets.) In the predecessors of Marvell, the figure seldom carries full conviction and seems rather to be awaiting its later consummation. When, for instance, it shows itself in Donne, some part of our surprise is not at the turn itself but at its being Donne who unexpectedly expects it to serve his turn:

> For thee, thou needst no such deceit,
> For thou thy selfe art thine owne bait.
> ('The Baite')

> And on the hatches as on Altars lyes
> Each one, his owne Priest, and owne Sacrifice.
> ('The Calme')

Both of those have something unfulfilled and prophetic, an unripeness. For the particular kind of half-convinced levity in those lines from 'The Baite' sounds more like a Caroline poet than the innermost Donne,[12] and the particular kind of half-convinced gravity in those lines from 'The Calme' sounds more like the Dryden of *Annus Mirabilis* than the innermost Donne. It is only in the sombre magnificence of the *Devotions* – 'But I doe nothing upon my selfe, and yet am mine owne *Executioner*; (*Twelfth Meditation*) – that Donne's imagination is profoundly stirred to an apprehension of ineradicable human perversity through the perversity of this figure of speech.

If for the moment we pass over Marvell and his contemporaries, we may sketch a literary history for the self-inwoven simile such as accords with the larger history as it has been argued by Eliot and Leavis. For this figure is a witty and mysterious one, and the eighteenth and the nineteenth centuries were both, in different ways, unhappy with the integration of wit and mystery characteristic of much seventeenth-century poetry. Augustan poetry has its favourite fascinations, exerted upon it and by it, in the matter of incongruity and surprise; but its 'common Sense' found pretentious and vulgar any large attempt to imagine this particular form of the unimaginable.

> And when the same Lady goes into the Bath, the Thought (as in justness it ought) goes still deeper.
>
> Venus *beheld her, 'midst her Crowd of Slaves,*
> *And thought* Herself *just risen from the Waves.*
>
> How much out of the way of common Sense is this Reflection of *Venus*, not knowing herself from the Lady?
>
> (*Of the Art of Sinking in Poetry*, 1728, ch. VII)

Yet notice how 'Reflection' – 'this Reflection of *Venus*' – almost concedes that there is a 'common Sense' explanation for, or at least intermediary towards, this two-in-one self-mistaking:

> And its yet muddy back doth lick,
> Till as a *Chrystal Mirrour* slick;
> Where all things gaze themselves, and doubt
> If they be in it or without.
>
> (*Upon Appleton House*, ll. 635–8)

Of the Art of Sinking in Poetry presses on:

> Of the same nature is that noble Mistake of a frighted Stag in full Chace, of which the Poet,
>
> *Hears his own Feet, and thinks they sound like more;*
> *And fears the hind Feet will o'ertake the fore.*
>
> So astonishing as these are, they yield to the following, which is *Profundity* itself,
>
> *None but* Himself *can be his Parallel.*
>
> [Theobald, *Double Distress*]

unless it may seem borrow'd from the Thought of that *Master of a Show* in *Smithfield*, who writ in large Letters, over the Picture of his Elephant,

This is the greatest Elephant in the World, except Himself.

Wittily done. Yet in simply ruling out, on simple principle, such turns (whether or not these particular ones are effective), such Augustan criticism was cutting itself off from a certain form of poetic apprehension which genuinely 'is *Profundity* itself'.

So hand in hand they passd, the lovliest pair
That ever since in loves imbraces met,
Adam the goodliest man of men since borne
His Sons, the fairest of her Daughters *Eve*.
(*Paradise Lost*, IV, 321–4)

So that the best Augustan uses of this figure are merely deft, unpretentiously and unmysteriously witty.

Such Piles of Buildings now rise up and down;
London itself seems going out of Town.
(James Bramston, *The Art of Politicks*, 1729)

That does not so much tease the mind, leave alone tease it at once into and out of thought, as tickle it. When Charles Dickens had recourse to the same turn, he gave it a context which is less wittily pointed but more poignantly mysterious, and more strongly related – as a reflexive image most revealingly may be – to the powers and the limitations of the imagination itself:

It [Washington] is sometimes called the City of Magnificent Distances, but it might with greater propriety be termed the City of Magnificent Intentions; for it is only on taking a bird's-eye view of it from the top of the Capitol, that one can at all comprehend the vast designs of its projector, an aspiring Frenchman. Spacious avenues, that begin in nothing, and lead nowhere; streets, mile-long, that only want houses, roads and inhabitants; public buildings that need but a public to be complete; and ornaments of great thoroughfares, which only lack great thoroughfares to ornament – are its leading features. One might fancy the season over, and most of the houses gone out of town for ever with their masters. To the

> admirers of cities it is a Barmecide Feast; a pleasant field for the imagination to rove in; a monument raised to a deceased project, with not even a legible inscription to record its departed greatness. (*American Notes,* ch. VIII)

Though the witty possibilities there are deliberately dampened, the profundity is at one with humour, a grounded lugubrious humour. Elsewhere Dickens used the self-infolded self-divided figure of speech in one of his greatest evocations of the self-infolded self-divided nature of guilty fear, in the true derangements of imagination that haunt the murderer Jonas Chuzzlewit:

> Dread and fear were upon him, to an extent he had never counted on, and could not manage in the least degree. He was so horribly afraid of that infernal room at home. This made him, in a gloomy, murderous, mad way, not only fearful *for* himself, but *of* himself; for being, as it were, a part of the room: a something supposed to be there, yet missing from it: he invested himself with its mysterious terrors; and when he pictured in his mind the ugly chamber, false and quiet, false and quiet, through the dark hours of two nights; the tumbled bed, and he not in it, though believed to be; he became in a manner his own ghost and phantom, and was at once the haunting spirit and the haunted man. (*Martin Chuzzlewit,* ch. XLVII)[13]

In its vital imagining of a nemesis of the short-circuited comparison in the short-circuiting that is madness,[14] this suggests that some particular triumphs were made possible by the nineteenth-century separating of such a figure from its witty possibilities; and yet it is characteristic of Dickens that even this grimmest instance should have its full nature only when it is seen as complementing the genuine though painful humour which has made play with the self-involved comparison throughout *Martin Chuzzlewit*:

> Mr Pecksniff . . . certainly did not appear to any unusual advantage, now that he was alone. On the contrary, he seemed to be shrunk and reduced; to be trying to hide himself within himself; and to be wretched at not having the power to do it. (ch. XXX)

> 'I want a man as is his own great-coat and cloak, and is always a-wrapping himself up in himself. And I have got him too', said Mr Tapley. (ch. XXXIII)

> He [Mr Nadgett] went about so stealthily, and kept himself so wrapped up in himself, that the whole object of his life appeared to be, to avoid notice and preserve his own mystery. (ch. XXXVIII)

So that when we come at last to 'He became in a manner his own ghost and phantom', we can take 'in a manner' as not merely meaning 'as it were', since we have seen some other manners in which a man may be self-infolded.

But the nineteenth-century propensity to isolate the witty (and the humorous) from the mysterious is evident in what mostly happens to the reflexive image. The poet to whom it came naturally, as Empson saw, was Shelley, but what also came naturally to Shelley was the disjunction of the figure's mystery from all possibility of wit or humour. Let me acknowledge an excellent essay by William Keach on 'Reflexive Imagery in Shelley'[15](though I had better add that it generously acknowledges as a spur to its thinking some thoughts of mine about Marvell, and I risk being suspected of self-infolded or short-circuited self-congratulation). Mr Keach sensitively shows that Empson does less than justice to Shelley in saying: 'when not being able to think of a comparison fast enough he compares the thing to a vaguer or more abstract notion of itself'; and likewise in saying: 'Shelley seldom perceived profitable relations between two things, he was too helplessly excited by one thing at a time, and that one thing was often a mere notion not conceived in action or in an environment.' For this not only does not do justice to Shelley, it does not do justice either to Empson's own intuition, since he at once added: 'But, even with so limited an instrument as the short-circuited comparison, he could do great things.' Keach is able to show how reflexive images in Shelley act 'as verbal representations' of the 'process of reflexive imaginative projection', by dramatizing sometimes 'a self-inclosed psychic experience', sometimes 'the mind's involuted descent into the depths of its own reflexiveness'. It is a strength of Keach's argument, as it is of Shelley's poetry, that this strange power of the imagination is shown by the same figure of speech to take both benign and malign forms. Imaginative self-sufficiency may be solipsism or madness. Yet it remains true, and is to my mind a grave limitation even of the best such images in Shelley, that their tone is itself obdurately self-enclosed, impervious to – though not invulnerable to – wit and humour. There is a self-gratification, an ease of continuity, in Shelley's use of the word 'mournfully', too at home with 'gloom' and 'shadow' and 'death':

> And others mournfully within the gloom
> Of their own shadow walked, and called it death.

Whereas Marvell's word 'mournful' has a various play of light against the surrounding words 'Shines' and 'Light', achieving a fluctuant iridescence:

> But gazing back upon the Skies,
> Shines with a mournful Light;
> Like its own Tear.

What Marvell achieves cannot, I believe, be justly caught in Keach's formulation about those lines: 'It is Marvell who sets the standard for the sheer intellectual wit reflexive images can yield.' For Marvell has a luminosity of pathos. And if we wish to use an antithesis of 'sheer intellectual wit' against 'psychic expressiveness', it is not in the seventeenth-century writers but in the nineteenth-century writers that such a choice, often misguidedly, is made. 'In emulation of Leander and Don Juan, he swam, I hear, to the opposite shores the other day, or some world-shaking feat of the sort, himself the Hero whom he went to meet' (Meredith, *The Ordeal of Richard Feverel*, ch. XXXV). The pun on Hero and the full iambic rounding – 'Himself the Hero whom he went to meet' – so plump out the reflexive image as to make it seem that it is not Richard Feverel, about whom those words are penned in a letter, or even Adrian Harley, who pens them, but the author of them, Meredith, who really breathes the air of self-congratulation. And at the opposite end, even Clough, who was creatively dissatisfied with the Victorian disjunctions, was able to animate only one half of this figure's paradoxical powers, the Shelleyan mournfulness:

Though tortured in the crucible I lie,
Myself my own experiment.
(*Adam and Eve*, I, ii)

When Eliot praised in Marvell 'this alliance of levity and seriousness (by which the seriousness is intensified)', he was urging the twentieth century to renew such an alliance in its poetry as in his own poetry. The self-infolded simile, moreover folding in itself both wit and mystery, has found itself at home again. As when Harold Massingham addresses the spider, with a felicity that is not the less comic in being rueful about the imagination:

You know the knack, don't you?
Imagination's envy.
You're your own yoyo, aren't you?
('Spider', *Black Bull Guarding Apples*, 1965)

Or as when the American poet David Ferry moves from the spider's self-infoldedness to the larger infoldings of love and duty, submission and self-submission, within a remarkable constellation of reflexive images:

Saturday afternoon. The barracks is almost empty.
The soldiers are almost all on overnight pass.
There is only me, writing this letter to you,
And one other soldier, down at the end of the room,
And a spider, that hangs by the thread of his guts,
His tenacious and delicate guts, Swift's spider,
All self-regard, or else all privacy.
The dust drifts in the sunlight around him, as currents
Lie in lazy drifting schools in the vast sea.
In his little sea the spider lowers himself
Out of his depth. He is his own diving bell,
Though he cannot see well. He observes no fish,
And sees no wonderful things. His unseeing guts
Are his only hold on the world outside himself.
I love you, and miss you, and I find you hard to imagine.
Down at the end of the room, the other soldier
Is getting ready, I guess, to go out on pass.
He is shining his boots. He sits on the edge of his bunk,
Private, submissive, and heedful of himself,

And, bending over himself, he is his own nest.
The slightest sound he makes is of his being.
He is his mother, and nest, wife, brother, and father.
His boots are bright already, yet still he rubs
And rubs till, brighter still, they are his mirror.
And in this mirror he observes, I guess,
His own submissiveness. He is far from home.
('The Soldier', *On the Way to the Island,* 1960)

Yet this, though a very fine poem, is an isolated instance; in so far as it calls up the same figure in other recent American poets such as Richard Wilbur, it calls them up too as instances rather than as a constellation. The more important affinity with Marvell and his contemporaries is the gifted group of recent Ulster poets: Seamus Heaney, Michael Longley, Derek Mahon, and Paul Muldoon. Like Marvell and his contemporaries, they write out of an imagination of civil war. But before speculating on the relation between civil war and the reflexive image, let me simply show how extraordinarily and variously pervasive is the self-infolded simile in these Ulster poets.

Seamus Heaney

The burn drowns steadily in its own downpour.
('Waterfall', *Death of a Naturalist,* 1966)

Then notes stretch taut as snares. They trip
To fall into themselves unknowingly.
('The Play Way')

The leggy birds stilted on their own legs,
Islands riding themselves out into the fog . . .

. . . things founded clean on their own shapes.
('The Peninsula', *Door into the Dark,* 1969)

The breakers pour

Themselves into themselves.
('Girls Bathing, Galway 1965')

Christopher Ricks

[of an eel]
. . . a wick that is
its own taper and light
through the weltering dark.
('A Lough Neagh Sequence: The Return')

You had to come back
To learn how to lose yourself,
To be pilot and stray – witch,
Hansel and Gretel in one.
('The Plantation')

The tawny guttural water
spells itself: Moyola
is its own score and consort.
('Gifts of Rain', *Wintering Out*, 1972)

like an eel swallowed
in a basket of eels,
the line amazes itself.
('Viking Dublin: Trial Pieces', *North*, 1975)

As if he had been poured
in tar, he lies
on a pillow of turf
and seems to weep

the black river of himself
('The Grauballe Man')

Michael Longley

a knife-thrower
hurling himself.
('The Corner of An Eye: Kingfisher',
An Exploded View, 1973)

Who bothers to record
This body digested
By its own saliva . . .
('Mole', *Man Lying on a Wall*, 1976)

I go disguised as myself, my own beard
Changed by this multitude of distortions
To stage whispers, my hair a give-away,
A cheap wig, and my face a mask only –
So that, on entering the hall of mirrors
The judge will at once award the first prize
To me and to all of my characters.
('Ars Poetica: 3')

I keep my own death-watch:
Mine the disembodied eye
At the hole in my head . . .
And no one there but myself,
My own worst enemy.
('Last Rites: Death-watch')

Derek Mahon

And heard, in the whispering gallery of his soul,

His own small, urgent discord echoing back.
('De Quincey in Later Life', *Night Crossing*, 1968)

To whom, in my will,

This, I have left my will.
('An Image from Beckett', *Lives*, 1972)

It is here that the banished gods are in hiding,
Here they sit out the centuries
In stone, water
And the hearts of trees,
Lost in a reverie of their own natures.
('The Banished Gods', *The Snow Party*, 1975)

Paul Muldoon

The snail moves like a
Hovercraft, held up by a
Rubber cushion of itself.
('Hedgehog', *New Weather*, 1973)

Its head in the clouds

Of its own breath.
('Thinking of the Goldfish')

I believed in your riding all night
Lathered by your own sweat.
('The Radio Horse')

Seeing the birds in Winter
Drinking the images of themselves
Reflected in a sheet of ice.
('Vampire')

You hold yourself as your own captive.
('Elizabeth')

[two stars]
They yawned and stretched
To white hides,
One cutting a slit
In the wall of itself
And stepping out into the night . . .

It had learned
To track itself
By following the dots
And dashes of its blood.
('The Year of the Sloes')

The girls in the poolroom
Were out on their own limbs.
('The Girls in the Poolroom', *Mules*, 1977)

I had gone out with the kettle
To a little stream that lay down in itself.
('Armageddon, Armageddon')

Many of those are creatively grateful to Marvell; Heaney's

and seems to weep
the black river of himself

may be bred from the union of 'Like its own Tear' and 'The River in it self is drown'd'. But so urgent and diverse a preoccupation with the same figure of speech, in poets who though close to each other are very different, is not likely to have arisen from a narrowly literary influence, let alone a single literary influence. It is more likely that there is at least some relevance in the deep affinity between Marvell's England and these poets' Ulster, racked by civil war that both is and is not religious. Christopher Hill's pioneering attempt to relate the conflicts within Marvell's poems to those of the Civil War might here be complemented.[16] There are indeed other important affinities between the poetry of Marvell's age and the poetry of this last decade, such as are obviously germane to the reflexive image: first, an intense self-reflexive concern with the art of poetry itself in poems; and second, a thrilled perturbation at philosophical problems of perception and imagination (Marvell's late-night reflexive wittiness is more than a joke: 'Th' *Astrologers* own Eyes are set', 'Two Songs at the Marriage of the Lord Fauconberg'). But to these should be added the way in which the short-circuited comparison is itself apt to civil war. It is not only a language for civil war (desolatingly two and one), but also, in its strange self-conflict, a civil war of language and of the imaginable. The peculiar attraction of the figure, though, is that while it acknowledges (as truth must) such a civil war, it can yet at the same time conceive (as hope must) a healing of such strife. For what Keach says of the reflexive image and the mind may be applied to the reflexive image and society:

> Reflexive images call unusual attention to the act of mind they presuppose, an act of mind which combines a moment of analysis and division, in which an aspect is separated from the idea to which it belongs, and a moment of synthesis and reunion, in which the separated aspect is put back into relationship with the idea: 'His eyes beheld / Their own wan light . . .' (*Alastor*, lines 469–470). 'Wan light' is simultaneously separate from 'eyes' and thus capable of becoming the direct object of what the eyes 'beheld', and inseparable from 'eyes', since their object is an aspect of themselves. . . . A reflexive image makes the reader aware of the mind's ability not only to perceive relationships but to create them in a context of unity and identity.

Reunion, unity, and identity: these may embody, as they do in the work of Marvell and of Heaney, not only philosophical and psychological hopes, but also civil and political ones.

The reflexive image simultaneously acknowledges the opposing forces and yearns to reconcile them. It is, like all paradoxes, 'a composition of contraries', and composition is not only a literary term but a civic one, of peace after differences. This is so whether or not the reflexive images in Marvell and in the Ulster poets deal directly with civil war, as they sometimes do and often do not. For the self-divided image flourishes in those unflourishing times when it will have to be said not only of the ignoble man but of the noble man that he

> Did thorough his own Side
> His fiery way divide.
> ('An Horatian Ode', ll. 15–16)

At its best, the wit of the self-infolded comparison is brave in its consciousness of danger or threat, and this is true even of the preposterous peril in Steinberg's drawings: a man putting a revolver to an apple on his own head, or a man sitting fishing on a whale which is about to swallow his bait. Those are as good as the report by the Food Standards Committee objecting to the digestive biscuit: 'To justify its name, said the committee's chairman, Professor Alan Ward, yesterday, the biscuit should have the power of digesting itself' (*The Times,* 12 May 1977). Or, in the words of Stanley Fish, *Self-Consuming Artifacts.*

When Marvell and his contemporaries, like the Ulster poets of the last ten years, were so wittily serious and resourceful with the self-infolded simile, they were at once recognizing and resisting the perverse infoldings and divisions, surmounting them with resilient paradox. Thomas Stanley's silkworm makes her destiny her choice, or at least her very being:

> See with what pains she spins for thee
> The thread of her own Destinie

– where 'pains' calls up pain but fends it off, in a way that consoles the lover for the pains he takes and receives.

Richard Lovelace's poems teem with everyday wonders that are comically *outré* and yet divertingly apt to human life and its large perplexities. When Lovelace goes to the ant, he sees a rebuke to the sluggard the oddity of which – 'Thou, thine own Horse and Cart' – goes beyond even the preposterous, since the preposterous (*praeposterus*, before–behind) means putting the cart before the horse, and how could that be posited of a creature who is his own horse and cart? The witticism, itself a compliment to witty nature, ushers in a serious anti-Aesopian fable. Again, the battle between 'The Toad and Spyder' jests about war (as does *Upon Appleton House*), but its alliance of levity and seriousness calls upon the short-circuited comparison, passing from a prayer to Athena ('Heaven's blew-eyed Daughter, thine own Mother!'), through a self-laceration ('Chaf'd in her own black fury wet'), to the climactic oddity:

> Till he but one new Blister is,
> And swells his own Periphrasis.

Yet the same figure of speech which may swell as a destructive excess of self may also be a valued feat of self-involvement, as when Lovelace praises Eldred Revett, 'That to thine own self hast the Midwife play'd'. And what is charming about that compliment to Revett's poems is that it infolds the very figure of speech which Revett delightingly shared with Lovelace – and with Marvell. For Revett's poems, when they come to life, are alive with the self-infolded comparison:

> And a winding river steals
> That with it self drunk curling reels.
> ('The Land-schap between two hills')

> Thou dost as it doth round thee flow
> In thine own cloud (invelop'd) go . . .
> As properly I might thee name
> Thine own fair picture in a frame.
> ('To a Lady with black hair')

> So a but peradventure fall
> Awakes the sleeping *Harpsychall.*
> Which since the Artist finger'd last,
> Lay lull'd in its own musick (fast).
> ('On *Mr. Gambles* composing of *Mr. Stanleyes* Odes')

When I retir'd back to her eyes to see,
If this were wanton prodigality;
But in those fair lights by some smarting wounds,
Their griefs seem'd carv'd by their own Diamonds.
('Lycoris weeping')

She is her *own close mourning in*
(At Natures Charge) a *Cypress skin* . . .
Thou dost not to our dear surprise
Thine own *white marble* statue rise.
('One Enamour'd on a *Black-moor*')

Rivers that chide upon their shelves
Caught, are made fetters for themselves.
('Winter')

And there is 'The Centaure':

Who usher to no Woman kind,
But *Ride before*, your *own behind*.
And when you over-ridden sweat,
Walk (your *own Hostler*) down the Heat.

Lovelace paid a compliment to Revett's Centaur in the opening of 'The Snayl', and then proceeded to outdo Revett in wit and substantiality.

So let me end, before I become my own periphrasis, with Lovelace's most acutely delightful eliciting of the powers latent within the self-infolded simile, his two poems on 'The Snayl':

Wise Emblem of our Politick World,
Sage Snayl, within thine own self curl'd.

Like Paul Muldoon with his snail, Lovelace himself creates a wise emblem, since he apprehends through this figure of speech so many of the taxing contrarieties of life, the self-divisions and self-infoldings, and yet suggests that the seriously witty imagination will rise to them and above them.

Compendious Snayl! thou seem'st to me,
Large *Euclids* strickt Epitome.

There is the largest life of nature, which is both distinct from us and yet alive in us, as when the snail is his own sunrise:

And thou from thine own liquid Bed
New *Phoebus* heav'st thy pleasant Head.

There is the life of family, which is both distinct from us and yet alive in us:

Thou thine own daughter then, and Sire,
That Son and Mother art intire,
That big still with thy self dost go,
And liv'st an aged Embrio.

There is death, strangely alive inside us and outside us:

And as thy House was thine own womb,
So thine own womb, concludes thy tomb.

Yet there is the religious life:

Now hast thou chang'd thee Saint; and made
Thy self a Fane that's cupula'd;
And in thy wreathed Cloister thou
Walkest thine own Gray fryer too.

Lovelace's second poem on the snail likewise opens out and clamps together the paradoxes not only of activity and passivity –

That moveth him by traverse Law,
And doth himself both drive and draw;

and of host and guest –

That when the Sun the South doth winne,
He baits him hot in his own Inne;

and of controller and controlled –

I heard a grave and austere Clark,
Resolv'd him Pilot both and Barque;

but also of the inconceivable ability to lift oneself up by one's own bootstraps:

Yet the Authentick do beleeve,
Who keep their Judgement in their Sleeve,
That he is his own Double man,
And sick, still carries his Sedan.

The snail carries himself in his own sedan chair; would Eliot have called this an image which supports nothing but its own misshapen body?

Marvell honoured Lovelace, as is clear from his celebratory poem, 'To his Noble Friend Mr. Richard Lovelace, upon his Poems', which speaks of what the Civil War had done to poetry: 'Our Civill Wars have lost the Civicke crowne' (l. 12). Marvell must have admired, that which his own art exemplifies, the alliance of levity and seriousness in the self-infolded simile which concludes Lovelace's second poem on the snail, a wistful weighty joke, at once personal and civic, about personal integrity and civil disintegration:

> But banisht, I admire his fate
> Since neither Ostracisme of State,
> Nor a perpetual exile,
> Can force this Virtue change his Soyl;
> For wheresoever he doth go,
> He wanders with his Country too.

Notes

1 *Seven Types of Ambiguity*, London, Chatto & Windus, 1930; 2nd rev. ed., 1947, pp. 160–1.

2 George Williamson, *The Proper Wit of Poetry*, London, Faber, 1961, p. 95.

3 *Paradoxia Epidemica*, Princeton University Press, 1966, p. 282.

4 *Some Graver Subject*, London, Chatto & Windus, 1960, p. 147.

5 Proust created his own hyperbolical version of this hyperbole, by making spectacles their own spectacle:

> 'But isn't the Princess on the train?' came in ringing tones from Brichot, whose huge spectacles, resplendent as the reflectors that laryngologists attach to their foreheads to throw a light into the throats of their patients, seemed to have taken their life from the Professor's eyes, and, possibly because of the effort that he was making to adjust his sight to them, seemed themselves, even at the most trivial moments, to be gazing at themselves with a sustained attention and an extraordinary fixity. (*Cities of the Plain*,

in *Remembrance of Things Past*, trans. C. K. Scott Moncrieff, London, Chatto & Windus, 1929 (reprinted 1941), VIII, p. 28).

6 *Swann's Way* in *Remembrance of Things Past*, II, pp. 20–1, 224.

7 *Marvell's Ironic Vision*, New Haven, Conn., Yale University Press, 1965.

8 Ted Hughes seems to me to subtract in force what he adds in violence, in 'A Kill' (*Crow*, London, Faber, 1970):

> Flogged lame with legs
> Shot through the head with balled brains
> Shot blind with eyes
> Nailed down by his own ribs
> Strangled just short of his last gasp
> By his own windpipe
> Clubbed unconscious by his own heart
>
> Seeing his life stab through him, a dream flash
> As he drowned in his own blood

9 'Illusion and Visual Deadlock' (1961), in his *Meditations on a Hobby Horse*, London, Phaidon, 1963; 1971 ed., p. 155.

10 'The Responsible Critic', *Scrutiny*, XIX (1953), p. 166.

11 'Andrew Marvell' (1921), in his *Selected Essays*, London, Faber, 1932; 1951 ed., p. 297.

12 'The Baite' imitates Marlowe's 'The Passionate Shepherd to his Love'; Walton described Donne's lines as 'made to shew the world that hee could make soft and smooth Verses, when he thought them fit and worth his labour'.

13 Thom Gunn uses the climax of this paragraph as the epigraph to Part 2 of *Jack Straw's Castle*, London, Faber, 1976.

14 Compare *The Diary of Alice James*, ed. Leon Edel, London, Hart-Davis, 1965, p. 149 (26 October 1890):

> As I used to sit immovable reading in the library with waves of violent inclination suddenly invading my muscles taking some one of their myriad forms such as throwing myself out of the window, or knocking off the head of the benignant pater as he sat with his silver locks, writing at his table, it used to seem to me that the only difference between me and the insane was that I had not only all the horrors and sufferings of insanity but the duties of doctor, nurse, and strait-jacket imposed upon me, too.

15 *Keats-Shelley Journal*, XXIV (1975), pp. 49–69.

16 'Society and Andrew Marvell' (1946), in his *Puritanism and Revolution*, London, Secker & Warburg, 1958.

6

Reversals transposed: An aspect of Marvell's imagination

John Carey

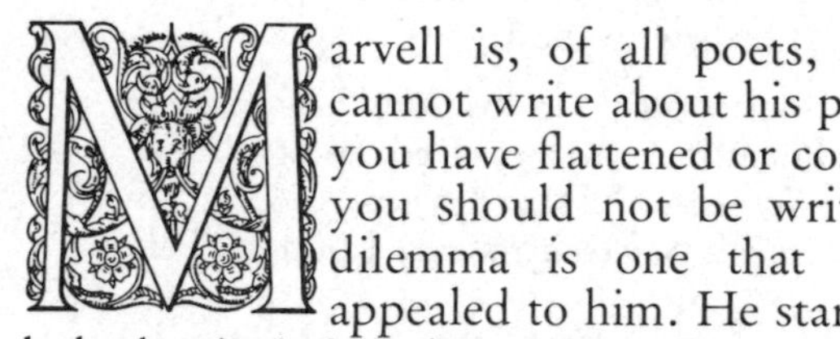

arvell is, of all poets, the critic's despair. You cannot write about his poetry without feeling that you have flattened or coarsened it – or if you can, you should not be writing about it at all. This dilemma is one that would have very much appealed to him. He starts his 'Epitaph' on a dead lady by insisting that, since all praise must be inadequate, the poem should stop straight away, before it has begun:

> Enough: and leave the rest to Fame.
> 'Tis to commend her but to name.

Ironically the lady's name is now lost. We don't know whose name it would have been enough to name before saying 'Enough'. That might appear to spoil the point of Marvell's lines, but in a sense it is a rather Marvellian mishap, for besides appreciating the difficulty of writing epitaphs, he seems to have been, for his period, exceptionally attuned to the hazards involved in naming things. We recall that little T.C., in her poem, 'tames / The Wilder flow'rs, and gives them names'. Once named, they are no longer wild, or not so wild as they were. They have been interfered with by language. Naming destroys the unnamed innocence of the thing itself. Perhaps that is why little T.C. is given only initials. Something of this sense lies too, I think, behind the ludicrous image in 'The Garden' of Marvell carving trees' names on trees:

Fair Trees! where s'eer your barkes I wound,
No Name shall but your own be found.
(ll. 23–4)

The officious and destructive aspect of naming is what the depredations of this blundering tree-lover remind us of. Human language falsifies and defaces what it describes. The danger, for trees, of such attentions had been made clear by Abraham Cowley, in a poem which Marvell no doubt intends us to remember:

I chose the flouri'shingst *Tree* in all the Park,
With freshest Boughs, and fairest head;
I cut my Love into his gentle Bark,
And in three days, behold, 'tis *dead.*[1]

An alternative version of Marvell's tree-cutting incident is given in 'Upon the Hill and Grove at Bill-borrow'. There the word which Fairfax engraves on the oak tree is '*Vera*', which, besides being a form of Lady Fairfax's maiden name, Vere, is also, conveniently for Marvell's purpose, simply an adjective meaning 'true' or 'genuine'. Thus the nearest Fairfax can come to naming a tree is to put the word 'true' on it, in Latin. It is, he learnedly and absurdly attests, truly whatever it is. That this linguistic effort is quite superfluous, Marvell points out: 'ere he well the Barks could part / 'Twas writ already in their Heart'. They were truly trees before he began cutting at them. It is not surprising that, with these misgivings about human language and trees, Marvell should announce in *Upon Appleton House* (ll. 561–76) that he has started learning tree language and is conversing with them in that – which means that he has given up words.

All this makes – or should make – the critic feel even more trepidation than he otherwise would about using his own words to give an account of Marvell's, and about the processes of transposition and paraphrase which that entails. In a sense, the fittest tribute to Marvell would be an hour's silence – or silent marvelling. However I am aware that this would be regarded as an inadequate, not to say fraudulent contribution to these tercentenary celebrations. What I shall try to do instead is to show how a particular kind of problem or dilemma keeps recurring in Marvell's poems. I think this is worth doing because his poems present such a miscellany of subjects and tones that it is hard to bring them into a single focus and see them as products of the same mind. What has the poet of, say, 'The Coronet' to do with the poet of 'To his Coy Mistress'? How do 'An Horatian Ode' and 'Ametas and Thestylis making Hay-Ropes' issue from the same imagination? We can start to answer this by noticing that a continual irritant in Marvell's poetry is the predicament of restriction – the condition of being thwarted, confined or enmeshed. Sometimes this is a poem's obvious subject, as with 'The Definition of Love'. The title, here, contains a pun. 'Definition' has, on the one hand, its modern sense – a precise statement of the essential nature of a thing. But Marvell's poem views love as essentially thwarted, restricted, and so exploits the older sense of 'definition' which was 'restriction', from the Latin *definire*, to restrict or limit. By compressing both meanings into a single word, Marvell makes the notion incontrovertible. Love is, by definition, a definition. To be, it must be thwarted. Love must be for something desired but not possessed. Being 'perfect' the lovers' loves are '*Paralel*'; being parallel, they can never be perfected. Frustration is thus inherent in the nature of reality, for the thwarting thing in the poem is not so much that their love is thwarted, as that it must be thwarted or it would not be love. Thestylis, making hay ropes, sees the same truth through a different image:

> Think'st thou that this Rope would twine
> If we both should turn one way?
> Where both parties so combine,
> Neither Love will twist nor Hay.
>
> (ll. 5–8)

Lovers, like the strands of a rope, are pulled together by being turned away from each other. Thwarting binds. The persistent lover in 'To his Coy Mistress' is, of course, a living proof of the binding power of being thwarted. Given world enough and time, denial would keep him loving for thirty thousand years. But he is trapped in another of reality's paradoxes, too. He is obsessed with the speed of time – 'at my back I alwaies hear / Times winged Charriot hurrying near' – yet if he gains his end, and wins the lady, he will only increase time's speed: 'though we cannot make our Sun / Stand still, yet we will make him run'. The faster you run away from time the faster you use time up.

The frustrating nature of reality is what Marvell feels as a religious poet, also. 'The Coronet' is about not being able to disentangle the business of writing religious verse from self-interest and desire for fame. The self cannot offer a selfless tribute and remain itself. The title, like the poem's whole effort, is thwarted, self-cancelling. Though labelled 'The Coronet', the poem explains that it is not a coronet, because its poet could not, in the end, make one. It is hardly surprising that Marvell's clearest exposition of the human predicament, 'A Dialogue between the Soul and Body', should be devoted to expounding the inevitability of frustration in life. Each disputant complains that it is always and essentially thwarted by the other.

It will be seen that Marvell's perception of the difficulties inherent in naming and language, which I touched on just now, is part of this same fascination with reality's frustration-mechanisms. Little T.C. names, but tames, the wild flowers. To know a thing, you must name it; but once you have named it, it is no longer the thing you were trying to know. Marvell repeatedly, as here, associates our manipulation of flowers with our manipulation of language. In 'The Coronet', arranging words is arranging flowers, and the countryside poems regularly take gardening as a model for the invasion of nature by culture, of which language is a part. What is frustrating, is that art, immediately it attempts to perfect nature, destroys its naturalness. 'Art', explains Marvell in *Upon Appleton House*, 'would more neatly have defac'd' what nature has 'laid so sweetly wast' (ll. 77–8). To put it like that brings out the dilemma. Art defaces but, on the other hand, nature lays waste. What is needed is a fusion of the two; yet fusion is impossible: 'Nature that hateth emptiness, / Allows of penetration less'. Fusion would entail creating a garden that was, at the same time, not a garden. As a matter of fact that is what the nymph in 'The Nymph complaining' thinks she has done:

> I have a Garden of my own,
> But so with Roses over grown,
> And Lillies, that you would it guess
> To be a little Wilderness.
> (ll. 71–4)

But perhaps you would be guessing right. Maybe it *is* a wilderness, though the nymph still calls it a garden. Since nature will not allow penetration, the nymph's garden, or wilderness, must be either a wilderness or a garden. Still, we can see why Marvell is attracted by the impossible balance between the two. It dispenses, for a moment, with the frustrating need for all creation (whether in language or gardening) to entail destruction – destruction of what was there before creation took place.

The couplet about nature not allowing penetration comes, of course, from 'An Horatian Ode', and helps us to see that that poem, apparently so different, shares the preoccupations of the garden poems. It does this not merely because Cromwell is depicted as a gardener, but rather because the Ode depicts the collision of two kinds of goodness, Cromwell's and Charles's, and for Marvell it is part of the restricting nature of reality that one good must destroy another, as gardens destroy wildernesses, or wildernesses gardens.

The nymph fancies her gardening has escaped this dilemma, and another way of pretending that art and nature have fused, though they can't really, is to make out that nature uses art:

> The low roof'd Tortoises do dwell
> In cases fit of Tortoise-shell.
> (*Upon Appleton House*, ll. 13–14)

What exquisitely contrived cases, we momentarily think – the ideal size for a tortoise, and of such appropriate material! But the fancy at once collapses into a joke. The tortoises are merely in their skins (an alternative meaning of 'cases'), and no one has been using any art, except, deceivingly, Marvell.

Being interested in restriction, Marvell is naturally drawn to write about containers – not just tortoise-shells, but enclosed gardens, and islands like the Bermudas, and buildings like Appleton House, in which 'Things greater are in less contain'd', and the 'curled trammels' of a girl's hair in which a soul gets caught, and the 'Iron gates' of life, and the bay of Santa Cruz which, as containers will, becomes a trap, fatally enclosing the Spanish fleet that sheltered there. Now one question that arises about containers is precisely what they contain. To put it another way, since nature does not allow penetration, each object may be seen as containing, or holding back, the space outside itself, as surely as it contains the space it encloses. A box contains, or restricts what is outside it, as well as what is inside. This seems to have intrigued Marvell. He makes his abbess in *Upon Appleton House* claim that her convent is just such an outward-shutting container:

> 'These Bars inclose that wider Den
> 'Of those wild Creatures, called Men.
> 'The Cloyster outward shuts its Gates,
> 'And, from us, locks on them the Grates.
> (ll. 101–4)

It is those outside who are enclosed. They, not the nuns, are under lock and key: locked out. Another instance of container and contained changing places in *Upon Appleton House* occurs when Marvell comes to talk about the river.

> See in what wanton harmless folds
> It ev'ry where the Meadow holds.
> (ll. 633–4)

The lines are surprising, since we should normally think of the meadow as holding the river, as a receptacle holds water. Marvell makes us see that the river equally holds, or contains, the meadow. It provides it with its limits, as well as meandering round bits of it. The second line of the couplet might just possibly be a poetic inversion – 'It . . . the Meadow holds' could mean the meadow holds the river. But the slipperiness of the syntax only compounds the confusion between container and contained which is Marvell's point, and in fact the river's 'wanton harmless folds' make it pretty clear that it is doing the holding. So, whether we seem to be inside or outside containers we are, Marvell shows us, equally contained – restricted. Restriction is everywhere.

An especially intriguing – and inescapable – kind of container is the container which contains itself. By simultaneously being restricted and restricting, it becomes the most economic (most restricted) exemplar of restriction possible. Marvell's 'Drop of Dew' is a container of this kind. We are told that it 'Round in its self incloses', and editors have worried about the line because 'inclose' is unprecedented as an intransitive verb, yet here it has no object. It doesn't need one, because having said what the dew drop contains its contents in ('its self'), Marvell has already named the contents. The dew drop encloses itself in itself, and 'Round' describes both the drop and the circular syntax.

There is a tendency for metallic images to gather round this predicament of restriction. 'Decrees of Steel' and 'Iron wedges' keep the lovers apart in 'The Definition of Love'. The lovers in 'To his Coy Mistress' must tear pleasure through life's 'Iron gates'. We feel, through these images, how rigorously we are bound. But because what binds us is largely impalpable – simply the frustrating nature of reality – Marvell specializes too in bonds that dissolve or disappear, though still binding. To take the word 'fetters', for example: fetters in Marvell can be composed of water, or of air, or of nothing at all, but bind none the less surely for that. Mary Magdalen fetters her redeemer's feet with tears – 'liquid Chaines' ('Eyes and Tears', ll. 31–2). 'The Fair Singer's' 'subtile Art', Marvell complains, 'invisibly can wreath / my Fetters of the very Air I breath' (ll. 11–12). And in 'A Dialogue between the Soul and Body' the fetter vanishes into the foot. The soul, because it is in the body, 'fetter'd stands / In feet' (ll. 3–4). The one fetter your foot can't get out of is a foot. By disappearing, the fetter has become utterly inescapable.

In the subtle trap which life thus becomes for Marvell, actions are constantly turning against themselves. This, it seems, is all they can do. Thus we find that the mower in the Mower Poems, who treasures the 'wild and fragrant Innocence' of the fields, is doomed by his very occupation continually to destroy it. He is a creature of contradictions. His mind, he says, 'in the greenness of the Grass / Did see its Hopes as in a Glass' ('The Mower's Song', ll. 3–4). But his hopes were for a good hay harvest, and so depended, for their fulfilment, on un-greening the greenness which made the grass a mirror of them. When he has been laid low by Juliana, he reproaches the grass for its gaiety:

> Unthankful Medows, could you so
> A fellowship so true forego,
> And in your gawdy May-games meet,
> While I lay trodden under feet?
>
> (ll. 13–16)

The indignant tone is absurd, because treading the grass under the feet, while *he* rejoiced, was what he intended all along. The grass has merely turned the tables on him. And he turns the tables on himself:

> The edged Stele by careless chance
> Did into his own Ankle glance;
> And there among the Grass fell down,
> By his own Sythe, the Mower mown.
> ('Damon the Mower', ll. 77–80)

It is this fatal reversibility of our actions that Marvell warns little T.C. about:

> Gather the Flow'rs, but spare the Buds;
> Lest *Flora* angry at thy crime,
> To kill her Infants in their prime,
> Do quickly make th'Example Yours;
> And, ere we see,
> Nip in the blossome all our hopes and Thee.
> (ll. 35–40)

If little T.C. picks blossoms, she will become a blossom and be picked. In 'The Nymph complaining for the death of her Faun', the faun eats the roses and lilies that grow in the nymph's garden, but the action turns round on itself, and by eating them he is gradually becoming them. 'Had it liv'd long, it would have been / Lillies without, Roses within' (ll. 91–2). It has already started to turn into the garden, which is why it is so well camouflaged:

> Among the beds of Lillyes, I
> Have sought it oft, where it should lye;
> Yet could not, till itself would rise,
> Find it, although before mine Eyes.
> For, in the flaxen Lillies shade,
> It like a bank of Lillies laid.
> (ll. 77–82)

The serpent in 'The Coronet', whose aim is similarly to lie hidden among flowers, also seems to find itself turning into them. 'Disguis'd', it folds around the flowers 'With wreaths of Fame and Interest' (ll. 15–16). 'Wreaths' meant a serpent's coils but also, of course, garlands. As we shift from one sense to the other, we see the snake becoming what it hides among. This is an essential part of the poem's meaning, and of Marvell's worry. What the snake represents is so deeply embedded in the 'flow'rs' of poetry, he fears, that snake and flowers may, eventually, be indistinguishable, and must flourish or perish together (ll. 22–4).

These situations in which an agent finds its actions shooting back upon itself – 'the Mower mown' – are curiously frequent in Marvell's poems once one starts to look. When the flood occurs in *Upon Appleton House,* Marvell presents the river as drowned in itself – 'The River in it self is drown'd' (l. 471). In 'Mourning', Marvell looks at a girl weeping, and thinks of the myth of Danae being rained on and seduced by a shower of gold. But this girl is both rained on and raining. 'She courts her self in am'rous Rain; / Her self both *Danae* and the Showr' (ll. 19–20). In 'An Horatian Ode' it is part of Cromwell's cunning that:

> twining subtile fears with hope,
> He wove a Net of such a scope,
> That *Charles* himself might chase
> To *Caresbrookes* narrow case.
>
> (ll. 49–52)

We see here how Marvell's apprehensions about traps and entanglements – the 'Net' and 'case' – connect with his sense of the self-defeating reversibility of our actions. Charles chases himself: is both pursuer and pursued. The dew drop in 'On a Drop of Dew' which, as we have already seen, is simultaneously both container and contents, is also, Marvell intimates, both weeping and wept. It 'Shines with a mournful Light; / Like its own Tear' (ll. 12–13). Marvell had, of course, found this in Crashaw:

> Each Ruby there,
> Or Pearle that dare appeare,
> Bee its owne blush, bee its owne Teare.[2]

He was on the lookout for these repercussive situations, we realize, in other poets as well as in life. Or, for that matter, in death. In 'Tom May's Death', Tom, the translator of Lucan, 'found he was translated' (l. 26), as Marvell puts it, on entering the underworld. Translation is what any translator in Marvell should learn to expect to undergo. There is an elaborate instance of this type of reversal in 'The Nymph complaining'. The nymph says at the end of the poem that she wants her statue cut in marble, and it must be the statue of a girl weeping:

> but there
> Th'Engraver sure his Art may spare;
> For I so truly thee bemoane,
> That I shall weep though I be Stone:
> Until my Tears, still dropping, wear
> My breast, themselves engraving there.
> (ll. 113–18)

The sculptor will not need to represent tears, because the tears, dropping on the statue's breast, will engrave replicas of themselves – be both engraver and engraving. They will also by wearing tear-shaped holes, dig their own little graves – 'themselves engraving' in that sense too. We recall, and presumably Marvell did, Shakespeare's Richard II and Aumerle dropping their tears 'still upon one place / Till they have fretted us a pair of graves' (III, iii, 166–7).

Agents who, through whatever devious or disastrous chain of events, end up achieving precisely the opposite end to that they intended have, inevitably, a rueful appeal to Marvell, given the angle on life we have isolated. The nuns in *Upon Appleton House* are a sorry instance of this. Their aim was to get Isabel Thwaites into the nunnery, and they do, but only at the expense of getting thrown out themselves. When the nunnery is secularized at the Dissolution, it becomes a Fairfax property, and Isabel has by this time married into the Fairfax family. What the nuns willed, Marvell points out, was thus ironically fulfilled: 'For if the *Virgin* prov'd not theirs, / The *Cloyster* yet remained hers' (ll. 277–8). Isabel has entered the cloister – indeed, entered into possession of it. The actions of Nature and Love in 'The Match' prove similarly self-defeating. Nature gathers and hoards her treasures in separate compartments, but their proximity makes them coalesce, which was the last thing she wanted. Love stores his explosives in an impregnable magazine, but so placed they are able to detonate each other, and turn his magazine into a bomb. The unfortunate Spanish fleet in 'Blake's Victory' finds itself in much the same fix.

What prevents it escaping is its own massive armaments. 'We to their Strength are more oblig'd then they' (l. 104), rejoices Blake. Marvell takes an involved pleasure in detecting these reversals of intention within the everyday fabric of reality. 'What in the World most fair appears,/Yea even Laughter, turns to Tears', he writes in 'Eyes and Tears' (ll. 13–14). It sounds, at first, like a solemn reminder of the transitoriness of mirth. But it is less, or more, than that. What Marvell has in mind is the simple physiological fact that prolonged laughter produces the symptoms of weeping. We do, given something laughable enough, laugh till we cry. The principle of reversion governs, in this case, our very glands and secretions. Attaining the exact opposite of one's intent may even be a kind of satisfaction, as Marvell indicates in 'The Coronet', where he invites Christ to trample on the flowers he has gathered. In this way, he says, they will at any rate crown Christ's feet, even if they couldn't crown his head:

> That they, while Thou on both their Spoils dost tread,
> May crown thy Feet, that could not crown thy Head.
> (ll. 25–6)

Christ wearing a crown on his feet is a model of all our reversed aims, and is clearly related to Marvell's salmon fishers wearing their shoes on their heads:

> But now the *Salmon-Fisher's* moist
> Their *Leathern Boats* begin to hoist;
> And, like *Antipodes* in Shoes,
> Have shod their *Heads* in their *Canoos*.
> How Tortoise like, but not so slow,
> These rational *Amphibii* go?
> (*Upon Appleton House*, ll. 769–74)

The salmon fishers are reversed in two respects: they have shod their heads, and they are speeded-up tortoises. T. S. Eliot, it will be recalled, objected to this stanza, using it to illustrate his claim that Marvell 'falls into the . . . error of images which are over-developed or distracting; which support nothing but their own misshapen bodies'.[3] This is badly wrong. The salmon fishers, putting shoes on their heads, are not distracting but central – germane to Marvell's whole outlook. We are all shoeing our heads in the long run, because our actions have a built-in reversibility, and the recognition of this lies at the root both of Marvell's desperation and of his amused tolerance. It hangs, for instance, behind his warning to Cromwell. 'The same *Arts* that did *gain* / A *Pow'r* must it maintain' ('An Horatian Ode', ll. 119–20). Force does not establish power; it establishes, simply, the need to use force.

We might expect that this eye for reversals in a poet would produce dialogue poems in which the arguments of each participant are persistently turned round by the other – and that is, of course, what we find in Marvell. But more often – and more intricately – Marvell's urge to reverse normal procedures affects not the plan of the poem but the behaviour of persons or objects within it. There is a pleasing instance in 'Bermudas' where, of the singers in the rowing-boat, we are told that: 'all the way, to guide their Chime, / With falling Oars they kept the time' (ll. 39–40). You would expect them to sing to keep their oars in time, to give rhythm to their rowing – since that is what rowers normally do, if they sing at all. In Marvell, typically, the reverse happens. The Bermudans row only to give time to their singing, which is perhaps why they took to their boat in the first place, before bursting into song. It is, as it were, an aquatic metronome. At any rate, no other explanation of what they are doing in the boat is given.

It is, of course, when two things coincide exactly – the time of a song and the time of oars – that they can most plausibly be made to change places like this, and Marvell is consequently drawn to such coincidences. They can happen in space as well as in time. The hill in 'Upon the Hill and Grove at Bill-borow' is, Marvell tells us, a peculiarly 'courteous' eminence, so self-effacing that it does not really want to be a hill at all: 'Nor for itself the height does gain, / But only strives to raise the Plain' (ll. 23–4). At a hill-top, the height of the ground and the height of the hill coincide precisely, needless to say. So one can either think of a hill as rising up on the level ground, or of the level ground as rising up on the hill, which obligingly lifts it. As with the rowers' song and oars, precise coinciding has led Marvell to think of role-reversal.

We also find in Marvell role-reversals which are virtually private jokes, since they turn on (and turn round) bits of his reading which will be unknown to most readers. The distant cows, for example, in *Upon Appleton House*, look small:

Such Fleas, ere they approach the Eye,
In Multiplying Glasses lye.
(ll. 461–2)

To the uninstructed reader it seems a needlessly elaborate simile. Distant cows look small, like fleas – agreed. But why should they look like fleas before the fleas have been magnified? Aren't unmagnified fleas simply fleas? It was J. B. Leishman who picked up the reference, noticing that James Howell in his *Epistolae Ho-Elianae* speaks of 'such glasses as anatomists use in the dissection of bodies, which can make a flea look like a cow'.[4] Howell claims magnified fleas look like cows; Marvell, that diminished cows look like fleas. He is making fun of Howell as well as reversing his example, of course. If fleas, when magnified, really look like cows, Marvell's argument runs, then it follows that unmagnified fleas can't look like fleas at all but like very, very tiny cows. In other words, what Howell had at the end of his 'Multiplying Glasses' was a midget dairy herd, and that is why Marvell, seeing a midget dairy herd, likens it not just to fleas but to fleas waiting in Howell's multiplying glasses to be magnified and identified by him as cows.

Another instance of specialized reading lurking behind a Marvellian reversal occurs, I think, in 'The Mower against Gardens'. Among the man-made reversals of nature that the mower there complains about, there is one that seems so far to have defied explanation: 'in the Cherry he does Nature vex, / To procreate without a Sex' (ll. 29–30). What does it mean? 'Like Grosart', admits Margoliouth, '"I do not know the garden-process to which this refers".'[5] Hugh Macdonald, in his edition, says that he has it on the authority of a Mr John Gilmour that the lines refer only 'to the practice of vegetative or asexual propagation of cherries and other fruits by budding and grafting which has, of course, been extensively practised for many hundreds of years'.[6] That plainly can't be right, though, for Marvell has already discussed grafting in his poem, and he presents what man does to the cherry as an additional and more dastardly perversion of nature: 'His green *Seraglio* has its Eunuchs too; / Lest any Tyrant him out-doe' (ll. 27–8). Marvell is, I believe, referring to the growing of stoneless cherries. 'Stone' meant, of course, 'testicle', for the seventeenth century, hence Marvell's eunuchs. In a gardening book of 1616, Gervase Markham's *The Country Farm*, we find elaborate directions for growing stoneless cherries:

> cut off a young Cherrie-tree within a foot of the earth, cleaving it also even to the root, take out the pith both of the one side and of the other, afterward joyne them together againe, and tye them close with a strait band, and a yeare after that this Cherrie-tree hath taken, graft therein a graft of a Cherrie-tree which never bare fruit, and the fruit which commeth of such a graft, will be without any stone.[7]

It is a double reversal of nature that Marvell's mower deprecates. Not only is the cherry tree, which usually has stones, made a eunuch, but, though a eunuch, it is made to bear fruit, to procreate. Incidentally, I am assured by expert horticulturalists that the method Markham recommends could not possibly work. Since it is nonsense, we may be sure Marvell got it from a book rather than from observation of cherry trees. Entailing such cruelty to a tree, it was bound to catch his eye.

We have noticed how Marvell likes swopping round things that coincide. This was bound to make him interested in mirror-images and in echoes – the most usual kinds of visual and aural coinciding. When a mirror-image swops round it vacates the mirror and becomes the object outside. The people and animals in *Upon Appleton House* aren't sure this hasn't happened. Their river is:

> as a *Chrystal Mirrour* slick;
> Where all things gaze themselves, and doubt
> If they be in it or without.
>
> (ll. 636–8)

Have they stepped through the looking-glass, and left only their reflections on the bank? They 'gaze themselves', Marvell writes (not merely 'gaze at themselves'). By the intensity of their looking they re-create themselves on the far side of the water surface. Tears are a topic which inevitably tempt Marvell to this sort of involved mirror-play. In 'Mourning':

Her Eyes confus'd, and doubled ore,
With Tears suspended ere they flow;
Seem bending upwards, to restore
To Heaven, whence it came, their Woe.
(ll. 5–8)

Tears, arrested below the girl's eyes, reflect her eyes, so look like eyes looking upwards. And since both eyes and tears look like eyes, or like tears reflecting eyes, it's difficult to tell which is which. Our eyes are 'confus'd' like the girl's. At the end of 'Eyes and Tears' this visual swop-over is further and enthusiastically encouraged:

Thus let your Streams o'reflow your Springs,
Till Eyes and Tears be the same things:
And each the other's difference bears;
These weeping Eyes, those seeing Tears.
(ll. 53–6)

The last line imitates the Latin *hic . . . ille* construction. Thus the tears ('These') will look like eyes weeping tears reflecting eyes. The eyes ('those') will look like tears reflecting eyes weeping tears. Since both tears and eyes mirror, what each mirrors is an infinite series of images, endlessly receding, in which tears and eyes interminably reverse and re-reverse their roles.

As for echoes, they are among Marvell's most resplendent things, especially when they do not exist. His finest echo is (or, rather, is not) in 'To his Coy Mistress':

Thy Beauty shall no more be found;
Nor, in thy marble Vault, shall sound
My ecchoing Song.
(ll. 25–7)

The instant we have heard that echo, we realize that it isn't there and never was. There will be no song, so no echo. It was the ghost of an echo we heard, deepening, as it dwindles into nothingness, the silence of the vault. A more cheery silent echo comes in *Upon Appleton House*, where the flowers are imagined as riflemen loosing off a salvo:

Well shot ye Firemen! Oh how sweet,
And round your equal Fires do meet;
Whose shrill report no Ear can tell,
But Ecchoes to the Eye and Smell.
(ll. 305–8)

The air round the flowers reverberates with colour and perfume. Stunned and dazzled, we feel the shock waves, after the explosion. But there was no explosion, and no echo, only flowers. In both these last examples echo, not original sound, is what Marvell gains his effect by concentrating on. As with his mirror-images, the echo (even when it doesn't happen to exist) becomes primary, usurping the place of what was mirrored or echoed. It is the same with the forest birds in *Upon Appleton House,* though here the echo is no longer silent. The trees rise like columns:

And underneath the winged Quires
Echo about their tuned Fires.
(ll. 511–12)

The clamorous and bewildering bird-filled grove is conveyed through the syntax. The birds do not sing, but echo, as if in the pulsating air echo extinguished song. And they echo 'about' themselves, flashing like fire through the grove, seemingly substanceless, with their noise not issuing from them but quivering in the atmosphere.

Finally, to return to where we started – with Marvell talking to trees – the reversal that seems to have appealed to him most was the chance of becoming a vegetable. As such one would retain, of course, only one's vegetable soul. This appealed, because it allowed an escape from the trap of being human, and its frustrations. What the rational soul brought with it was sin and sexual awareness – 'the Pestilence of Love', as the Body calls it in 'A Dialogue' (l. 35). The body lying flat in the grass is Marvell's way of indicating a return to the vegetable level of existence. Little T.C., in her poem, is still innocent of sex, which is why Marvell says she loves to lie horizontally in the grass. All the green things admire her. 'Every verdant thing / It self does at thy Beauty charm' (ll. 25–6). The wording is curious but significant. Each green thing charms *itself* when looking at the little girl, as if it were looking in a mirror. And, in effect, it is. The child reflects the plants' innocent level of being. Likewise in *Upon Appleton House*, when the flowers fire a salute to the General and his Lady, they don't fire one for Maria: 'for She / Seems with the Flow'rs a Flow'r to be' (ll. 301–2). She's one of them. In 'The Garden' Marvell imagines his own vegetable body and rational soul being able to come apart. The body ('the humane flow'r', as Marvell calls it in 'On a Drop of Dew') falls flat in the grass, and the plants welcome it back:

> The Nectaren, and curious Peach,
> Into my hands themselves do reach.
> (ll. 37–8)

They recognize a close relation.

So joining the vegetables is one way of escaping sexual complications. Making love to a girl-vegetable is another. When Marvell tells Clora in 'The Gallery' that he likes best to picture her 'Transplanting Flow'rs from the green Hill, / To crown her Head, and Bosome fill' (ll. 55–6), the odd word 'Transplanting' makes us suspect that the flowers are to continue growing on Marvell's imagined girl, induing her with their green life. In 'Young Love' Marvell pays courts to a female baby, but does so because he regards her as a species of vegetable:

> Whose fair Blossoms are to green
> Yet for Lust, but not for Love.
> (ll. 11–12)

The baby is still an 'Infant' (l. 1) – unable to speak – so she can't understand Marvell's love-making any more than a vegetable could, which makes it completely innocent (as well as, of course, completely futile).

Whether these fancied escapes from adult sexuality tell us anything about Marvell's personality, we can only surmise. He seems to associate sex with faithlessness and cruelty. Lovers are at best 'am'rous birds of prey' – beaked predators. They are cruel, too, to vegetables. They cut trees with knives; and when Marvell thinks of little Maria Fairfax growing up and getting married, he portrays her as a '*sprig of Misleto*' waiting to be 'cut' (*Upon Appleton House*, ll. 739–42).

Ultimately, though, Marvell's trepidation about sex is only part of that larger awareness which we have observed – an awareness of reality as a restriction, a trap, and of the thwartings and reversals that attend upon action. Why did he feel this? One answer might, I suppose, be given by reference to the growing sense, in the mid-seventeenth-century mind, that nature was ruled by laws as immutable as those of mathematics. Marvell's fascination with the intractability of geometrical figures – parallel lines, spheres – would plainly be relevant here. Alternatively we might point to Marvell's political predicament in the early 1650s. He was trapped in history: caught between the 'antient Rights' and the attractions of the hero who had swept them aside. In the previous decade action had issued in disaster: the 'dear and happy Isle' had been laid waste. But now it appeared that only Cromwell's 'active Star' could redeem the situation. What we have found in the poems is the meticulous and intricate and often playful manufacture of reversed intentions and self-defeating activities, with, over all, a potent feeling of constriction. This suggests, I think, a calculating and urbane mind preparing itself to take a decisive, and perhaps misguided, step, yet feeling itself forced to take it. In effect that step meant, it seems, the abandonment of poetry for politics, and of that there was unfortunately no reversal.

Notes

1 'The Tree', ll. 1–4 (in *Poems*, ed. A. R. Waller, Cambridge, 1905, p. 140).
2 'Wishes. To his (supposed) Mistresse', ll. 52–4 (in *Poems*, ed. L. C. Martin, Oxford University Press, 1957, p. 196).
3 *Selected Essays*, London, Faber, 3rd ed., 1951, p. 297.
4 *The Art of Marvell's Poetry*, London, Hutchinson, 1966, p. 222.
5 *The Poems and Letters of Andrew Marvell*, ed. H. M. Margoliouth, Oxford University Press, 2nd ed., 1952, vol. I, p. 225.
6 *The Poems of Andrew Marvell*, ed. Hugh Macdonald, London, Routledge & Kegan Paul, 2nd ed., 1956, p. 172.
7 Gervase Markham, *Maison Rustique, Or, The Countrey Farme*, 1616, p. 361. Markham was, as usual, refurbishing an earlier work,

namely Richard Surflet's *Maison Rustique or The Countrie Farme*, 1600, in which the passage quoted is at p. 460, and Surflet was himself translating *L'Agriculture et Maison Rustique de Mm. Charles Estienne, et Jean Liebault,* Lyons 1594, in which the directions for stoneless cherries occur on p. 203. They also appear in another of Markham's refurbishings: *Foure Bookes of Husbandry, collected by M. Conradus Heresbachius . . . Newely Englished, and increased, by Barnabe Googe Esquire,* 1577, was republished by Markham as *The Whole Art of Husbandry . . . First written by Conrade Heresbatch . . . then translated by Barnaby Googe Esquire, and now Renewed, Corrected, enlarged,* 1631. The stoneless cherries are on p. 95 of Googe's translation and p. 183 of Markham's republication. In Googe's original, *Rei Rusticae Libri Quatuor . . . Auctore DD.Conrado Heresbachio,* Cologne, 1570, they are to be found on p. 173, and the method of growing them, which is exactly that given by Markham, is attributed to Martial. This is, of course, not the epigrammatist but Quintus Gargilius Martial, who must, so far as I know, take the credit for starting the tradition. The fragments of his work on horticulture which survive are for the most part embedded in the *De re rustica* of Palladius, the Latin agricultural writer of the fourth century, which was first published in 1472 in Venice, and was very popular in the Middle Ages. Markham's method of growing stoneless cherries is given by Palladius in Book XI, Section 12, and ascribed to Martial (*Palladii Rutilii Tauri Aemiliani . . . Opus Agriculturae*, ed. J. C. Schmitt, Leipzig, 1898, p. 221). I am informed by Professor A. F. Posnette, CBE, ScD, FRS, Director of the East Malling Research Station, Kent, that 'apart from it being intrinsically unlikely that such a method would affect the fruit of the scion, stoneless cherries are unheard of'.

7

Andrew Marvell: The aesthetics of inconclusiveness

Balachandra Rajan

The danger of a paper on the aesthetics of inconclusiveness is that it may end in an inconclusiveness that is anything but aesthetic. I had thought of safeguarding myself against this danger by subtitling my essay 'Some Preliminary Evasions'. This kind of anticipatory deflation, it will be remembered, was regarded by the New Critics as a sign of maturity. However recklessness is more in vogue today than ironic self-insurance and so, like Marvell, though without Marvell's agile elegance, I must proceed to definitions that are 'begotten by despair / Upon Impossibility'. Indeed in the interests of controlled overstatement, I shall proceed to talk of forms of inconclusiveness, disdaining the more prudent word, 'types'.[1]

Let us begin unexpectedly with Dante. *The Divine Comedy* will seem unpromising terrain for a searcher after inconclusiveness but reflection will show that the very structure of the *terza rima* encloses an ongoing lack of completion. The rhyme sandwich, if one may use so disrespectful a description, contains or, better still, prophesies the next rhyme and the infinite linkages which are thereby solicited make the pattern a pioneering model of open form. The verse calls for continuation out of its nature. Continuation is not necessarily inconclusive though it is insistently so in the second section of Eliot's *The Dry Salvages.* In Dante we have not yet reached the point where there is no end but addition. But continuation posits a local inconclusiveness from which one can advance into finality, or towards a receding horizon, or into a world which is all before one where to choose but where no choice can be trusted to lead anywhere. The journey can be differently perceived; but something has been said once and for all by a rhyme structure the very nature of which predicates the journey.

Milton elaborates the poetry of continuation with firm closes that point beyond themselves, providing a model for Eliot's final finding that 'to make an end is to make a beginning'. The endings undermine their own conclusiveness with the 'bright harnessed' angels of the 'Nativity Ode' 'in order serviceable' for the greater work ahead, the 'uncouth swain' of 'Lycidas' facing the future with 'eager thought', Adam and Eve wandering hand in hand into an open world of peril and opportunity and Christ returning to his mother's house on earth, having stood on the pinnacle of the father's house of heaven. The 'private' return, the scaling down to the world of the ordinary, advises us of what lies beyond the poem for its hero and of what can also lie beyond it for ourselves. The open endings of the poetry help to remind us that the remaking of the self is a continuing enterprise which the acts of the imagination both mirror and help to advance. Milton tells us in *Areopagitica*, through the Osiris image, that history moves to a conclusion but that the conclusion will be outside history. The poem as an act of mimesis fully responsive to this understanding, is both an affirmation and an inquiry, a statement of the pattern so far as it is known and a movement of finding by which the pattern is both verified and advanced towards completion. 'Calm of mind all passion spent' is by no means an attainment of autumnal tranquillity. It suggests rather gathering into a much-needed clarity, a necessary reassurance of design before the bafflement of the actual is once again faced. There is of course a difference between the open form of truth and the uncompletable yet growingly self-evident structure which Milton makes real in the shape of his work. But the consolidations which end his poems are not conclusions. They are opportunities to renew the effort of self-making.

In Eliot the endings are disasters subverted into significance as Prufrock drowns, as Gerontion is driven to his sleepy corner, and as the thunder intones its benediction in an alien language over the cultural clutter assembled by the poem's bewildered hero. The *oeuvre* advances through catastrophes that arrange themselves to make new beginnings possible. Failure is the ironic form of enlightenment. All defeats are inconclusive, not only because defeats in the waste land manifest themselves less as heroic frustrations than as the continuance of aimlessness, but also because of the gathering consolidations that are found to be taking place under what initially seems the 'drifting wreckage'. We can see this in Section II of *The Dry Salvages* where the fall of progression into addition, of continuity into stark repetitiveness, is brought out by a rhyme structure totally and destructively open which seems capable only of being endlessly echoed. Such purified pointlessness might be difficult to bear if it were not in its turn undermined by the movement of significance which it does not wholly succeed in excluding. Meaning does not prevail; but at least it can be said that it survives and by surviving rules out the inverse conclusiveness of a world built around the absence of meaning.

It should be apparent by now that both the confident close and the stuttering irresolution are more than what they seem to be. The *oeuvre* builds itself on the awareness that the stuff of experience is not fully revealed in its texture, that the part is seen differently through its membership of the whole. Vehement finalities can conclude a poem by subjecting it to a boundary; but their very vehemence may summon into existence another poem with a contrary field of force. A characterization of Yeats will be detected by many in this preamble and it must be acknowledged that Yeats is indeed the master of a poetry of stances on a wheel of possibilities. A poetry of stances is basically inconclusive since every stance is formed by acts of exclusion which become in their turn the origin of other stances. Poems in patterns of continuity, open into other poems by taking into themselves elements which they do not fully organize, or by reaching into a centre which other forms of insight are used to penetrate. In an *oeuvre* of stances, on the other hand, a poem summons other poems into being by virtue of what it omits. Poems respond to and complete themselves by the creative enmities they seek and by the alliances of undermining into which they enter. If man can embody truth but cannot know it, then one man in his time must play many parts.

Hitherto we have looked at poems or structural units which are inconclusive because they promise or threaten something beyond themselves. The advance into understanding, the arrival at understanding by different routes which reshape the arrival, the interlocking of stances vigorously limited, the partially open rhyme schemes of consummation and the totally open rhyme schemes of numbing additiveness, the baffled self-consciousness decoding itself by dint of its own bewilderments, all present us with local events within structures of continuity. They are inconclusive because they require relationship with the overall embodiment which they help to bring into being. One could oppose to a poetry of continuity a poetry of arrest to which the 'Ode on a Grecian Urn' might be a crucial example. Frozen potentiality is the form of this 'cold pastoral'. The other side of fulfilment can be extinction. Yeats recognizes this relationship in declaring that 'The herald's cry, the soldier's tread / Exhausts his glory and his might' but for him there is tragic joy in the exhaustion, as well as the knowledge that any new movement of creativeness must find its birth amid the ruins of an old one

Whatever flames upon the night
Man's own resinous heart has fed.[2]

Yeats, to use Marvell's phrase, makes the sun run, exulting in what he elsewhere calls the thundering away of time. The urn attempts to make the sun stand still. Its unravished achievement touches rather than enters becoming, teasing us out of thought by teasing us into shapes of possibility. The town it portrays can be by a river, by the sea-shore, or amid the mountains. It does not divulge the reason for its emptiness. The poem poses questions which are aesthetically pleasing because they admit of more than one answer. Refraining from the narrative force of history, the urn is nevertheless a sylvan historian, capable of intimating wild ecstasy through the withdrawals of its quietness. Keats is too considerable a poet not to be aware of the losses that are necessary as the urn maintains its distance against what Yeats was later to call the 'pushing world'. If the lover is spared the ravages of time, he is also denied the fulfilment of the moment. More significantly, the town, emptied of its populace on a happy morning, is bleakly described as 'desolate'. Indeed the very nature of the urn invites us to contemplate the spectacle of the permanence of art perpetually confronting the permanence of mortality. The 'foster child of silence and slow time', adopted rather than generated in that hushed tenuousness with which being approaches becoming, bears witness continually to the triumph of time and of the uncreating silence. Art is constituted around its own undoing. One can thus read sadness as well as felicity into the urn's abstentions from history. The point is that one can revise one's reading even as one makes it. The poem is like the object which it contemplates, interpreting it, but arresting its interpretation, poised between detachment and entry with a precariousness that seems the condition of its cogency.

Inconclusiveness can be apparent, or be detected under apparent conclusiveness because more remains to be said. It can also be justifiable because everything has been said. When Kretschmar, the music professor in Mann's *Dr. Faustus,* explains why Beethoven's Opus III lacks a final movement, his point is that when the possibilities of the genre have been exhausted, the genre must be abandoned even in mid-gesture.[3] Nevertheless, the unfinished is not typically an exhaustion of possibilities. It is like the urn a refraining from possibilities. It calls on the reader or viewer to become a participant in an act of completion from which the creator abstains. The unfinished nature of a work can also suggest that it is less a declaration of form than an endeavour towards form, apprehended in becoming, like the actuality it purports to represent.

The reader's response can be an important element in a work of calculated inconclusiveness. Herbert writes 'Prayer' as a catalogue, carefully omitting those verbs which are in language the main instruments of narration and causality. It is a poem purified by being without an argument. The final 'something understood' calls on the reader to discover within himself the implied cohesion between the prayer's components. Thus the phrase covers not only the structure of relationship but the act of making by which the structure is reached. We are brought to the eventual and essential understanding that prayer must be an act and not a recital. Herbert's lyric is a striking early example of a genre which might be titled the 'do-it-yourself' poem and Eliot, who quotes it for a different purpose,[4] may not have forgotten it in minimizing his own use of connectives in *The Waste Land*. The 'do-it-yourself' poem is inconclusive because it solicits completion by the reader. When more than one way of completion is made available the possibilities of inconclusiveness can be particularly intriguing.

In outlining various forms of inconclusiveness, the accommodations of the word may seem to have been stretched. Some stretching is perhaps desirable if we are to free ourselves from the containment of the Aristotelian postulate that a whole must have a beginning, a middle and an end. Much of poetry can be read as a quiet questioning of this postulate, a resistance against it as much as a contribution to it. Actuality, even when freed from what are classically called 'accidents', does not always exhibit those plot structures which the work of art is supposed to discover in it. An aesthetic of inconclusiveness serves a corrective purpose because it can be more receptive to the obstinacies of the actual, to the ongoing nature of the poem of process, to the ironic response, the response that is 'vacillating' in Yeats's sense, or the response seeking to formulate itself.

We now come to the curious case of Marvell. Perhaps it should be made clear at the outset that the statements which follow do not apply to all of Marvell's work but only to certain poems, frequently anthologized, which are widely regarded as distinctively Marvellian. There can be little doubt that these poems are inconclusive. 'Coolly elusive', the phrase so often used to evoke the quality of Marvell's accomplishment, testifies to the difficulties of adequate characterization. Joseph Summers, in introducing a selection from Marvell's work, offers three readings of each of the better-known Marvell poems, making clear by his language which reading he prefers, but indicating that the other readings are possible and even plausible.[5] Even the titles of two fairly recent books on Marvell – *The Resolved Soul* and *Marvell's Ironic Vision* – suggest radically different assessments, both sustained by attentive scholarship, of the kind of poet with whom we are dealing.[6] These wide variations in reading have a point to make. It can be argued in response to them that Marvell's poems are not inconclusive because they take place within larger patterns of settlement that are to be negotiated by the poet, or negotiated between the poet and the reader. They are inconclusive because a controlled uncertainty is the objective of the poem rather than its enmeshment, because the play of forces within it is so arranged that the poems can settle down in more than one way.[7]

'Ironic' is another term frequently applied to Marvell's poetry, but irony in poems often prescribes its own weight, or exists in order to be overcome by affirmative forces which the irony serves to validate. The alliance of levity and seriousness is supposed to intensify and not overturn the seriousness. With Donne and Yeats the deflationary risk-taking is intended to dramatize the range of facts with which the overall understanding is able to coexist. The poem as a performance is made convincing by the degree to which it undertakes to threaten itself. Nevertheless when the performance is over, there should be no doubt about what has been performed. The revisionary energies of 'Lycidas', the poem's anguished dismantling of its assumptions, raise the stakes for which thc game is being played.[8] Eager thought becomes not only possible but significant when one has confronted and civilized the power of the meaningless. With Marvell it is not easy to agree upon the nature of the understanding that has emerged, prevailed, or survived. In fact it is not clear whether the purpose of his poems is to arrive at a finding or to display a pattern of forces.

Marvell's most celebrated poem provides a spacious arena for compliment. From the Humber to the Ganges and from the deluge to the Last Judgment gives room enough for the expertise of praise. It is in fact the very size of the exaggeration which undermines the enterprise, putting before us with amused civility the disproportion between means and ends. 'Vegetable love' grows with the slow pace of empires, though not through conquest as an empire does and as a lover hopes to do.[9] There is a touch of monstrosity here to contend with the surface elegance. Yet the hyperboles of praise are esteemed as well as dismissed. 'Lady you deserve this State; / Nor would I love at lower rate' is at once an urbane concession to the postponements of the love game, a reminder that the suitor is fully adept at playing it, an appreciation of the lady's reticence, a mockery of that reticence, a recommendation to inhabit a world of reality rather than one of convention and an acknowledgment that reality might be barbarous were it not for the civilizing force of convention. This is the characteristic Marvell tone, complex and even treacherous, subverting what it alleges and at the same time questioning its own subversion.

Carpe diem exercises do not begin with the *blason*. Marvell starts with a convention and then proceeds to dismantle it (in the carefully qualified way which has been outlined) before making his approach to another convention. The tactics put us on notice that 'realism' is not necessarily to triumph. The *carpe diem* injunction is in any event unusual because of its incorporation of the metaphysical shudder in a manner that is generally and justly admired. In thus turning from urbanity to grimness the poem confronts us with the destructive forces that loom behind all ceremonies whether of sophistication or, as Yeats would have it, innocence. Space is a desert now, instead of a fertile land of compliments. The epochs of praise now stretch into a sterile eternity.[10] Time's winged chariot hurries threateningly closer in an image that seems mockingly ornate as if conventions of embellishment previously played with were offering the poem their deadly consequences. Spaciousness shrivels into the narrow grave. The 'none I think, do there embrace', savagely conjectural, metamorphoses polished bantering into macabre taunting. Yet we have to ask what is implied by a situation in which honour and lust are alike exposed to mortality and in which lust is declared as the probable driving force behind an earlier zeal for compliment. The Biblical echoes of dust and ashes provide no sanction for the satisfying of desire. It is the triumph of time that lives at the heart of the poem. That triumph cannot be thwarted. All that can be done is to retrieve the moment from it and intensify the meaning of the moment. The *carpe diem* exercise always had desperation as a suitably muted context, but Marvell endows that context with predatory urgency while proceeding again, in typically Marvellian fashion, to undermine the retrieval that he offers.

As Eliot and others point out,[11] the poem might have ended here. In other writers the exhortation to seize the day has not called for an anatomy of seizure. But a previous convention has been set up to be dismantled and the one that has replaced it is not any more sacrosanct. It is deconstructive energy that characterizes the poem rather than the choice of one possibility or another. To devour time may be to turn on one's tormentor. But it is also to become the enemy. At point after point the imagery suggests that liberation can be the subtlest of victimizations, that we are born again as that which we repudiate. The winged chariot is responded to by 'am'rous birds of prey' who 'sport' presumably in those very deserts from which the courage to act had purported to deliver us. To actively 'devour' rather than to passively 'languish' is not to escape the end but to accelerate its arrival. If we console ourselves by declaring that we have at least taken charge of our destiny, the destructive comment is that our destiny may have altered because of the manner in which we were permitted to take charge of it. We may concentrate all our strength and sweetness (the ingredients of Samson's riddle) into the 'ball' which is the substitute sphere of perfection,[12] but there is little sweetness in the 'rough strife' and the tearing, the forcing of those 'Iron gates' which as 'Iron wedges' in 'The Definition of Love' contributed so elegantly to love's geometry. 'Tear', 'devour', 'strife', and 'prey' provide a telling reiterative context for 'am'rous'. The savagery of engagement and the frivolity of abstention from engagement dispose themselves around that mocking grave which is now seen as common to both courses. The poem ends with what it is able to salvage. We can make the sun run, even if we are not able to make it stand still. To abstain from action is to surrender one's destiny to time. To act is to discover that self-realization cannot be wrested from the space of seizure, the intense moment when the flame should burn at its brightest. If the sun runs, then time reasserts itself even in our command of it. We declare ourselves only in what we accomplish; but the accomplishment is always a betrayal of the intention.[13]

'To his Coy Mistress' is probably Marvell's most destructive poem. Its strength is that having turned against itself in the expected manner of ironic poems, it then turns against its own internal objections, leaving us with the desert that is the poem's centre. It is inconclusive because of its consistent, subversive energy. Marvell's other poems do not demolish themselves as thoroughly as 'To his Coy Mistress' and one might even say that the typical objective is the stalemate or stand-off as much as the demolition. But even in poems that press less close than this one to the desolation of reality Marvell remains the most accomplished of English subversives. I make the remark with this restriction only because I am insufficiently acquainted with the sophistications of subversion in Continental and American literature.

'The Definition of Love' is an exercise in geometry, countering Donne's 'Valediction' where separation argues for relationship.

Here Fate and Love, opposition and conjunction, the outreaching soul and the separating wedges, co-operate to design a pattern of forces in which neither alliance can be perceived as dominant. Hemispheres mirror each other in Donne and join together in the perfection of the sphere. In Marvell, parallel lines mirror each other and remain endlessly separated by the perfection of their mirroring. The definition might seem a salvaging from defeat (or a witty refusal to agree to a lover's demands) until we allow ourselves the possibility that the poem, because of its basic inconclusiveness, can find its locus of satisfaction only in its geometry. Fulfilment would collapse that very geometry in which inconclusiveness is stylized and celebrated.[14] So too would the directing of the design by hope and that is why the poem spurning reliance on hope's 'Tinsel Wing' chooses instead to generate its diagram from despair. One makes these statements on the basis that the poem is not simply about star-crossed lovers[15] but to some degree about a world the nature of which is that the ideal cannot be completed in the actual. On this basis we can see how the presence of absence and the creative potential of impossibility are put before us in the modern manner as forces on which definitions may reliably depend. We may prefer a solution or a failure that is more heroic but the poem presses the advantage of a fictive world that is not corrupted by success or failure, where the diagram of forces can be studied without the distraction of the triumph of either force.

In the 'Horatian Ode' the force of change embodied in Cromwell is presented in images of catastrophe the effect of which is

> To ruine the great Work of Time
> And cast the Kingdome old
> Into another Mold.
> (ll. 34–6)

The pleading of 'antient Rights' in this context is a complaint by 'Justice against Fate'. Change may be desirable but the cost of change is not to be minimized. And if progress (or that creative change which the poem officially celebrates) is put forward in images of disaster, resistance to progress is presented in images of decorum and self-control. This double undermining haunts the remainder of the poem notwithstanding its celebration of Cromwell's victory over the Irish, his coming victory over the Scots and his Adamic union of 'contemplation and valour'.[16] There are ironic reversals as one might expect with Marvell. He who stood for Fate against Justice is now both good and just. He who relinquished the 'inglorious Arts of Peace' must now maintain his power by the same '*Arts*' by which he gained it.[17] Milton's sonnet to Cromwell should echo in the reader's mind but Marvell's version is befittingly ambiguous. Perhaps the poem invites us to admire a final figure who has recovered some of what he gave up in himself and who has assimilated some of what is praiseworthy in his opponents. But the poem's underminings are extensive enough to leave uncertain how much weight is to be given to the poem's official statement and how much to the subversion of that statement.

This discussion can be further complicated and a complication is duly suggested. Cromwell is, as is often observed, presented as a force of nature. Charles is a '*Royal Actor*' on a '*Tragick Scaffold*'.[18] Marvell's underlining ought to advise us that the king is a participant in a work of art. The nature–art relationship cross-biases (to use Herbert's helpful word)[19] the poem's other relationships, making a statement of its 'findings' even more difficult. Art, we may say, must answer to nature; but nature, particularly when it is that 'rude heap together hurl'd' that lies outside the boundaries of Appleton House must also answer to the civilizings of art. Perhaps one cannot creatively ruin the great work of time if one has not planted bergamots in gardens. If tradition is linked to art, then the nature–art relationship comments upon the relationship between tradition and the new in ways that further modify the main ways of the poem.

Gardens trouble Marvell as well as soothe him and it is not just to his troubles to say that he is a poet of pastoral sensibilities or even a poet putting the pastoral mode to ironic use. The relationship between the garden and the world outside it echoes the relationship between reality and a fictive world and invites us to ask what fictionalizing accomplishes. We can say, probably rather emptily, that gardens are organically related to nature. We might add, slightly more specifically, that gardens represent a co-operation of the natural and the human. Marvell, as a subversive, is not reluctant to suggest that man, the ordering force in the garden, is also the principal force of disorder in it, whether as 'Luxurious Man' contriving unnatural relationships, or as the mower doing to the grass and eventually to himself what Juliana does to him. Art too has its displacements and misplacements in addition to its purer renderings. But it is the protective garden, the enclosed and therefore manageable space, with which Marvell is concerned as a counterpart to the protective fiction. The organic relationship sustains us here in insisting that art cannot escape from life. The space of enclosure reconstitutes what it nominally excludes. Thus in *Upon Appleton House*, the formal gardens ironically re-enact the Civil War while the wilder, less explored areas beyond provide a background of history – the deluge, the passage through the Red Sea and the Crucifixion. The vantage-point in the journey through history is, in the modern manner, that of the experiencing self, so that the meaning of the landscape is not described but discovered – through Alice-in-Wonderland alterations of scale that become convincing as part of the fictive experience.

At this point we ought to be able to tell ourselves consolingly that the worlds of withdrawal and involvement, or in aesthetic terms of the fictive and the actual, are different in degree rather than in kind. But the simulation of the Crucifixion makes us wonder not just whether the distance of withdrawal is too great, but whether the impulse to withdraw does not always create too great a distance of withdrawal. This likelihood becomes manifest in the garden of Marvell's poem of that title where the 'enormous bliss' of Milton's Paradise is reduced to the comic prodigality of 'What wond'rous Life in this I lead'. All things served man in the original garden but they did not do so by crushing themselves against his open mouth. If it is objected that the fish in 'To Penshurst' exhibit similar behavioural characteristics and that this is a respectable classical trope, one can only reply that it needed a Marvell to expose its latent outrageousness.

The mind is its own place and can only be lessened by responses limited to external stimulations.[20] The next stage of withdrawal is to the Paradise within, the ocean of imagination, the interior garden of Adonis, the repository of the forms of all created things.

The mind is now not tied to that exterior reality which it has succeeded in originating fully within itself. It can, in Bacon's reproving phrase, 'join that which Nature has severed and sever that which Nature has joined'[21] much in the manner of 'Luxurious Man'. It can also create its own 'seas' which are other than the ocean of the forms of the actual and its own worlds which are other than golden counterparts to bronze ones. The capabilities of the imagination here verge on the irresponsible and we are made aware of the hubris latent in the creative enterprise. The world of art is a mimesis of the real world, but through its inherent auto-intoxication, it is also a continuing subversion of that mimesis. 'Annihilating all that's made / To a green Thought in a green Shade' puts before us the achieved harmony of the work of art through its counterpart, the creative tranquillity of the garden, but we are not expected to forget the still-persistent force of 'annihilating'. Nevertheless and despite its comic undertones, the world of withdrawal can remain a place where the soul, like a bird about to take flight, can wave the 'various Light' in its plumes, preparing to blend the colours into the white light of eternity. Thus the poem negotiates its subtly shifting balances between the affirmation and the undermining. It undermines itself again in the mildly preposterous suggestion that to live alone in Paradise is to possess two Paradises in one. There is a text in Genesis to challenge this proposition of which *Paradise Lost* has made even the modern reader aware. Adam's eloquent plea for companionship in Eden which is Milton's elaboration of the Genesis text makes evident the demand of the human identity for enrichment and completion in acts of social relationship. That society is 'all but rude' to the 'delicious Solitude' of the garden is not exactly a statement that the fictive world is anti-social. Nevertheless the word 'delicious' does comment on the latent self-indulgence of the artistic impulse, just as 'annihilating' comments on the latent destructiveness of what begins as a withdrawal from destructiveness. On the other hand we have to remember that poetry can have its beginning in disengagement and even in the refinement of disengagement into solitude. The inconclusive conclusion is that the energies which constitute the fictive world are also instrumental in undermining what they create. The fictive and the actual stand in what is potentially a reinforcing rather than a contending relationship; but the nature of mind may be such that it contributes to the contention in seeking the reinforcement, brings about the mimesis in constructing the protection and subverts the validities of withdrawal through the very manner in which withdrawal is made.

It is apparent that 'The Garden' is another one of those poems which must be resignedly described as 'elusive'. That word in Marvell criticism has come to connote exasperation as well as admiration. Marvell might not have been displeased with this mixed response which is not irrelevant to the piece of work that is man. The fact is that poems which seek to display a field of force rather than to pass judgment on its dispositions must resist conversion into that poetic argument which the reader seeking conclusiveness attempts to win from the work. Marvell achieves this resistance through extensive underminings which themselves contribute to the depiction of the field. However when poems are as fully subverted as Marvell's, it becomes difficult to ascertain whether the centre of gravity lies in the surface understanding or the overturning effort; and one's sense of the centre of gravity may reasonably shift from reading to reading. An inconclusive poem of this kind, moreover, permits the reader to cast himself in more than one role and to enter the poem as the potential ally of either the proposition or the subversion. The resultant elasticity of interpretation will not console the seeker after tidiness, though Marvell is anything but an untidy poet. Yet there is a justice in a strategy which presents the fictive world as subverted by the very impulse of withdrawal which forms it and as calling for a correction by the actual which is in turn self-subverting, necessitating a retaliatory correction by the fictive. Since Marvell's tone is ironic rather than absurdist the indecisiveness of this disposition of forces is not driven to its conclusion of futility. Indeed the containing form of the poem, its elegance of enclosure, leads to a degree of aesthetic and actual acceptance which is far other than the diagram might cause one to expect.

Art begins in a counter-thrust against the 'pushing world',[22] a withdrawal into an enclosure of order where the force of the actual can be reflected, but diminished in intensity to what the form can tolerate. Marvell can put before us the comedy and even the irrelevance of withdrawal; but it is a fictive world which he both seeks and mocks. It requires a more powerful poet to tell us that the betraying fictions may be not those of art but of existence, the banalities of a life measured with coffee spoons, and to find the poetic commitment demanding an advance from a time 'reckon'd with herbs and flow'rs' to one threateningly measured 'under the oppression of the silent fog'. These statements point to Eliot, but it is Yeats who has given us the most uncompromising account of the deconstructive onslaught of the mind against those fictions which are its assurance of safety.

> Civilisation is hooped together, brought
> Under a rule, under the semblance of peace
> By manifold illusion; but man's life is thought,
> And he, despite his terror, cannot cease
> Ravening through century after century,
> Ravening, raging and uprooting that he may come
> Into the desolation of reality

The 'desolation of reality' stands in a line of descent from Keats's core of 'eternal fierce destruction'[23] and Marvell's deserts of eternity. Keats wished not to look too far into that core. Yeats is telling us that the tragic nature of man leaves us with no choice but to look. 'We have put a golden stopper into the neck of the bottle. Pull it Lord! Let out reality.'[24] No text expounds more eloquently than 'Meru' the compulsive terror of the passion to demystify and no poet shows more convincingly than Yeats how the imagination seeks the dream and the dream's destruction. 'Desecration and the lover's night', the repeated line that ends 'A Full Moon in March', confesses much through its violent juxtaposition.

Marvell does not fare forward, like Eliot, into the meaning that can lie only beyond the perilous flood. He does not, like Yeats, advance to 'an act of faith and reason' that enables one to 'rejoice in the midst of tragedy'.[25] His is the cautious tenancy of an uncertain middle ground, between the betrayals of withdrawal and the treacheries of involvement. The desolation of reality is a presence and sometimes a threatening presence in this middle ground; but it is kept within limits by the propitiations of irony. An area of inconclusiveness is thus occupied and made into a proper space for poetry. If Marvell is conscious of the fictive comedy, he is conscious also of how it can protect us.

> Stumbling on Melons, as I pass,
> Insnar'd with Flow'rs, I fall on Grass.

Notes

1 The pages which follow profit from Barbara Hernstein Smith's *Poetic Closure*, University of Chicago Press, 1968, and from Frank Kermode's *The Sense of an Ending*, New York, Oxford University Press, 1968.

2 W. B. Yeats, *Collected Poems,* London, Macmillan, 1950, p. 240.

3 Thomas Mann, *Dr. Faustus*, trans. H. T. Lowe Porter, New York, Alfred Knopf, 1968. For Kretschmar's origins see Mann, *The Genesis of a Novel*, London, Secker & Warburg, 1961, p. 40, and Patrick Carnegy, *Faust as Musician*, London, Chatto & Windus, 1973, p. 14.

4 T. S. Eliot, 'George Herbert', *British Writers and Their Work No. 4*, ed. Bonamy Dobrée and J. W. Robinson, Lincoln, University of Nebraska Press, 1964, p. 65.

5 Joseph H. Summers, ed., *Marvell*, New York, Dell Publishing Co., 1961, pp. 14–15.

6 Harold E. Toliver, *Marvell's Ironic Vision*, New Haven, Conn., Yale University Press, 1965; Ann E. Berthoff, *The Resolved Soul*, Princeton University Press, 1970.

7 It is, of course, now argued by several critics that all poems settle down in more than one way. Such critics would have to distinguish a Marvellian poem from others by the range of permissible settlements which it demarcates and by the strategies of demarcation.

8 This sentence refers to a view of the further development of 'Lycidas' by the present author in *The Lofty Rhyme*, London, Routledge & Kegan Paul, 1970, pp. 45–55.

9 Notwithstanding Legouis (*The Poems and Letters of Andrew Marvell*, ed. H. M. Margoliouth, rev. Pierre Legouis and E. E. Duncan-Jones, Oxford University Press, 1971, p. 253), 'vegetable love' does seem to refer to the Aristotelian division of the soul into

vegetative, animal and rational. In terms of this division, a vegetable love is an impropriety. Since growth is the property of the vegetable soul, Marvell's use of the impropriety to suggest the corpus of praise expanding inertly like some enormous cabbage seems expertly comic.

10 'Vast Eternity' picks up and grimly consummates the 'Vaster than Empires' of line 12.

11 T. S. Eliot, 'Andrew Marvell', *Selected Essays*, London, Faber & Faber, 1934, p. 296.

12 In the introduction to his selection of Marvell criticism, John Carey lists eight differing explanations of the 'one ball'. The possibility offered here is not among them. (*Andrew Marvell*, ed. John Carey, Harmondsworth, Penguin Books, 1969, p. 63.)

13 Christopher Hill quotes Bishop Joseph Hall: 'A good man must not be like Ezechia's sun that went backward, nor like Joshua's sun, that stood still, but David's sun, that (like a bridegroom) comes out of his chamber, and as a champion rejoiceth to run his race' (*Puritanism and Revolution*, London, Secker & Warburg, 1958, p. 347; quoted Carey, as above (note 12), p. 82). Legouis (Margoliouth, as above (note 9), p. 255) comments that 'the difference between David's sun, which runs of its own accord, and Marvell's, which will be compelled to run, strikes me more than the resemblance'. It is not clear that an allusion to Psalm 19: 4–5 is intended; if it is we would have to recognize the contrast between a situation in which the sun runs so that the firmament can display the glory of its maker and one in which it runs to signify the limited (and perhaps self-destructive) control over events that is possible in the desert of reality. We therefore cannot take it that the conclusion of the poem endorses Bishop Hall's advice, or for that matter that it rejects Milton's consistent curbing of the temptation to seize the day, evident not only in *Comus* and in *Paradise Regained* but also in Sonnet VII ('How Soon Hath Time . . .') and Sonnet XIX ('When I consider . . .'). Marvell's poem is designed to resist simplification and like other poems which are fundamentally self-critical it is also a critique of its own allusiveness.

14 Stanza VI envisages in suitably catastrophic terms the possible collapse of this sustaining geometry.

15 J. B. Leishman, *The Art of Marvell's Poetry*, London, Hutchinson, 1966, p. 65.

16 *Paradise Lost*, IV, 297.

17 Occurrences of the thought, which is a commonplace, are noted by Margoliouth and Duncan-Jones, as above (note 9), pp. 302–3. But

here as in 'To his Coy Mistress' a critique of the thought is called for by the questioning and supporting dispositions of the poem. Professor Kermode notes that Lucan and Horace

> also celebrated at a crucial moment of history, the destruction of ancient rights and the casting of the State into another mould . . . certain ancient rights have been repressed, the king has died well but his manners were those of an *ancien régime*, now superseded. (*The Classic*, London, Faber & Faber, 1975, p. 65)

What must be must be; the problem is to determine the weight which Marvell gives to the costs and risks of its being. The reference to 'Justice' and 'Fate' makes the response that is invited more complex. We are kept aware, via the classical connection, that Olympian justice was subject to fate. A Christian god, on the other hand, can declare that 'What I will is Fate' (*Paradise Lost*, VII, 173). It is tempting to argue, as Professor Wallace does, that justice must yield to providential will (John M. Wallace, *Destiny His Choice*: *The Loyalism of Andrew Marvell*, Cambridge University Press, 1968, pp. 69–84; see also *The Selected Poetry of Marvell*, ed. Frank Kermode, New York, New American Library, 1967, Intro. XI–XV). The main difficulty facing this reading is that (apart from the exemptions of mercy) the divine will stands above fate to implement justice rather than overrule it. We can circumvent this difficulty by 'demoting' justice to the civic and social level, while raising fate to the status of divine providence. Unfortunately Marvell's capitalization of both terms, for what it is worth, resists our placing them on separate planes.

18 The word play with *'Scaffold'* which, according to Margoliouth (as above (note 9), p. 299), was 'in use to denote "stage" ', strengthens the theatrical metaphor and the connection between the lived and the dramatic.

19 Herbert, 'Affliction' (1), l. 53.

20 Margoliouth (as above (note 9), p. 268) reads these lines as describing a withdrawal from the lesser (physical) to the greater (intellectual) pleasure. Leishman (as above (note 15), p. 312) agrees and adds that the language reflects the Aristotelian division between pleasure and happiness. He nevertheless concludes that 'Marvell's clumsy inversion, here as often elsewhere, has produced an unintended ambiguity'. Rosalie Colie agrees that the primary meaning is 'from lesser pleasure' but also argues for Empson's 'diminished by pleasure' (*My Ecchoing Song*, Princeton University Press, 1970, p. 149). The

Empsonian view and its subversive consequences are part of the effect here; the ambiguity is anything but clumsy.

21 'The Advancement of Learning', *The Works of Francis Bacon*, ed. Spedding Ellis and Heath, vol. III, London, Longman, 1859, p. 343.

22 W. B. Yeats, 'Certain Noble Plays of Japan', *Essays and Introductions*, London, Macmillan, 1961, p. 224.

23 'To T. H. Reynolds, Esq.', *The Poems of John Keats*, ed. Miriam Allott, London, Longman, 1970, p. 325.

24 *The Ten Principal Upanishads* put into English by Shree Purohit Swami and W. B. Yeats, London, Faber & Faber, 1937, pp. 16–17.

25 *Letters on Poetry from W. B. Yeats to Dorothy Wellesley*, New York, Oxford University Press, 1940, p. 13.

8

The politics of Paradise: 'Bermudas'

Philip Brockbank

Shakespeare's art had visited the Bermudas discreetly, allowing only a passing direct reference by Ariel to 'the still-vexed Bermoothes' and requiring the island of *The Tempest* to lie somewhere between Italy and Tunis. The play nevertheless is consonant with much in the island's early history to which Marvell too had ready access. When Admiral Sir George Somers died in 1610 while on his second visit to Bermuda, his body, says Captain John Smith,[1] was brought back to Dorset and three men and a dog were left in possession. 'Those three Lords,' says Smith, 'the sole inhabitants of all those Ilands, began to erect their little common wealth for a while with brotherly regency, repairing the ground, planting Corne, and such seeds and fruits as they had', and for a time all went well. Then they 'chanced upon the greatest peece of Amber-greece was ever seene or heard of in one lumpe', and now 'being rich, they grew so proud and ambitious, contempt took such place, they fell out for superiority, though but three forlorne men, more than three thousand miles from their native Country, and but small hope ever to see it againe'. They fall to blows and one of them is bitten by his own dog, 'as if the dumbe beast would reprove them of their folly'. The island persists, as it were, in allegorizing itself, in functioning as a metaphor for the larger world. The men 'recover their wits' but put themselves at greater risk by resolving to build a boat 'and therein to make a desparate attempt for Virginia, or New found

Land'. They wanted to abandon the paradisal island (where they had at first chosen to stay) and cash in on the ambergris. They are saved from their folly by the arrival of the first permanent settlers under Richard More.

Forty years later, as Lefroy records,[2] the Grand Inquest of the Bermudas is taking note 'of the unhappy divisions that hath fallen amongst us the Inhabitants of these Islands which have come to pass by the misgovernment of it chiefly'. In the hope of restoring unity and love it asks that all men should be willing, each 'according to their abilities, to give a rateable proportion of what they have to make up what they have taken from them'. The history of exploration, settlement and empire in the Renaissance is at once a story of aspiration and exploitation; going to heaven and grabbing the loot.

In confining my attention almost exclusively to 'Bermudas' I hope to have scope to clarify a little some of its imaginative and historical resonances, some familiar, others less so, and to read the poem both as a moment of art and as a sign of the time. 'Bermudas' is usually associated with that period of Marvell's life when he was acting as tutor to Cromwell's ward and staying at Eton in the house of the Puritan divine, John Oxenbridge. The two surviving letters from Eton are dated 28 July 1653 and 2 June 1654. Oxenbridge had fled the tyranny of Archbishop Laud and had memorializes both the visit and the return in the Latin epitaph he wrote for Jane Oxenbridge in April 1658. These circumstances invite us to see the poem as the nostalgic commemoration of a voyage to a promised land, undertaken some twenty years before. Oxenbridge had fled the tyranny of Archbishop Laud and had returned to England, as the epitaph would have it, when consciences there were again free, at the end of 1641. The disarming historical setting for the poem may suffice for one of its meanings and effects; like others, I doubt if it serves for all.

Turning from its historical to its literary context, it has been recognized that the poem keeps company with Horace's Epode XVI. '*Nos manet Oceanus circumvagus*', says Horace,

> the encompassing ocean waits for us. Let us seek the happy fields and the islands of the blest, where every year the unploughed land yields corn, the vine always blooms

> unpruned . . . the dark fig graces its native tree . . . and the goat comes without asking to the milking pail.[3]

But the poem begins on a different note, '*Altera iam teritur bellis civilibus aetas*': 'Already a second generation is being ground to pieces by civil war.' One translation gives for title, 'The Woes of Civil Strife. A Remedy'; another has it, 'Iron and Golden Age'. Marvell's poem is apparently free from the Horatian irony which led Swift to recall the Epode in *An Argument against Abolishing Christianity*. To stand up for 'real', as distinct from 'nominal', Christianity, says Swift,

> would be full as absurd as the proposal of *Horace*, when he advises the *Romans*, all in a Body, to leave their City, and seek a new Seat in some remote Part of the World, by Way of a Cure for the Corruption of their Manners.[4]

Marvell's poem is apparently a golden one. Its forty lines may measure the forty days that the spies of Moses took to return from Canaan with the grapes, figs and pomegranates of Canaan. Its professed locus is the Summer Islands but its covert one the enclosed gardens of the Song of Solomon. It offers both the satisfaction of arrival and the poignancy of expectation, and it is a richly sensual poem uncomplicated by what Donne once called 'The queazy pain of loving and being loved'. To those who have come through the hazards of the voyage it offers the security of the land, or rather the island, for the land in the very structure of the poem is islanded between the seas past and seas anticipated, the Atlantic and the Mexique Bay.

To admire the skill of the poem it is almost enough to recognize the subtleties of its movement, playing the metronomic beat of the oars against the swell and wave-break of the ocean; and to listen to the echoing rhymes, tuned to the 'hollow seas that roar'. It is only slightly disconcerting that the island we seem to have reached in earlier lines is still being approached in the last. But Marvell with great tact has floated his poem between the ship at anchor and its longboat coming ashore. The singers have arrived, but they are still travelling hopefully.

Such an innocent account of the poem, however, no matter how refined and extended, is unlikely to appease those who, like Mr R.

M. Cummings, are concerned with 'The Difficulty of Marvell's "Bermudas"'.[5] 'Unfortunately', says Cummings, 'what is known of the real Bermudas not only does not support Marvell's (or the singers') idealization of them but actually contradicts it.' The innocent poem seems still to wait for an experienced response, and such it would have received from one of its first readers – John Oxenbridge. It has become usual in recent years for us to remind ourselves that a poem created by a poet is re-created by its reader. 'Bermudas' gives us the chance to put that critical relationship into focus. For Oxenbridge had every reason to know that for more than forty years Bermuda had been exposed to a succession of frustrations, ordeals and crises, and that for twenty years many who had sought asylum in the Bermudas now looked for refuge from them. What was known to Oxenbridge was also likely to be known to Marvell, and much of the catastrophic record is set down by Captain John Smith, whose *Generall Historie* encapsulated earlier accounts, including some that served Shakespeare for *The Tempest*. Thus it comes about that from the innocent, golden poem 'Bermudas' it is possible to conjure the spectre of an experienced, iron one. Such contrarieties are essential to the early literature of the Bermudas. Marvell, like Shakespeare, would have read how Somers's ship was at the height of the storm fixed between rocks, before a sudden calm allowed the party to take to the boats and 'with extreme joy, even almost to amazednesse, arrive in safetie, though more than a league from the shore'.[6] Expecting 'the most dangerous, unfortunate, and forlorne place in the world' they found it 'the richest, healthfullest and pleasantest they ever saw'. Shakespeare allows the desolate island to the vision of Sebastian and Antonio, and the fortunate one to Gonzalo's. For an auspicious view more immediately in touch with fact, Marvell could have read (perhaps in Oxenbridge's library) Lewis Hughes's *A plaine and true relation of the Goodness of God towards the Sommer Islands, written by way of exhortation, to stirre up the people there to praise God* (1621).[7] Hughes says much that fosters Gonzalo's dream, 'Nature should bring forth, / Of its own kind, all foison, all abundance, / To feed my innocent people'. But he does not share the delusion that 'All things in common Nature should produce / without sweat or endeavour'. Like William Strachey in the *True Reportory of the Wreck* (published in

Purchase his Pilgrimes, 1625), Hughes believed that '*Dei laboribus omnia vendunt*, God sels us all things for our labour, when Adam himselfe might not live in Paradice without dressing the Garden'.[8] Strachey and Hughes would have been disconcerted by Marvell's poem, finding in it intimation of disaster: for 'loyterers' who will not 'sow with providence' will reap 'the fruits of too deere bought repentance'.[9]

Whatever ironies and instabilities may be intimated in the poem, however, do not advertise themselves but must be elicited from the reaction of the poem's language upon our literary, historical and experiential awareness.

> Where the remote *Bermudas* ride
> In th' Oceans bosome unespy'd,
> From a small Boat, that row'd along,
> The listning Wind receiv'd this Song.

In the first line Marvell sets his islands floating – they *ride* as if at anchor; and it is not perhaps clear whether in the second line it is the singers or the island that lie 'unespy'd'.[10] Horace anticipates the floating rocks in Epode XVI (925–6), for only when that miracle happens will it be time to return to Rome. In the golden poem the 'unespy'd' boat can be the more secure; but the unespied islands were a disastrous hazard for voyagers to Virginia. As Fulke Greville has it, in his fifty-eighth sonnet to Caelica:

> Yet this isle poison-like, by mischief known,
> Weans not desire from her sweet nurse, the sea;
> But unseen shows us where our hopes be sown.

The felicities promised by the sweet nurse, the sea, are in Fulke Greville's vision on the other side of the Bermudas:

> For who will seek the wealth of western sun,
> Oft by Bermuda's miseries must run.

In Marvell's golden poem the ship rides safely at anchor while the party rows ashore. In the iron one the ship could be wrecked on an unespied reef while the survivors take to the boats; but I think the poem is not as iron as that. The suggestion, a muted one, is of the 'sea-change' that attends the end of the voyage. I borrow the phrase from Shakespeare, as one might for *The Tempest* borrow from Marvell; where the Soul in 'A Dialogue between the Soul and Body', seeking to escape from the persecuted state of being in the body, grieves at how hard it is to die:

> And ready oft to Port to gain,
> Am Shipwrackt into Health again.

For the small boat, rowing along, however, we need not look towards the after-death island of Elysium, but rather to the arrival of Sir Richard More in 1612 'upon the south side of Smiths Ile'. One of the party wrote:[11]

> As soon as wee had landed all our company, we went all to prayer, and gave thankes unto the Lord for our safe arrivall, and whilst we were at prayer, wee saw our three men come rowinge downe to us, the sight of whom did much revive us; so that welcoming us and we the like to them againe, we sang a Psalm and praised the Lord for our safe meeting.

We have met those three men before – those who quarrelled about the ambergris – and within a short time of More's arrival he had two of them imprisoned. The singing of the psalms, however, has undiminished validity. Many stories are told of the coexisting piety, greed and heroism of Elizabethan and Jacobean sailors.[12] In Marvell's version there is also an Orphic suggestion of the 'listening winds' responding to the song, as in Shakespeare's (or Fletcher's) 'Even the billows of the sea, / Hung their heads and then lay by'.[13] What Psalms More and his party sang is not recorded, but I would expect a choice from 32, 33, 66, 67, 104, 114 and, of course, 107, for those 'that go down to the sea in ships':

> For he commandeth, and raiseth the stormy wind, which lifteth up the waves thereof. They mount up to the heaven, they go down again to the depths; their soul is melted because of trouble. They reel to and fro and stagger like a drunken man, and are at their wits' end. Then they cry unto the Lord in their trouble and he bringeth them out of their distresses. He maketh the storm a calm, so that the waves thereof are still.

Marvell is writing his own psalm:

What should we do but sing his Praise
That led us through the watry Maze,
Unto an Isle so long unknown,
And yet far kinder than our own?

The 'watry Maze' could allude to the high seas, to the reeling and staggering through storm and wave that the psalmist sings about or to the crossing of the Red Sea;[14] but for its more local significance we should need to consult an admiralty chart. For the Bermudan harbours were notoriously difficult of access, as Lewis Hughes writes, making the hazards defences to the island:

> God hath so compassed them about with fearfulle rockes, as shippes are not able to come neare, but in two channels, that leads into two goodly and large harbours. . . . The channels are so narrow and curious, as ships must come in very leasurely, one after another, so as the forts on both sides the channels may sinke them with ease by the helpe of God.

Another notion – of the intricacy of the divine order – may linger behind 'Maze'; 'This is as strange a maze as e'er men trod', says Alonso, led a dance, one might say, by Prospero's art; '*Quo Fata Ferunt*' – where the Fates bear us – says the islands' heraldic motto.

Lewis Hughes was glad to reflect 'That the Islands have been kept from the beginning of the World for the English nation and no other'; and even though the 'long unknown' Bermudas had taken their name in the first instance from Juan Bermudez who discovered them in 1515, and there were several later Spanish visits to the islands, the English were the first settlers and natives. 'And yet far kinder than our own' expresses the conviction of the refugees and is perfectly consistent with the first impressions recorded by Jordain and Hughes:[15]

> The aire is very holsome, and not subject to such contagious infections as it is in England . . . the earth is very fertile, and so mellow and gentle, as it needeth neither plowing nor digging, so that after the wood is taken off, and the grass and weeds be burnt . . . men shall live heere in much ease, without much moiling and toyling as in *England*.

Hughes, for all his formidable exhortations to work, dreams of a prospect – within reach – of a life in which, as in *Paradise Lost*, 'the greatest labour will be in worming and pruning some plants, which children may doe as well, and better than men'.[16] The comparison with England is a reminder that England too was counted among the Fortunate Isles – 'In a great pool a swan's nest', 'This other Eden, demi-paradise'. But it is not the more benign climate only that makes the Bermudas kinder:

> Where he the huge Sea-Monsters wracks,
> That lift the Deep upon their Backs.
> He leads us on a grassy Stage;
> Safe from the Storms, and Prelat's rage.

Oxenbridge, we are often reminded, left England under pressure from Archbishop Laud. The specific circumstances, however, do not encourage us to believe that the poem is remembering them. Oxenbridge was dismissed from his Magdalen Hall tutorship by Laud (then Chancellor of Oxford) because he exacted from his scholars an oath of 'obedience in hair and clothes, studies, performace of religious duties, company and recreations'.[17] The prelate's rage, therefore, was directed at Oxenbridge's eagerness to impose a stricter regimen than the university's regulations required. The incident has its place in the general history of the Bermudas and of America as religious asylums. The Spaniard Don Pedro Menendez, for example, called at the Bermudas in 1563 (in search of his son) and went on to exterminate the Huguenot colony in Florida; and for a century before the poem was written, religious aspirants and refugees alike had been moving west. The significant fact for the poem is that the movement was still under way in 1653. When Oxenbridge first arrived in the Bermudas he proved himself a vigilant member of the established church, and it was not until reports of Laud's fall reached the island that he and his zealous brother-in-God, Nathaniel White, became openly active in the Puritan and Independent cause. Richard Norwood, himself a refugee from Laud, wrote to the governor of the Bermudas Company, in 1642, specifically about the activities of Oxenbridge and White, complaining that he was 'quite out of love with the government of the clergy'.[18] The ministers had set up a system of catechism which encouraged children to report delinquent lapses on the part of their parents. Oxenbridge, probably seeing ampler career prospects under Parliament, returned to England in 1641, leaving White to be proclaimed 'supreme governor of this church, next and immediately under Christ'. Outraged members of the Church of England in Bermuda submitted a petition to Parliament in 1645 pleading that many had gone to the islands as 'a sanctuary against the avengers of non-conformity' and now they wished to be allowed to worship 'quietly, freely and peacably'.[19] Parliament, at a time when Milton was raging that 'new presbyter is old priest writ large', upheld the petition and ordered that 'the inhabitants of the Summer-Islands . . . shall, without any molestation or trouble, have and enjoy the liberty of their consciences, in matter of God's worship, as well in those parts of Amiraca where they are now planted . . .'.[20] In the same year Laud was beheaded and five years later his estates were appropriated in order to finance the fleet sent to effect the 'reduction' of Barbados, Bermudas and Virginia, all in some degree disarrayed by news of the king's execution.[21]

In the Bermudas a military group, with popular support, had dispossessed the Independents and put Nathaniel White in prison. Among the signatories of a letter sent from the Bermudas Company in London to Captain Forster, the newly appointed governor, in 1650, was John Oxenbridge, or so it seems, as only 'John Ox' is still legible on the damaged manuscript.[22] It begins with an expression of anxiety about the 'generall and religious concord of the Island', but, more significantly for an experience of the poem, it speaks of those refugees who had recently fled the Bermudas under a former governor, William Sayle, to establish a new sanctuary upon a long-abandoned island in the Bahamas that was now re-named Eleutheria. The island, Forster says in his reply to the Company's letter, 'is a most barren rock, shallow Earth, not hopeful to produce food for the Inhabitants'. For a more ample account than Forster's, however, there is the History of Massachusetts by its contemporary governor, John Winthrop:[23]

> [Sayle's] first article was for liberty of conscience, wherein they provided that the civil magistrate should not have cognizance of any matter which concerned religion: but every man might enjoy his own opinion or religion without control

> or question (nor was there any word of maintaining or professing any religion or worship of God at all.)

It is clear that Sayle and his followers hoped to escape from both prelate and Independents, although those who joined him were a very mixed bunch. A certain Captain Butler

> made use of his liberty to disturb all the company. He could not endure any ordinance or worship . . . and when they arrived at one of the Eleutherian Islands and were intended there to settle, he made such a faction as enforced Captain Sayle to remove to another Island, and being near the harbour the ship struck and was cast away.

What follows is a curious mockery of the expectations awakened by Marvell's poem:[24]

> The persons were all saved, save one, but all their provisions and goods were lost, so as they were forced (for divers months) to lie in the open air, and to feed upon such fruits and wild creatures as the Island afforded. But finding their strength to decay and no hope of any relief, Captain Sayle took a shallop and eight men, with such provisions as they could get, and set sail, hoping to attain either the Summer Islands or Viginia.

He arrived in fact at Virginia where he found the church 'in a state of persecution' and set off back for Eleutheria, taking a number of Virginians with him. As Lefroy remarks, 'the experience of these advanced secularists affords little encouragement to imitators'.

Oxenbridge continued to be fully informed about events in Eleutheria and in June 1653 he was appointed to a commission 'for governing and carrying on the affairs of the Somer Islands'. He was still actively concerned when the party from Eleutheria was invited back to the Bermudas in 1655. By the time Whitehall moved, however, in December 1656, to rescue the 'sixty Protestant English' who had been driven from the Somer Islands by 'violent persecution', they had already left. Sayle, like Marvell himself, eluded fanatical commitment to either Puritan or royalist factions. His impulse to get away made him friends and enemies of both parties. He offered sanctuary to the deposed supreme head of the Church after Christ – Nathaniel White – but left his Bermudan estates in the care of the governor, Trimingham, who led the royalist rising. A Whitehall committee in 1658 reported Sayle's opinion that the execution of the king was 'a treacherous and murderous act' and therefore pronounced him unfit to govern the islands; but he carried on for another four years.[25]

The singers in the small boat, it seems, therefore, could commemorate a choice of fugitives and settlers: Somers's party in 1609, Richard More's in 1612, Oxenbridge's in the *Truelove* in 1635 or, more obliquely, William Sayle's Eleutherian voyages beyond Bermuda and back again from 1650 to 1655. The poem does not invite us to alight at any one moment in Bermuda's past. The deliverer that it praises is, like the God of the Psalmist, the seas' creator: 'The earth is full of thy riches. So is this great and wide sea. . . . There go the ships; there is that Leviathan, whom thou hast made to play therein.' The poem is an answering creation, while the reader re-creates it:

Where he the huge Sea-Monsters wracks,
That lift the Deep upon their Backs.

Much of the poem's serene persistence comes from that metrical trick of letting a more than usually strong beat fall early in the line, usually on the second syllable: 'The listning Winds receiv'd this Song'; but a few, like the first, are suspended between equable opening and closing stresses; and a few others break, as it were, at the wave's end. So it is later with 'And makes the hollow seas, that *roar*', and here, with '*wracks*'. In Pliny's account of the Fortunate Isles (specifically the Canaries)[26] the carcasses of putrefying whales are washed up on to the beach. Cummings, not unreasonably, sees an irony here and adds that 'all attempted whaling adventures in the Bermudas failed', while Smith does not say that whales were stranded on Bermudan beaches. It is true that early attempts to get whaling under way were a failure, but a few decades after Smith, in 1670, about the time when Marvell himself was appointed to a committee of inquiry into the affairs of the Bermudas,[27] Sir John Heydon issued a proclamation declaring that the inhabitants were suffering extreme annoyance 'by the Carcasses of Whales, turned adrift after they have been used for peoples most advantage'.[28] The psalmist's leviathan is created for play; Marvell's monsters are created and wrecked, by the swell of the sea, with an effect of splendid but gratuitous power. The Bermudan and Pliny would have said, 'Oh, you mean those stinking whales.'

A response to the poem would have been further complicated by any recollection the reader might have had of Waller's celebrated poem, 'The Battle of the Sommer Islands', published in 1645. In the poem a whale and her cub are caught between reef and shore and have to fight for their lives before a flood tide carries them back to sea. Waller too had served on a parliamentary committee for the Bermudas, to consider a 1628 petition against the increase in tobacco tax. His poem is heroically ironic about the cruelty of men in comparison with whales (compare Lamentations 4: 3) and about paradisal trade:

> The naked rocks are not unfruitful there,
> But at some constant seasons every year
> Their barren top with lucious food abound,
> And with the eggs of various fowls are crown'd
> Tobacco is the worst of things in which they
> To English Land-lords as their Tribute pay;
> Such is the mould, that the blest Tenant feeds
> On pretious fruits, and pays his rent in weeds.

Waller's poem reminds us how Marvell keeps his distance from direct allusion to the economic resources of the islands, and to their exploitation and spoliation Marvell's island in comparison is a symbolic, not an actual, destination. Yet symbol and actuality keep in touch.

The cedars that Marvell speaks of were not in fact, in the Bermudas, of the Lebanon kind; the poem recalls the temple and the gardens of Solomon, with pomegranates, grapes and figs. The Bermudas cedars were, shall we say, highly valued, and were therefore depleted at such a rate that a dozen or more proclamations were issued in Oxenbridge's time to try to conserve them.[29] From the Grand Inquisition of June 1652 we learn that the palmettos had been cut down to make bibby and aquavita for the base and deboshed populace, that the poor had been dispossessed by greedy settlers who 'strive to get as much land into their hands as they can', and the exotic fruits were so raided by the children of the deboshed parents that 'it will end by some fruits being worn out of the island'.[30] In early days, however, before what Smith calls 'the wonderful confusion of rats', Captain Daniel Tucker (said to be the 'Dan, Dan, dirty old man' of the nursery rhyme) was planting hedges of fig trees and pomegranates. The orange trade flourished to the extent that it threatened the cedars – required for boxes; and from time to time the Company expressed interest in more exotic fruits grown on the island, including pineapples and melons.

In the poem the fruits express the prolific, magical fecundity of the created world, and are there for nourishment and delight. 'There seemes to be a continuall Spring', says Smith, 'which is the cause some things come not to that maturity and perfection as were requisite.' Cummings thinks that Marvell's 'eternal spring' carries a similar implication. But I would prefer the phrase to be differently suspended. Horace, in the seventh ode of Book IV, reminds us that the seasons' cycle is not unqualified solace: 'spring is trampled under foot by summer, destined to go in its turn when fruitful autumn has poured out its harvest, and lifeless winter soon returns again'. The epitaph upon Sir George Somers puns upon his seasonal name, perhaps with a memory of Horace: Smith's English version runs:

> Alas Virginia's Summer so soone past,
> Autumn succeeds and stormy Winters blast,
> Yet England's joyfull Spring with joyfull showers,
> O Florida, shall bring thy sweetest flowers.

Marvell would have noticed that 'England's joyfull Spring' was an abbreviated translation of '*At ver perpetuum nascetur, et Anglia laeta*'. The epitaph's Latin has summer passing through autumn and winter to a perpetual spring. As in the epitaph on Jane Oxenbridge and in the sonnet to Caelica, felicity is beyond death and beyond the Bermudas. Summer and Somers alike die into life; it is the *Tempest* experience again, that Eliot will remember in *The Waste Land*.

'He sends the Fowls to us in care, / On daily visits through the air' may remind us of the 'remote' ordeal of Elijah, fed by the ravens and the brook of Cherith – a spring which dried up; or we may think of those, shortly before the poem was written, wrecked on Eleutheria, fed by the birds. But the assuring solicitude survives these associations, in the poem's rhythm and in that metaphor which we reach, as it were, at the next pull upon the oars:

> He hangs in shades the Orange bright,
> Like golden Lamps in a green Night.

We are reassured about the creator's, and the poet's, capabilities to transfigure the darkness into greenness, the greenness into fruit, the fruit into life and light. The light is 'golden' and so is the fruit, with a suggestion of perpetual and fabulous artifice – like Yeats's Byzantium (we may now feel), or, as the poem has it, like the jewels of Ormus, the gospel's pearl, and the apples of the Hesperidean gardens. These oranges must not be crated; but they were; and in a different dimension of our thoughts, we are glad of it. Yet they must remain 'enammeled', by the 'eternal spring' and by the poet's art. They must remain inviolable for, like the apples to come, 'no Tree could ever bear them twice'. Some, with an eye on Smith's description, say the apples are pineapples, leaving others to point out that pineapples don't grow on trees; Marvell's word 'plants' perhaps suggests indeed that trees would find them an embarrassment. It is necessary for the poet never to do again what he or others have done before; but he must keep returning to the same truths; thus, as others have noticed, Spenser's Bower of Bliss and Garden of Adonis can come upon us as we read of Marvell's paradise:

> At last farre off they many Islands spy . . .
> Both faire and fruitfull, and the ground dispred
> With grassy greene of delectable hewe. . . .

'Here', says Cummings, 'is the origin of Marvell's "grassy stage".' I am less confident. The bay nearest the old governor's house on the south-east side of the island is called 'Grassy Bay', and 'stage' is a word used by Smith for 'landing-stage'; the reefs once past, the small boats within the bay could run ashore. But the Bower of Bliss is still, as it were, *ethically* present in the poem's evocations. Both, as Cummings says, are a 'Port of rest from troublous toil'. Marvell, in Keats's phrase about the Grecian urn, 'teases us out of thought'. He knows he is writing in the tradition of Jonson's 'To

Penshurst' which is about the fruitfulness and plentitude of a well-cultivated country estate. But he knows that Paradise and the Promised Land and the territories of Solomon are inescapable presences in the language he has inherited.

The pomegranate was a symbol of the diversity and unity of the church, but in later seventeenth-century painting it is a common theme for still-life studies which attend to their complex inner structure; along with melons and figs they are treated as prolific boxes of seeds.

Marvell chooses to make his pomegranate a jewel casket – 'Jewels more rich than *Ormus* shows'. Ormus, alas, is not without its iron and irony. Marvell could have read about it in Hakluyt: 'Ormus is an Island in circuit about five and twentie miles . . . and is the driest island in the world'. Nothing grows there, but it offers 'great store of pearls' and a rich variety of jewels. 'Very shortly after our arrival', says the narrator, 'wee were put in prison.'[31] But the fame of Ormus had a more parochial history for the Englishman, as its sacking was the centre of a major scandal involving the king in the time of James II. For the poem, however, it is enough that one image of treasure should foil another.

The created riches of the island – in one sense, the treasure in heaven – still have their commercial history, and Marvell was well aware of it. One of the more ruthless exploiters of the islands, whose activities led finally to official confiscation of his property, was a certain Perient Trott; and Marvell wrote epitaphs for two related Trotts who were shareholders in the Bermudas Company. He dealt, among other things, in ambergris. When Richard More's psalm-singers came to the island in 1612 it was in hope, not of arriving in Elysium, but of getting 13*s*.4*d*. per ounce for ambergris. The three lords of the island (and their dog) had by this time accumulated 120 lb of it, and their story (as we have partly noticed) is a fit theme for Conrad. Ambergris, says the Encyclopedia, 'occurs as a biliary concretion in the intestines of a sperm whale'; it was, and is, used in the preparation of perfumes. The poem's 'hollow seas', in another great wave-break, '*proclaime* the Ambergris on shoar'. As the poem approaches land it grows, as it were, more conscious of the roar and echo of the re-sounding coast. Smith tells of its remarkable caves, and Marvell may well connect the sea-sound in caves with the sound of voices singing in temples – the stone temples, too, which Pliny finds upon the Fortunate Isles. If we think of Richard More and the three lords of the island, and the joy of that arrival, the echo beyond the Mexique Bay is a delightful hyperbole about the full-throated singing of the psalm. If we think of Oxenham's arrival and his missionary dream, the gospel may (perhaps) be carried farther west to the territories of Spain's aspirations. But thinking of William Sayle's less fortunate oarsmen, they (perhaps) will still be rowing and singing, across the Gulf of Mexico, in hope's eternal spring, looking for Eleutheria.

The 'Gospels Pearl' is, in Matthew's text of the Sermon on the Mount, not to be 'cast before swine'. Cummings thinks that the island's early reputation for black hogs is in the deep shade of Marvell's mind, 'and that the voyagers may have to make do with the allegoric pearl of the gospel's message, when the island's oysters prove fruitless'. But the wryer irony is in 'of which we rather boast'. Sayle, we remember, had been driven out, and Norton alienated, by the zealous regimes of prelate and Independents alike. That the gospel aspirations of the Puritans in Bermuda had been bitterly disappointed was clear in 1645 (when Lefroy supposes the poem was written) and again between 1653 and 1655. Had Sayle been a boy in Donne's congregation of 1622, at a sermon preached for the Virginian Plantation,[32] he would have heard that 'God taught us to make Ships, not to transport our selves, but to transport him'. Sayle would not have thought instantly of pigs, reading that the gospel pearl was *cast* upon the coast; 'cast' would keep company with 'wrack'. Donne says 'let not the riches and commodities of this World, be in your contemplation'. But Donne works as skilfully as Marvell, and will not let the mind come quite to rest. The poem, we may remember, is probably written within a year or two of the expected Second Coming – a prospect that entertains Marvell in 'To his Coy Mistress'.[33] Donne warns the Virginia Company that Christ's kingdom is not of this earth, but we reach it through this earth. The Apostles, he makes it clear, chose to question Christ at a most inconvenient moment – just when he was ready to ascend 'when one foot was upon the Earth, and the other in the cloud that tooke him up'. Thus, says Donne, when men are 'upon the wing for heaven, men tie lead to their feet'.

Long musing upon the sermon alongside the poem would, I think, convince many that Marvell's abstention from arrival, together with his many verbal enlistments of the senses, is an imaginative insight into the nature of our irrepressible and continuing millenarian hopes.

The poem is sometimes thought to offer a puzzle at the close; for it is supposed odd that the singers keep time with their oars rather than with their song.[34] But the oars can as well 'chime' with the song as the song with the oars. It is a last suggestion of an in-tune, harmonious relationship between the working community in the English boat and the poet's song. Together they move towards the attainable but never-attained golden world – the aesthetics, to recall Professor Rajan's phrase, of inconclusiveness.

I cannot expect my iron reflections, or indeed those of others, to make a significant difference to the way the poem is experienced. For there is a sense in which, whatever our knowledge of Bermudan history, the poem has always pulled both away from and towards our dashed expectations. Oxenbridge's hopes and frustrations are more specifically relevant than the great diversity of our own, but they need not be supposed different in kind. It was apparently with hope still live and still unrealized that Oxenbridge set out again as a refugee for the New World; 'in the general shipwreck that befel non-conformists we find him swimming away to Surinam', says an early history.[35]

The last sermons, delivered in Boston in the early 1670s, still had vision enough to make an acknowledged contribution to that long Puritan tradition which in a later phase was represented by Emerson. He was, as it were, still rowing. Had he set out north of Boston he would have passed islands that have since become, to very different effect, a sign of the times – the Dry Salvages. In Eliot's poem hope and purpose are no longer kept up by a vision of arrival but by obscure, sub-heroic persistence:

> Where is the end of them, the fishermen sailing
> Into the wind's tail, where the fog cowers?
> We cannot think of a time that is oceanless
> Or of an ocean not littered with wastage
> Or of a future that is not liable
> Like the past, to have no destination.

We have to think of them as forever bailing,
Setting and hauling, while the North East lowers
Over shallow banks unchanging and erosionless
Or drawing their money, drying sails at dockage;
Not as making a trip that will be unpayable
For a haul that will not bear examination.

Marvell's poem allows us a destination, and its creating (not merely communicating) art makes satisfying things that are from the world but not to be possessed in it. Or, in another sense of the word, their possession is a feat of the imagination, and about such possession economics can tell us nothing. But as the old voyagers knew, '*Dei laboribus omnia vendunt*', God gives everything to the workers.[36] The real and the ideal must coexist; we must stand, like Donne's Jesus, one foot on earth and the other in the cloud that takes us up.

Notes

1 John Smith, *Generall Historie of Virginia, New England and the Summer Iles,* 1624; references are to Smith, *Works,* ed. E. Arber, London, 1884, 2 vols.

2 J. H. Lefroy, *Memorials of the Discovery and Early Settlement of the Bermudas or Somers Islands, 1511–1687,* London, 1877–9, 2 vols. For the Grand Inquest referred to, see II, p. 31.

3 Quotations are from the Loeb edition, ed. C. E. Bennett. See also Herrick, 'The Apparition of his Mistresse calling him to Elizium', a poem with other elements of the Elysian mode in common with 'Bermudas'.

4 *Prose Writings of Jonathan Swift,* ed. Herbert Davis, Oxford, Blackwell, 1966, II, pp. 27–8.

5 In *Modern Philology,* LXVII (1969–70), pp. 331–40.

6 Smith, I, p. 342.

7 For extracts, see Lefroy, II, pp. 577–80.

8 For a convenient text of Strachey, see Frank Kermode's Arden edition of *The Tempest*, London, Methuen, 1954, pp. 135–40.

9 Both Strachey and Hughes report that some of the stranded sailors chose to eat their fish raw rather than fetch wood for fires to cook them.
10 Rosalie L. Colie supposes the singers unespied; see 'Marvell's Bermudas and the Puritan Paradise', *Renaissance News,* X (1957), p. 75. Her article makes an important contribution to my theme.
11 See Lefroy, I, pp. 65–6.
12 See, for many examples, Louis B. Wright, *Religion and Empire,* Chapel Hill, University of North Carolina Press, 1943. For some characteristic conjunctions of piety and commerce see the commission sent to Richard More by his sponsors, in Lefroy, I, pp. 58–62.
13 *Henry VIII,* III, i, 10–11. See also Milton's 'Lycidas', where Christ is 'the Pilot of the Galilean Lake' and Lycidas is commended to 'the dear might of him that walkt the waves'.
14 A suggestion hard either to admit or exclude; Bruce King makes much of it in his *Marvell's Allegorical Poetry,* Cambridge and New York, Oleander Press, 1977, pp. 39–46.
15 Lefroy, II, p. 579.
16 Much in the early Puritan tracts of the seventeenth century is concerned with the paradisal satisfaction that will come of hard work in the New World. A comparable creative innocence is apparent in revolutionary China, as manifest in the exhibition catalogued as *Peasant paintings of the Hu county, Shensui Province,* London, Arts Council, 1976.
17 H. C. Wilkinson, *The Adventurers of Bermuda,* London, Oxford University Press, 2nd ed., 1958, p. 254.
18 Ibid., p. 256.
19 Ibid., p. 258.
20 *Proceedings and Debates of the British Parliament respecting North America,*ed. Leo Francis Stock, Washington, DC, 1924, I, p. 169.
21 Ibid., p. 219.
22 Lefroy, II, pp. 2–8.
23 See Lefroy, II, pp. 11.
24 Lefroy, II, p. 11.
25 Lefroy, II, p. 118.
26 *Historia naturalis,* IV, xxxvii, 202–5.
27 *Proceedings* (as above, note 20), p. 411. For an ironical postscript to the political history of the period, see Richard S. Dunn, 'The Downfall of the Bermuda Company: A Restoration Farce', *The William and Mary Quarterly,* XX (1963), pp. 487–512.
28 Lefroy, II, p. 310.
29 See, for example, Lefroy, II, p. 51.

30 Lefroy, II, p. 30.
31 Richard Hakluyt, *The Principal Voyages of the English Nation,* 1600; Everyman's Library, 1908, III, p. 284.
32 *The Sermons of John Donne,* ed. G. R. Potter and E. M. Simpson, Berkeley, University of California Press, 1959, IV, pp. 264–82.
33 In his allusion to the related event, 'the conversion of the Jews', which was expected in about 1653 (see *The Poems and Letters of Andrew Marvell,* ed H. M. Margoliouth, rev. Pierre Legouis and E. E. Duncan-Jones, Oxford University Press, 1971, p. 253).
34 See, for example, Cummings (as above, note 5), p. 331.
35 Mather, *Magnalia Christi Americana,* 1702, *apud DNB,* s.v. 'Oxenbridge'.
36 Compare R. L. Stevenson, *Virginibus Puerisque,* VI, 'El Dorado': 'To travel hopefully is a better thing than to arrive, and the true success is to labour.'

9

Marvell and Herrick: The masks of Mannerism

Louis L. Martz

In associating Marvell with Herrick and with Mannerism, I have in mind a partial dissociation of Marvell from the metaphysical line. I mean to suggest, first, Marvell's much closer alliance with the Sons of Ben, and thus with the Cavaliers, but more important, I would like to explore the possibility that Herrick and Marvell, along with Carew and Lovelace, form a school of English mannerist poets. Now, as several wise critics have reminded us, Mannerism is not a fact that exists: it is only an hypothesis that we have invented to describe certain aspects of late Renaissance art and literature.[1] It is a term that we use for purposes of exploration and affiliation, a term that may expedite discussion – if we can settle upon a satisfactory definition.

Accounts of Mannerism have multiplied amazingly in recent years, ranging from Arnold Hauser's stress on tension, neurosis, and anxiety, to John Shearman's opposite view of the art as simply one of *maniera*, high style, the 'stylish style'.[2] In between we have the more judicious view of S. J. Freedberg, expressed in several works, but most recently set forth in his volume in the Pelican History of Art: *Painting in Italy, 1500 to 1600.*[3] With those dates we might reasonably expect to find as frontispiece a painting by Raphael or Michelangelo, or even Leonardo; instead Freedberg had chosen the *Deposition* of Pontormo; and in the paperback revision of 1975 he has added, as background for the title page, the

Madonna dal Collo Lungo of Parmigianino. The illustrations thus dramatize the rapid rise in estimation and attention given to the mannerist painters, an attention not much less than that accorded the great masters of the High Renaissance from whom they learned their art.

What, then, is Mannerism? My own definition, indebted to many critics, will emerge gradually in the course of this paper. It is, first of all, an art that deliberately recalls the lessons of the masters, and then proceeds to use those lessons in a way that departs from the effects of rational harmony and idealized beauty characteristic of the High Renaissance. Let us consider a few examples. First, *The Virgin and Child with St Anne* of Leonardo, (London, National Gallery), where the figures, the faces, and the folds of drapery all blend together in a scene of harmonious grace, focused upon the divine child, while the central curve moves along the Virgin's right arm, through the Christ child's body and arm, upward to the mysteriously coloured hand of St Anne, pointing heavenward. Next, the *Entombment* of Raphael (Rome, Borghese Gallery: Plate 9.1), an early work in which the rational construction is particularly clear.[4] There can be no doubt about the focus of the painting: the body of Christ is framed by the opposed, slanting lines of the bearers, while in between them the sorrowful gaze of Mary Magdalene directs our attention firmly to the features of Christ, rigid in pain. The figure of Mary the mother at the right is deeply subdued: her fainting body recedes into the background. Meanwhile a placid sunlit landscape casts an aura of calm upon the scene of sorrow.

But when we turn from these to consider the *Deposition* of Pontormo (Florence, S. Felicità: Plate 9.2), we find that the flowing draperies are swirling in a radiance of costume that reminds us somewhat of a courtly masque; and the swirling effect is caused by the fact that here the two chief heads are not bound close together in endearment and devotion, but are indeed separated as two contending centres of interest, to such an extent that Mary Magdalene turns her back upon the dead Christ to comfort Mary, while the two apostles bearing the body look out towards us in anguished appeal. We notice too that, unlike the Raphael, the painting bears no iconography, no cross in the background, no haloes. Even the wounds of Christ are hardly visible. This might be called a universal masque of sorrow, in which the dead Christ evokes the postures of human woe in many guises. These faces that grow out of the drapery are highly individual, and indeed one of them, at the far right, is the visage of Pontormo himself. Yet with all this individuality of detail, we have the utmost elegance and grace of garb and posture, a refined beauty of face, skin, arm, and torso, and all this combines to create a delicate, tense, and unstable moment of drama.

Instability, this would be the second point in my developing definition – a precarious, uneasy design that coheres, fluently, around the centre marked in Pontormo's painting by the handkerchief held by the graceful arm of Mary Magdalene. The contrast with the almost geometric firmness of the High Renaissance is clear, even while the debt to the great masters appears in every face and every fold of drapery. Instability, then, is one of the prime qualities of mannerist art, well described by Freedberg in his account of Giulio Romano's achievement in the Sala di Costantino, where the art is based upon a principle of 'stressed contrasts':

> The levels of experience we are presented with are not only multiple but disparate, and they shift. The whole visual and intellectual situation is beyond ambivalence: it is a calculated multivalence, and its meanings are disjunctions or emphatic contrasts. It is as if the synthesis of classical style had been thrown into a centrifuge and its separated elements recombined, but into an opposite totality of which complexity and antithesis have become the motive principles.

Allowing for the great difference in scale and subject, we would not, I think, go very far astray to find such an effect in the totality of Herrick's *Hesperides*, where, as in the work of Giulio, 'there is a complication of spatial levels so ambiguously interrelated and so multiplied as to leave no fixed plane of reference the spectator can grasp; and an exceptional diversity of figure-scales works with a similar effect'.[5] Thus in Herrick's book poems celebrating the utmost delicacy of refined beauty are placed side by side with scatological and grotesque epigrams; Mab and Oberon and their tribe mingle with pilfering Shark and 'Mistresse Katherine Bradshaw, the lovely, that crowned him with Laurel', while a substratum of Christian culture is at first seen subtly to underlie, and then is openly appended to, the celebration of pagan joys in wine and 'fresh and fragrant Mistresses'. Had Herrick been a mere imitator, instead of a true creator, it would have been easy for him to have gathered together into one section or book his varied epigrams, satiric, gnomic, funereal, or complimentary, as his master Jonson had proudly done before him. Instead, he deliberately disperses them, not quite at random, throughout his book, as he has done with other poems that might easily have been grouped together, such as the Oberon poems or the several poems to each mistress. We might at least expect some such divisions as the editor had given John Donne's poems: Songs and Sonnets, Epigrams, Elegies, Epithalamions, Satires, (Verse) Letters, Epicedes and Obsequies, Divine Poems.

Herrick's book instead creates the impression of design by dispersion, joy in incongruity, 'Delight in Disorder', to cite the popular poem that contains this central principle of Herrick's art. In fact the principle is stated frequently throughout the *Hesperides*, in his various demonstrations of the beauty of 'cleanly-*Wantonnesse*', 'wild civility', 'pleasing transgression', and 'sweet disorder'.[6] Thus in 'What kind of Mistresse he would have' we find this requirement:

> Be she shewing in her dresse,
> Like a civill Wilderness;
> That the curious may detect
> Order in a sweet neglect. . . .

Such a principle is of the very essence of Mannerism, avoiding classical regularity and seeking instead a fluent ('diffused')[7] diversity of parts that nevertheless somehow flow together. All depends, Herrick implies, upon the 'curious' reader or viewer: 'curious' in the old sense of 'attentive', 'careful as to the standard of excellence', or, most important, 'taking the interest of a connoisseur in any branch of art' (*OED*). Only such a viewer, he indicates, can be trusted to find the order in this 'sweet neglect': 'sweet' not in any sentimental modern sense, but 'sweet' in the old sense of 'pleasing', 'yielding pleasure or enjoyment; agreeable, delightful, charming' (*OED*).

A sweet fluency of parts, pieces juxtaposed in a unity

perceivable only to the curious viewer – here is a third aspect of mannerist art, as found for example in the *Joseph in Egypt* of Pontormo (London, National Gallery: Plate 9.7). Here details from the whole vocabulary of Renaissance art, both in Italy and in the north, are set together in a great diversity of scale and incident; Joseph appears four times in the painting. Nevertheless the composition flows together as the stairway curves upward, with Joseph moving half-way up the stairs, his presence accentuated by the column above him; it is as though he were inviting the curious viewer to trace his movement from lower left to lower right to upper right.

One may glimpse an analogy to this artistic method in Herrick's 'Argument of his Book', where he prophesies the ways in which his creation will fall together – in groupings that overtly come together only in this poem, but which may be found dispersed and may then be connected by memory and association as the curious reader proceeds:

> I sing of *Brooks*, of *Blossomes, Birds*, and *Bowers*:
> Of *April, May*, of *June*, and *July*-Flowers.
> I sing of *May-poles, Hock-carts, Wassails, Wakes*,
> Of *Bride-grooms, Brides*, and of their *Bridall-cakes*.
> I write of *Youth*, of *Love*, and have Accesse
> By these, to sing of cleanly-*Wantonnesse*.
> I sing of *Dewes*, of *Raines*, and piece by piece
> Of *Balme*, of *Oyle*, of *Spice*, and *Amber-Greece*.

Piece by piece: Herrick allows his garden to grow together out of flowers and blossoms treated to individual tribute; likewise he does not celebrate a single Corinna or Lesbia, but rather a dozen mistresses, and each of them celebrated for their parts: instep, skin, hair, lips, voice, breath, nipples, breasts, feet, teeth, legs, voice, eyes, even their fragrant sweat. And then their clothing: 'Put on your silks; and piece by piece / Give them the scent of Amber-Greece' – lace, cuff, petticoat, shoe-string, 'ribands', 'a black Twist, rounding the Arme'. In sum, 'How rich and pleasing thou my *Julia* art / In each thy dainty and peculiar part!'[8]

This emphasis upon the perfectly made detail brings us back to the source of all accounts of Mannerism, Vasari, especially in the famous preface to the third part of his *Lives*, where he gives what might be called a self-portrait of Mannerism, as he singles out the qualities that he most admires in his contemporaries and their immediate predecessors.

> And then the artist achieves the highest perfection of style by copying the most beautiful things in nature and combining the most perfect members, hands, head, torso, and legs, to produce the finest possible figure as a model for use in all his works; this is how he achieves what we know as fine style ['bella maniera'].[9]

Earlier ages, he says, could not achieve this perfection because they lacked 'a certain freedom' which 'might be able to exist without causing confusion or spoiling the order; which order had need of an invention abundant in every respect, and of a certain beauty maintained in every last detail'. That last phrase is most significant for our analogy with Herrick: 'd'una certa bellezza continuata in ogni minima cosa'. Hence Vasari's insistence on 'a certain finish and finality of perfection' in the feet, hands, and hair – 'that minuteness of finish which is the perfection and bloom of art' – from which, he says, follow the 'delicacy, refinement and supreme grace' that mark this perfection. Thus he praises Correggio for painting hair in such fine detail that it appears 'soft and feathery, with each single hair visible', so that 'they seemed like gold and more beautiful' than the living thing. And the same, he adds, should be said of Parmigianino, who excelled Correggio 'in many respects in grace, adornment, and beauty of manner' – 'di bella maniera'. The aim, in short, is to achieve, by the utmost finish of detail, 'una graziosissima grazia'. That phrase, surely, must be an essential part of our still-developing definition.

But this aspect of the definition may not seem to allow for what happens when Herrick displays that 'certain freedom' in arranging his poems. Piece by piece the poems dance their way in delightful disorder, with the result that the delicate poem 'Upon Mistresse Elizabeth Wheeler, under the name of Amarillis' is placed between the epigram on Glasco's false teeth and the epigram on Furze's bad breath. Thus the fragrances of the mistresses are continually interfused with the foul smells of baser creatures, and indeed the dainty and the foul may sometimes come together in the same poem:

Jane is a Girle that's prittie;
Jane is a wench that's wittie;
Yet, who wo'd think,
Her breath do's stinke,
As so it doth? that's pittie.

Similarly the epitaph on the commendable virtues of 'the much lamented, Master J. Warr' is followed by the epigram on Gryll, who won't say grace for his roast. And the epigram on Brock's 'clammie Reume' and his 'mouth worse furr'd with oathes and blasphemies' is immediately followed by the graceful pastoral lyric 'To Meddowes'.

It may well seem at first that Herrick's book will never fulfil the mannerist ideal represented in 'To Perenna': 'When I thy parts run o're, I can't espie / In any one, the least indecencie' – 'indecencie' in the sense of inelegance, lack of comeliness in form. The book may seem not to fulfil his 'Vow to Minerva': 'For to make the Texture lye / Each way smooth and civilly', or to follow his advice to Master Henry Northly and 'the most witty Mistresse Lettice Yard': 'Do all things sweetly, and in comely wise.' 'Comely', we should note, is one of Herrick's favourite words: it indicates a particular kind of attractive grace, fair and pretty, well made, agreeable in all proportions, but not overwhelming, not audacious, not 'handsome'. But how, we may well wonder, can a comely edifice of many parts contain such a horror as 'Jollies wife':

First, *Jollies* wife is lame; then next, loose-hipt:
Squint-ey'd, hook-nos'd; and lastly, Kidney-lipt.

But the inclusion of such apparent indecencies is allowed for in the mannerist principle of 'disjunction' that I have earlier described – the principle expressed in Herrick's poem 'Upon his gray haires': 'This begets the more delight / When things meet most opposite.' It is not simply that the satirical epigrams bring the salt of reality to offset the sweetness and artifice of the mistresses. The crude epigrams are truly opposite: as far from reality as are these comely ladies draped with lawn. The best of the vile epigrams have their own perverse version of 'comeliness': all their parts fit together to create a ludicrous caricature of human indecency. The elements of reality lie elsewhere, partly in the tributes to identifiable men and women and places, as in 'His tears to Thamasis', which, near the end of the book, sums up an atmosphere of rarefied and exalted actuality:

> Never againe shall I with Finnie-Ore
> Put from, or draw unto the faithful shore:
> And Landing here, or safely Landing there.
> Make way to my *Beloved Westminster*:
> Or to the *Golden-cheap-side*, where the earth
> Of *Julia Herrick* gave to me my Birth.
> May all clean *Nimphs* and curious water Dames,
> With Swan-like-state, flote up and down thy streams:
> No drought upon the wanton waters fall
> To make them Leane, and languishing at all.
> No ruffling winds come hither to discease
> Thy pure, and *Silver-wristed Naides*.

Cheapside is of course the haunt of goldsmiths – but the place becomes golden for Herrick in a much more glowing way, while the classical water deities mingle with exquisite Dames who float elegantly upon the water in their barges.

A more significant and more difficult element of actuality lies in Herrick's bland and tantalizing use of Christian reference, as in the famous poem to Corinna: 'Wash, dresse, be briefe in praying: / Few Beads are best, when once we goe a Maying'. The pressure of a Christian context runs from beginning to end of Herrick's *Hesperides*, where the first poem concludes: 'I write of *Hell*; I sing (and ever shall) / Of *Heaven*, and hope to have it after all'; and the last reminds us that the pagan visions are but play: '*Jocond his Muse was, but his Life was chast*'.[10] The appendix of *Noble Numbers; or, his Pious Pieces*, expurgated from the main body of the volume, serves to stress the interplay between pagan and Christian that runs throughout. The point is covertly made in the Greek motto on the title page of *Noble Numbers*, where Herrick quotes the words the Muses speak to Hesiod at the outset of his *Theogony*: 'We know how to speak many false things as though they were true; but we know, when we will, to utter true things.'[11]

This interplay between the feigned and the true may be seen at its best in the brief poem, 'His embalming to Julia':

> For my embalming, *Julia,* do but this,
> Give thou my lips but their supreamest kiss:

(Does 'supreamest' carry a suggestion of extreme unction?)

> Or else trans-fuse thy breath into the chest,
> Where my small reliques must for ever rest:

(The word 'trans-fuse' is used in the basic sense of 'pouring a liquid out of one vessel into another'; at a first reading the 'chest' might appear to be the chest of the dead man, but it turns out to be the coffin, where his bones, now sanctified by her breath, will for ever rest.)

> That breath the *Balm,* the *myrrh,* the *Nard* shal be,
> To give an *incorruption* unto me.

Herrick italicizes 'incorruption' so as to stress the allusion to St Paul: 'For this corruptible must put on incorruption' (I Corinthians 15: 53). The explicit Biblical reference casts a glancing light backward over the whole poem, tending to confirm our sense that other Christian and Biblical echoes may be lurking here. The balm and myrrh and nard seem to imply more than burial preservatives, for all these spices are redolent of the Bible: the Song of Songs, with its myrrh and spikenard; the merchants 'bearing spicery and balm and myrrh' to Egypt (Genesis 37: 25: the Joseph story); and even the spikenard with which Mary Magdalene anointed Christ. But which way is the emphasis falling? Does the Christian allusion exalt the pagan ceremony, or does it subtly undermine that ceremony by suggesting that all this is only a witty play in the realms of art?

But the word 'only' will not apply to the attitude towards art conveyed in Herrick's *Hesperides.* 'Saint Ben' is the patron saint of this region, where the moralistic fervour of the master has been refined and transmuted, in the mannerist way, into something that might be called a religion of art – a religion summed up in Herrick's 'Apparition of his Mistresse calling him to Elyzium', where his 'Father *Johnson*' stands in the foreground, 'As in a Globe of Radiant fire', while all the poets of Greece and Rome stand in the background, with Anacreon singing Herrick's own verses.

This masking of Christianity by paganism, or rather, this effect of translating Christian culture into a realm where the values of art predominate – this too is a tension found in the mannerist painters, especially in the paintings of Parmigianino upon religious themes. His sacred ladies display a strange, absorbing elegance, a distillation of fleshly beauty and courtly fashion. Their comely breasts are glimpsed through the silkiest of tissue, while their hair, richly jewelled, is endowed with the most elegant of curled coiffures. They stand or sit or kneel in the most artful postures of exaggerated worldly grace. The figure of St Catherine in Parmigianino's *Mystic Marriage* (London, National Gallery: Plate 9.5) says it all.

A related effect may be seen in Parmigianino's *Vision of St Jerome* (London, National Gallery: Plate 9.4), so fortunately placed in the same room with Raphael's *Ansidei Madonna* (Plate 9.3). In Raphael the Madonna is modestly clothed, with her hair veiled, while she and her son gaze humbly downward towards the book. Meanwhile, at the left, the Baptist gazes devoutly at the pair, pointing discreetly at the child. The contrast with Parmigianino is startling. Here the Virgin still has something of Raphael's modesty in her downward gaze, but otherwise she is transmuted into the sensuous, elegant beauty of Mannerism. And the divine child, so elegantly curled, poses like a dancing putto. Below, the Baptist strikes a muscular, unnatural pose reminiscent of Michelangelo, while he invites the curious viewer to respond. With what? With a feeling of Christian joy and gratitude? Hardly that, but rather with an admiration for the painter's art, who has given us here, surely, a vision that St Jerome, asleep in the lower background, would never have dreamed. Are such paintings, then, irreligious, or a-religious, or improper for an altar? Possibly not, if we can believe that the artist is paying his tribute to God by painting all the beauty he can paint: glorifying God by demonstrating the talents the deity has given to this man. And yet an ambiguity remains: the worldly beauty of the vision shows a pride in the painter's art that conflicts with traditions of religious humility. As Andrew Marvell says of his effort to weave a coronet for his Saviour's head:

And now when I have summ'd up all my store,
  Thinking (so I myself deceive)
  So rich a Chaplet thence to weave
As never yet the king of Glory wore:
  Alas I find the Serpent old
  That, twining in his speckled breast,
  About the flow'rs disguis'd does fold,
  With wreaths of Fame and Interest. (ll. 9–16)

Nevertheless the mannerist writer or painter must do what he can: create those forms of polished elegance as the only tribute his spirit can summon. As Freedberg says of Parmigianino,

> Though there is no overt religiosity in Francesco's altar, there is a high and intense spirituality in its very aestheticism, and this is in effect a private substitute for the devotion that the Roman Church of Clement's time could not command from individuals of Francesco's sophisticated and questing stripe.

The spirituality of such artists, he adds, 'might choose uninstitutionalized ways to express itself, and in this time of scepticism the making of aesthetic experience in art became an important one among these ways' (p. 220).

Some such tendency may be found in the sophisticated and questing spirit of Andrew Marvell when he comes to deal with overtly religious themes. Consider 'On a Drop of Dew', where the conceit is so beautifully, so coolly, so deliberately worked out that religious feeling seems attenuated by intellectual control. The poem is neat, well made, graceful, artful, comely, and yet when all is said of its elegance and polish and wit, the poem may still seem rather like its own manna: 'White, and intire, though congeal'd and chill'. Much the same effect may be felt in reading the poem that opens Marvell's posthumous volume of 1681, 'A Dialogue between The Resolved Soul, and Created Pleasure'. It is easy to read the soul's lines in such a way as to suggest pertness:

My gentler Rest is on a Thought,
Conscious, of doing what I ought.

A Soul that knowes not to presume
Is Heaven's and its own perfume.
(ll. 23–4, 29–30)

But one need not read the lines in this way; the soul's answers may be read in a tone of gentle, intelligent security, of polite, smiling, patient firmness. With its Chorus singing in the middle and at the close, this poem might almost be seen as the performance of a courtly masque of virtues and vices.

A performance: here is yet another salient attribute of mannerist art: the effect of staged performance which reaches its apogee of artifice in the mannerist courts of the Medici, and of Charles I. As part of the ambiguity of Marvell and his age, we should recall that he wrote, was presumably commissioned to write, two highly artificial songs in the mythological and pastoral mode for the marriage of Cromwell's daughter to the Lord Fauconberg. Here again the use of the Chorus at four points creates a masque-like effect, reminding us that new Puritan was sometimes old Cavalier writ large, as in Milton's Ludlow 'Maske'. The arts of the mannerist court of Charles did not entirely die, but held a place in the cultural memory, as Marvell remembers the king's great collections in 'The Gallery' – a poem that suggests Marvell's broad acquaintance with Continental painting, as well as with Marino's *La Galeria.*

'The Gallery' is a poem that stands forth almost as a definition of mannerist art. It begins with the invitation to attend closely to the performance, to watch and judge the writer's art:

> *Clora* come view my Soul, and tell
> Whether I have contriv'd it well.

For his soul, he says, is now made up of his lady's various attitudes and postures, seen as in a portrait gallery. First she appears in the conventional Petrarchan guise of a 'Murtheress', tormenting with 'Black Eyes, red Lips, and curled Hair'. Next, as some great nude Venus by a Giorgione or a Titian:

> Like to *Aurora* in the Dawn;
> When in the East she slumb'ring lyes,
> And stretches out her milky Thighs;
> (ll. 18–20)

in a pastoral landscape where, at her feet, 'the wooing Doves / Sit perfecting their harmless Loves'. Next she appears in a guise that might suggest an engraving by Dürer or one of his followers, with an 'Enchantress' who, in an obscure light, performs the rites of divination over her lover's entrails in a cave. Next, like a Botticelli of '*Venus* in her pearly Boat', or perhaps the Galatea of Raphael. All these and many more, he says, create 'a Collection choicer far / Then or *White-hall's,* or *Mantua's* were'. The past tense seems to cast a backward glance upon the royal collection, augmented by the purchase of the great collection of the Duke of Mantua – ruthlessly sold off by parliamentary order shortly after Charles's death. But of all these pictures, he concludes,

> That at the Entrance likes me best:
> Where the same Posture, and the Look
> Remains, with which I first was took.
> A tender Shepherdess, whose Hair
> Hangs loosely playing in the Air,
> Transplanting Flow'rs from the green Hill,
> To crown her Head, and Bosome fill.

This is hardly praise of her simplicty, for here too is a Posture and a Look; pastoral, it is often said, is the most artificial of genres. What one should stress is the eclectic quality of the paintings in these panels: parts and pieces from the old masters set together to create the impression of a constantly shifting and evasive lady whose existence nevertheless depends entirely upon the art through which the poet has 'contriv'd' her existence in his mind.

Such an effect is true of mannerist portraiture: one has the impression that the image had been contrived in the painter's mind in such a way that the Posture and the Look form a world of art, but in the process mask the actual personality of the sitter, by moulding the subject into an image of aristocratic distance and reserve. Especially in Bronzino the face of the sitter (and this is true of his religious paintings too) resembles a mask rather than a breathing human countenance. This effect is so persistent that Freedberg three times uses the analogy of the mask in describing Bronzino's art. The painter, he says,

> makes a fine record of the surface of the countenance but goes no deeper, accepting – preferring, indeed – that it should have the fixity and the impenetrability of a mask. The very attitudes of body that the sitters take intensify the sense of

PLATE 9.1 Raphael, *The Entombment*, 1507

PLATE 9.2 Pontormo, *The Deposition*, *c.* 1526

PLATE 9.3 Raphael, *Madonna and Child with St John the Baptist and St Nicholas of Bari* ('The Ansidei Madonna'), 1505

PLATE 9.4 Parmigianino, *Madonna and Child with St John the Baptist and St Jerome* ('The Vision of St Jerome'), 1526-7

PLATE 9.5 Parmigianino, *The Marriage of St Catherine* (detail), *c.* 1526

PLATE 9.6 Bronzino, *Lucrezia Panciatichi*, *c.* 1540

PLATE 9.7 Pontormo, *Joseph in Egypt*, *c.* 1518

PLATE 9.8 Bronzino, *An Allegory* ('Venus, Cupid, Folly, and Time'), *c.* 1545

> constraint: their behaviour is according to a precisely controlled, willed, personal *maniera,* of which the high artifice serves as a mask for passion or as an armour against it. (p. 432)

Bronzino's use of colour, he adds, sometimes creates a tone of

> cold intensity, high-keyed, in which sensuous value is distilled away. . . . Each preciously articulated effect of design conveys the quality of tight and precise elegance, yet at the same time gives the sense that this constrains a high-pitched, fine-wrought, complication. (p. 433)

It seems an apt description of Marvell's 'To his Coy Mistress' – a poem that seems to me not to convey passion, but rather to constrain passion, a poem that reveals, within a witty distancing, the harshness and the desperate futility of passion.

Consider Bronzino's portrait of Lucrezia Panciatichi (Florence, Uffizi: Plate 9.6). The scarlet gown, the red hair speak of passion; the pale yet glowing cheeks seem to cover an inner tension suggested by her uneasy, forward-pitched posture. On the links of the gold chain around her neck can be read the words 'Amour Dure Sans Fin' – 'Love lasts for ever'. Yet the book on which her right hand rests seems to be an illuminated prayer book. What is this love which seems to glow, under severe discipline, within her far-reaching gaze? There is something of religious exaltation in her face – yet could it not, perhaps, constrain the longing for an earthly love?

Masks: the word itself, in several senses, seems to describe the whole corpus of Bronzino's work. For what is the famous *Venus, Cupid, Folly and Time* (London, National Gallery: Plate 9.8) if it is not an elegant allegorical performance, a dramatized, ambivalent and multivalent riddle? Masks, literally, lie at the bottom right of the work; perhaps they belong to the bland-faced figure with the bestial body who lurks above in the background, representing the deceptiveness of pleasure. And that face at the upper left, expressing distaste and horror at the scene, seems itself to be a mask, for it may be hollow; and yet it is not only a mask, for it is attached to a body that has active hands, and black hair seems to cover the top of the ear. Does it represent the mysteries of Truth, as Panofsky argues, or does it represent only emptiness, as Levey thinks?[12] Does it suggest a doubt that Truth exists? And is old Time moving the curtain forward or backward? Is he revealing or hastening to conceal the scandal? For scandal it is: Cupid inviting his mother. And that brandished arrow poised so elegantly in Venus' right hand: has she, as Levey thinks, disarmed Cupid, or is the arrow a phallic symbol suggesting her consent? At the same time we may feel a wicked echo here, for the posture of Venus, several critics have noted, echoes the posture of the Madonna in Michelangelo's *Doni Tondo*.

So too in Marvell, one often finds it hard to settle upon the subject behind the masks. In 'The Unfortunate Lover' lies an enigma no one has unravelled, nor ever will. To some it has spoken of secular love, but to me this seems impossible, because the opening stanza seems to set a sure distinction between secular lovers, 'Sorted by pairs', sponsored by Cupid – and this unfortunate lover, born in a shipwreck, amid a storm of thunder and lightning, a 'masque of quarrelling Elements'. I have sometimes thought these properties suggested the Crucifixion, which might be seen as the birth of Christian love, always at its best in suffering. And the 'Corm'rants black' that both feed and famish the lover – are these then the priests of the Roman church, in accordance with the common Protestant version of Christian history? 'And now', as the scene shifts from the past to the present tense, now, at the present moment,

when angry Heaven wou'd
Behold a spectacle of Blood,
Fortune and He are call'd to play
At sharp before it all the day . . .

See how he nak'd and fierce does stand,
Cuffing the Thunder with one hand;
While with the other he does lock,
And grapple, with the stubborn Rock:
From which he with each Wave rebounds,
Torn into Flames, and ragg'd with Wounds.
And all he saies, a Lover drest
In his own Blood does relish best.

(ll. 41–4, 49–56)

Those last two lines, much debated, I would interpret thus: all the lover says in his torment is this: 'a lover dressed in his own blood does please (the viewer) best'. Or, what the emblem here presented says is this: 'a lover willing to sacrifice himself presents the most pleasing image of love'. At the same time the lines imply that all this emblem says will be best appreciated by a lover who has himself endured a similar suffering. For this kind of lover, the final stanza says, is the only true knight ('*Banneret*') of love; only he, 'Forced to live in Storms and Warrs', rules now the whole realm of history and romance: 'In a Field *Sable* a Lover *Gules*', with a shield of black, white, and red. Is Marvell saying that now, once again, Christian love is being forced to enact a bloody emblem? Is this Marvell's comment on the Civil Wars? We shall never be sure. Marvell has masked the subject too securely.

When we turn to consider *Upon Appleton House* all these facets of Mannerism may be seen coalescing in a poem that might be regarded as a mannerist work in six panels, and as a masque of constantly shifting, though never quarrelling, elements. The masque-like qualities of the last three sections are indeed stressed by Marvell in such lines as 'No Scene that turns with Engines strange / Does oftner then these Meadows change' (ll. 385–6), or 'Then, to conclude these pleasant Acts, / *Denton* sets ope its *Cataracts*' (ll. 465–6). The speaker himself becomes a masker in the wood as, under his '*antick Cope*' of oak leaves and ivy, he moves 'Like some great *Prelate of the Grove*' (ll. 591–2). Then at the close all the shifting scenes and panels of the poem are drawn together in the image of Maria, Marvell's young pupil, who appears accompanied by the hues of the halcyon, in blue of Mary's colour, with 'Azure dy' and '*Saphir-winged Mist*', reconciling, dominating, ordering the landscape: '*She* yet more Pure, Sweet, Streight, and Fair, / Then Gardens, Woods, Meads, Rivers are.' Just so at the close of a court masque the king or queen appears, to dominate the changing pageantry of masque and anti-masque.[13]

I have, throughout this paper, deliberately fused and confused two related meanings of this word 'mask', meanings distinguished in print by the spellings 'masque' and 'mask'. It is a fusion inevitable in any discussion of mannerist art, for the element of performance is inseparable from the wearing of a disguise. The court masque presented an allegorical enigma. The mannerist painter of religious themes covered the scenes of Biblical humility with an aura of radiant courtly grace. The mannerist painter of portraits covered the inner being of his sitters with a mask of the most elegant costume, the most aristocratic posture, the most reserved and even disdainful countenance. Yet all these postures, all these looks (some directly into our eyes, as though daring us to communicate) seem to convey a basic insecurity and instability. The tension of the forms is so extreme that the creation seems to stand on the very verge of breaking down. Guarded and protective, the mannerist artist tends to encamp his mind at a distance, so that passion may be muted, discreet, inferred, but seldom directly glimpsed. Thus Marvell, in his mannerist 'Picture of little T. C. in Prospect of Flowers', prefers to regard beauty from the shade: to admire very young beauty, before it arouses passion, as he has done with his image of Mary Fairfax, and as he has done in his poem 'Young Love', where he explicitly sets forth an aversion from mature passion. This does not make Marvell a candidate for the current British controversy over paedophilia; it is only an expression of his constantly guarded and distanced attitude towards passions of every kind, religious, political, or erotic. (It is interesting to recall, in this context, that among these painters Bronzino excelled in the painting of children, as in his superb portrait of little Pia de' Medici, aged about six or seven, in whose face and posture and dress one can already read the ensigns of command.)

Marvell's guarded posture in the face of passion is found at its best in his poem on Milton's *Paradise Lost*, where the mannerist writer, in trim couplets, explains his reluctance to encourage the grand passions of the baroque:

When I beheld the Poet blind, yet bold,
In slender Book his vast Design unfold . . .
the Argument
Held me a while misdoubting his Intent,
That he would ruine (for I saw him strong)
The sacred Truths to Fable and old Song . . .
Yet as I read, soon growing less severe,
I lik'd his Project, the success did fear;
Through that wide Field how he his way should find

O're which lame Faith leads Understanding blind . . .
   Pardon me, *mighty Poet*, nor despise
My causeless, yet not impious, surmise . . .
   That Majesty which through thy Work doth Reign
Draws the Devout, deterring the Profane. . . .
   Where couldst thou Words of such a Compass find?
Whence furnish such a vast expense of Mind?

Thus the sceptical, guarded, constrained, ambiguous, elegant art of Mannerism was soon to be overwhelmed by the daring, vast, and soaring assertions of a faith and a mission that defied the restraints of earlier forms.

But, one may ask, am I implying that there was a direct relation between mannerist art in Italy of the sixteenth century and English poetry of the seventeenth? Such a relation may exist. Italian Mannerism was introduced into England early in the seventeenth century through the agency of Inigo Jones, who brought back from Italy an intense concern with mannerist art, as his notebooks and his drawings for the masques reveal. In the Caroline court Mannerism became almost a way of life, and also a way of death, if we may believe Marvell's account of Charles's execution, which he describes in a way that can only be called a tribute to mannerist principles enacted on a bloody stage:

He nothing common did or mean
Upon that memorable Scene:
   But with his keener Eye
   The Axes edge did try:
Nor call'd the *Gods* with vulgar spight
To vindicate his helpless Right,
   But bow'd his comely Head,
   Down as upon a Bed.
('An Horatian Ode', ll. 57–64)

The pathos of that scene is increased by our awareness that a dozen years before, in the Cambridge days of peace, Marvell had written a Latin poem of congratulation to the same king, in verses of a similar Horatian mould: his 'Ad Regem Carolum Parodia', an imitation (or parody in the sense of transmutation) of the second ode of the first book of Horace. To choose the Horatian mode for his later poem of double tribute is a tactic of irony and ambivalence typical of mannerist art.

My chief point lies in tracing a possible analogy of temperament, attitude and situation. The conditions were indeed similar. Both the Italian painters of the mid-sixteenth century and the English poets of the mid-seventeenth century worked under turbulent political and religious conditions, represented by the Sack of Rome in 1527 and by the execution of the king in 1649. And both groups of artists worked under the shadow, as well as the inspiration, of the great masters who had just preceded them:

Ah *Ben*!
Say how, or when
Shall we thy Guests
Meet at those *Lyrick* Feasts,
Made at the *Sun*,
The *Dog*, the triple *Tunne*? . . .

My Ben
Or come agen:
Or send to us,
Thy wits great over-plus;
But teach us yet
Wisely to husband it;
Lest we that Tallent spend:
And having once brought to an end
That precious stock; the store
Of such a wit the world sho'd have no more.
(Herrick, 'An Ode for [Ben Jonson]')

Thus mannerist art, with all its beauty, creates the effect of recording the end of an era; an art of such refined elegance can go no further. Nothing conveys this sense of the end of an era better than Herrick's series of poems to King Charles, beginning, very early in the *Hesperides*, with the poem 'To the King, Upon his comming with his Army into the West', where Herrick attempts to give comeliness to the very face of battle: 'War, which before was horrid, now appears / Lovely in you, brave Prince of Cavaliers!' Then, two poems later, we have 'To the King and Queene, upon their unhappy distances', a poem on the separation caused by the Civil Wars: 'Woe, woe to them, who (by a ball of strife) / Doe, and have parted here a Man and Wife'. From here on allusions to the Civil Wars are frequent, occurring sometimes as celebrations of the few victories that the royal forces achieved, or as expressions of belief and hope in victory, or as brief gnomic epigrams upon the troubles that beset kings. Finally, near the close of the *Hesperides*, in one of the very latest poems ever written by Herrick, we have the poem 'To the King, Upon his welcome to Hampton-Court', where Herrick celebrates the return of Charles, under the watchful eye of the parliamentary army, as though it were a welcome for a victorious emperor who has won for his realm the joys of an Augustan peace:

> Welcome, *Great Cesar,* welcome now you are,
> As dearest Peace, after destructive Warre:
> Welcome as slumbers; or as beds of ease
> After our long, and peevish sicknesses.
> O *Pompe of Glory*! Welcome now, and come
> To re-possess once more your long'd-for home.
> A thousand Altars smoake; a thousand thighes
> Of Beeves here ready stand for Sacrifice.
> Enter and prosper, while our eyes doe waite
> For an *Ascendent* throughly *Auspicate*. . . .

The qualification implicit in the last two lines is sufficient to indicate the poet's knowledge of the true situation. But he speaks of what should be, not of what is. Never was the distance between the ideal and the real covered with a stronger or more gracious mask of loyalty. The poem marks the end of the doctrine of the divine right of kings and all that claim entailed. It marks the end of the most artistic, most highly cultivated court that England had ever seen, and the end, too, of a monarch whose devotion to art greatly excelled his devotion to the practical work of government. It is appropriate, then, that his virtues should have been celebrated, in such different ways, by the two best English poets of the mannerist school.

Notes

1 See Henri Zerner's essay in *The Meaning of Mannerism*, ed. Franklin W. Robinson and Stephen G. Nichols, Jr, Hanover, N.H., University Press of New England, 1972, p. 114. Also E. H. Gombrich's introduction to the symposium on 'Recent Concepts of Mannerism' in *The Renaissance and Mannerism; Studies in Western Art: Acts of the Twentieth International Congress of the History of Arts*, 4 vols, Princeton University Press, 1963, II, pp. 163–5.

2 Arnold Hauser, *Mannerism: The Crisis of the Renaissance and the Origin of Modern Art*, 2 vols, London, Routledge & Kegan Paul, 1965; John Shearman, *Mannerism*, Harmondsworth, Penguin Books, 1967.

3 Harmondsworth, Penguin Books, 1971; revised paperback edition, 1975; all citations of Freedberg are made to the 1975 edition.

4 See the discussion of this painting by John Pope-Hennessy, *Raphael: The Wrightsman Lectures*, London, Phaidon, 1970, pp. 50–8.

5 Freedberg, p. 205.

6 Quotations from Herrick are taken from *The Complete Poetry of Robert Herrick*, ed. J. Max Patrick, New York, Norton Library, 1968. I do not, however, observe italics in quoting titles. For the above quotations see 'The Argument of his Book', 'Delight in Disorder', 'Julia's Petticoat', and 'Art above Nature, to Julia'.

7 See Herrick, 'To Perenna': 'But every Line, and Limb diffused thence, / A faire, and unfamiliar excellence'.

8 For the quotations see 'To his Mistresses', 'Upon a black Twist, rounding the Arme of the Countesse of Carlile', and the opening lines of 'To Julia'. Court ladies are frequently treated in the same terms as the imaginary mistresses.

9 Giorgio Vasari, *The Lives of the Artists*, selection translated by George Bull, Harmondsworth, Penguin Books, 1965, pp. 249–50. For the subsequent passages, however, I have turned to the more literal translation by Gaston DuC. DeVere in the edition of the *Lives* published by the Medici Society, 10 vols, London 1912–14, IV, pp. 80–3. For the Italian original I have used *Le Vite* in the edition of the Istituto Geografico de Agostini, 9 vols, Novara, 1967, III, pp. 377–82.

10 Though Herrick on his general title page used the word *Hesperides* to include his *Works both Humane & Divine*, he clearly distinguishes his main 'Booke' from his *Pious Pieces*; to keep the

two separate, I use *Hesperides* to refer only to the first part, the 'pagan' part.

11 *Theogony*, 27–8, in the translation by Hugh G. Evelyn-White, *Hesiod*, London, Loeb Library, 1914, p. 81.

12 See Erwin Panofsky, *Studies in Iconology*, New York, Oxford University Press, 1939, pp. 86–91; and Michael Levey's essay in *Studies in Renaissance & Baroque Art presented to Anthony Blunt*, London, Phaidon, 1967, pp. 32–3. The two interpretations are opposed, in detail and in general, with Panofsky seeing the work as a critique of 'Luxury', in the sense of sexual indulgence, while Levey, denying this, stresses the dominant, triumphant posture of Venus. Yet her piquant expression may suggest that there is more than one way of 'disarming' a seducer. The triumphs of Venus may tend to conceal jealousy, deception, disease, remorse, and incest. Truth is traditionally masked; as Thomas Carew said, 'Wise Poets that wrap't Truth in tales, / Knew her themselves, through all her vailes'. The whole painting requires an ambivalent interpretation. Philip Brockbank has pointed out to me an analogous vision of Venus and Cupid at play in Herrick's 'How Lillies came white'.

13 For an excellent, detailed account of the masque-like qualities in the last three sections of *Upon Appleton House* see Ann E. Berthoff, *The Resolved Soul: A Study of Marvell's Major Poems*, Princeton University Press, 1970, pp. 163–93.

10

Marvell's mind and mystery

Robert Ellrodt

Marvell's poetic elusiveness is widely acknowledged but I find him elusive in a very personal sense. I can imagine what it must have felt like to be John Donne or George Herbert, Richard Crashaw or Henry Vaughan. I do not claim, of course, that what I imagine (with sympathy or distaste) is the actual truth about these poets. I only mean I can make a consistent picture out of the facts of their lives and the ideas and emotions expressed in their writings: even their contradictions or conversions seem to fit in. With Marvell the facts known mainly relate to his public career and allow different interpretations. What the poems disclose or suggest about his opinions and experiences is not only controversial: they leave out some essential aspects of the man's personality and inner life. To me his very portrait is mute. Donne's effigies are speaking pictures of his eloquent self, but Marvell's inquisitive eyes look out of an expressionless face with sensual lips which, like his conversation before strangers,[1] betray no secret.

Pierre Legouis and John M. Wallace have traced the poet's political career and shown in slightly different ways that his shifting attitudes were unsurprising in the circumstances. He may have been, indeed, a constitutional monarchist who acted throughout the Commonwealth and the Restoration out of a 'devotion to strong and responsible government'.[2] Yet all doubts have not been laid. Admitting that 'it is very difficult to place

Marvell in a clearly defined political category', Donal Smith chose to place him among the Trimmers; and to Isabel Rivers 'unlike the revolutionary Milton or the conservative Dryden, Marvell had no commitment to an ideal of political life'.[3]

The 'Horatian Ode' has been a battleground for critics and historians. The case for the covert expression of royalist sympathies in ironical praise of Cromwell[4] is undoubtedly weak and the contrast between the Ode and 'Tom May's Death' does not create a serious problem.[5] Within the Ode itself the alleged contradiction between reverence for Charles and admiration for Cromwell has been removed by Wallace: 'there is no reason to suppose that a poet could not write an ode to Cromwell and retain a profound regret for Charles's murder'.[6] Yet the host of parallels offered for a willing compliance with 'the forced Pow'r' should not blind us to a difference in approach and in tone. The Engagers argued for 'the right to obey an unlawful government in lawful things';[7] they spoke like casuists and often sound apologetic. Marvell is not concerned with justification of any sort. Neither the death of 'the *Royal Actor*' nor the ruin of 'the great Work of Time' call for a bad conscience. The strange power of the Ode lies in the very fact that it does not engage emotions of pity, love or fear but only invites a controlled exultation in the display of power – 'angry Heavens flame' – or tragic dignity on 'that memorable Scene'. The poet is a detached spectator of history in the making who makes a dispassionate evaluation of character and destiny.

Since the later 'Poem upon the Death of O.C.' shows 'all the force of Marvell's sentiments for Cromwell' after years of loyal service,[8] it must be out of prudence rather than indifference that the Member for Hull refrained from any expression of grief or indignation when relating how the carcasses of Cromwell, Bradshaw, Ireton and Pride were to be 'hanged up for a while & then buryed under the gallows'.[9] Yet the callous mention makes a strange contrast to the outraged and anguished allusion in *Samson Agonistes* to God's unfair dismission of His servants, 'thir carkasses / To dogs and fowls a prey' (ll. 693–4). It cannot be denied, however, that Milton's friend acted honourably and courageously on many occasions 'under change of times'. Besides, the sincerity of his various political poems – from eulogy to satire – has hardly been impugned. Had he not been sincere at the time, there would be no problem! When other poets praised Charles I, Cromwell and Charles II in turn, some of the tributes at least could be dismissed as lip-service. But if the variations in Marvell's political statements or attitudes reflect genuine convictions his consistency has to be vindicated. Can we define its exact nature?

Legouis stressed Marvell's religious and patriotic convictions: he was always 'ready to welcome any régime, whether authority resided in "a single person" or in "a representative" (assembly), provided all Protestants were safe and the greatness of England assured'.[10] To Wallace, Marvell was 'among the few . . . who believed that moderation was the very essence of government'; hence his 'adherence to the ideal of balance' and the flexibility of policy which would be necessary to achieve it while retaining 'the standard of decency'.[11] But deeper motivations for this flexible consistency may be found in the conjunction of intellectual freedom, active will, and a belief in 'a necessity . . . that was pre-eternal to all things'.[12] Marvell never opposes Fate since 'all things . . . happen in their best and proper time'.[13] Yet while disclaiming 'officiousness', he passes judgment. Ancient rights 'do hold or break / As Men are strong or weak' (ll. 39–40), and men of will are not to be resisted or blamed when they are the instruments of Fate. But though Marvell, like Shakespeare's Octavius, will 'let determined things to destiny / Hold unbewailed their way', he knows that tactics and manoeuvres may be required to open up the way.[14]

Fate to a Christian could only mean the Providence of God. But the profuse evidence we have about Marvell's Protestant convictions, his abhorrence of popery and the Anglican prelacy, is mainly negative. As Legouis observed, 'we can tell more easily what he attacks than what he approves'.[15] Besides, neither his prose nor his religious lyrics supply the kind of information about his spiritual life that Donne and George Herbert give us in their divine poems: 'a picture of the many spiritual conflicts that have passed between God and my soul'.[16] Donne and Herbert, in different ways, speak to God. Crashaw and Traherne, again in different ways, celebrate Him rapturously. Only in 'The Coronet' does Marvell address God. His praise is heard in but two of his poems, and it is sung not by the poet but by the pilgrims of

'Bermudas' and the pastoral Chorus of 'Clorinda and Damon'. We have no sense of intimacy between the poet and his God. The lyrics have no doctrinal emphasis and, unlike the prose and the political poems, they are remarkably free from allusions to contemporary religious issues, apart from the glance at the 'Prelat's rage' in 'Bermudas' and the nunnery episode in the history of Nun Appleton. The other poems could have been written by any Christian. Yet they prove disconcerting. One of them goes further than the Renaissance humanists did in the pastoral allegorization of Christianity. Christ had earlier appeared in the guise of Pan but the 'Dialogue between Thyrsis and Dorinda' ends in a strange conjunction of mystic longing and pagan euthanasia. Other Christian poets have used sacrilegious language but only Marvell in the seventeenth century wrote about death and heaven in terms meant to be spiritual and yet definitely not Christian.[17] The moods expressed in religious lyrics may be various and conflicting but we are confronted here with a fundamental contradiction. In 'The Dialogue between The Resolved Soul, and Created Pleasure', as in 'On a Drop of Dew', spiritual elevation implies an outright rejection of the world of the senses. Yet the same spiritual values seem to be attained in 'Bermudas' and in 'The Garden' through the acceptance of pleasures afforded by the senses – sensuous pleasures supposed to be free from sensuality like the delights of the Appleton poet 'languishing with ease . . . On Pallets swoln of Velvet Moss' but safe against Beauty's 'useless Dart' (sts 75–6).

The love poems bring us no nearer the heart of the poet. Most of the situations in Donne's dramatic lyrics may be of imagination all compact, but we know at least that he is not speaking of love and sex, ecstasy or disgust, without any experience of such emotions. Marvell did not marry. We have no record of any love affair and there are only rumours about his sex life – rumours of impotence or homosexuality. In his religious poems he never showed the intense sin-consciousness paraded by Donne when the author of the *Holy Sonnets* remembered his 'profane mistresses'. But there is as little evidence for the kind of chastity that must have been Crashaw's addressing his wishes only to 'his (supposed) Mistresse'. Yet it seems naïve to argue that the daring language used in 'To his Coy Mistress' suffices 'to settle contemporary doubts cast on the poet's virility, and to prove that he was at least once in love – body and soul – with a real live mistress'.[18] The final lines do convey the breathless urgency of physical passion, but it is a passion that seeks no more than the spending of sexual energy. There is only one other invitation to love, the slight lyric 'Ametas and Thestylis'. In 'The Match', 'The Definition of Love' and 'The unfortunate Lover' the poet seems to be more interested in the hyperbolical or emblematic expression of love than in the passion itself. Love conventions are handled in an ironical or semi-burlesque way in 'Mourning', in 'Daphnis and Chloe', and even in 'The Gallery'. The love theme is subservient to an interest in Nature in the Mower Poems. In the other pastoral poems human love is rejected, as in the dialogues between Clorinda and Damon or Thyrsis and Dorinda, or simply excluded, as in 'The Garden' and *Upon Appleton House*. The exclusion of 'lust' and womanhood is no less conscious in 'Young Love' and 'The Picture of little T.C.'. The variety Legouis claimed for Marvell as a love poet cannot be found in a wide range of moods, comparable to Donne's, but only in the diversity of literary motifs and art forms.

It is tempting, indeed, to consider Marvell as a poet mainly interested in the craft of poetry. Besides, whereas Donne usually seeks to be original in form as in matter, Marvell has been described as an 'inveterate imitator' 'trying his hand at almost every kind of poetry that his contemporaries and immediate predecessors had been writing'.[19] When Leishman offered a profusion of parallels with Latin, Neo-Latin, Renaissance and seventeenth-century poetry he only confirmed T. S. Eliot's terse description of Marvell's 'best verse' as 'the product of European, that is to say Latin, culture'.[20] In this 'Ecchoing Song', as Rosalie Colie observed, 'sometimes it seems as if Marvell deliberately tried to write a single poem which could summarize and surpass all that had gone before'.[21] From this angle even the problems of political allegiance that have puzzled us would vanish, as in this view of the 'Horatian Ode': 'nothing makes the *Ode* a political declaration, such as must be defended in resulting argument or controversy, rather than a view of Cromwell appealing to Marvell's thought and imagination as engaged in the making of a *poem*'.[22]

Yet if Marvell is to be thought of as a literary artist mainly concerned with overdoing what had been done before, why was he so little solicitous about what he himself had achieved? Crashaw and Vaughan had their poems printed in their lifetime. George Herbert is said by Walton to have left the decision to Nicholas Ferrar but he must have known his friend was unlikely to 'burn' his *Temple*. Donne, though he sometimes affected the pose of the gentleman who does not condescend to print, projected an edition of his poems in 1614.[23] Lovelace, an aristocrat and Marvell's friend, prepared his poems for publication while in prison. Marvell apparently took no steps either to let his profane or religious lyrics come into print or to preserve them for posthumous publication. Though a manuscript copy of 'To his Coy Mistress' has recently come to light, there is no evidence that he allowed his unpublished poems to circulate as freely as other amateur poets did. Can this attitude be reconciled with the 'professionalism' and the 'preoccupation with poetry's problems' emphasized by Rosalie Colie and others?[24]

If Marvell wrote his non-political poems and the 'Horatian Ode' only to please himself or a narrow circle (his patron Fairfax and his friends), it does argue a genuine delight in poetry for its own sake, but the kind of delight that will lead an amateur poet, unlike a professional, to write as he chooses and therefore to betray his own inclinations even when seeking to emulate or excel his predecessors. On this assumption rested my attempt to build out of recurrent associations a coherent pattern for Marvell's world of imagination. There is nothing mysterious about his perceptions of space and time which hardly call for further exploration.[25] More obscure are the relationships between various aspects of his sensibility. I still feel there is a natural harmony between a number of distinctive features: the rejection of 'Passions heat' in so many poems; the obvious attraction to girls 'too green / Yet for Lust, but not for Love' ('Young Love'); the persistent opposition of the world of plants and innocence and the world of women and experience; the keen delight in the lusciousness of fruit and the sweetness of flowers as a substitute for the gratification of the sexual instinct; even the preference insistently expressed for shade and coolness in the very evocation of Paradise.[26] The recurrence of these predilections, joined to Marvell's command of style and rhythm, is responsible for the uniqueness of poems which are often so little original in theme or even in diction.

Whether such associations can be explained in psychological terms, ascribed to the repression of desire or latent homosexuality, need not concern us. What I find important is the network of imaginative relationships and the correspondence between such modes of sensibility and the nature of the poet's religious feeling. The obsession with purity is all the more remarkable for not being characteristically Puritan, nor even essentially Christian. Marvell does not call to God like Donne to 'breake, blowe, burn, and make him new' (*Holy Sonnets,* XIV). He describes the soul as 'Trembling lest it grow impure' in contact with the world ('On a Drop of Dew', l. 16), and the beautiful exclamation before a pastoral fountain, 'Might a soul bath there and be clean' ('Clorinda and Damon', l. 15), suggests the removal of some outward stain, not the kind of 'purging' or 'new-fashioning' often urged by Donne or Herbert. Marvell's imagery of pollution and ablution seems to imply a spontaneous inclination to dream about the 'natural' purity of the soul rather than keep in mind its corruption through original sin (with the one exception of 'The Coronet'). The same mode of imagination is disclosed by the poet's longing for a 'natural' innocence, preserved in childhood and recaptured in the 'garden' – 'a place so pure' – by the mere exclusion of woman and society.[27]

This longing for purity and Marvell's acknowledged emphasis on the dual nature of man may proceed from the same inner necessity, the same structure of personality. The Incarnation was the central mystery for Donne in his profane and religious poems alike: he thought of the spirit and the senses in terms of conjunction. Only an over-ingenious and misguided search for allegorical meanings can turn Marvell's poems into emblems of Christian mysteries.[28] This kind of systematic approach defeats itself and hardly calls for refutation. One should also refrain from erecting a philosophical superstructure over poems of lyric grace and witty playfulness. Because of the very elusiveness and allusiveness of the poet it has proved easy to read into the 'light *Mosaick*' of his verse whatever 'Phancy weaves' (*Upon Appleton House,* st. 73). Of late, indeed, philosophical criticism has 'set ope its cataracts' and it may be urgent to retire from the flood of learned commentaries and interpretations.

Some of Marvell's poems are undoubtedly suffused with

Platonic idealism and may be read in the light of a philosophy which has pervaded Renaissance literature. It does not mean either that their author was deeply read in Plato or Plotinus (not to speak of Hermes or St Bonaventura) or that he was under the tutelage of the Cambridge Platonists, a theory exploded by Muriel Bradbrook in her review of D. M. Friedman's *Marvell's Pastoral Art.*[29] When I spoke of an unresolved conflict between an ascetic Platonic idealism and a sensuous 'Edenic ideal' (a conflict often found in the Platonic tradition), I only intended to characterize Marvell's poetic inspiration and relate some formal features of his poetry with this fundamental form of thought and sensibility. The substitution of sharp antithesis for the Incarnation-like paradoxes cultivated by Donne and George Herbert is not a mere change of style.[30] In the same way the cleavage between sense and spirit invited a comparison between the structures of poetic thought in Marvell and Cartesian dualism. But only the discovery of unmistakable echoes (which I am unable to trace) would justify the confident assertion that Marvell in 'The Garden' is 'playing with the fascinatingly new and radical concepts of Descartes'.[31]

Scepticism may be carried further. J. B. Leishman objected to my own 'psychologizing' about time:

> an elaborate attempt to isolate Marvell's conceptions of time and eternity and to contrast them with Donne's and Herbert's seems to be based mainly on passages in 'To his Coy Mistress' and 'The Garden' and on a light-hearted couplet in 'Thyrsis and Dorinda'. . . .[32]

The thinness of the poetic corpus, I agree, made my attempt hazardous. But my purpose never was to define 'Marvell's *conception* of time': I sought to characterize his spontaneous intuition and poetic expression of time as something experienced: 'un temps senti', 'felt time'.[33] The free play of the poetic imagination may discover structures of which the poet himself is not aware, and their unconscious workings do not imply any intellectual speculation. Such an approach allows us to 'philosophize' about the '*easie Philosopher*' (*Upon Appleton House,* l. 561) without warping his own playful intention in his lighter moods.

The error of many critics may have consisted in taking Marvell's poetry too seriously or too lightly, an error the poet himself never committed when dealing with a subject.[34] Developing T. S. Eliot's hint about 'intense levity', Frank J. Warnke has shown how Marvell's 'playful seriousness' is 'his chief vehicle for conveying his sense of the contradictions of experience'.[35] The sanest critics seem to agree that historical, philosophical and religious overtones are 'not meant to supply another level of significance parallel to, or expressed through, the literal surface meaning but to intensify that "meaning" '.[36] Some of them, however, in their insistence on the presence of 'an enormous background of thought and of emotional association',[37] still tend to overfreight the poet's pinnace 'With wares which would sinke admiration'.

The 'play attitude' is an aspect of the poet's self-consciousness. In his faculty of critical detachment Marvell comes closest to Donne, yet his peculiar irony is more objective than Donne's: it often lies in the perception of contrasts and discrepancies between words or attitudes and actual feelings or behaviour.[38] It dissolves the false appearances of passion, and this cool exposure of the empty violence or solemnity of speech and gesture – obvious in the parting words of Daphnis or the closing image of 'Mourning', ambiguous in 'The unfortunate Lover' – even seems to cast a doubt on the reality of an inner life whose 'bottom' one may not 'sound'.

Marvell's 'Puritan inwardness' has been stressed but the assertion must be qualified.[39] To call him an 'essentially extrovert poet', as Leishman did in contrasting his technique with Donne's, is another overstatement, but I had called attention to the lack of evidence in his prose and poetry alike for the kind of self-interest and self-analysis which is so characteristic of Donne and George Herbert.[40] In his translation of a chorus from Seneca's *Thyestes* he no doubt condemns the man 'Who expos'd to other Ey's,/Into his own Heart ne'r pry's'. But the poet's own heart is not Herbert's 'Busie enquiring heart' ('The Discharge'), nor Donne's 'naked thinking heart' ('The Blossome') or his 'perplexed, labyrinthicall soul'.[41] Even when he calls up all the temptations that besiege the 'Resolved Soul' he describes the objects and pleasures offered, asserts his moral resolution but does not convey the hesitations or the strain of a soul in conflict. When he seeks to 'define' love, what is defined is the dramatic situation rather than the passion: envious

Fate preventing the lovers' union. The 'unfortunate Lover', whatever the meaning may be, is a projection of emotions into pictures. When the poet opens his soul to Clora, he only presents her with a 'gallery' of paintings. In the Mower Poems we have a reflection of the passions in the landscape and incidents. In *Upon Appleton House* the poet mainly plays the part of a spectator and commentator.

'Christianity', Marvell observed in *The Rehearsal Transpros'd*, 'has obliged men to very hard duties, and ransacks their very thoughts.'[42] As a Protestant of Puritan inclination he was bound to be aware of the dangers of self-deception. The deceitfulness of man's heart had been stressed by Calvin.[43] A whole treatise devoted by Daniel Dyke to *The Mystery of Self-Deceiving* was published in 1614 and showed the convergence of the religious and profane interest in self-knowledge since it drew on both the *Confessions* of Augustine and the *Epistles* of Seneca;[44] it was twice translated into French and may have influenced La Rochefoucauld. 'The Coronet' discloses a keen awareness of impure motives 'When wee are mov'd to seeme religious / Only to went wit . . .', as Donne had phrased it in 'The Litanie'. The discovery is not surprising and the poem derives its power from the mastery of form, not from any subtlety of psychological analysis. Marvell's originality lies in an introspectiveness of a different nature: an intuition of pure thought reached through the contemplation of the world.

Some of Donne's poems, notably 'The Good-Morrow', 'The Sunne-Rising' and 'The Canonization', were characterized by an intense and simultaneous awareness of the self and the world, but the world was something to be apprehended through the beloved. For the world well lost for love was also a world well won, triumphantly possessed through the lovers' union: 'Let us possess our world, each hath one, and is one'. The language may be Platonic but the living emotion is the intuition described in our own days by Jean-Paul Sartre:

> the world must be revealed through the beloved – he makes a world spring into being – his function is to impart existence to all things in order to give them all to his lover who will compose a world out of them. . . . Instead of being an object

> perceived against the background of the world, he is himself the background against which the world stands.[45]

Marvell is also intensely aware of the world, but the world is only a setting in 'To his Coy Mistress' and in 'The Definition of Love' its expanse defeats the union of the lovers. It is only in solitude and in the very act of contemplation of the surrounding scene that an original intuition of the world as representation emerges – the world enclosed in the sphere of consciousness.

In his famous lines in 'The Garden' on

> The Mind, that Ocean where each kind
> Does straight its own resemblance find

the poet may or may not allude either to 'the Platonic doctrine of the correspondence of forms as objects of thought with forms as they exist in their own realm' or to the Cartesian 'theory of representative perception in which thought possesses a symbolic relation to object',[46] but he undoubtedly expresses in the context of the poem his living awareness of the interiority of perception. Thomas Traherne later described the same experience when writing: 'And evry Object in my Soul a Thought / Begot, or was . . .' ('My Spirit', st. 3). Now, since the world is seated in the mind by the very act of perception, the creations of the mind will be as real as the reflected world and the poet can write:

> Yet it creates, transcending these,
> Far other Worlds, and other Seas;
> Annihilating all that's made
> To a green Thought in a green Shade.

Again this may or may not be a 'Cartesian' reduction of the world to 'a *res cogitans* and a *res extensa*', but I take it to be first the expression of the concrete experience of the poet looking at the natural scene. The next stanza shows him lying 'at the Fountains sliding foot, / Or at some Fruit-trees mossy root'. His eyes must be filled with greenness. The 'green Thought' may have all the connotations of freshness, innocence or hope ascribed to it in various readings. I still think the first and foremost meaning is the actual sensation of greenness which pervades, fills and satisfies the poet's consciousness in the quiet bliss of contemplation. This interpretation may sound jejune and unphilosophic and I admit Marvell himself intellectualized his experience but I claim that the experience, not its intellectual elaboration, makes the lines imaginatively convincing.

In such a state of quiescence the contemplating mind will lose all sense of confinement to the body. That there is no distance between the mind and the object in the act of perception, as Berkeley and Whitehead will variously argue, Traherne, probably taking a cue from Plotinus,[47] has expressed in his own way in 'My Spirit':

> It Acts not from a Centre to
> Its Object as remote,
> But present is, when it does view,
> Being with the Being it doth note.
> (st. 2)

There is, of course, no conscious expression of this philosophic view in 'The Garden', but the poet's projection of his soul into the green boughs seems to rest on the same experience. Anyone lying under a tree and dreamily gazing on the sunlit foliage will forget his body and have the impression of being among the boughs, 'immanent there', as Whitehead would have phrased it:

> Casting the Bodies Vest aside,
> My Soul into the boughs does glide:
> There like a Bird it sits, and sings,
> Then whets, and combs its silver Wings.
> ('The Garden', ll. 51–4)

Marvell did not anticipate the idealism of Traherne but there is in his poetry a consciousness of the perceiving mind which relates him to the Divine Philosopher. His own use of the term is characteristic in such lines as:

> How safe, methinks, and strong, behind
> These Trees have I incamp'd my Mind;
> (*Upon Appleton House*, ll. 601–2)

My Mind was once the true survey
Of all these Medows fresh and gay;
And in the greenness of the Grass
Did see its Hopes as in a Glass;
('The Mower's Song', ll. 1–4)

Reflections in water have attracted many Baroque poets. However, when Marvell describes a river as 'a *Chrystal Mirrour* slick; / Where all things gaze themselves, and doubt / If they be in it or without' (*Upon Appleton House*, ll. 636–8), this doubt at once reminds us of Traherne's 'Shadows in the Water' and seems to herald a more philosophical interrogation: are the things reflected in the mind without it or within? To trace individual modes of apprehension may be more rewarding than to search for borrowed concepts. In this perspective even the comparison of the soul with a drop of dew may take on a richer significance. The drop that fell from 'the clear Fountain of Eternal Day', 'recollecting its own Light',

Does, in its pure and circling thoughs, express
The greater Heaven in an Heaven less.
In how coy a Figure wound,
Every way it turns away;
So the World excluding round,
Yet receiving in the Day.
('On a Drop of Dew', ll. 25–30)

Through his world-awareness Donne reached a higher self-awareness. Marvell shuts out the world of men when 'incamping' his mind behind the trees and at times excludes even the world of nature; but he more often contemplates the outer world as mirrored in his consciousness. In both cases attention turns to the thinking mind in its act of perception or creation.

What emerged as a fleeting intuition in the poems of Marvell became a constant illumination in the 'divine philosophy' of Thomas Traherne. In varying degrees they both bear witness to an important development in the history of thought – or rather of the way in which men looked upon the operations of their own minds. Throughout the Middle Ages and the early Renaissance the life of the mind had been described as an interplay of forces and faculties endowed with an objective reality.[48] The Renaissance and the Reformation resulted in a heightened self-consciousness, but the self-examination practised – whether religious or profane – was a dissection of the heart, an anatomy of the passions of the soul. In his interest for the workings of the mind Lord Herbert of Cherbury – a philosopher and a poet – was truly a pioneer when he criticized the schools for judging matters which refer to the forms of apprehension by means of 'discursive thought'. He invited 'a careful attention to the testimony of consciousness', insistently 'referred the Reader to his inner consciousness', for 'inner perception is more trustworthy than external perception, and the latter more trustworthy than discursive thought'.[49] With Donne introspection meant an attempt to define his emotions and his own self: a self 'Meteor-like, of stuffe and forme perplext, / Whose *what*, and *where*, in disputation is'.[50] With Lord Herbert, and occasionally with Marvell, it came to mean a turning in of the mind upon itself which can be described as 'reflexive consciousness' rather than 'self-consciousness'.[51]

Locke will later claim that it is 'impossible for anyone to perceive without *perceiving* that he does perceive'.[52] But though the statement could be reconciled with earlier theories of perception (including the Aristotelian 'common sense') the conscious experience of perceiving that one does perceive is by no means constant nor even common in our daily life. In literature, as far as I know, Traherne first called attention to an experience on which he founded his Gospel of Felicity; Marvell, I admit, offers no more than an adumbration of it. With the Cambridge Platonists, as with Traherne, the 'reflex acts' of the soul opened the way to a contemplation of the divine in man: a way not unknown to Plato, Plotinus and the mystics.[53] What was really new and original in the seventeenth century was the way in which some minds began to exercise their reflexive faculty in the contemplation of the outer world. The 'reflex act' is then no more than the awareness of perceiving all natural objects as objects of the mind, seated in the mind itself.

With Marvell this kind of introspection allowed a simultaneous involvement in and detachment from Nature and the world of the senses. He could indulge in a Keatsian 'life of sensation' and yet retire into a 'thought', since sensations could also be apprehended as 'ideas' of the mind in the Lockean sense. Reflection would show him the vanity of men's labours 'To win the Palm, the Oke, or Bayes' ('The Garden', l. 2) and yet allow his involvement in the world of action since, in the service of Cromwell and later in Parliament, he could remain, 'in busie Companies of Men' as in retirement, a detached observer of the social and political scene. Thus the poet's awareness of his thinking mind may prove a key to the mystery of his personality and account for the seeming contradictions and the elusiveness of his poetry.

Notes

1 He was . . . of very few words; and though he loved wine, he would never drink hard in company, and was wont to say that he would not play the good-fellow in any man's company in whose hands he would not trust his life. He had not a general acquaintance. (Aubrey, *Brief Lives*)

2 Wallace, *Destiny his Choice: The Loyalism of Andrew Marvell*, Cambridge University Press, 1968, p. 144.

3 Smith, 'The Political Beliefs of Andrew Marvell', *University of Toronto Quarterly*, XXXVI (1966–7), p. 55; Rivers, *The Poetry of Conservatism 1600–1745*, Cambridge, Rivers Press, 1973, p. 108.

4 The well-known thesis of Cleanth Brooks has been revived by J. M. Newton who even assumes that 'Tom May's Death' was written to show that Marvell was not a turncoat and 'had been arraigning successful crimes' ('What Do We Know About Andrew Marvell?' *Cambridge Quarterly*, VI (1973), pp. 125–46). Marvell, indeed, had not been oblivious of 'ancient Rights' in the Ode, and the recurrence of the phrase in 'Tom May's Death' is striking; but no reading of the Ode can turn it into the kind of public arraignment of 'successful crimes' expected from the poet in the later satire.

5 Marvell's authorship is denied by George de F. Lord, but Legouis tends to accept it in his revision of Margoliouth, *The Poems and Letters of Andrew Marvell*, Oxford University Press, 1971, I,

p. 304. I incline to Margoliouth's hypothesis of 'a topical adaptation in 1661 of an earlier MS'. Some phrases – e.g. 'the World's disjointed Axel' – seem to me distinctly Marvellian but 'the political mystery remains' (Legouis) unless the poem was written or revised after the Restoration.

6 Wallace, as above (note 2), p. 79.

7 Ibid., p. 47: see the whole of the first chapter.

8 Ibid., p. 143.

9 *Poems and Letters* (see note 5), II, p. 7.

10 P. Legouis, *Andrew Marvell*, Oxford, The Clarendon Press, 1960, p. 147.

11 Wallace, as above (note 2), pp. 205, 213.

12 Isabel G. MacCaffrey, 'Some Notes on Marvell's Poetry, Suggested by a reading of his Prose', *Modern Philology*, LXI (1963), p. 265.

13 Marvell, *Complete Works*, ed. A. B. Grosart, London, 1872–5, III, pp. 212–13.

14 The surprising praise from Cromwell's alleged stratagem in lines 49–52 of the Ode, and Marvell's own tactics under the Restoration, may proceed from the same conviction.

15 Legouis, as above (note 10), p. 221.

16 Herbert's words in Walton's *Life*.

17 On the 'un-Puritan' and 'un-Christian' nature of Marvell's pastoral inspiration, see L. Lerner, 'Pastoral *versus* Christianity', *The Uses of Nostalgia*, London, Chatto & Windus, 1972, pp. 181–96.

18 Legouis (as above, note 10), p. 34.

19 J. B. Leishman, *The Art of Marvell's Poetry*, London, Hutchinson, 1966, p. 202.

20 T. S. Eliot, 'Andrew Marvell' (1921); reprinted in John Carey's anthology, *Andrew Marvell*, Harmondsworth, Penguin Books, 1969, p. 47.

21 Rosalie Colie, *'My Ecchoing Song': Andrew Marvell's Poetry of Criticism*, Princeton University Press, 1970, p. 20.

22 A. J. N. Wilson, 'Andrew Marvell: An Horatian Ode . . . the Thread of the Poem and its Use of Classical Allusion', *Critical Quarterly*, XI (1969), p. 326.

23 See Helen Gardner's edition of *The Elegies and the Songs and Sonnets*, Oxford, The Clarendon Press, 1965, p. lxxxii; and on Donne's general attitude to poetry: my *Poètes métaphysiques anglais*, Paris, Corti, 1960, III, pp. 112–17 – hereafter cited as *PMA*.

24 Colie (as above, note 21), pp. 105, 137.

25 *PMA*, II, pp. 114–27; partly translated in Carey's anthology (as above, note 20), pp. 151–5.

26 Ibid., pp. 136 ff. To this 'complex' belongs the interest in cold substances, things 'congeal'd and chill' and '*Nature . . . vitrifi'd*': ibid., p. 121.
27 See ibid., II, pp. 139–46.
28 Bruce King, *Marvell's Allegorical Poetry,* New York, Oleander Press, 1977, p. 88 and *passim.*
29 In *Renaissance Quarterly,* XXIV (1971), pp. 584–5.
30 See *PMA*, II, pp. 146–7.
31 Daniel Stempel, 'Marvell's Cartesian Ecstasy', *Journal of the History of Ideas,* XXVIII (1967), pp. 99–114.
32 In *Review of English Studies,* XIII (1962), p. 307.
33 *PMA*, II, pp. 116–17.
34 'His errors of taste . . . never consist in taking a subject too seriously or too lightly' (T. S. Eliot, as above, note 20).
35 Frank J. Warnke, *Versions of Baroque*, New Haven, Conn., Yale University Press, 1972, p. 23.
36 Karina Williamson, 'Marvell's "The Nymph" . . . A Reply', *Modern Philology,* LI (1953), p. 271. Cf. *PMA*, II, p. 164.
37 Colie (as above, note 21), p. 103. Though acknowledging that Marvell 'managed to play with ideas', Colie still discovers a 'philosophical content' (pp. 303, 166).
38 As in 'Daphnis and Chloe' or 'Mourning': *PMA*, II, pp. 132–3.
39 MacCaffrey (as above, note 12), p. 261.
40 Leishman (above, note 19), p. 69; and *PMA*, II, pp. 128–35.
41 In a letter quoted by Sir Edmund Gosse, *Life and Letters,* London, 1899, I, pp. 62–3.
42 Marvell, as above (note 13), III, p. 391.
43 'C'est certes un excellent et singulier profit, quand, toutes cachettes découvertes, le coeur est produit en lumière, bien purgé de cette méchante infection d'hypocrisie': 'Préface' of the 'Commentaire sur les Psaumes', *Oeuvres Choisies,* Geneva, 1909, p. 9.
44 The Dedication also brings together Augustine and Persius: 'Here shall they (the readers) find that dangerous Art of selfe-sophistry displayed . . . ., And so by seeing their selfe-deceit, shall come to their selfe-knowledge. A knowledge never more neglected. *Ut nemo in sese temptat descendere nemo*' (London, 1614, fol. A3v).
45 *L'être et le néant*, Paris, Gallimard, 1943, pp. 434, 449.
46 Stempel (as above, note 31), pp. 106, 107.
47 See *PMA*, II, pp. 305–8. I first called attention to the kinship between Marvell and Traherne (II, p. 126) recently stressed by Don P. Norford in 'Marvell and the Arts of Contemplation and Action', *Journal of English Literary History,* XLI (1974), p. 72.

48 A comparison of Donne's self-analysis with the psychology of Dante or Cavalcanti will show the difference: see *PMA*, III, pp. 204–7.
49 *De Veritate*, trans. M. H. Carré, Bristol, 1937, pp. 154–5, 153, 234.
50 'To the Countesse of Bedford at New-yeares Tide', ll. 3–4.
51 In French I opposed 'conscience de soi' and 'conscience de conscience': see *PMA*, II, pp. 415–17.
52 *An Essay Concerning Human Understanding*, II, xxvii, p. 11; ed. Alexander C. Fraser, New York, Dover Publications, 1959, 1, p. 449.
53 On 'reflex acts' and 'self-reflexion' see Nathaniel Culverwell, *Discourse of the Light of Nature*, London, 1652, pp. 102, 156, and John Smith, *Select Discourses*, London, 1660, IV, p. viii (3rd ed., 1821, p. 118).

11

The meadow-sequence in Upon Appleton House: *Questions of tone and meaning*

Frank J. Warnke

About halfway through *Upon Appleton House*, the narrator-protagonist of Marvell's longest non-satiric poem passes from the garden, which he has been describing in pyrotechnically witty conceits, to the meadows adjoining the estate. There he observes, and to some extent participates in, a series of events which are, if natural, none the less surrounded by a penumbra of mystery, magic, and nameless potency. The central position of the meadow-sequence is probably significant. The earlier portions of the poem – description of the house, historical digression on the Fairfax ancestors, evocation of the garden – bestow praise on Lord Fairfax and his family rather in the manner of Jonson's 'To Penshurst' and other 'great house' poems, with the poet effectively reduced to a pair of observing eyes and a panegyric voice. (Early in the poem Marvell is more anonymous even than Jonson: the first-person singular does not appear at all until the meadow-passage, the earlier portion being articulated through the first-person plural.) In the later portions of *Upon Appleton House*, after the meadow-passage, the poet (or his persona) becomes the focus of interest as he withdraws from the flooded meadow to the sheltering wood, undergoes his experience of nature, goes fishing, and is interrupted by the monitory figure of his pupil, Maria Fairfax. The activity of praise continues, indeed reaches its apogee in the tribute to Maria, but within a context in which the projected personality of the narrator is strongly present.

I should like to suggest that the occurrences in the meadow have something to do with this shift of emphasis, and that the mysterious quality that hovers about them operates in such a way as to turn outside to inside, observer to celebrant, panegyric poem to sacramental experience.

The meadow-sequence begins, as Rosalie Colie and others have noted,[1] with violent disruptions of perspective and proportion:

And now to the Abbyss I pass
Of that unfathomable Grass,
Where Men like Grasshoppers appear,
But Grasshoppers are Gyants there:
They, in their squeking Laugh, contemn
Us as we walk more low then them:
And, from the Precipices tall
Of the green spir's, to us do call.
(st. 47)

'Unfathomable' in both a literal and a figurative sense (i.e., 'without an ascertainable bottom' and 'incomprehensible, mysterious'), the grass constitutes an abyss, a pit into which one may fall with danger of annihilation. Such annihilation is hinted at by the reversal of normal relationship brought about by the elevation of the scornful grasshoppers and the attendent shrinking of the human figures; it is overtly stated in the stanza that follows:

To see Men through this Meadow Dive,
We wonder how they rise alive.
As, under Water, none does know
Whether he fall through it or go.
But, as the Marriners that sound,
And show upon their Lead the Ground,
They bring up Flow'rs so to be seen,
And prove they've at the Bottom been.

The grass is an abyss, but it is also a sea, and, like the sea, it can swallow up those who venture into it. Hence the speaker's wonder at the fact that the sojourners in the grass return alive. But the meadow-sea is not exclusively a domain of threat; the divers return with flowers, an image of beauty won from the depths of the abyss.

Maren-Sofie Røstvig and a number of other critics have found yet more strongly positive implications in the image of the sea-meadow: its greenness is the *benedicta viriditas*, the colour of hope and of the creative spirit, and the passage through the meadow signifies the death and rebirth of baptism.[2] Whether or not the assertion of such a specific symbolism is justified, it seems likely that the general direction of the reading is just, and that submersion in the meadow is in fact a spiritual experience of formidable power. Worth noting, for example, is the way in which the narrator moves from his – or 'our' – wonder at the return from oblivion to the wonder he ascribes to the divers themselves, who have experienced a sense of submarine dislocation, or loss of bearings, related to the disrupted perspectives of the initial stanza but related also to the motif of that loss of self which is the indispensable condition of the finding of self: '. . . under Water, none does know / Whether he fall through it or go'.

The perplexing unreality of this experience of natural reality is underscored by the theatrical imagery which opens the next stanza:

> No Scene that turns with Engines strange
> Does oftner then these Meadows change.
> For when the Sun the Grass hath vext,
> The tawny Mowers enter next;
> Who seem like *Israalites* to be,
> Walking on foot through a green Sea.
> To them the Grassy Deeps divide,
> And crowd a Lane to either Side.
>
> (st. 49)

As Margoliouth has pointed out, the 'Engines strange' are surely to be associated with the elaborate machinery employed in court masques.[3] And, like the stage-set of the masque, the meadows are specialized in metamorphosis. When the appropriate season arrives – and the one day's tour of Appleton House magically embraces the whole seasonal year – the mowers come on stage to put on their act: parting the sea, like Moses, and, as we shall shortly note, massacring the grass as Pharaoh and his troops were massacred. Many readers of the poem, most notably Don Cameron Allen, have drawn our attention to the 'grim pastoralism' of this part of the poem and have suggested the presence of an allegory of the recently concluded Civil War.[4] Allen, in particular, extends an allegorical reading to the subsequent stanza:

> With whistling Sithe, and Elbow strong,
> These Massacre the Grass along:
> While one, unknowing, carves the *Rail,*
> Whose yet unfeather'd Quils her fail.
> The Edge all bloody from its Breast
> He draws, and does his stroke detest;
> Fearing the Flesh untimely mow'd
> To him a Fate as black forebode.

According the Allen, the rail, or corncrake, traditionally known as the *roi des cailles,* the 'king of quails', represents the slain Charles I (whose execution Lord Fairfax had strongly condemned), and the action of the mowers is thus a representation of the entire civil conflict, including the regicide.[5] However this may be – and I have some reservations – the actors in the scene have a variety of responses to the slaughter: the mower, as we have seen, 'detests his stroke', finding in it an omen of his own mortality, while the narrator, in a later stanza, moralizes the episode. In between, however, another voice is heard, expressing a quite different attitude:

> But bloody *Thestylis,* that waites
> To bring the mowing Camp their Cates,
> Greedy as Kites has trust it up,
> And forthwith means on it to sup:
> When on another quick She lights,
> And cryes, he call'd us *Israelites*;
> But now, to make his saying true,
> Rails rain for Quails, for Manna Dew.
>
> (st. 51)

Allen and Røstvig agree in associating Thestylis with Bellona, as a bloody – and bloody-minded – goddess of battle.[6] I'm not so sure. Thestylis is primarily interested in the rail's edible properties, and, when she finds another unfortunate bird, her emphasis is surely culinary rather than sanguinary. Whatever she may be allegorically, on the literal level she's a farm-girl entrusted with preparing dinner for the mowers.

She's a very sophisticated farm-girl, however, as she demonstrates by casually cracking the frame of fiction so carefully crafted by the narrator. '. . . he call'd us *Israelites*', she says, with a glance in his direction. What are we to make of this? We have been in a familiar and comfortable position *vis-à-vis* the poet: as his audience, we have been sitting back listening to him describe for us his scene, his characters, his actions. All these have, quite decorously, gone about their business in decent ignorance of the fact that they were being talked about. Now, all at once, one of the characters peers from the frame, speaks from the stage – speaks, presumably, to us as she comments on the poet's witty Scriptural allusion and develops it further with a Scriptural citation of her own. As in the first stanza of the meadow-sequence, but even more radically and disturbingly, perspective and proportion are thrown into chaos. The meadow which we have entered with the poet is an enchanted theatre in which a very curious kind of play is being played – a play in which identity shifts disconcertingly from moment to moment, and in which all things – including slaughter, whether of grass or little birds – may turn out to be different from what they seem.

The pathos which so many commentators have found in the death of the rail is, if present anywhere, to be found in the next stanza, spoken by the narrator:

> Unhappy Birds! what does it boot
> To build below the Grasses Root;
> When Lowness is unsafe as Hight,
> And Chance o'retakes what scapeth spight?
> And now your Orphan Parents Call
> Sounds your untimely Funeral.
> Death-Trumpets creak in such a Note,
> And 'tis the *Sourdine* in their Throat.
>
> (st. 52)

His lament carries over into the next stanza, but after one line it shifts, with an abruptness emphasized by rhyme, into a savagely jubilant panorama of the completed mowing:

Or sooner hatch or higher build:
The Mower now commands the Field;
In whose new Traverse seemeth wrought
A Camp of Battail newly fought:
Where, as the Meads with Hay, the Plain
Lyes quilted ore with Bodies slain:
The Women that with forks it fling,
Do represent the Pillaging.

The imagery is, of course, consistently military, but I do not find the stanza 'grim': as I have remarked elsewhere, and as Rosalie Colie has confirmed, the violent activities associated with the mowing are, if an allegory of war, an allegory with innocuous and life-giving implications, the activities being presented as part of the natural process.[7] In discussing this poem, I have called the mowing-scene 'a played equivalent of . . . war, violence metamorphosed into a life-giving ritual of fertility'.[8] It might be more accurate to turn things around and see war as a kind of perverted play, a destructive version of the ultimately beneficent activity of the mowers – who may be seen as enacting the agonistic structure that Johan Huizinga sees as the 'root-principle of existence'.[9]

My reading of the mowing-scene as positive and joyful in tone is supported, I think, by the next stanza:

And now the careless Victors play,
Dancing the Triumphs of the Hay;
Where every Mowers wholesome Heat
Smells like an *Alexanders sweat*.
Their Females fragrant as the Mead
Which they in *Fairy Circles* tread:
When at their Dances End they kiss,
Their new-made Hay not sweeter is.
(st. 54)

If I am responding accurately to the overall tone, how are we to account for the pathos elicited by the bird's death? Allen, Røstvig, and Colie all find that pathos authentic, the last-named critic employing such phrases as 'heroic and tragic' and, more cautiously, 'near tragic' to characterize the relevant passages.[10] It is once again, I believe, a question of shifting focus, of wrenching perspective. For a moment after the accidental slaying, the mower feels regret mixed with apprehension; for rather more than a moment, the narrator feels the delicious pangs of a sympathy mingled with sententiousness, then forgets them – and the bird – in the spectacle of the completed mowing and the celebration that crowns it. The mowers' dance is a ritual of fertility, and properly so, for fertility is what the mowing has been all about. In the context of the vast movements of the natural cycle, the death of the baby rail – an obligatory blood-sacrifice, perhaps – is worth a fugitive tear from the sensitive observer, but nothing more than that. Perhaps, indeed, in the context of *Upon Appleton House*, all death is worth no more than that.

With a characteristic foreshortening of time, the next stanza shows us the meadow with the hay piled in stacks, the speaker's conceited imagination viewing the landscape as a seascape:

When after this 'tis piled in Cocks,
Like a calm Sea it shews the Rocks:
We wondring in the River near
How Boats among them safely steer.
Or, like the *Desert Memphis Sand*,
Short *Pyramids* of Hay do stand.
And such the *Roman Camps* do rise
In Hills for Soldiers Obsequies.

The military imagery, one notes, is sustained. As we shall see, the identification of the meadow with first the sea and then the desert sand anticipates what will very shortly be an actual metamorphosis. As the theatrical imagery returns, the field is swept free of its haycocks and assumes the empty flatness of the world at creation – an imaginative reversion in time which I take to be extremely important:

This *Scene* again withdrawing brings
A new and empty Face of things;
A levell'd space, as smooth and plain,
As Clothes for *Lilly* stretch to stain.
The World when first created sure
Was such a Table rase and pure.
Or rather such is the *Toril*
Ere the Bulls enter at Madril.

For to this naked equal Flat,
Which *Levellers* take Pattern at,
The Villagers in common chase
Their Cattle, which it closer rase;
And what below the Sith increast
Is pincht yet nearer by the Beast.
Such, in the painted World, appear'd
Davenant with th' Universal Heard.
(st. 56–7)

The scene, in its flat blankness, resembles the world at creation, but it is further analogized to more particular images of beginnings: the stretched canvas before the noted miniaturist Sir Peter Lely applies his paints to it, the bull-ring before the start of the *corrida*, society as the radical Leveller movement of the time would wish it – stripped free of all the structures and institutions of tradition. The first two images are, significantly, of art, and when the poet continues his description with the appearance of the grazing cattle, they too are visualized doubly in terms of art – Sir William Davenant's description, in *Gondibert*, of a painting of a herd of cattle. Nakedness, art, and – at this moment in the seasonal cycle – once again disjunction and disruption of perspective:

They [i.e. the cattle] seem within the polisht Grass
A Landskip drawen in Looking-Glass.
And shrunk in the huge Pasture show
As Spots, so shap'd, on Faces do.
Such Fleas, ere they approach the Eye,
In Multiplying Glasses lye.
They feed so wide, so slowly move,
As *Constellations* do above.

The general topsy-turviness reaches its climax as the River Denton concludes the 'Acts' (which I also take in a theatrical sense) by overflowing its banks and flooding the meadow, as is its yearly wont:

Then, to conclude these pleasant Acts,
Denton sets ope its *Cataracts*;
And makes the Meadow truly be
(What it but seem'd before) a Sea.

For, jealous of its *Lords* long stay,
It try's t'invite him thus away.
The River in itself is drown'd,
And Isl's th' astonish'd Cattle round.
(st. 59)

As Colie points out, this stanza and the one that follows it constitute a rendition of the 'world-upside-down' topos so thoroughly investigated by Curtius.[11] Here, however, the disruption of order is neither sinister nor dangerous: it is vital, restorative, and, most of all, comic:

Let others tell the *Paradox*,
How Eels now bellow in the Ox;
How Horses at their Tails do kick,
Turn'd as they hang to Leeches quick;
How Boats can over Bridges sail;
And Fishes do the Stables scale.
How *Salmons* trespassing are found;
And Pikes are taken in the Pound.
(st. 60)

These lines conclude the meadow-sequence; the stanza that follows moves the narrator into his forest sanctuary, where (conditioned, I would contend, by his meadow experiences) he becomes the focus of the poem as he experiences communion with nature and full participation in its reality:

But I, retiring from the Flood,
Take Sanctuary in the Wood;
And, while it lasts, my self imbark
In this yet green, yet growing Ark;
Where the first Carpenter might best
Fit Timber for his Keel have Prest.
And where all Creatures might have shares;
Although in Armies, not in Paires.

It is beyond the scope of this paper to deal in detail with the events of the rest of the poem, although I shall have a few suggestions to make about how Marvell's final emphases are related to the mysterious actions in the meadows. What I have been implying is that the meadow-sequence is a ritual of fertility, that the mowers' actions, including the slaying of the rail, should be seen as steps performed in order to assure the continuation of fertility, the vital recharging of the seasonal cycle. To do this they must – as the poet must – enact chaos, for without the return of chaos no new creation is possible. But the 'Acts', specifically including the disorder-bringing flood, are 'pleasant', and the poet's mood is one of sustained, if quiet, joy, for creation will emerge again from the life-bringing chaos.

Mircea Eliade writes,

> The creation of the world . . . is reproduced every year. . . . Any form whatever, by the mere fact that it exists as such and endures, necessarily loses vigor and becomes worn; to recover vigor, it must be reabsorbed into the formless . . . it must be restored to the primordial unity from which it issued; in other words it must return to 'chaos' (on the cosmic plane), to 'orgy' (on the social plane), to 'darkness' (for seed), to 'water' (baptism on the human plane, Atlantis on the plane of history, and so on).[12]

In the same context he mentions the 'very close connections between the ideas of Creation through water (aquatic cosmogony, deluge that periodically regenerates historical life, rain), birth, and resurrection'.[13] Eliade is describing a primordial, *pre*-historic world-view, basing his description on his study of archaic and primitive societies, but his description seems eerily accurate as an account of the meadow-sequence in *Upon Appleton House* – one of the most sophisticated works of the most sophisticated poet of the English Baroque.

Maren-Sofie Røstvig, as already noted, sees the 'green' of the Appleton House meadows as a *benedicta viriditas* that symbolizes renewal and hope, that constitutes, actually, the creative principle itself. In Marvell's metamorphoses, the meadow becomes water (first, we might note, metaphorically; then metamorphically), the element of death and rebirth. For Røstvig, then, the passage of the mowers through the meadow becomes baptism.[14] I see what she is getting at, and, indeed, in many ways her approach to the poem is similar to mine. I would, however, want to avoid a reading in which the mysterious forces of the meadow 'stand for' anything in a precise or one-to-one relationship. I do not, in other words, regard *Upon Appleton House* as being in any sense allegorical. The grass (which is also flesh) does not *represent* baptism, but the rite of baptism comes from the same curious part of the human mind that makes Marvell see the grass as water and the annual mowing as a ritual experience of chaos in order to participate in creation.

This sounds all very quaint and mythy, but can it be justified, in terms of the text or in terms of the thought of Marvell's age? To begin with, the poem as a whole has to mean more than meets the eye. Not merely a 'great house' poem in the manner of Jonson, not merely a topographical poem in the manner of Denham's *Cooper's Hill*, it repeatedly suggests to us, through its allusiveness and through its complex figuration, that witty description and casually meandering reflection are its method, not its meaning. Virtually all commentators on *Upon Appleton House* have assumed and attempted to demonstrate the nature of hidden meanings in the work: Allen sees it as an historical and political allegory urging Fairfax's return to public life from retirement and prophesying the coming of God's wisdom (represented by Maria as Athena-Sophia) to restore England to peace and health; Røstvig sees it as an Hermetic fable of regeneration, both personal and collective; Colie sees it as being many things at the same time, not least important of which is a virtuoso study in the possibilities of *genera mixta*.[15] All these readings are correct as far as they go, but no one of them is sufficient to account for all aspects of the work. Perhaps no one reading can. Among other things, the interpretations referred to do not deal adequately with the mysterious goings-on in the meadow and the mysterious tone with which the narrator presents them.

As my earlier remarks have indicated, most commentators on *Upon Appleton House* see the meadow-sequence as constituting a grim and bitter recapitulation of the Civil War, with the slaying of the rail as either an allegorical representation of the slaughter of the king, or a near-tragic exercise in pathos, or both. But the voice of the narrator is not bitter, and it is only fleetingly pathetic; on the contrary, that voice expresses a sustained and positive sense of joy, a joy in no way undercut by the presence of the warfare imagery. For at Appleton House – '*Paradice's only Map*', as we are later told (l. 768) – all things are innocuous, and the war is only a play war – as, in 'The Garden', one can eat fruit, stumble, be ensnared, and fall, with no harm done, none at all.

If the mowing is indeed a fertility ritual, a return to vital chaos undertaken to assure the re-creation of the earth, then, like all ritual, it is *played,* that is to say: another identity is feigned and assumed and, having been assumed, takes on a reality that calls original identity into question; violence and conflict are exhibited, but with a kind of transcendent jocularity that blunts their danger; the self – compromised by the play-attitude, swept into the chaos of a nature being destroyed that it may be reborn, annihilated, therefore, as self – is paradoxically reaffirmed and emerges with a stronger identity than it originally possessed.[16]

Christian doctrine, Hermetic philosophy, the rich heritage of the emblem books – all these things were, we know, a part of Marvell's intellectual heritage. We cannot, with confidence, make such a claim for the ideas about ritual enactment of chaos which I have been expounding. The poet was not, presumably, familiar with twentieth-century anthropology, depth psychology, or mythography. Nevertheless, that fact does not invalidate those ideas as an instrument for unearthing some of the meanings of *Upon Appleton House.* C. L. Barber has demonstrated the degree to which Shakespeare's early and middle comedies recapitulate the patterns of traditional holiday festivity,[17] patterns that Barber sums up in the formula 'through release to clarification'. The fact that neither Shakespeare nor his contemporaries are likely to have seen the patterns in quite the same terms as would a twentieth-century person does not deny the presence of the patterns – in either the holiday festivities or the plays (or, for that matter, in the poems in which Robert Herrick employs details drawn from traditional rural observances). Marvell, too, lived in a world imbued and coloured with traditional practices of great antiquity and a ritual cast; like Shakespeare, he transformed them into art.

But I should not like to suggest that Marvell didn't know what was going on in his own poem, that the central meanings of that poem emerged exclusively from the poet's unconscious, or the collective unconscious, or any other hidden recess of the psyche. It would be foolhardy to ascribe too hastily any variety of unconsciousness to Andrew Marvell. The representation of nature in such a way as to invoke her chthonic power, with a full awareness of the ritual implications of such invocation, is, I believe, the result of consciously held attitudes of Renaissance and Baroque poets.

In his *Mythomystes* (*c.* 1633), Henry Reynolds follows the traditions of Italian Neoplatonism in asserting that the prime end of poetry is the representation of the hidden processes of nature. Admitting that ancient poetry – and his subject is almost exclusively ancient poetry – sometimes conveys an ethical content in symbolic terms, he lays far more stress on the way in which such poetry conveys a knowledge of the workings of nature. Thus, of the three areas in which, as Jean Seznec has demonstrated to us, the 'survival of the pagan gods' was effected – the historical, the physical and the moral[18] – Reynolds emphasizes the physical to the virtual exclusion of the other two. Let me quote a few passages from his essay:

> I will graunt they have in their Poesies, as I have said mingled much Morality with their Ethick doctrines. . . . Yet questionlesse infinite many more of their fables then these, (though even these and the rest of this kind want not among our best Mythologians their Physick as well as Ethick meanings), as all those of their gods and goddesses, with their powers and dignities, and all passage of affinity and commerce betweene themselves, and betweene them and others, were (as I have said before) made to meane meere matter of Nature, and in no possibility of Sense to bee wrested to the doctrine of Manners, unlesse a man will withall bee so inhumane as to allow all those riotts, rapes, murders, adulteries, incestes, and those *nefaria* and *nefanda,* unnaturally-seeming vices that they tell of them, to bee, litterally or Morally taken, fit examples of Manners or wholesome instructions for the lives of men to be levelled and directed by.[19]

He goes on to give us some examples:

> Whereas, on the contrary side . . . who can make that Rape of *Proserpine,* – whom her mother *Ceres* (that under the Species of Corne might include as well the whole Genus of

the Vegetable nature) sought so long for in the earth, – to meane other then the putrefaction and succeeding generation of the Seedes we commit to *Pluto*, or the earth, whome they make the God of wealth, calling him also *Dis quasi dives* (the same in Latine that *Pluto* is in Greeke), rich or wealthy, because all things have their originall from the earth, and returne to the earth againe? Or what can *Iupiters* blasting of his beloved *Semele,* after his having defloured her, and the wrapping of his sonne he got on her (*Bacchus* or wine) in his thigh after his production, meane other then the necessity of the Ayres heate to his birth in the generation, and (after a violent pressure and dilaceration of his mother the Grape) the like close imprisoning of him also, in a fit vessell, till he gaine his full maturity and come to be fit aliment?[20]

Reynolds is, of course, arguing for an allegorical reading of classical mythology – like Bacon in *De sapientia veterum* or Sir Thomas Browne in *The Garden of Cyrus.* (It is interesting to note that Reynolds takes Bacon to task for having suggested that allegorical interpretations were not intended by the ancient poets but were devised later; such a suggestion destroys his entire theory of poetry.) Like most English Metaphysical poets, Marvell avoids classical mythology, banishing, in Carew's phrase, 'the goodly exiled train / Of gods and goddesses',[21] and putting in their place a wealth of reference to Scripture. It doesn't make too much difference, from a point of view like that of Reynolds. The figures of pagan myth are nothing more than the figures of Scriptural history under different names:

all those *dij maiorum gentium* from Saturne to *Deucalions* deluge were but names for *Adam, Caine*, *Lamech*, and the rest of their successors to *Noahs* floud. . . . What other can *Hesiod's Pandora, the first and beautifullest of all women, by whome all evils were dispersed and spred upon the earth*, meane then *Moses* his *Eve*? . . . What was the Poets *Bacchus* but his *Noah*, or *Noacchus,* first corrupted to *Boacchus,* and after, by remooving a letter, to *Bacchus,* who (as *Moses* tells us of *Noah*) was the first likewise in their accompt that planted the vine and taught men the use of wines soone after the universall deluge?[22]

In other words, Scriptural figures and figures from pagan myth may alike be used to body forth the mysteries of nature.

But I have denied that *Upon Appleton House* is an allegorical poem in the sense of being a work in which implied terms may be substituted, in a one-to-one manner, for terms overtly present. How, then, can Reynolds's extravagantly allegorical theory help us to understand any of the workings of Marvell's poem? The point is, I believe, that Marvell, although sharing Reynolds's Neoplatonic view of poetry as an expression of the vital workings of nature, writes not as a poet of the Renaissance but as a poet of the Baroque: his imagination is, in the characteristic Baroque manner, essentially lyric–dramatic rather than narrative–didactic, and nature, in his great poem, is not something to expound but something to enact, not something to be understood but something to be participated in. *Upon Appleton House* is not an allegorical poem; it is a symbolic poem.

In the course of the meadow-sequence the narrator beholds the sea of the meadow, the actions of the mowers, the death of the rail, the reduction of the landscape to a simulacrum of the world before creation, and, finally, the coming of the chaos – and life-bringing flood. Conditioned by this ritual experience, he withdraws into the forest and, as he tells us in the transitional stanza, 'imbarks' himself, while the flood lasts, in the 'green, yet growing Ark' of the wood. By imbarking himself on an ark he stays above the destructive element of the water yet is at the same time, poetically, afloat on the water, in touch with its life-giving properties. Also, of course, when he 'imbarks' himself he covers himself with bark, becomes, as it were, one with the trees, the dark, dense, and all-embracing quality of which is powerfully evoked in the stanzas which follow. Throughout the forest-sequence the narrator is fused with nature – identified with the birds, the plants, and the trees (ll. 562–4); endowed with a knowledge of the language of nature (ll. 571–2); able to construe '*Sibyls* Leaves' (l. 577); become a 'Prelate of the Grove' (l. 592); and, finally, bound in woodbines and ecstatically crucified by brambles and briars (ll. 615–16). The meadow-sequence dealt with the enactment of life-giving chaos (the equivalent to the plot-confusions that make up the middle of a Shakespearean festive comedy); the forest-sequence deals with rebirth as experienced.

His consciousness enriched by the *participation mystique* of the meadow, he has, like the most vital of Shakespeare's comic heroes and heroines, undergone the loss of identity only to emerge with a stronger, re-defined identity. Having engaged the mysteries of nature, he is able, at length, to prophesy rather than merely to praise.

It is in this light, I think, that we should view the appearance of Maria, the final episode of the poem. Maria has been seen as many things – as Athena-Sophia, a figure of redemptive divine wisdom, as 'the archetypal pattern of beauty responsible for each separate manifestation of beauty in her own environment', as 'the Form of the world . . . the image of God restored', as, simultaneously, the propagatress of the Fairfax virtues and Andrew Marvell's girl-student.[23] She is all these things, and she is also, as the female principle, the epitome of all that has been learned in the meadow and the forest. In praising her, Marvell is able to praise, in finally appropriate terms, Appleton House and all that it symbolizes as a world where fertility and virtue are united:

'Tis *She* that to these Gardens gave
That wondrous Beauty which they have;
She streightness on the Woods bestows;
To *Her* the Meadow sweetness owes;
Nothing could make the River be
So Chrystal-pure but only *She*;
She yet more Pure, Sweet, Streight, and Fair,
Then Gardens, Woods, Meads, Rivers are.
(st. 87)

Notes

1 Colie, *'My Ecchoing Song': Andrew Marvell's Poetry of Criticism*, Princeton University Press, 1970, pp. 211–12.
2 Røstvig, *The Happy Man*, 2nd ed., Oslo, Norwegian Universities Press, 1962, I, p. 180.
3 *The Poems and Letters of Andrew Marvell*, ed. H. M. Margoliouth, 2nd ed., Oxford, The Clarendon Press, 1952, I, p. 233.

4 Allen, *Image and Meaning*, rev. ed., Baltimore, The Johns Hopkins Press, 1968, pp. 201–12.
5 Ibid., p. 209.
6 Ibid., pp. 208–9; Røstvig, as above (note 2), p. 189.
7 Colie, as above (note 1), p. 202; Frank J. Warnke, 'Play and Metamorphosis in Marvell's Poetry', *Studies in English Literature*, V (1965), i, p. 30.
8 Ibid.
9 *Homo Ludens*, English trans., Boston, Mass., Beacon Press, 1955, p. 116.
10 Colie, as above (note 1), p. 242.
11 Ibid., p. 201; E. R. Curtius, *European Literature and the Latin Middle Ages*, trans. W. R. Trask, New York, Pantheon, 1953, pp. 94–8.
12 Eliade, *Cosmos and History*, trans. W. R. Trask, New York, Harper, 1959, p. 88.
13 Ibid., p. 63.
14 Røstvig, as above (note 2), p. 180.
15 Allen, as above (note 4), pp. 187–225; Røstvig, as above (note 2), pp. 172–90; Colie, as above (note 1), pp. 181–294.
16 See Frank J. Warnke, *Versions of Baroque*, New Haven, Conn., Yale University Press, 1972, pp. 90–129.
17 *Shakespeare's Festive Comedy*, Princeton University Press, 1959.
18 *The Survival of the Pagan Gods*, trans. Barbara F. Sessions, Princeton University Press, 1972.
19 *Mythomystes*, in J. E. Spingarn, *Critical Essays of the Seventeenth Century*, Bloomington, Indiana University Press, 1957 (first published 1907), I, p. 169.
20 Ibid., p. 170.
21 In his 'Elegy upon the Death of the Dean of Paul's, Dr John Donne'.
22 Reynolds, as above (note 19), p. 175. Røstvig, as above (note 2), pp. 157–9, suggests Reynolds's relevance to Marvell but does not discuss *Upon Appleton House* in that connection.
23 Allen, as above (note 4), pp. 220–5; Rostvig, as above (note 2), p. 189; Barbara K. Lewalski, *Donne's Anniversaries and the Poetry of Praise*, Princeton University Press, 1973, p. 367; Warnke, as above (note 16), pp. 121–2.

12

Marvell as religious poet

Barbara Kiefer Lewalski

Andrew Marvell has written only a handful of lyrics which can be called religious or devotional in any strict sense, but these few are among his most impressive poems, remarkable even in an era noted for its magnificent religious poetry. A religious lyric, I take it, must treat centrally and seriously the speaker's stance towards or relationship with God. This definition eliminates from the category several of Marvell's poems which make significant use of Biblical allusions or theological concepts but which are fundamentally about something else – e.g. the nature of man or of the good life ('A Dialogue between the Soul and Body', 'The Garden', *Upon Appleton House*); the losses and pain of the fallen condition as experienced by fully dramatized pastoral personae ('The Nymph complaining', 'The Mower's Song', 'Damon the Mower'); the somewhat comic misconceptions of religious truth by naïve shepherds ('Thyrsis and Dorinda'). Setting aside such poems, we find the canon of Marvell's religious lyrics to be comprised of just those poems which the contemporary editor placed first (no doubt for this very reason) in the posthumous first edition of the *Miscellaneous Poems*: 'A Dialogue Between The Resolved Soul, and Created Pleasure', 'On a Drop of Dew' (with its Latin counterpart, 'Ros'), 'The Coronet', 'Eyes and Tears', 'Bermudas', and 'Clorinda and Damon'.[1]

We have learned how to respond to witty religious poems – Donne's outrageous conceits or Herbert's hieroglyphs – but Marvell's religious poems create difficulties of a different order, because of large uncertainties about their purpose, mode, and meaning. One problem is their discreteness: they seem unrelated to each other, and they are certainly not linked together through the familiar seventeenth-century meditative mode, in which a single, self-conscious, self-probing speaker is understood to be expressing his various spiritual emotions and states of soul in various poems. Also, few as they are, Marvell's religious poems represent a very wide range of contemporary genres – meditation, emblem poem, debate, pastoral eclogue, hymn of praise – and they often call upon the données of genre and the familiar store of Biblical allusions, tropes, and symbols in disconcerting ways. We might be tempted to regard these poems simply as generic and thematic experiments were it not for their evident seriousness of tone and subject.

My question here is whether Marvell's religious poems, taken together, exhibit characteristics which give them some coherence as a group, and impart to him a distinct identity as a religious poet. The movement of criticism in the past decade or so from consideration of individual poems to comprehensive synthesis has produced several versions of the essential Marvell: Toliver's Platonist–Puritan who presents, through dialectic, multiple and ironic perspectives on nature and art; Ellrodt's metaphysical poet who views reality in terms of balance and antithesis rather than unifying paradox; Cullen's and Friedman's pastoralist who makes extensive and various use of pastoral idiom and, more fundamentally, of the pastoral mode as a means of viewing nature and art from different perspectives; Berthoff's allegorist who presents under a variety of allegorical guises the resolved soul confronting the dilemmas of its life in time; and, perhaps most suggestively, Colie's supremely sophisticated artist whose poems are themselves critiques of the generic stances and assumptions carried by their forms.[2] Such studies, and most recently Annabel Patterson's account of the Protestant poetics implicit in 'The Coronet' and 'Bermudas',[3] provide a basis for an exercise in synthesis specifically directed to the religious poems.

I suggest that Marvell's six religious poems are characterized by the following qualities. First, all of them focus upon the dilemma created by the Christian's simultaneous life in two spheres, the order of nature and the order of grace, and together they present a full range of possible Christian responses to that dilemma. These are: Christian warfare against and conquest over all the goods of nature ('The Resolved Soul'); firm, unyielding resistance to the pollutions of the natural order ('On a Drop of Dew'); renunciation and sacrifice of natural gifts and their products as inevitably corrupt ('The Coronet'); repentance as a means to clearer vision about the natural order and its goods ('Eyes and Tears'); conversion of all aspects of the natural world to Christian meaning and use ('Clorinda and Damon'); and thanksgiving for a singular providential example of the restoration of nature by grace to its Edenic state ('Bermudas').

Second, despite the thematic congruence suggested by this formulation, Marvell's religious poems are not allegories of the Christian soul meeting its dilemma in various ways, nor yet are they simply six possible aesthetic variations on a single theme. Rather, each particular Christian response requires the poet to find an appropriate art in which to embody that response, leading him in the several poems to quite different generic choices, poetic strategies, and stances towards audience and material. There are always three, or perhaps really four, terms to be considered in these poems: nature, grace, and the art produced by or proper to each order.

Third, in these religious poems the basic dichotomy, nature and grace, and the various antitheses related to it – body and soul, flesh and spirit, this world and heaven, the fallen and the Edenic state – are very sharply drawn, but yet the resolutions achieved (in contrast to such poems as 'A Dialogue between the Soul and Body' or 'The Definition of Love') seem finally unambiguous, inevitable, and satisfying. This is so because the resolutions are fully adequate to the poems' complexities, and provide welcome release from the great tension generated by the poems' antitheses. Such resolution and release are provided in a number of literary ways – through the management of tone, through a magnificently apt image or symbol, through typology – but in almost every case these devices also open the poem out to the future, as the only locus for the full and complete resolution of the human dilemma.

'The Coronet' invites consideration first, because of its direct thematic concern with the problems inherent in writing religious poetry, and because this poem stands at one pole, the harshest, on

Marvell's scale of poetic responses to the nature–grace antithesis, proposing the renunciation and sacrifice of all that pertains to or results from the flawed natural order and from corrupted human nature. The poem is related to a popular Protestant meditative kind, an analysis of the motives and motions of the sinful self;[4] and the generic choice results (uniquely in Marvell's religious poems) in the speaker making himself and his dilemma as fallen man and Christian poet the very centre of his poem. Specifically, the poem is a member of a special sub-genre of seventeenth-century meditative poetry, poems in which the speaker strives to present a wreath or crown of poetic praises to God and in so doing confronts problems arising from Protestant convictions about the worthlessness of all human acts or arts or works in God's sight, and Protestant anxieties about adulterating divine truth and humble devotion by human art and artfulness.[5] But the issue in 'The Coronet' is broader still: when the speaker apostrophizes himself as 'foolish man' he recognizes that his special problem as Christian poet results directly and inevitably from his situation as fallen man corrupted by the 'Serpent old'. The question then becomes whether, and how, an art which must be derived from the fallen natural order can find any place in the order of grace.

The wreath / crown poems collectively recall an emblem figure often positioned among the final plates in popular sixteenth- and seventeenth-century emblem books, signifying the tribute of praise accorded to notable achievement and, often, the reward of the Christian who perseveres to the end.[6] Donne's seven interlinked 'La Corona' sonnets create and offer to Christ a poetic crown interweaving the two primary modes of Christian devotion, prayer and praise; for this poetic crown, the speaker begs as reward Christ's crown of glory gained by his thorny crown, and renounces the crown of bays which rewards poetry in this world.[7] The speaker of these sonnets is confident of his motives: the crown is woven in his 'low devout melancholie', and it is not tainted with sinfulness or deceit, being the product of his 'muses white sincerity'. Moreover, the poetic sequence is a fully achieved crown of prayer and praise: by repeating the last line of one sonnet as the first line of the next, each sonnet is interlaced with that which precedes and follows it; the final line of the last sonnet repeats the opening line of the first sonnet to complete the round; and subtle uses of repetition, ploce, and antithesis weave lines and half-lines together within individual poems and in the entire sequence. Herbert's twelve-line poem, 'A Wreath', is also devised as an emblematic 'Wreathed garland of deserved praise' for Christ, by means of a closely interwoven structure of repeated sounds, words, and phrases.[8] But the speaker soon recognizes that this winding structure is both emblematic of and a product of his own 'crooked winding wayes', which contrast all too sharply with the straight path properly emblematic of God's ways. Despite this recognition, the speaker completes and offers his wreath, even as he prays for the simplicity and straightness of life which could, paradoxically, enable him to replace it at some future time with a more appropriate and more valuable circlet: 'then shall I give / For this poore wreath, give thee a crown of praise'. Vaughan's 'The Wreath' is less closely woven than Herbert's poem, but its final eleven lines are formed into a poetic wreath by means of repeated sounds, words, and phrases;[9] Vaughan's speaker contrasts this 'twin'd wreath of *grief* and *praise*' (the appropriate tribute to Christ's crucifixion, woven from the matter of his own stormy, wintry days) with the joyful praises he will someday sing, amid 'cloudless Quires' and 'without tears'.

Marvell's 'The Coronet' relates itself self-consciously to these earlier poetic wreaths, but incorporates a harsher judgment upon and a more sweeping renunciation of the inevitably flawed natural order and all its artistic products. By some repetitions of words and sounds, the speaker begins in the first eight lines to weave, rather loosely, his poetic crown:

When for the Thorns with which I long, too long,
    With many a piercing wound,
    My Saviours head have crown'd,
I seek with Garlands to redress that Wrong:
    Through every Garden, every Mead,
I gather flow'rs (my fruits are only flow'rs)
    Dismantling all the fragrant Towers
That once adorn'd my Shepherdesses head.
(ll. 1–8)

At this point, however, he abruptly gives over the wreath-weaving. Some of the misapprehensions inherent in the misguided effort simply to transfer to sacred uses the materials and structures of secular pastoral are intimated in these lines: the supposition that the wounds made by the crown of thorns can be 'redressed' (made up for, bandaged, covered over) by a wreath of flowers; the supposition that pastoral flowers (the product of corrupt nature and once used in ostentatious elaborate headpieces for shepherdesses)[10] can be appropriate for this sacred purpose; the supposition that flowers of rhetoric (rather than the fruits of good works which ought properly to spring from the regenerate soul) can be a pleasing offering to Christ. The speaker now voices his culminating – and prideful – self-delusion: that this poetic wreath made from 'all my store' will be a richer chaplet than any yet worn by the 'king of Glory'. This statement reveals a flaw much more serious than the expectation that art derived from fallen nature (flowers, pastoral conventions, flowers of rhetoric) can do this; the speaker now perceives that the 'Serpent old' (the original sin of pride) is so intricately folded around and disguised among the flowers in 'wreaths of Fame and Interest' as to seem to provide the very frame of the wreath – even as a serpent's body provides the frame for a wreath of fruits and flowers in an emblem figure by Paradin.[11] At this point the speaker admits his folly and gives over the attempt to bridge by an art based on nature and human nature the chasm between nature and grace: a coronet made of 'mortal Glory' can only debase 'Heaven's Diadem'.

The speaker considers two possible resolutions of his dilemma, both of which depend, as they must, upon Christ's action rather than his own, and specifically upon Christ's role as destroyer of the old serpent – the antitype of Hercules, the serpent-crushing seed of the woman. Christ might unbind the serpent from the poetic wreath, 'his slipp'ry knots at once untie, / And disintangle all his winding Snare'. Though this would clearly be an enterprise of great difficulty, and quite unlikely to be accomplished 'at once' because of the serpent's involvement in the very structure of the wreath, the art resulting from such unbinding would presumably present nature restored by grace – perhaps indeed a sanctified pastoral such as 'Bermudas'. The more probable resolution is the crushing beneath Christ's heel, as the spoils of his victory, both the serpent himself and that which contains him – the wreath's 'curious frame':

> Or shatter too with him my curious frame:
> And let these wither, so that he may die,
> Though set with Skill and chosen out with Care.
> That they, while Thou on both their Spoils dost tread,
> May crown thy Feet, that could not crown thy Head.
> (ll. 22–6)

Though these lines seem to repudiate both this poem and the possibility of sacred poetry, the speaker's willing and uncompromising stance of sacrifice at last resolves the dilemma in terms consonant with its complexity. As Christ's passion, his crown of thorns, was the means of his conquest over the 'Serpent old', so the speaker's offer to sacrifice poetic wreath and self is finally a proper tribute to, and a mimesis (as far as may be) of that sacrifice. As such it intimates that life and art may be redeemed. As Christ's crown of thorns was transmuted into a glorious heavenly diadem truly fit for the King of Glory, so the final line of Marvell's poem suggests that a poetic crown, produced in some paradoxical way from flowers detached from the curious frame and by the agency of Christ's treading rather than his own curious setting out, might become a humble crown for Christ's feet. The repetition of the word 'crown' in the last line – 'May crown thy Feet, that could not crown thy head' – marks a return to the weaving technique of the first eight lines, and this device of closure reinforces the possibility that a new and properly humble poetic crown for Christ may be produced on these new terms. Perhaps it is not too far-fetched to suggest that a poetic crown of this sort might involve poems on just the Marvellian topics: the virtuous soul's conquest over or resistance to the goods of nature in mimesis of Christ's conquest over the old serpent; the sacrifice of self and works in mimesis of Christ's sacrifice; the analysis of penitence and conversion as a means to view and value the natural order rightly, in relation to the order of grace.

In 'A Dialogue, Between The Resolved Soul, and Created Pleasure', the response to the nature–grace dichotomy is Christian warfare against and victory over all the sensory pleasures and created goods pertaining to the order of nature. The speaker understands that the combat is designed to exhibit and prove the soul's elect state, its participation in the order of grace: 'Now, if thou bee'st that thing Divine, / In this day's Combat let it shine' (ll. 7–8). The battle proceeds by thrust and parry, temptation and rejoinder: pleasure first invites indulgence in the sensory delights of taste, touch, smell, and sight, associating these respectively with sins of gluttony, sloth, presumption, and pride; the climactic appeal (not in itself sinful) is to the pleasures of music and verse ('sweet Chordage') offered to the sense of hearing. When all these are categorically refused, the goods of the Platonic *scala* are offered – beauty in women, wealth, glory, knowledge. When these are also scorned, the soul's resounding victory is proclaimed by a heavenly chorus.

By its title and dialogic form the poem is related to one variety of medieval soul-body debate, which a virtuous soul overcomes and chastises a guilty and spiritually obtuse body.[12] Marvell has also, in his 'Dialogue between the Soul and Body', a witty and complex version of the other major variety of such debate, that in which the Soul shares guilt with the Body and often deserves more blame. Other seventeenth-century dialogic poems related to these kinds include Herbert's 'Dialogue-Anthem' between the Christian and Death, and Vaughan's 'Death', 'Resurrection and Immortality', and 'The Evening-watch', between the Soul and a naïve or ignorant Body. Normally, such poems present the collision of intellectual positions, with one or the other interlocutor winning a rhetorical victory. In 'The Resolved Soul', however, these generic features are transformed almost beyond recognition by the associations evoked by the controlling topos of Christian warfare, introduced in the opening lines and developed throughout:

> Courage my Soul, now learn to wield
> The weight of thine immortal Shield.
> Close on thy Head thy Helmet bright.
> Ballance thy Sword against the Fight.
> See where an Army, strong as fair,
> With silken Banners spreads the air.
> Now if thou bee'st that thing Divine,
> In this day's Combat let it shine:
> And shew that Nature wants an Art
> To conquer one resolved Heart.

The *Miles Christi,* wielding the arms of a Christian man described in Ephesians 6: 13–17, is a familiar figure in contemporary sermon and tract literature as well as in allegorical romance – e.g. Red Cross Knight, Christian in *Pilgrim's Progress.* But the topos is surprising in lyric treatments of temptation. What could be less martial than Herbert's light-hearted little allegory, 'The Quip', whose speaker meets all temptation by a lilting refrain which casts all responsibility upon Christ:

> First Beautie crept into a rose,
> Which when I pluckt not, Sir, said she,
> Tell me, I pray, Whose hands are those?
> *But thou shalt answer, Lord, for me.*
> (ll. 5–8)

By contrast, Marvell's poem is characterized by the pervasive warfare metaphor, the martial tone, and generic allusions to similar temptation episodes in allegorical romance and brief epic (Spenser's Guyon in the Cave of Mammon, Christ tempted by Satan in Giles Fletcher's *Christs Victorie, and Triumph*, and in Milton's *Paradise Regained*). Accordingly, the opening lines do not prepare us for a meditation in which the speaker will analyse his own performance in the battle with temptation; rather they display a curiously detached though hardly disinterested speaker assuming the posture of a spectator at a knightly joust or gladiatorial contest, advising and cheering on one of the combatants. After this first speech he is not heard from again, and the Soul appears as a separate entity, an exemplary character whose paradigmatic trial pertains to all Christian souls. By eschewing the meditative stance the speaker both universalizes the encounter and avoids seeming to celebrate himself.

The Soul's categorical, iconoclastic rejections ought to seem harsh and anti-humanistic. That they do not may be explained in part by the fact that the Soul's victory is not only a conquest of grace over nature, but of one mode of art over another. The combat is designed to demonstrate that 'Nature wants an Art / To conquer one resolved Heart'; in fact it demonstrates also that the gracious soul has an art to overcome the finest art which nature, in the role of created pleasure, can produce.[13] Pleasure's art is exhibited in trochaic heptasyllables, evoking the qualities and delights of the various senses and worldly goods. Tempting the sense of touch, Pleasure invites:

On these downy Pillows lye,
Whose soft Plumes will thither fly:
On these Roses strow'd so plain
Lest one Leaf thy Side should strain.
(ll. 19–22)

The Soul's art, the art of the order of grace, is displayed in octosyllabic couplets, epigrammatic in their point and brevity but intimating precisely what sins Pleasure's offers entail, and indicating also the Soul's own higher values – often by punning on the very terms supplied by Pleasure. Answering the above temptation, the Soul's trenchant couplet glances not only at the sinful sloth the offer conceals, but also points to the more important rest sought by the spirit:

My gentler Rest is on a Thought,
Conscious of doing what I ought.
(ll. 23–4)

Again, answering the temptation addressed to the olefactory sense and associated with the presumptuous enjoyment of incense proper only to God, the Soul's witty rhyme connects the object offered and the sin:

A Soul that knowes not to presume
Is Heaven's and its own perfume.
(ll. 29–30)

Or again, responding to the Glory temptation, the Soul by the neatest of antitheses can turn Pleasure's offer of half the world as friend and half as slave back on itself:

What Friends, if to my self untrue?
What Slaves, unless I captive you?
(ll. 67–8)

The Soul punningly refuses to be bound by the 'sweet Chordage' of nature's sensory music, but it perfects its own brilliant and witty plain-style epigrams. These couplets display the ease and elegance of the Soul's victory, causing us to delight in a victory won by superior art.

Another source of satisfaction, indeed exhilaration, in the combat and its resolution lies in the martial *élan* sustained throughout the fast-paced, highly stylized exchanges. The excitement rises to a first climax as a heavenly chorus (of angels and saints, we assume) celebrates in ringing tones the Soul's victory over the senses and then encourages it to further efforts: '*Earth cannot shew so brave a Sight / As when a single Soul does fence / The Batteries of alluring Sense, / . . . Then persevere: for still new Charges sound*' (ll. 45–9). Rising to a higher pitch, the Chorus celebrates the soul's final and total victory with a rousing triumphal hymn:

Triumph, triumph victorious Soul:
The World has not one Pleasure more:
The rest does lie beyond the Pole,
And is thine everlasting Store.
(ll. 75–8)

As the poem comes to rest upon the term, 'store', the dichotomy is resolved and the tension is suddenly exploded: having scorned created pleasures, the Resolved Soul is now granted all the rest – the uncreated pleasures which cannot be enumerated or analysed or gained piecemeal, but simply and wholly and for ever enjoyed.

In 'On a Drop of Dew' the nature–grace dichotomy evokes the response of anxious resistance to the pollutions of the natural order so as to preserve spiritual integrity. The soul in this poem has nothing whatever of the martial or combative about it: emblematized by a dew drop holding its spherical shape carefully intact (by surface tension) as it lies within a blowing rose, the soul is tense, anxious, fearful, fragile – an exile in the material and temporal order, desiring only to return unblemished to its proper spiritual sphere. Though this is one of Marvell's most Platonic poems, it is invested with profoundly Christian meaning by the symbolism of the manna and by the image of the soul's release, not through its own striving but through the pity of, and into the glories of, the 'Almighty Sun'.

The emblem genre is employed with stunning success in this

poem, in that the fit between the precisely described *pictura* (the dew) and the *significatio* (the soul) seems well-nigh perfect, inviting the supposition that there must be close emblem-book analogues for Marvell's poem. In fact this is not the case: the closest analogue, the Protean dew in Henry Hawkins's *Parthenia Sacra*, has associations diametrically opposed to Marvell's dew drops, in that Hawkins's dew takes on the colouration and quality of everything around it:

> The *Deawes* . . . wil easily comply with everie thing they meete with; and likely seeme to put-on the forme, the garb, and qualities of every one. . . . It is the *Deaw* . . . that metamorphosies itself, heere into flowers, there into leaves, and then to fruits in sundrie sorts; it is even the *Protheus* and *Chamaeleon* of creatures, clothing itself with the liverie of al the rarest things; heer scarlet, there milk, heer the emerald, the carbuncle, gold, silver, and the rest.[14]

Marvell may well have intended a correction of Hawkins's emblematics, but more important, he obviously intended and accomplished a revision of certain emblem-poem conventions, notably the employment of a meditative or hortatory stance. Several of Vaughan's poems – 'The Showre', 'The Storm', 'The Tempest', 'The Palm-tree', 'The Timber', 'The Rain-bow', 'The Water-fall' – are devised as meditations. As does Marvell, Vaughan's speaker takes an object in nature as emblem of divine truth and interprets its signification, but unlike Marvell, he applies that meaning to his own spiritual state, as meditative theory prescribes.[15] Again, while Marvell's hortatory opening line, 'See how the Orient Dew', may suggest that the speaker intends to draw out specific lessons for his audience (as Herbert does in 'The Church-floore'), in fact he does no such thing. To be sure, there is a lesson implied regarding the soul's proper stance towards the seductions of nature, but the speaker gives no direct advice to others, and makes no application to himself. Instead, he presents himself as a careful observer of nature and its meanings, and this disinterested, detached stance invites confidence that his reading of the relation of dew drop and rose, spirit and matter, truly presents the nature of things.

The dichotomy between the two orders seems to force distressingly rigorous and sweeping rejections. The dew drop in the blowing rose is placed within the very symbol of earthly beauty and sweetness and love (though also of transience), but it 'slights' and scarcely touches the purple flower, holding itself globe-like, tear-like, trembling, 'unsecure', until it is inspired back to the skies by the warm sun. The soul, similarly placed in a 'humane flow'r . . . / Shuns the sweet leaves and blossoms green', straining always to return to that 'clear Fountain of Eternal Day' whence it came (ll. 20–3). Yet for all this, Marvell bridges and at length resolves the nature–grace dichotomy and the steadily mounting tension it creates, in poetic ways which are satisfying and pleasing. For one thing, he emphasizes the perfect fit between the emblem in nature and the soul by a structural balance in which eighteen lines describe the dew drop and eighteen lines the soul, and the language of each description translates precisely to the other. We can recognize the effect of such emphasis upon the way in which the natural and spiritual orders are seen to be related, by examining the quite different development in Vaughan's 'The Water-fall', which J. B. Leishman rightly identified as the closest contemporary emblem-poem analogue to Marvell's 'On a Drop of Dew'.[16] Vaughan's speaker also finds many analogies between his emblematic waterfall and the soul's situation – the murmuring, hesitating, falling water images mankind's fear of death; the circularity of the water's flow images the soul's restoration to the stream of light whence it came; the falling water breaking upon the banks intimates man's passage to an unseen state. But at length Vaughan repudiates the nature emblem as wholly unable to represent the soul's final situation:

> O my invisible estate,
> My glorious liberty, still late!
> Thou art the Channel my soul seeks,
> Not this with Cataracts and Creeks.
> (ll. 37–40)

However, Marvell's dew drop can figure every stage of the soul's life, including its final, glorious exhumation. This fact, reinforced by the pervasive imagery of sphericity which links dew drop, soul, world, the heavenly spheres, and the Almighty Sun, forges links between the natural and spiritual orders on the basis of analogy and correspondence, which span the gulf that divides those orders.

Second, both dew drop and soul are involved in artful creation, not merely passive and tense resistance: they respond to and seek to reflect a beauty and brightness far surpassing the material beauty of roses or bodies. The dew drop attempts to encapsulate that higher beauty within itself: 'and in its little Globes Extent, / Frames as it can its native Element' (ll. 7–8). The soul's artful movement attempts a mimesis of, response to, and reflection of the eternal beauty, the heavenly light of which its nature partakes; it 'Does, in its pure and circling thoughts, express / The greater Heaven in an Heaven less' (ll. 25–6). Moreover, the openness and love characterizing the soul's movements and its responsiveness to heaven are shown, through a series of antitheses, to be far more potent than the more negative emotions dictating resistance to nature:

> In how coy a Figure wound,
> Every way it turns away:
> So the World excluding round,
> Yet receiving in the Day.
> Dark beneath, but bright above:
> Here disdaining, there in Love.
> (ll. 27–32)

Subsequent lines render in almost kinesthetic terms the soul's freedom and grace of movement as it strains towards heaven – rather like a ballerina *en pointe*:

> How loose and easie hence to go:
> How girt and ready to ascend.
> Moving but on a point below,
> It all about does upward bend
> (ll. 33–6)

In the final two couplets both dew drop and soul are brilliantly and perfectly assimilated to the overarching and authoritative symbol of the Biblical, dew-like manna showered upon the Israelites in the desert: it came at dawn as 'small as the hoar-frost' (calling up associations of chillness), and it retained its form only in that cold state, for 'when the sun waxed hot, it melted'.[17] This

Scriptural symbol authenticates the speaker's interpretation of his emblem from nature, and the three-way analogy suddenly releases all the tensions of the poem. Dew, soul, and manna, which have alike been tense, wary, self-enclosed, chill, and congealed on earth in order to preserve their integrity, now dissolve joyously into the essential fire and light and glory of God:

> Such did the Manna's sacred Dew destil;
> White, and intire, though congeal'd and chill.
> Congeal'd on Earth: but does, dissolving, run
> Into the Glories of th'Almighty Sun.
> (ll. 37–40)

'Eyes and Tears' explores penitence as the fitting Christian response to fallen nature from the standpoint of the order of grace and, specifically, as the only means to see nature accurately and value it properly. The dichotomy between eyes and tears or, more properly, between the use of eyes for seeing and for weeping, corresponds to that between nature and grace. Seeing is of the order of nature simply: all use eyes to 'see, or sleep'; but only human eyes wise enough to do so can weep. As the opening lines suggest, tears are dictated by nature itself – 'How wisely Nature did decree, / With the same Eyes to weep and see!' – but penitence promotes the blurring and transformation of natural seeing by weeping, a process which leads to truer and more penetrating spiritual vision of all things.

This is also a species of emblem-poem. It invites comparison with the most famous English example of the mode, Crashaw's 'The Weeper',[18] a series of elaborate conceits on that favourite Counter-Reformation saint of penitence, the weeping Magdalen. But the differences are more remarkable than the similarities. In Crashaw's poem there is no tension, as in Marvell, between eyes and tears: both have the same qualities and value as emblems of the Magdalen's sorrow for sin. The eyes are 'Thawing crystall', 'Heavens of ever-falling starres', nests of milky doves, faithful fountains, walking baths, compendious oceans, weeping gates, mines of silver. The tears are stars, pearls, breakfasts for cherubs, balsam, watery blossoms, wine for heaven's feast, floods, beads. Crashaw's emblem *pictura* showing the saint with weeping eyes and winged, enflamed heart provides a suitable key to that poem's terms. But for Marvell's poem, which gives only a single quatrain to the Magdalen as an eminent example of the right use of eyes and tears,[19] the appropriate visual emblem would be a disembodied eye or eyes with tear drops falling from it – rather like the large, disembodied, weeping eye above a landscape in Henry Peacham's emblem collection, *Minerva Britanna.*[20] Moreover, in Marvell's poem, 'eyes' and 'tears' are opposing terms, representing the dichotomy between natural and spiritual vision, and the poem's images are logical and spare rather than sensuous and ornate.

In this poem also the speaker's stance in regard to his central emblem does not quite meet our expectation that emblem-poems be meditative or didactic. The poem obviously is not (as in Crashaw) a meditation upon the Magdalen's penitence, nor yet upon the speaker's own spiritual state – though he does draw upon his own experience in white, red, and green gardens to support his observations, and he applies his conclusions to himself, as Protestant meditative theory requires. But he does not probe his own soul and psyche here (as he does, for example, in 'The Coronet'), and he makes no effort to stir up his affections to grief and sorrow for sin – the expected culmination of a meditation on penitence. Rather, he remains curiously distanced as he analyses his disembodied emblem, and recommends tears to himself as the appropriate intellectual response to that analysis. As in the poem 'On a Drop of Dew', this strategy serves to reinforce his authority as an observer of things as they are: he seems himself to embody that clear spiritual vision which is the primary concern of the poem and which provides the resolution of the eyes–tears dichotomy.

The opposition between the two uses of eyes and the two kinds of vision resulting from them is emphasized throughout most of the poem. Natural eyes, looking at corrupted nature, must necessarily be deluded by false values, worldliness, vanity: their objects are vain, sight is self-deluding, heights must needs be measured in a false angle; the world only appears fair. Humble tears, falling downward, measure things better with their 'wat'ry Lines and Plummets' (l. 8), and properly weigh out in sorrows the cost of every joy. Tears truly reveal the essence of things: all laughter turns to tears; jewels melt into tear-pendants; worldly gardens yield only the honey of tears, even the all-seeing Sun in distilling the world finds its essence to be 'only Showers', which he draws back to himself. The conclusion is that weeping – seen as eye-bath and purge – is the only means to gain a true perspective on nature:

> Yet happy they whom Grief doth bless,
> They weep the more, and see the less;
> And, to preserve their Sight more true,
> Bath still their Eyes in their own Dew.
> (ll. 25–8)

The Magdalen exemplifies a further, more creative, power in tears – to approach and somehow to appropriate the divine order. Paradoxically dissolving her 'captivating eyes' in tears, Mary forges from them 'liquid Chaines' to 'fetter her Redeemer's feet'; she thereby binds to herself by tears the God she could not possibly see or attach to herself with eyes. Subsequent stanzas reinforce the value and power of tear-drenched eyes: they are pregnant with more good than chaste wombs or full-bellied sails; they quench lovers' desires and the hissing lightning of divine judgments; incense has worth only because its wisps of perfume rise to heaven as tears, and stars are only valued as 'Tears of Light'.

This last assertion intensifies the dichotomy by focusing upon the contrasting perceptions of natural beauty dictated by the eyes of nature and those dictated by the tears of grace. But at the same time it points towards a resolution of the problem, in that the true essence of beauty (a vital matter for the poet) may be known only through penitence. The resolution begins with the speaker's desire to transform his eyes into ever more abundant and active sources of water, which, by degrees, can be wholly transmuted into the water they produce: his eyes should become clouds dissolving drop by drop; or two fountains trickling down; or two floods that 'o'return and drown' their banks; and finally, streams which entirely overflow their springs. Building upon this progression, the concluding lines wholly satisfy the terms of the problem by means of oxymorons which collapse the nature–grace dichotomy into paradoxical unity, linguistic and conceptual. Eyes and tears are now identified, transmuted into each other, and take over one another's functions; and in this way the speaker can achieve true vision:

Thus let your Streams o'reflow your Springs,
Till Eyes and Tears be the same things:
And each the other's difference bears;
These weeping Eyes, those seeing Tears.
(ll. 53–6)

In 'Clorinda and Damon' the response explored is one of conversion – from a life defined entirely by the pastoral goods of the order of nature to one exhibiting the spiritual goods and values of the order of grace. Several conversions are displayed in the poem. Damon alludes to his recent conversion when '*Pan* met me', and every word he speaks is dictated by that transforming experience. His dialogue with Clorinda is the means to, and results in, her own conversion to those new spiritual values. And the dialogue between these two reinterprets familiar pastoral emblems, converting them from the meanings they customarily carry in the pastoral world to spiritual significations which testify that the pastoral world also belongs to and reveals God. The final conversion is that of pastoral art: though Damon's oat is too slender to present Pan's message it does sound his praises, and Clorinda's voice joins the song in harmony with the entire choir of nature.

This poem presents a more humane resolution of the dichotomy between nature and grace than do the poems heretofore discussed: the opposition seems less severe, and nature is more amenable to restoration and dedication to gracious ends. In part this more hopeful attitude is dictated by the response explored, conversion, and in part by the genre chosen, the pastoral eclogue. The generic choice permits the poet to develop his subject in relation to particular characters whose conversion produces changes in their vantage-point upon nature, rather than in terms of abstractions representing the two orders themselves. Moreover, pastoral speakers can achieve a simpler resolution than that available to the sophisticated, self-analytic poet-speaker of 'The Coronet'. Given these considerations, we are not forced to conclude that this must be an early poem because it looks towards conversion and reconciliation, but only that, once again, Marvell has achieved a fine meshing of subject, stance, and genre. The generic choice relates the poem to a very wide contemporary literary field. As a pastoral eclogue utilizing debate and persuasion in discussions of 'Great Pan' and of Christian pastoral values, the poem most obviously recalls *The Shepherd's Calendar*, particularly the May, July, and September eclogues. Moreover, specific verbal allusions relate the 'grassy Scutcheon' Clorinda offers to Acrasia's Bower of Bliss, and associate the final pastoral song in which '*Caves eccho, and the Fountains ring*' (l. 28) with that exalted hymnic celebration of all nature's harmony, Spenser's *Epithalamium*.[21] Also, as Donald Friedman has acutely observed, the poem is an inversion of the pastoral 'persuasion to love':[22] instead of a passionate shepherd wooing a coy shepherdess to lie and live with him and prove all the pastoral pleasures, a passionate shepherdess invites a hitherto willing shepherd to continue in the usual way, only to find herself being persuaded through witty dialectic to 'meet' with him on quite other terms – those of Great Pan's values and praises. Finally, this dialogue invites comparison and contrast with other Marvellian dialogues which do not lead to comfortable resolutions: 'Thyrsis and Dorinda' in which the shepherds' naïvety leads them to seek Elysium through suicide rather than conversion and divine praises; and the 'Dialogue between the Soul and Body', which ends in a stalemate of recriminations concerning the evils each party brings to the other.

In 'Clorinda and Damon', the pastoral lovers' contrasting interpretations of emblematic objects in the familiar landscape emphasize the dichotomy between nature and grace, but this very contrast becomes the means of resolution, in that Damon's more adequate explanations rather transform than negate the signification of pastoral. To Clorinda's invitation to 'drive thy flocks this way', he alludes to their straying, and thereby to the Christian's responsibility to guard his own faculties from a similar state. To Clorinda's invitation to repose in a grassy and flowery meadow (Flora's scutcheon), wherein she proposes with idolatrous *double entendre* to offer flowers for Damon's 'Temples', he responds by echoing Isaiah and also a long line of pastoral lovers, 'Grass withers, and the Flow'rs too fade'.[23] Clorinda promptly makes the proper pastoral response to this sentiment – *Carpe floream* – directing Damon to a private cave nearby that is well suited for love. The cave, with its intimations of Plato's cave of illusions, is then subjected to several stichomythic reinterpretations: Damon associates it with common carnality – 'That Den'; Clorinda terms it the Temple of Love – 'Loves Shrine'; and Damon again, with reference to the spiritual effect of the act it would shelter, labels it 'Virtues Grave'. The sun is the next object of interpretation: Clorinda rejoices that the cave is safe from the heat of the sun, but Damon refers to the divine light that sun emblematizes – 'Not Heaven's Eye'. Clorinda then recalls a pleasing fountain which tinkles in the cave, and Damon alludes to the spiritual uses of fountains as emblems of baptismal washing and of the grace flowing forth from Christ: 'Might a Soul bath there and be clean, / Or slake its Drought?'[24] At this point Clorinda, thoroughly mystified, asks for explanation, and Damon laconically reports his conversion – '*Pan* met me'. Clorinda imitates the immediacy of that conversion in her own, and both see implications for their pastoral song as well as their life. Damon's poetic skill cannot rise to the heights needed to render Pan's words, but he is wisely content simply to sound Pan's name on his oat – and that sound of itself seems to win others to partake the song:

C. What did great *Pan* say?
D. Words that transcend poor Shepherds skill,
But He ere since my Songs does fill:
And his Name swells my slender Oate.
C. Sweet must *Pan* sound in *Damons* Note.
D. *Clorinda's* voice might make it sweet.
C. Who would not in *Pan's* Praises meet?
(ll. 20–6)

The simple concluding song resolves the nature–grace dichotomy pleasantly, for Clorinda and Damon do 'meet', albeit in Pan's praises rather than in their cave. Their song celebrates the perception the eclogue has worked towards, that to the converted spiritual vision all nature testifies of and celebrates God, so that the shepherds' life and art together with all the emblem-objects of pastoral nature are also caught up in that all-encompassing harmony. But the shepherd singers recognize also that their abilities, and nature's, to perceive and participate in that harmony arise not from their own skill but from divine inspiration:

Of *Pan* the flowry Pastures sing,
Caves eccho, and the Fountains ring.
Sing then while he doth us inspire;
For all the World is our *Pan's* Quire.
(ll. 27–30)

Marvell's 'Bermudas', with its fusion of travellers' exotic descriptions of the actual Summer Islands and the paradisiacal or millennial gardens of Biblical myth, has invited two quite contradictory interpretations. It is most often read as a celebration of the Bermudas as a Puritan paradise in which nature has been restored by a gracious Providence to near-Edenic conditions, and to which the Puritan inhabitants respond with a lovely psalm-like Hymn of Thanksgiving.[25] But some have read the poem ironically, finding warrant for this in the frame supplied by the first and last lines which distance speaker and reader from the singers; in the emphasis upon sensuous delights, personal righteousness, and material goods, which presumably differentiates the Bermudans' hymn from its psalmic models; and in the less-than-idyllic realities of Bermudan life which the hyperboles of the hymn might seem designed to recall – the Laudian sympathies of the majority of the inhabitants, the history of shipwrecks near the island, the dangers from whales, the disappointments over the paucity of ambergris and pearls.[26] Yet whatever the force of these considerations, the poem will not finally sustain an ironic reading: the exalted tone and exquisite beauty of the hymn is against it; so is the fact that in essential attitudes as well as details of language the hymn is modelled closely upon those psalms identified as Thanksgivings for God's Benefits;[27] so also is the fact that the speaker himself pronounces the hymn 'holy' and 'cheerful'. But we cannot ignore the perspective upon the singers and their hymn which the frame provides, or the fact that the psalm of thanksgiving and praise is not the speaker's psalm, or the profound ambiguities caused by tense changes and by the seeming confusion as to the location of the singers in relation to their island. The poem, I suggest, explores the Christian response of thanksgiving and praise for a vision of nature redeemed and transformed by grace, but all this is controlled by a typological perspective which points up the relation of, but also the distance between, present hopes and future realizations, types of Eden and the true antitypical millennial paradise.

The singers see their Bermudan paradise in typological terms as a recapitulation of Eden and as a version of the Garden of Canticles (understood allegorically to figure the Garden of the Church):

> He gave us this eternal Spring,
> Which here enamells every thing;
> And sends the Fowl's to us in care,
> On daily Visits through the Air.
> He hangs in shades the Orange bright,
> Like golden Lamps in a green Night.
> And does in the Pomgranates close,
> Jewels more rich than *Ormus* show's.
> He makes the Figs our mouths to meet;
> And throws the Melons at our feet.
> But Apples plants of such a price,
> No Tree could ever bear them twice.
> With Cedars, chosen by his hand,
> From *Lebanon,* he stores the Land.
> (ll. 13–26)

Here is imagery long associated with the topos of the Edenic garden – the eternal spring, the 'enamelled' and marvellously abundant fruits, the fowl in tributary service to man.[28] Some of it recalls the Genesis account of the glories of the creation pronounced good by God: the garden in Eden in which God planted 'every tree that is pleasant to the sight, and good for food'; the fowl brought to Adam for naming, the lights hung in the firmament of the heavens to give light in darkness, the apples (from the Tree of Life) absolutely unique in their provenance and value.[29] Other imagery – the figs, the cedars of Lebanon, the pomegranates enclosing rich jewels, the oriental sensuousness and lushness of the whole scene – recalls verses from Canticles: 'his fruit was sweet to my taste'; 'The fig tree putteth forth her green figs, and the vines with the tender grapes gave a good smell'; 'Thy plants are an orchard of pomegranates with pleasant fruit'; 'His countenance is as Lebanon, excellent as the cedars'.[30] Moreover, the singers' posture of journeying to a paradise from over the sea, singing thanksgivings ('What should we do but sing his Praise / That led us through the watry Maze', ll. 5–6), indicates that they see themselves as fulfilling Isaiah's millennial prophecies of deliverance (commonly applied by American Puritans to their own errand into the wilderness to find a new Promised Land):

> For the Lord shall comfort Zion: he will comfort all her waste places; and he will make her wilderness like Eden, and her desert like the garden of the Lord; joy and gladness shall be found therein, thanksgiving, and the voice of melody. . . .
>
> Art thou not it which hath dried the sea, the waters of the great deep; that hath made the depths of the sea a way for the ransomed to pass over?
>
> Therefore the redeemed of the Lord shall return, and come with singing unto Zion; and everlasting joy shall be upon their head.[31]

The song itself, with its numerous reminiscences of psalms of thanksgiving for benefits, relates this millennial and miraculous deliverance to God's ongoing providential care for his people, and asserts the continual duty of praise and thanksgiving according to the psalmic model. We are reminded of several thanksgivings for God's bounty in the earth's fruitfulness: 'He causeth the grass to grow for the cattle, and herb for the service of man . . . / And wine that maketh glad the heart of man . . . / The trees of the Lord are full of sap; the cedars of Lebanon, which he hath planted' (Psalm 104: 14–16). The fowl sent daily 'in care' recall the raven sent to Elijah and the quail sent to the Israelites in the wilderness: 'The people asked, and he brought quails, and satisfied them with the bread of heaven' (Psalm 105: 40). The hymn also recalls psalmic thanksgivings for deliverance: 'he sent me from above, he took me, he drew me out of many waters. / He delivered me from my strong enemy, and from them which hated me' (Psalm 18: 16–17). Or again, the deliverance from the threat of whales recalls the thanksgiving for deliverance from Leviathan, the embodiment of evil: 'Thou brakest the heads of the dragons in the waters. /

Thou brakest the heads of leviathan in pieces' (Psalm 74: 13–14).

The frame for the hymn – the first four and and last four lines – clarifies and extends the typological perspective. That frame makes clear that neither the speaker nor indeed the singers actually equate the Bermudas with Eden fully restored: rather, since the signs of providential care and blissful natural conditions in the Bermudas recapitulate Eden in some respects, the islands are thereby a type of the Edenic paradise. Because of the 'Gospel pearl' upon these coasts and the temple for God's praise in these rocks, the island paradise is also a version of the Garden of the Church allegorized in Canticles. Also, this particular deliverance from enemies and restoration to an Eden-like state is a type of the final millennial deliverance and restoration to come. All this is clearly indicated by certain deliberate ambiguities. Though the song itself, reviewing the delights of the place in the past and present tense, indicates that the singers have already arrived and taken up residence in their Eden, yet the opening lines place them in a small boat, approaching the islands:

> Where the remote *Bermudas* ride
> In th'Oceans bosome unespy'd,
> From a small Boat, that row'd along,
> The listning Winds receiv'd this Song

The point is of course that the singers know what they will find and experience even before they arrive: since their island is a type, it must necessarily exhibit the characteristics of the great and familiar Biblical antitypes. Moreover, as the first line makes clear, the Bermudas themselves 'ride' in the ocean as if they are themselves boats bound upon a journey: this elegant metaphor catches up both the singer-travellers and their island goal into God's typological scheme, showing both to be a part of an ongoing progress towards the final place of rest, the true millennial and heavenly paradise. The final lines, completing the frame, fix the singers in the only posture possible to Christians in this world – a posture of approach rather than arrival, of hope rather than present enjoyment, of steady, regular, rhythmic motion towards the true paradise, aided by, and aiding, their psalmic hymn of praise:

Thus sung they, in the *English* boat,
An holy and a cheerful Note,
And all the way, to guide their Chime,
With falling Oars they kept the time.

The speaker regards the scene from some distance. He does not presume to make the hymn his own, or to locate himself among the singers – perhaps because (as 'The Coronet' suggests) he dares not claim that he has himself produced sanctified pastoral; perhaps because the singers, having approached a type of the Edenic and millennial renewal of nature, believe the millennium to be much closer than he does. His stance afar off, recording the song and praising the singers as they testify to their own faith and hope, reinforces the sense of the distance to be travelled before the vision of the hymn can be realized, but yet affirms the reality of that vision to the eyes of faith. Through this shared vision, and through their remarkable rhythmic effects, these final lines provide a wholly satisfying resolution to the tension arising from the distance between anticipation and fulfilment, type and antitype, the singers' perspective and the speaker's. For the speaker's verses now seem to sound in rhythmic accord with the singers' rhythmic rowing, as, together, they keep the time on their psalmic voyage towards Paradise.

We can then appropriately speak of Marvell as a religious lyric poet, and recognize by that title that his poems in this kind display something of the coherence and depth and range exhibited by major seventeenth-century religious poets such as Donne, Herbert, and Vaughan – albeit in a much smaller compass. Marvell's religious poems all centre upon the nature–grace dichotomy, but they explore a very wide spectrum of Christian responses to that dichotomy. Though few in number they include an impressive variety of kinds, for Marvell makes subtle and effective use of the nuances of genre in exploring each particular response: the poems accordingly resist attempts to collapse them into broad categories of allegory or of personal meditation. Finally, in his religious poems Marvell is more than a poet of antithesis: these poems close with various, though in each case satisfying, resolutions which release the tensions generated by the nature–grace dichotomy by subsuming or dissolving all antitheses within some comprehensive perception of wholeness and integrity. This perception is at once a vision and an experience – future in time, but present to hope and faith.

Notes

1 The poems are published in this order in the first edition (1681) and in *The Poems and Letters of Andrew Marvell*, ed. H. M. Margoliouth, rev. P. Legouis and E. E. Duncan-Jones, Oxford University Press, 1971.

2 Harold E. Toliver, *Marvell's Ironic Vision*, New Haven, Conn., Yale University Press, 1965; Robert Ellrodt, *L'Inspiration personelle et l'esprit du temps chez les poètes métaphysiques anglais*, II, Paris, J. Corti, 1960, pp. 107–65; Patrick Cullen, *Spenser, Marvell, and Renaissance Pastoral*, Cambridge, Mass., Harvard University Press, 1970, pp. 151–202; Donald M. Friedman, *Marvell's Pastoral Art*, Berkeley and Los Angeles, University of California Press, 1970; Ann E. Berthoff, *The Resolved Soul: A Study of Marvell's Major Poems*, Princeton University Press, 1970; Rosalie L. Colie, *'My Ecchoing Song': Andrew Marvell's Poetry of Criticism*, Princeton University Press, 1970.

3 Annabel Patterson, ' "Bermudas" and "The Coronet": Marvell's Protestant Poetics', *Journal of English Literary History*, XLIV (1977), pp. 478–99.

4 See, e.g., Thomas Taylor, *The Practice of Repentance*, London, 1629; Thomas Gataker, 'The Spiritual Watch', *Certaine Sermons*, London, 1637; James Ussher, *A Method for Meditation*, London, 1657; Richard Sibbes, *Divine Meditations and Holy Contemplations*, London, 1638. See also Norman Pettit, *The Heart Prepared: Grace and Conversion in Puritan Spiritual Life*, New Haven, Conn., Yale University Press, 1966.

5 The place of Marvell's poem in this tradition has been recognized in several studies: Margaret Carpenter, 'From Herbert to Marvell: Poetics in "A Wreath" and "The Coronet" ', *Journal of English and Germanic Philology*, LXIX (1970), pp. 50–62; Joseph Summers, ed., *Andrew Marvell: Selected Poems*, New York, Dell, 1961, p. 14; Patterson, as above (note 3).

6 See, e.g., the three intersecting wreath-crowns of laurel, olive, and oak with the motto 'His Ornari aut Mori', in Joachim Camerarius, *Symbolarum et Emblematorum Centuriae Tres . . . Accessit Novites Centuria* [Nuremberg], 1605, p. 101; Claude Paradin's individual emblems of laurel, grass, and oak crowns in his *Devises Heroiques*, Lyons, 1557, pp. 248–51; and George Wither's final plate showing the hand of God holding forth a wreath to the Christian – 'Dabitur Perseveranti' – in *A Collection of Emblemes*, London, 1635, p. 258.

7 All these terms are developed in the first of the seven sonnets. See *John Donne: The Divine Poems*, ed. Helen Gardner, Oxford, The Clarendon Press, 1952, pp. 1–2.

8 The poem is placed just before a sequence on last things which ends the volume of lyrics, *The Church*. See *The Works of George Herbert*, ed. F. E. Hutchinson, Oxford, The Clarendon Press, 1959, p. 185.

9 Vaughan's poem, also among the last poems of his *Silex Scintillans*, gives two quatrains to the problem of wreath-making, but then proceeds to the eleven-line construction. See *The Works of Henry Vaughan*, ed. L. C. Martin, 2nd ed., Oxford, The Clarendon Press, 1957, p. 539.

10 As J. E. Hardy points out in 'Andrew Marvell's "The Coronet": The Frame of Curiosity', in *The Curious Frame*, Notre Dame (Indiana) University Press, 1962, pp. 47–9.

11 Paradin, as above (note 6), p. 191.

12 See Michel-André Bossy, 'Medieval Debates of Body and Soul', *Comparative Literature* XXVIII (1976), pp. 144–63.

13 See also Harold E. Toliver, 'The Strategy of Marvell's Resolve against Created Pleasure', *Studies in English Literature*, IV (1964), pp. 57–69.

14 Hawkins, *Parthenia Sacra* (1633), facs. Menston, The Scolar Press, 1971, pp. 59–60, 63.

15 See, e.g., Joseph Hall, *The Arte of Divine Meditation*, London, 1606, pp. 16–17: 'God is wronged if his creatures bee unregarded; our selves most of all if wee reade this great volume of the creature, and take out no lesson for our instruction.'

16 *The Art of Marvell's Poetry*, London, Hutchinson, 1968, pp. 196–203.

17 Exodus 16: 14, 21.

18 The comparison is developed in some detail in Leishman, as above (note 16), pp. 38–45. Crashaw's poem, 'The Teare', also provides an analogue to Marvell's poem.

19 This stanza is also translated into Latin elegiacs at the end of the poem.

20 1st ed., 1612; facs, Menston, The Scolar Press, 1973, p. 142.

21 The specific allusions are noted by Leishman, as above (note 16), pp. 117–19.

22 Friedman, as above (note 2), p. 51.

23 Isaiah 40: 6, 8: 'All flesh is grass, and all the goodliness thereof is as the flower of the field. / . . . The grass withereth, the flower fadeth: but the word of God shall stand for ever.'

24 Damon's reference to the spiritual significance of fountains alludes to such Biblical passages as Canticles 4: 15, 'A fountain of gardens, a well of living waters', allegorized as Christ's grace given to the church, and John 4: 13–14, 'Whosoever drinketh of this water shall thirst again; / But whosoever drinketh of the water that I shall give him shall never thirst; but the water that I shall give him shall be in him a well springing up to everlasting life'. The concept was a frequent subject for emblem plates, e.g. Benedictus van Haeften [Haeftenus], *Schola Cordis,* Antwerp, 1629, II.14, p. 216. A similar symbolic interpretation of a fountain in a landscape is supplied in Vaughan's 'Regeneration', ll. 49–52.

25 See, e.g., Pierre Legouis, *Andrew Marvell,* Oxford, The Clarendon Press, 1965, p. 96; as above (note 2): Toliver, pp. 100–3, Cullen, pp. 162–5, Friedman, p. 160; Rosalie Colie, 'Marvell's "Bermudas" and the Puritan Paradise', *Renaissance News,* X (1957), pp. 75–9; Patterson, as above (note 3), pp. 486–90.

26 See, e.g., R. M. Cummings, 'The Difficulty of Marvell's "Bermudas" ', *Modern Philology,* LXVII (1969–70), pp. 331–40; Tay Fizdale, 'Irony in Marvell's "Bermudas" ', *Journal of English Literary History,* XLI (1975), pp. 203–11.

27 See, e.g., George Wither, *A Preparation to the Psalter,* London, 1619, p. 54: 'those psalms that are intituled *Halleluiah,* are *Hymns* also, mentioning particularly the praises of God for benefits received'; and Theodore Beza, *The Psalmes of David,* trans. Anthonie Gilbie, London, 1581, pp. 304–5, identified the fifteen Gradual Psalms (Psalms 120–35) as a special group of praises and thanksgivings for benefits, notably for the return of the Israelites from Babylon.

28 See the discussion of this topos in A. Bartlett Giamatti, *The Earthly Paradise and the Renaissance Epic,* Oxford University Press, 1966, pp. 11–86; and Joseph E. Duncan, *Milton's Earthly Paradise: A Historical Study of Eden,* Minneapolis, University of Minnesota Press, 1972.

29 Michael Wilding, ' "Apples" in Marvell's "Bermudas" ', *English Language Notes*, VI (1969), pp. 254–9, argues that the 'Apples plants of such a price, / No Tree could ever bear them twice' refers not to the pineapples indigenous to the Summer Islands, but to the apples of the Tree of Knowledge. Since this is an earthly paradise restored, and a type of the millennial garden, the likelihood is rather that the apples are of the Tree of Life. See Revelation 22: 2.

30 Canticles ['The Song of Solomon'] 2: 3, 13; 4: 13; 5: 15. For discussion of the Canticles garden as a literary topos see Stanley Stewart, *The Enclosed Garden: The Tradition and the Image in Seventeenth-Century Poetry*, Madison, Wisconsin University Press, 1966.

31 Isaiah 51: 3, 10–11. See Sacvan Bercovitch, *The Puritan Origins of the American Self*, New Haven, Conn., Yale University Press, 1975.

13

Perplexing the explanation: Marvell's 'On Mr. Milton's Paradise lost'

Joseph Anthony Wittreich, Jr.

'Tributes from . . . contemporary writers are revealing if we interpret them cautiously.'[1]

It is an axiom of Marvell criticism: the poet's reputation was revived in the nineteenth century and secured in our own. Yet to speak of a revival is misleading; for Marvell's name was known, though not in relation to the metaphysical poets we place him with today and not in association with the works we currently admire him for – 'The Garden', *Upon Appleton House*, the Mower lyrics and Cromwell poems. His reputation, rather, was more narrowly based, sustained by his polemics and by one poem, '*On Mr.* Milton's *Paradise lost*',[2] which was published four times in the seventeenth century and many times again in the succeeding century:

When I beheld the Poet blind, yet bold,
In slender Book his vast Design unfold,
Messiah Crown'd, *Gods* Reconcil'd Decree,
Rebelling *Angels*, the Forbidden Tree,
Heav'n, Hell, Earth, Chaos, All; the Argument
Held me a while misdoubting his Intent,
That he would ruine (for I saw him strong)
The sacred Truths to Fable and old Song,
(So *Sampson* groap'd the Temples Posts in spight)
The World o'rewhelming to revenge his Sight.
　Yet as I read, soon growing less severe,
I lik'd his Project, the success did fear;
Through that wide Field how he his way should find
O're which lame Faith leads Understanding blind;
Lest he perplext the things he would explain,

And what was easie he should render vain.
Or if a Work so infinite he spann'd,
Jealous I was that some less skilful hand
(Such as disquiet alwayes what is well,
And by ill imitating would excell)
Might hence presume the whole Creations day
To change in Scenes, and show it in a Play.
Pardon me, *mighty Poet*, nor despise
My causeless, yet not impious, surmise.
But I am now convinc'd, and none will dare
Within thy Labours to pretend a Share.
Thou hast not miss'd one thought that could be fit,
And all that was improper dost omit:
So that no room is here for Writers left,
But to detect their Ignorance or Theft.
That Majesty which through thy Work doth Reign
Draws the Devout, deterring the Profane.
And things divine thou treatst of in such state
As them preserves, and Thee inviolate.
At once delight and horrour on us seize,
Thou singst with so much gravity and ease;
And above humane flight dost soar aloft,
With Plume so strong, so equal, and so soft.
The *Bird* nam'd from that *Paradise* you sing
So never Flags, but alwaies keeps on Wing.
Where couldst thou Words of such a compass find?
Whence furnish such a vast expense of Mind?
Just Heav'n Thee, like *Tiresias*, to requite,
Rewards with *Prophesie* thy loss of Sight.
Well mightst thou scorn thy Readers to allure
With tinkling Rhime, of thy own Sense secure;
While the *Town-Bays* writes all the while and spells,
And like a Pack-Horse tires without his Bells.
Their Fancies like our bushy Points appear,
The Poets tag them; we for fashion wear.
I too transported by the *Mode* offend,
And while I meant to *Praise* thee, must Commend.
Thy verse created like thy *Theme* sublime,
In Number, Weight, and Measure, needs not *Rhime*.

Romantic notice of Marvell's poetry may widen the base of his reputation; but it begins by focusing upon a conjunction of names and, moreover, upon the poem that fixed that conjunction in the new literary consciousness. Wordsworth's celebration of Marvell is widely known:

> Great men have been among us; hands that penned
> And tongues that uttered wisdom – better none:
> The later Sidney, Marvel, Harrington,
> Young Vane, and others who called Milton friend.

Not so well known is Alexander Gilchrist's report of Blake, that 'no man less resembled the vulgar radical. His sympathies were with Milton, Harrington, and Marvel'.[3] And less known still are two imaginary conversations between Milton and Marvell, and three between Marvell and Bishop Parker, wherein Walter Savage Landor first brings the two poets together in dialogue and later, in the conversations with Parker, allows Marvell to assume the stance of Milton's defender, here identifying Marvell at the outset as the author of 'On *Paradise Lost*'. These conversations provide a convenient starting-point for examining what was still, in the Romantic period, Marvell's most famous poem – a poem that embodies both 'the virtuosity and multiple intellectual and moral stances' that we have come to associate with Marvell's major poetry, and that, like the Cromwell poems, is 'no panegyric . . . but an unflinching analysis' of Milton and his *Paradise Lost*.[4]

I

> our learning raiseth up against us many enemies . . ., yet doth it invest us with grand and glorious privileges, and confer on us a largeness of beatitude. . . . we enjoy sailing on a wish from world to world.[5]

'On *Paradise Lost*' is not Marvell's only 'critical' poem: he wrote two others – 'Tom May's Death' in the spirit of diatribe and 'To his worthy Friend Doctor Witty' in the spirit of praise – neither of which achieves the delicate ambiguities that mark the poem on Milton. Nor is 'On *Paradise Lost*' Marvell's only critical pronouncement on Milton. Years before this poem, Milton sent his friend three copies of *Defensio Secunda*, one of them intended for Marvell himself. Subsequently Marvell dispatched a letter to Milton, saying

> I shall now studie it even to the getting of it by Heart: esteeming it . . . as the most compendious Scale, . . . the Height of Roman eloquence. When I consider how equally it turnes and rises with so many figures, it seems to me a Trajans columne in whose winding ascent we see imboss'd the severall Monuments of your learned victoryes. (Margoliouth, *The Poems and Letters of Andrew Marvell*, II, p. 293)

Marvell also promised, but apparently never provided, 'minutes' of Milton's life for a contemporary biography. Already evident in the letter is Marvell's awe at the 'Scale' of Milton's achievement, as well as his interest in Milton's artistic presence. These concerns persist, though Milton's post-revolutionary status in England caused Marvell's praise to modulate into the apologetics of both *The Rehearsal Transpros'd: The Second Part* (1673) and 'On *Paradise Lost*' (1674). The poem especially, which has been characterized by its 'cautious and crabbed remarks', invites questioning of David Masson's conclusion that 'Marvell's discipleship to Milton . . . is perfect and exceptionless to the last'.[6]

The story of Marvell's role in exacting Milton's release from prison and eventual pardon hardly needs rehearsing; yet it should be remembered that the part Marvell played here is responsible for the sniping at him – and for the sniping at Milton through him – in the post-revolutionary era. The onslaught of criticism levelled against both poets, particularly by Samuel Parker and Richard Leigh, provoked Marvell into composing Part II of *The Rehearsal Transpros'd* which is at once a sustained defence of himself and an exoneration of Milton from playing any part in Marvell's own polemical warfare.

The immediate effect of Marvell's *The Rehearsal Transpros'd* (1672), prompted by Samuel Parker's Preface to Bishop Bramhall's *Vindication of Himself* (1672), was to open old wounds and thereby subject both himself and Milton to a new barrage of criticism. As early as 1647, Milton had been numbered among the erring spirits of his time; soon he would be accused of heresy both in politics and religion and, thereafter, dubbed a fanatic, an agent of the devil – a murderer whose faculties are united in wickedness and whose blindness is evidence of divine retaliation against the polemist.[7] These old charges are renewed by Parker in *A Reproof to the Rehearsal Transpros'd* (1673), where he complains that Marvell, in his work of the year before, affords 'as good Precedents for Rebellion and King-Killing, as any we meet with in the writings of J[ohn] M[ilton] in defence of the Rebellion and the Murther of the King' (p. 212). Richard Leigh, supposed by Marvell to be Parker issuing still another reproof, had also published *The Transproser Rehears'd* (1673) which, after ridiculing Milton's tactics in his prose works, chides Marvell for learning 'the Moods and Figures of Railing' from Milton himself (p. 32). Marvell is thus judged guilty by association, and his own writings condemned as being 'nothing but *Iconoclastes* drawn in Little, and *Defensio Populi Anglicania* in Miniature' (p. 72). Marvell who 'has . . . clubbed' with this enemy of bishops and hater of kings, says Leigh, uses Milton's pen, sucking from it the 'black . . . Poyson' with which he writes his own libellous prose. And Leigh concludes: 'There are many *Miltons* in this one Man', Marvell (p. 147). But there is also one Milton who is *not* comprehended in Marvell, a point Leigh makes as he turns from Milton the polemist to the poet of *Paradise Lost*. It is in these remarks that Leigh unwittingly gives shape to the poem that Marvell did write in Milton's defence.

Leigh advances the proposition, however facetiously, that 'dark Souls may be illuminated with *bright* and shining thoughts' as instanced by 'the *blind* Author of *Paradise lost* . . . [who] begins his third Book . . ., groping for a beam of *Light*':

> Hail, holy Light, off-Spring of Heav'n first born,
> Or of th' Eternal Coeternal beam.

And a little later:

> thee I revisit safe,
> And feel thy sov'raign vital Lamp; but thou
> Revisitst not these eyes, that rowl in vain
> To find thy piercing Ray, and find no dawn;
> So thick a drop Serene hath quencht their Orbs,
> Or dim suffusion veil'd.

Turning these lines against Milton, Leigh issues two rebukes: first, this poem, supposedly full of light, is riddled with dark meanings; and second, it violates its own poetic procedures, using such internal rhymes as 'Eternal Coeternal' (pp. 41–2). Milton is thus ridiculed as 'the *blind Bard* . . . who can by no means endure a Rhyme any where but in the middle of a Verse' (pp. 42, 133). This criticism of Milton turns quickly into an attack on Marvell; for though a '*Schismatick* in *Poetry*' and 'though *nonconformable* in point of Rhyme' (p. 43), Milton could have led Marvell into the great tradition of Christian and epic literature – a tradition that, sanctioning rhymeless verse, subverts the current fashion, practised by Marvell himself, of tagging every line. Its heterodoxy aside, there is something 'authentick' about *Paradise Lost* that is missing from modern poetry, including Marvell's own; for it is the great epic poets and the 'untoucht' works of Scripture, says Leigh, that teach 'the World the Mysteries of Handicraft, the Principles of Arts and Intrigues of Government' (p. 43). As Milton had done, Marvell should have grounded his poetry in these traditions – not in the minor, incidental, trivial literature of his time, which, from Leigh's point of view, has made those writings the equivalent of transversing the weekly newspapers.

These charges provoke Marvell into augmenting his earlier *Rehearsal Transpros'd* and into authoring the poem, 'On *Paradise Lost*'. The first is an exoneration of Milton and a defence of Marvell; and the second, ostensibly an encomium, is actually a defence of both poets. The element of self-interest in both these works suggests a double reason for reading each of them: they are reflections on Milton's writings and revelations of Marvell's own mind and art, and both become increasingly comprehensible as we probe the circumstances and motives that caused Marvell to write them.

In his comments on Milton in *The Rehearsal Transpros'd*, Marvell is extremely guarded, speaking simultaneously of 'His Majesties happy Return' and of Milton's 'misfortune, living in a tumultuous time' and being 'toss'd on the wrong side' from which he wrote '*Flagrante bello* certain dangerous Treatises' (p. 312). No *defence* of Milton, these remarks constitute instead an appeal for a man, now 'expiat[ing] himself in a retired silence' (p. 312), to be left alone. Marvell's apology for Milton is thus postponed for a poem in which, saying nothing at all about Milton's prose writings, he mounts a counterstatement to Leigh's criticism of *Paradise Lost*. The praise once bestowed upon Milton in Marvell's letter acknowledging receipt of *Defensio Secunda* now stands in marked contrast to the defence of the poet presented in 'On *Paradise Lost*'. Neither here, nor for that matter in *The Rehearsal Transpros'd*, can Marvell's tone be described as it once was – as that of 'a disciple, anxious to please, grateful for attention, quick to admire'.[8] 'On *Paradise Lost*' is simply anxious – and uneasy. It is a poem that, in Arnold Stein's words, 'observes a careful distance which seems to be more than a ceremony of good manners' and that in its own 'cautious distrust', as Lawrence Hyman explains, contrasts sharply with the visionary grandeur of Milton's poem.[9] It is a wonder, therefore, that Milton agreed to having this poem printed with his own.

Modern readers of 'On *Paradise Lost*' have often thought differently. But there have also been demurrals from the widely held view that Marvell is 'the chief of the surviving partisans who constituted the really fit among Milton's earliest audience'; and they are founded upon an understanding like Marjorie Nicolson's that in crucial instances 'the two poets stand at opposite poles in theological interpretation'.[10] Dismissing the contention that in this poem 'doubts are . . . submerged in . . . approval', J. B. Broadbent, for example, argues that Marvell's 'retraction of . . . doubts is not quite wholehearted, and his statement of the excellencies of *Paradise Lost* continues to hint at . . . difficulties'.[11] At least one eighteenth-century reader of Marvell's poem felt similarly, for he emended the following couplet – 'I too transported by the *Mode* offend, / And while I meant to *Praise* thee, must Commend' (ll. 51–2) – to read:

> I too transported by the mode commend
> And while I meant to praise thee must offend.[12]

Ironically, these lines, emended to reinforce Marvell's uneasiness with his subject, are the very ones the poet wrote intent upon removing the traces of uneasiness from his poem.

Marvell's lines are typically read as an example of self-mockery coming from a poet who finds himself hemmed in by the custom of rhyme: he means to '*Praise*' (on that word the accent should fall); but the convention of rhyme observed throughout the poem and here governed by 'offend' in the previous line cripples the verse, enabling Marvell only to commend. 'While Marvell would like to use the word *praise*', the argument goes, 'he must be content with the lesser word *commend*, because his rhyme calls for it.'[13] Yet this typical reading misses the wit of a couplet whose point is that commendation is actually the ultimate form of praise: many are the recipients of praise, but only a few are commended – that is, according to the *OED*, set off to special advantage by the 'added' grace and lustre which accompany commendation. Moreover, the word 'commend' as it relates to a person involves an expression of faith and confidence on the part of the bestower who ascribes glory but, more importantly, places the person commended under his own protection. The intention of shielding Milton from adverse criticism is as much a part of Marvell's poem as it was of the earlier prose tract. But lurking between its lines and manifesting itself in this couplet is the motive of self-justification as well. The wit of the couplet conveys the idea that rhyme need not be an encumbrance but, when employed skilfully, may be an advantage to the poet. Thus even as Marvell commends Milton for observing the decorum of sublime poetry, he asserts the possibility of doing something else – of employing rhyme with considerable ingenuity and to great effect.

The point made here is restated by the poem as a whole. While assiduously observing the rhyming conventions of English heroic verse, Marvell abandons the discipline of the stanza, his verse units becoming a scaled-down image of Milton's blank-verse paragraphs. Correspondingly, Marvell simulates the syntax and the sweep of the Miltonic period and, simultaneously, makes his own poem an analogue to a Miltonic structure. The circling effects achieved by Milton's erratic use of rhyme and by his symmetrical balances are approximated by Marvell through the matching lengths of his first and last verse paragraphs (each is ten lines long) and through the device of turning endings back upon beginnings. 'On *Paradise Lost*' divides into two unequal units, lines 1–44 and lines 45–54: the first is Marvell's defence of Milton, which in its concluding phrase, 'thy loss of sight', turns back upon the first line, 'the Poet blind'; and the second is Marvell's defence of himself, which in its culminating reference to 'Number, Weight, and Measure' circles back upon the poem's second line and the theme of Milton's 'vast Design'. Endings and beginnings merge, then, circumscribing a poem that, unfolding Milton's intentions, is a justification of their apparent boldness and that, in its own seven-part structure, is a replication of the seven-fold visionary design of Milton's epic. Not in any strict sense a facsimile of *Paradise Lost*, Marvell's poem, none the less, emblematizes Milton's, through its form projecting the vision that, in lines 3–5, it condenses into signatures. Through this shorthand, Marvell represents both the shape and the scope of Milton's achievement.

The fact remains, though, that to the extent that 'On *Paradise Lost*' has elicited critical attention, that attention has been riveted to a few lines from the poem's concluding section:

> Well mightst thou scorn thy Readers to allure
> With tinkling Rhime, of thy own Sense secure;
> While the *Town-Bays* writes all the while and spells,
> And like a Pack-Horse tires without his Bells.
> Their Fancies like our bushy Points appear,
> The Poets tag them; we for fashion wear.
>
> (ll. 45–50)

Oddly, this poem is remembered chiefly for these verses wherein Marvell is said to take a stand with Milton, and against Dryden, in the ongoing controversy over rhyme. The statement, 'The Poets tag them', has ever since David Masson been thought to be reminiscent of Milton's reported response to Dryden ('Well, Mr. Dryden, it seems you have a mind to tag my points, and you have leave to tag them').[14] Now commonplace, such an interpretation is probably an extension of Dr Johnson's suggestion that lines 21–2 refer to the division of *Paradise Lost* into scenes and the rendering of it as a play – a project undertaken by Dryden in *The State of Innocence* (1674, 1677). Whatever its ultimate origin may be, however, such an interpretation is directly traceable to David Masson, who infers that the story of Dryden's asking Milton for permission to tag *Paradise Lost* (relayed to Marvell, he believes) inspires this section of the poem. 'Tags in those days of elaborate dressing', Masson explains,

> were the metal points or knobs, gold or silver if possible, at the ends of laces or cords with which dresses were fastened. They were partly for ornament, partly to keep the ends of laces from fraying. Blank verse, therefore, in Marvell's clever momentary fancy, consisted of lines in their natural state, or *untagged*, and to make them rhyme as Dryden had proposed, was to *tag* them, or put on the fashionable shining points at the end.[15]

Masson here elucidates Marvell's figures; but, as Henry Lippencott suggests, by particularizing '*Town-Bays*' to Dryden, Masson also obscures the more likely possibility that Marvell, primarily concerned with the main issues of the rhyme controversy and perhaps even inspired by Milton's own observations on the verse form of *Paradise Lost*, probably would not 'stoop to incidental *Ad hominem* attack on Dryden'. Lippencott's argument, that *Town-Bays* is 'a personification of hack poets generally',[16] finds strong support, some of it in unexpected quarters.

It is well known that the Duke of Buckingham, in *The Rehearsal* (1672), ridicules Dryden in the character of Bayes, having him say: 'I transverse it; . . . if it be prose, put it into verse . . . ; if it be verse, put it into prose' (I, i). In *The Rehearsal Transpros'd*, Marvell simply appropriates the name of Bayes for Samuel Parker, his point being that the term is more fittingly used as an abstraction than as a cover for a proper name. 'Bayes' stands for the anonymity that Parker allows himself but disallows others: Parker, Marvell objects, 'writes under the greatest security', never identifying himself but giving the initials of other men's names (p. 9). Understood in this light, the phrase '*Town-Bays*' refers to rhymsters generally – is a generic term. It is the meaning not the name that Marvell calls – a rhetorical procedure, not a person, that he declaims against. Richard Leigh, it should be noted, offers a corroborating explanation in *The Transproser Rehears'd*, insisting that Marvell employs the name in an effort to 'frame a Character of bulky *Universals*', thereby '*Summing up an Army in one Man*'. As used by Marvell, Leigh determines, the name is simply part of an endeavour at 'Representation by *Symbols*, and Hieroglyphical Signatures' (pp. 16–17). What is true for this prose tract is likely true for Marvell's poem, which, intended to release one poet from personal abuse, for strategic reasons probably would not heap it upon another. In the very act of dissociating himself from the name-calling tactics of his adversaries, Marvell could thus demonstrate his superiority to them. When the motive of self-interest is recognized as an integral part of this poem and when it is realized that Marvell is here responding to criticism levelled against both Milton and himself, even those lines cited by Dr Johnson – 'Might hence presume the whole Creations day / To change in Scenes, and show it in a Play' (ll. 21–2) – seem to ask that a new construction be placed upon them.

Leigh had accused Marvell of being too well read in Sir William Davenant – of being more in sympathy, finally, with current fashions than with the aesthetic underpinnings of Milton's epic. It is precisely this linkage of Marvell with Davenant that lines 21–2 are meant to defy. Dryden's effort to render *Paradise Lost* as a play is less relevant to them than the critical theory set forth by Davenant, in his 'Preface to *Gondibert*', which sanctions all such efforts – which would turn heroic into dramatic poetry by 'proportioning . . . Books to *Acts & Canto's* to Scenes', thereby 'repealing' the old laws of epic poetry, both classical and Christian, by the new laws of 'the English . . . *Drama*'.[17] Even if mutedly, 'On *Paradise Lost*' contains a self-defence within a poem that purports to be an explanation and appreciation of Milton's epic.

However conventionally ceremonial, the poem in its virtuosity invites us to register a disclaimer against any view that restricts its statement to an assertion of Marvell's inferiority to Milton. Marvell says something other than that 'Only Milton is truly "free" in his verse',[18] his intention being not to acquiesce in Leigh's criticism of his own art but to discredit that criticism by devising a poem that, even if it employs the device of rhyme, is marvellously flexible and various. To Milton himself, Marvell will say (as Landor has him say a century and a half later) that 'I will not be pegged down . . ., not follow any walk'. Milton may himself oppose the 'agrarian law', the 'inclosure act' of rhyme, refusing 'to square the circle of poetry';[19] but Marvell, taking a similar stance, also refuses to square the circle of his own poem, even if it is commendatory, with the principles enunciated by Milton in his introductory remarks to *Paradise Lost*. Marvell's poem is thus a triumph not over, but within, the conventions of rhyme.

II

PARKER: . . . there are many who, like yourself, see considerable merit in his poems . . . I can only hope that he has now corrected what is erroneous in his doctrines.

MARVELL: . . . he hath never changed a jot, in acting or thinking.

PARKER: ... correction of error is the plainest proof of energy and mastery. ... Let us piously hope, Mr. Marvel, that God in his good time may turn Mr. Milton from the error of his ways, and incline his heart to repentance ... that so he may fully be prepared for death.[20]

Marvell's view of Milton, here expressed in an imaginary conversation, differs decidedly from the view of the poet that emerges from both *The Rehearsal Transpros'd* and 'On *Paradise Lost*'. There Milton is portrayed as *expiating* himself by recanting his earlier heterodoxy, by repressing his nonconformist spirit; but here he is represented as a man of indomitable will and unaltering opinions – as a Samson who, in his epic no less than in his prose works, would hurl down the most oppressive forms of religion and politics. Marvell may raise the same questions that are later entertained in Landor's conversations, but he also offers alternative answers to them.

'On *Paradise Lost*' makes its initial appearance in that 'slender Book' (l. 2) – a reference to the fact that the large quarto edition of 1667 is reduced in 1674 to an octavo volume. Marvell's poem is situated between Samuel Barrows's Latin encomium and Milton's remarks on his rhymeless verse. From this position, it looks backward and forward: Barrows claims for Milton's poem the universal vision that Marvell particularizes, while in the concluding lines of his poem Marvell seems to be responding directly to Milton's own explanation of the verse form he gives his epic, providing here, according to Lippencott, 'a poetic paraphrase' of it.[21] Having once shown an aptitude for transprosing, Marvell here displays adeptness at transversing. As Émile Saillens has observed, it is as if Barrows and Marvell 'had consulted each other', first the one poet, then the other, celebrating the immensity of *Paradise Lost*;[22] then, as Marvell turns to the verse form of Milton's epic, he enters into consultation with its poet.

It might be objected that Marvell, just as Dryden was to do, forces a linear design upon Milton's anti-linear narrative; but it should also be acknowledged that he identifies the aesthetic system that points the way to Milton's achievement. Unexpectedly, it is Richard Leigh with whom Marvell seems to be in agreement here, both men, concurring that Scripture sanctions those departures from the literary norms that have so often been cited to discredit *Paradise Lost*. Marvell's poem, importantly, both begins and ends by forging a link between *Paradise Lost* and Biblical poetics: the references to 'his vast Design' (l. 2) and to Solomon's temple (l. 54) point to what S. K. Heninger has called a 'poetics of making'.[23] This tradition of art, Landor's Marvell will later contend, enables Milton to carry 'the Word of God against the traditions of men':

> I know that Milton, and every other great poet, must be religious: for there is nothing so godlike as a love of order, with a power of bringing great things into it. This power, unlimited in the one, limited . . . in the other, belongs to the Deity and the Poet.[24]

In this imaginary conversation, Marvell's words make Parker 'shudder', as does the fact that, from Parker's point of view, Milton was a Samson who shook the pillars of Christianity, reducing religion to ruins. Landor's strategy here is identical to Marvell's in his poem, for both artists are responding to, and then attempting to correct, the historical record; both confront the very propositions that were set forth about Milton by his detractors, in his own lifetime. Milton's theological radicalism, his Samson-like tactics, his blindness – these were the principal concerns of Milton criticism from its very beginnings in the 1640s, and they are all focused for Marvell by the recent attacks of Parker and Leigh. He certainly knew that these assaults, for which he must have felt largely responsible, did nothing to enhance Milton's reputation or to ease the circumstances of Milton's last years; he must have known, too, that Milton himself contemplated a rejoinder to Leigh that never saw print.[25] It is obvious enough that Marvel's poem is meant to release Milton's from this whole tradition of hostile criticism, and credible to suppose that Marvell lets his poem take the form of a rebuttal to Leigh and in it, we may speculate, follows lines of argument suggested, and perhaps used, by Milton himself.

In its very first line, therefore, Marvell confronts head-on a fundamental supposition of Miltonoclasts: 'I beheld the Poet *blind*' (my italics). William R. Parker reminds us that the royalists 'had long pronounced Milton's blindness as evidence of divine retaliation' so that the problem for Milton's friends in 1660 had been 'to persuade the excitable Commons that justice had already been done'.[26] So common was this accusation that Richard Leigh begins and ends his most sustained critique of *Paradise Lost* by reformulating it, and so troublesome was it to Milton that he uses the prologue to the third book of his epic as a defence of himself against the widely accepted implications of his blindness. Two figures of the past, says Milton, are equal to him in fate, '*Tiresias* and *Phineus* Prophets old' (III, 36) – and equal to him in reward: both to them and to Milton comes 'Celestial Light' that, shining inwardly, irradiates their minds (ll. 51–5). The very terms used by Leigh to mock Milton are the ones appropriated by Marvell to honour him; indeed, the terms of approbation are provided by Milton himself. Beginning his formal defence of Milton by acknowledging the poet's blindness, Marvell terminates that defence by proclaiming: 'Just Heav'n . . ., like *Tiresias,* . . . / Rewards with *Prophesie* thy loss of Sight' (ll. 43–4).

In his poem, Marvell must take a position on prophecy fundamentally different from Parker's own. An opponent of enthusiasm, in *A Reproof* Samuel Parker speaks belittlingly of those who declare themselves to be prophets, revealing their own 'Impudence and Vanity' (p. 327); and in the Preface to Bishop Bramhall's *Vindication*, Parker describes prophecy as the device of 'the dissenting *Party*' whose 'PREACHERS fill the peoples heads with . . . Dreams and Visions'; it is also the agent of revolution utilized 'to dissolve and unravel the establish'd frame of things' (pp. 47, 54). One of its chief Biblical representatives, Marvell and Parker both understood, was Samson. Both may have remembered, too, that Samson was the much touted hero of the Puritan revolutionaries and that Milton himself had earlier been celebrated in terms of the Samson story:

> I answer with learned *Milton* that if God commanded these things, 'tis a sign they were lawful and are commendable. . . . Neither *Sampson* nor Samuel alleged any other cause or reason for what they did, but retaliation, and the apparent justice of the actions themselves.[27]

The poet who believed, as Marvell remarks in *The Rehearsal Transpros'd*, that the causes behind the Puritan Revolution were 'too good to have been fought for' (p. 135) clearly would resist any effort to associate Milton with Samson. The two are heterogeneous figures who only by violence can be yoked together.

It is an oddity of literary criticism that Marvell's lines containing the Samson reference have been so uniformly misread:

> the Argument
> Held me a while misdoubting his Intent,
> That he would ruine (for I saw him strong)
> The sacred Truths to Fable and old Song,
> (So *Sampson* groap'd the Temples Posts in spight)
> The World o'rewhelming to revenge his Sight.
> (ll. 5–10)

Rosalie Colie says of these verses that they are 'perhaps a compliment to the poet's preoccupation with another sacred story of figural and personal significance'; and she concludes: 'the comparison to Samson makes all well: "*Sampson* groap'd the Temples Posts in spight," but the "spight" was God-sent, and the destruction redounded to Israel's glory'.[28] The unstated hypothesis here is made explicit by Arnold Stein: 'A blind poet, if he is also a prophet, may succeed in his project. But the strength . . . first worries Marvell. The blindness suggests a motive and the analogy of Samson (not Milton's Samson) . . .' .[29] If not *Milton's* Samson, then whose Samson? Both critics seem to agree: the lines, meant to associate Milton with his Biblical prototype, draw their meaning from Scriptural commentary. What neither critic acknowledges, however, is that the meaning each attaches to 'spight' is without historical authority. The word, according to the *OED*, refers to hostile or malignant feeling, to contempt, hatred, and ill-will, to rancorous and envious malice – meanings substantiated here by reference first to *Paradise Lost* ('to spight his maker') and then to Marvell's *The Rehearsal Transpros'd* ('his spight against the Nonconformists').

These lines, thought by Colie and Stein to advance a comparison, plainly assert a contrast. Marvell is confused over Milton's intent, fearing that as a 'strong' poet Milton will ruin his Biblical source because, like Samson, he may be acting out of 'spight' to revenge his blindness. Given Marvell's own intention of releasing Milton from the retributive associations affixed to his blindness, a comparison between Samson and Milton would hardly seem apt, especially in view of the fact that when Milton invokes the Samson story (just once in *Paradise Lost*) he does so by way of elucidating the paradox: 'thir Eyes now op'n'd, and thir minds / How dark'n'd' (IX, 1053–

4). Marvell would rather exploit, as Milton had earlier done, the reverse of that paradox; and so, understandably, he chooses to distinguish Samson the false prophet and destroyer from Milton the true prophet and creator, the one figure losing his life, the other being providentially spared his.[30]

Marvell's chief claim for Milton, that he did not violate his Scriptural sources, countering Richard Leigh's complaint in *The Transproser Rehears'd* that Milton 'has both *excus'd* and *hallow'd* his Obscenity . . . by pleading Scripture for it' (p. 136), is founded upon a cardinal principle of Marvell's own art. That principle is formulated most explicitly in the poem, 'To his worthy Friend Doctor Witty', where Marvell allows that translators have grown into authors and argues that 'ill Translators make the Book their own':

> Others do strive with words and forced phrase
> To add such lustre, and so many rayes,
> That but to make the Vessel shining, they
> Much of the precious Metal rub away.
> He is Translations thief that addeth more,
> As much as he that taketh from the Store
> Of the first Author. Here he maketh blots
> That mends; and added beauties are but spots.
> (ll. 9–16)

Marvell's harshest accusation against Parker – 'Forgery . . . of Scripture and Religion' – rests upon just this principle. 'May a curse . . . belong to him who shall knowingly add or diminish in the Scripture', Marvell says in *The Rehearsal Transpros'd* (p. 87); and addressing Parker, he later declares:

> your Printed books debase . . . the value of the Bible under the scornful name of *the English Bible*; and not only Satyrize the Non-conformists Sermons, but traduce all Preaching, and make it seem unnecessary, that so the Liturgy might be sufficient for Salvation. (p. 275)

This is exactly the argument that had been advanced by Milton's detractors against his prose tracts: repeatedly, Milton was said to have distorted Scripture by lifting passages from context and using them to espouse the very positions they were meant to disclaim; and typically, he is numbered among those dissenters, described by

Parker in *A Reproof*, who made 'horrid work . . . with the Word of God', who 'shamefully did . . . urge the Prophecies of the Old Testament, in defiance to the Precepts of the New' (p. 396). There is little doubt, from the perspective formulated by Parker in his Preface to *A Vindication*, that Milton is among those who would 'model new Bodies of Orthodoxy' (p. 8).

In his poem, Marvell tries to discredit such arguments – but only in terms of *Paradise Lost*. 'Misdoubting' Milton's intent, Marvell begins to fear that Milton may perplex what he would explain and, subsequently, that ill-imitating Milton's poem some other poet will do with it what Milton skilfully avoided doing. Not until midway through his defence do Marvell's doubts and fears subside. They were 'causeless', he says; for first of all, omitting 'all that was improper', Milton has 'not miss'd one thought that could be fit'; and second, in its exhaustive completeness, *Paradise Lost* leaves 'no room . . . for Writers . . . / But to detect their Ignorance or Theft' (ll. 24, 27–30). In this enormous compass, Marvell concludes, Milton, rewarded with the gift of prophecy, has interpreted Scripture without violating it: 'things divine thou treatst of in such state / As them preserves, and Thee inviolate' (ll. 33–4). The certainty here, contrasting with Marvell's earlier doubts, causes this poem, as Arnold Stein has said, to 'waver in its clarity'.[31] Marvell may excuse Milton, but not himself, from perplexing an explanation.

All points of Marvell's argument converge upon an assertion of the orthodoxy of *Paradise Lost*; even the ascription of a prophetic character to Milton's epic is withheld until Marvell has stripped the genre of its incipient radicalism. Prophecy was widely understood to be God's vehicle for 'subversion', to involve a rejection of the established reality – of the forms and structures, aesthetic and institutional, of a corrupt civilization. 'At odds with the course of history', prophecy, it was believed, 'confoundeth all traditions, and subverteth all constitutions'.[32] Such ideological underpinnings Marvell knocks away from both *Paradise Lost* and its generic model. Thus, like Marvell's earlier self-defence in *The Rehearsal Transpros'd*, 'On *Paradise Lost*' urges that Milton not be numbered among the non-conformists, that he 'not be . . . mistaken for one of them' (p. 186).

Ironies reverberate. *Paradise Lost* will wield a power over later literature, no small part of which will produce the Romantic explosion of works that invoke Milton's poem as precedent for their own heterodoxy. Moreover, as Milton's epic accrues a tradition of commentary, critics will repeatedly turn back on *Paradise Lost* the question that, in its uneasiness with its subject, Marvell's poem turns back upon itself: is *Paradise Lost* a monument to Christian orthodoxy, or is it rather designed to subvert the very system of religion that Marvell thinks it supports? That question, at the very heart of Milton criticism through the centuries, is initially formulated by Marvell's poem, which perennial in its concerns, is also strikingly modern in its idiom. Prophets and prophecy, imitation and influence, strong poets and weak ones, and more cryptically Biblical poetics versus the emerging neoclassical aesthetic – these are the terms of Marvell's criticism and, equally, the concerns of the new Milton criticism.

That is why we should read 'On *Paradise Lost*', but we should also inquire with Arnold Stein, 'How to read the poem?' Stein urges, as he prepares his own answer to this question, that we try to imagine Milton's response in this way:

> There could not have been much news here for Milton to read, though that tone of admiring deference, combined with the demonstrated credentials of intelligent insight and appraisal, must have been gratifying. Prolonged and lonely effort is never quite answered by applause for the beautiful results; only shared insight into the nature of the difficulties confronted and the ways taken to overcome them can speak to the poet in the poem.[33]

Marvell's poem must have been 'gratifying' to Milton – not, as Stein thinks, because Marvell's claims for the poet's religious subserviency conform to the spirit of *Paradise Lost*, but because the poem was a timely defence of Milton composed by a loyal friend: one, as Milton surely realized, whose criticism was sometimes astute and at other times, in fundamental ways, misguided; one who perceived and was discomfited by the place Milton was destined to assume in the history of English poetry; and one who was no less concerned with carving a niche for himself in that tradition. Milton must have noticed, in an attitude of toleration, that Marvell denied him what most he aspired to: a place at the very head of a new tradition of English poetry and a role in the formation of a new Christianity. He must also have recognized, with appreciation, that even if held in servitude by the historical moment Marvell's poem attempted to mediate between *Paradise Lost* and an audience that, antipathetic to Milton, would be unreceptive to his poem. The initial publication of *Paradise Lost* was allegedly threatened by the censors.[34] This threat alone would have alerted Milton to the reality that history demanded of Marvell the kind of defence he provided. That defence may not be true to the objectives of *Paradise Lost* (possibly it is not even a precise rendering of Marvell's actual understanding of Milton's poem); but it is all that the year 1674 would concede to either poet. Thus a poem written expressly for the 1674 edition of *Paradise Lost* and published with it, presumably with Milton's approval, was allowed to become a measure for all time of the limitations of criticism and of the extent to which future generations would evolve an understanding of a poem that Milton's contemporaries – the very best of them – were slow to penetrate or, like Marvell, either unwilling or unable to countenance. Later history would reassemble the truth about *Paradise Lost* that Milton's own times – by dismantling the poem's vision, snaring its political and religious radicalism in the nets of a narrow orthodoxy – would repress.

Like most of Marvell's poetry, which is a 'poetry of criticism',[35] 'On *Paradise Lost*' is a scrutiny of literary tradition. The poet's task, Marvell had made clear in 'Tom May's Death', is to fight 'foresaken Vertues cause':

> He, when the wheel of Empire whirleth back,
> And though the World's disjointed Axel crack,
> Sings still of ancient Rights and better Times . . . .
> (ll. 67–9)

The poet's capacity to do this is the measure of his achievement, here judged by Chaucer and Spenser whose 'dust does rise' against Tom May to expel him from their side (ll. 85–7). Within twenty years of this poem, one of Marvell's contemporaries will rise up and join the august company of Chaucer and Spenser, becoming a third among these English sons of light. Not just Marvell's contemporary, Milton is also his poetic rival and, some would say, his superior, which explains for one reader the contrary impulses of 'On *Paradise Lost*': on the one hand, its 'identification' with Milton; and on the other, its 'recoiling comment on . . . [Marvell's] own place in relation to a greater master'.[36] The poem, clearly, portrays Milton as a master-poet; but it is less clear on other matters – on whether, for example, Milton is 'a greater master' and on the kind of relation Marvell is willing to strike with this master. What Marvell does not say here may be more revealing than what he does say: unlike Spenser in a similar situation, he does not say: 'I follow here the footing of thy feete' (*The Faerie Queene*, IV, ii, 34). We are left to speculate on 'why?'.

Marvell and Milton both served apprenticeships as poets, preparing for some greater flight that Milton accomplished but that Marvell never undertook. 'On *Paradise Lost*', therefore, makes no extravagant claims for Marvell's achievement; but the poem everywhere implies the integrity of that achievement, in the process showing Marvell playing Theocritus to Milton who is his Homer. Like Theocritus, Marvell seems to regard his poems as an alternative to the epic tradition that from Theocritus' perspective had been exhausted by Homer and that from Marvell's was now brought to an end by Milton. The poet who is said to be 'without retrospective',[37] in 'On *Paradise Lost*' invites a retrospective glance at his own poetry. With his major verse now behind him and with Milton's own canon virtually completed, Marvell insinuates his own place in poetic tradition, finding a continuity between his writings and Milton's not in epic but in pastoral tradition.

It is noteworthy, as Lawrence Hyman has observed, that to enter into the imaginative world of *Paradise Lost* Marvell reverts to an image he had used in 'The Garden'. In 'On *Paradise Lost*' Milton's soul, like the bird of paradise, is said to have soared 'above humane flight . . . / With Plume so strong' (ll. 37–8), contrasting with that of 'The Garden' poet:

> My Soul into the boughs does glide:
> There like a Bird it sits, and sings,
> Then whets, and combs its silver Wings;
> And, till prepar'd for longer flight,
> Waves in its Plumes the various light.
> (ll. 52–6)

Marvell's editors have long recognized that the poet bypasses tradition in 'On *Paradise Lost*' by giving the bird of paradise wings that, hithertofore, no one thought it possessed. His point, of course, is that not a mythical but an historical poet, Milton – not always but on the occasion of *Paradise Lost* – soared. At other times, in his early lyrics for example, Milton, like Marvell, was earth-bound.

In *Paradise Lost*, Milton moves beyond the pastoral world that he once inhabited and that had circumscribed most of Marvell's major poetry. In poetry as in politics, Marvell has managed, it would appear, to be no more than an apprentice to Milton; yet he also manages, in 'On *Paradise Lost*', to draw attention to just those attitudes that, whether or not they reflect Milton's intentions, are exact reflections of Marvell's own. The conforming spirit and Biblical aesthetics celebrated here are the foundation stones of Marvell's art; and while the former characteristic is well documented, the latter one is of special interest, because seeming to provide an identity between Marvell and Milton it, more importantly, focuses a distinction.

Marvell, we should remember, declares *Paradise Lost* a prophecy only after he dispels from the reader's consciousness the notion that the poem harbours nonconformist doctrines. He thereby divests prophecy of its revolutionary ideology and of its radical aesthetic implications as well. This genre is founded upon a notion of ongoing revelation and consequently posits a theory of poetic relationships such as is epitomized by Wordsworth when, in *The Prelude*, he speaks of poets as prophets being 'each with each / Connected in a mighty scheme of truth' (XIII, 301–2). It is this idea – along with the corollary belief that each new prophet because he extends the vision of his precursor soars beyond him – that finally accounts for Marvell's uneasiness with *Paradise Lost*. Milton's representation of himself as a second Moses about to eclipse even the Biblical prophets and as a new poet about to out-do his epic forebears exhibits a pride that Marvell recoils from. Commenting on 'The Coronet', Annabel Patterson speaks pertinently:

> The poem describes the conversion of poetry from profane to sacred subject, followed by the discovery of a new and more insidious error, that of doing the right thing for the wrong reason. The more assiduously the poet strives to perfect his praise of God, to surpass the . . . efforts of others by producing something 'never yet' offered, the more secretly he desires his own praise and

> admires his works. We recognize, in the discovery of pride, the most universal influence of the 'Serpent old'. . . . Marvell's poem is partly a comment on that particular brand of pride which, as Thomas Taylor put it . . ., makes a man 'sacrifice his owne net, and ascribe things to his owne powre, wisdome, and industry'.[38]

Not just 'The Coronet', but 'On *Paradise Lost*' – at its profoundest level – implies such a comment. Marvell's distancing of himself from Milton, his evident uneasiness with his subject, his modesty in the face of Milton's achievement – all are strategies calculated to portray Marvell as a poet different in kind from Milton, with an integrity of his own, and an honour. What has seemed to so many readers a self-effacing poem is, at least covertly, a self-justifying one. Milton took the flight for which Marvell spent a lifetime preparing. Marvell knows that and openly acknowledges it. But he also hides in his poem these clandestine questions: should the poet ever take that flight? does presumption begin where preparation ends? Marvell's poems may not be 'openly *personal explorations*',[39] but these questions indicate that, while fastening attention to another subject, Marvell is able to glance over his shoulder, as it were, at himself and his own poetic achievement. They should remind us, too, of that axiom of criticism which, rather than challenging, 'On *Paradise Lost*' confirms: 'we can only understand a poet's criticism of poetry in relation to the poetry he writes'.[40]

It has been said that Marvell's dedicatory verses 'are, or ought to be, in all modern editions' of *Paradise Lost*.[41] But they may also be read as a headpiece to Marvell's own poetry, offering a perspective on both its ideological character and its aesthetic intentions. A shrewd critic in his own right, Milton would not have missed this third dimension of Marvell's statement. Having given the world a poem of such vastness, Milton, moreover, would have been touched by the awe with which Marvell regarded *Paradise Lost*, as well as by Marvell's impulse to set forth the integrity of his own achievement, albeit on a diminished scale. The poet of 'Lycidas', after all, who entered into the 'greater Heaven' in *Paradise Lost*, would have sympathized with another poet's quietly turning back upon his own work, 'recollecting its own Light', however different that may be from Milton's, and feeling that that work 'Does, in its pure and circling thoughts, express / The greater Heaven in an Heaven less'

('On a Drop of Dew', ll. 24–6). In this respect, the composing of 'On *Paradise Lost*' constitutes Marvell's tribute to Milton; and the decision to print that poem, Milton's final (and equally moving) tribute to Marvell.

Notes

1 William R. Parker, *Milton's Contemporary Reputation*, Columbus, Ohio State University Press, 1940, p. 3.

2 When first published with the 1674 edition of *Paradise Lost*, this poem appeared as 'On *Paradise Lost*'. Hereafter I shall use this abbreviated title when referring to Marvell's poem. As late as 1843, it was still said that Marvell 'is better known as a prose writer than a poet' and still common to accent his 'association with Milton in friendship and in public service' (see, e.g., Robert Chambers, *Cyclopaedia of English Literature*, Edinburgh, 1843, I, p. 342).

3 For both Wordsworth's and Blake's comments, see *The Romantics on Milton: Formal Essays and Critical Asides*, ed. Joseph Anthony Wittreich, Jr, Cleveland, Press of Case Western Reserve University, 1970, pp. 96, 111.

4 See both Joseph H. Summers, 'Marvell's Nature', in *Andrew Marvell: A Critical Anthology*, ed. John Carey, Harmondsworth, Penguin Books, 1969, p. 139, and, in the same volume, Cleanth Brooks, 'Marvell's *Horatian Ode*', p. 193.

5 Milton speaking to Marvell in Walter Savage Landor's *Imaginary Conversations*, in *The Complete Works of Walter Savage Landor*, ed. T. Earle Welby, London, Chapman & Hall, 1927–34, IV, p. 175.

6 For the characterization of Milton's poem, see Lawrence W. Hyman, *Andrew Marvell*, New York, Twayne Publishers, 1964, p. 117; and for David Masson's remark, see *The Life of John Milton*, London, Macmillan Co., 1881–94, VI, p. 716.

7 See W. R. Parker, as above (note 1), especially pp. 77, 83, 87, 99–103, 107.

8 William R. Parker, *Milton: A Biography*, Oxford, The Clarendon Press, 1968, I, p. 451.

9 See both Stein, *The Art of Presence: The Poet and Paradise Lost*, Berkeley, University of California Press, 1977, p. 3, and Hyman, as above (note 6), pp. 116–17.
10 James H. Hanford, *John Milton, Englishman*, New York, Crown Publishers, 1949, p. 251; Nicolson, *John Milton: A Reader's Guide to the Poetry*, New York, Noonday Press, 1963, p. 275. See also Stein (previous note), pp. 10, 18.
11 Hanford, as above (note 10), p. 252, and Broadbent, *Some Graver Subject: An Essay on Paradise Lost*, London, Chatto & Windus, 1960, p. 64.
12 The emendation appears in *The Works of Milton*, ed. Thomas Newton, 1759, I, p. lxv. The correction is penned into the copy in my own Milton collection.
13 Henry F. Lippencott, Jr, 'Marvell's "On *Paradise Lost*" ', *English Language Notes*, IX (1972), p. 272. See also Pierre Legouis who describes 'praise' as 'the plainer and stronger' of the two words (*Andrew Marvell*, Oxford, The Clarendon Press, 1965, p. 122).
14 I quote this story as reported by Parker, above (note 8), I, p. 635. The story had led to the now commonplace supposition that Marvell ends his poem with 'an effectual kick to Dryden' (Émile Saillens, *John Milton: Man, Poet, Polemist*, Oxford, Basil Blackwell, 1964, p. 342). It should be noted, though, that, seeming to follow John Aubrey's account ('Mr. Milton received him [Dryden] civilly, & told him he would give him leave to tagge his Verses'), in his reference to 'points', Parker indicates that, actually, he is following a version of this story published anonymously in *The Moniter* (1713). Given this date, together with the fact that Aubrey's notes, compiled in the early 1680s, were not published until 1813, the evidence here is inconclusive: it is uncertain whether lines 45–50 are influenced by the story of Milton's encounter with Dryden or whether, as I suspect, those lines provided the materials for embellishing later reports of that encounter.
15 Masson, as above (note 6), VI, p. 709.
16 Lippencott, as above (note 13), p. 270.
17 Quoted from *Critical Essays of the Seventeenth Century*, ed. J. E. Spingarn, 1957; reprinted Bloomington, Indiana University Press, 1963, II, p. 17.
18 Rosalie L. Colie, '*My Ecchoing Song*': *Andrew Marvell's Poetry of Criticism*, Princeton University Press, 1970, p. 8. Saillens also believes that Marvell, representing himself as 'a modest poet using a minor literary form, must not venture into blank verse' (as above (note 14), p. 342).
19 Landor, as above (note 5), IV, pp. 178, 181.

20 Ibid., IV, pp. 207, 251–2. In a conversation between Milton and Marvell, however, Landor does have Milton say, probably on the authority of this poem, that 'My opinions in theology have undergone a change' (IV, p. 187).

21 Lippencott, as above (note 13), p. 272.

22 Saillens, as above (note 14), p. 262.

23 See Heninger's 'Sidney and Milton: The Poet as Maker', in *Milton and the Line of Vision*, ed. Joseph Anthony Wittreich, Jr, Madison, University of Wisconsin Press, 1975, especially pp. 68, 89–90; see also his *Touches of Sweet Harmony: Pythagorean Cosmology and Renaissance Poetry*, San Marino, Huntington Library, 1974. William G. Riggs provides a concise explanation of Marvell's phrase and its Biblical associations in *The Christian Poet in Paradise Lost*, Berkeley, University of California Press, 1972, pp. 42–3, 164–5.

24 Landor, as above (note 5), IV, pp. 214–15.

25 See Parker, as above (note 8), I, p. 630.

26 Ibid., I, p. 571.

27 William Allen, *Killing, No Murder* (1659), quoted by W. R. Parker, as above (note 1), p. 97.

28 Colie, as above (note 18), p. 6.

29 Stein, as above (note 9), p. 3; cf. William Kerrigan, *The Prophetic Milton*, Charlottesville, University Press of Virginia, 1974, p. 161.

30 The treatment of Samson in Biblical commentary undergoes a significant change in the 1650s and 1660s. Once the hero of the revolutionaries, Samson is now portrayed as a villain, as a type of Antichrist. For a review of that portion of Biblical commentary to which Milton's tragedy and Marvell's poem seem most responsive, see chapter II, 'Variations on the Paradigm', in my study, *Visionary Poetics: Milton's Tradition and His Legacy*, San Marino, Huntington Library, 1978.

31 Stein, as above (note 9), p. 3.

32 Edmund Chishull, *The Great Danger and Mistake of All New Uninspir'd Prophecies, Relating to the End of the World*, 1707, p. 12. See also Rupert Taylor, *The Political Prophecy in England*, New York, Columbia University Press, 1911, pp. 105–6; Marjorie Reeves, *The Influence of Prophecy in the Later Middle Ages: A Study of Joachimism*, Oxford, The Clarendon Press, 1969, p. 291; and my own study, as above (note 30), ch. I, 'The Politics of Vision'.

33 Stein, as above (note 9), p. 11.

34 See Parker, as above (note 8), I, pp. 600–1, and II, p. 1107.

35 I borrow the phrase from Rosalie Colie who uses it as the subtitle for her superb study of Marvell, *'My Ecchoing Song'*, as above (note 18),

especially pp. xi–xii, 3–4. Significantly, Colie uses 'On *Paradise Lost*' as a preludium to her study. Noting that Marvell left 'few comments on his own art', John Carey mentions 'On *Paradise Lost*' as 'the longest of them (above (note 4), p. 21). V. Sackville-West is still more restrictive, quoting sixteen lines from 'To his worthy Friend Doctor Witty' and the last ten lines from 'On *Paradise Lost*' and saying these two quotations represent 'the entire stock of Marvell's literary criticism' (*Andrew Marvell*, London, Faber & Faber, 1929, pp. 49–50).

36 Colie, as above (note 18), p. 8.

37 I quote from the portion of Robert Ellrodt's commentary on Marvell which is reprinted by Carey, as above (note 4), p. 151.

38 Annabel Patterson, '"Bermudas" and "The Coronet": Marvell's Protestant Poetics', *Journal of English Literary History*, XLIV (1977), p. 491.

39 S. L. Goldberg, 'Marvell: Self and Art', in Carey, as above (note 4), p. 173.

40 T. S. Eliot, *On Poetry and Poets*, 1943; reprinted New York, Noonday Press, 1961, p. 204.

41 Masson, as above (note 6), VI, p. 714.

14

Sight and insight in Marvell's poetry

Donald M. Friedman

In the middle of the third decade of the seventeenth century Father Christoph Scheiner, a German Jesuit astronomer, dissected the eyeballs of a sheep and an ox before a fascinated audience of Roman scientific virtuosi.[1] His purpose was to demonstrate that rays of light entering the eye were brought together as they reached the retina, and that they formed upon it a reduced image of the external object from which they had originally been reflected. The hypothesis of the experiment was that the part of the eye known as the crystalline humour functioned exactly as did an optical lens, whose properties of transmission and refraction had become increasingly well known in the previous quarter of a century. Scheiner wanted also to provide confirmation of optical theories advanced by Johannes Kepler some years earlier by illustrating their correspondence to facts of the physiology of vision.[2] Kepler's work on the optical properties of telescopes had led him to assert that the eye must behave as any dioptric lens, receiving a selection of the many emanations of light from the object it has focused upon, refracting those emanations, and finally resolving them into an image within the eye corresponding to that object, except for being smaller, inverted, and reversed. So much of the theory had been published by the opening years of the century, although there was no general agreement about the process through which the internal image was transmitted to the brain, that image which is what we refer to when we talk about what we 'see'.

But Scheiner's demonstration did more than simply to provide physical evidence to support Kepler's geometrical proof; it also marked the first occasion when the relationship between the external world and internal human consciousness could be witnessed, and then described it in the new universal language of the physical sciences. Moreover, in showing that the eye produced a retinal image, Scheiner made it possible and therefore necessary for the eye to see itself as it functioned. Like Milton's God looking down from his heavenly throne 'His own works and their works at once to view',[3] the intellect – whose contemplation of itself had long been a theme of Western philosophic speculation – was presented with an analysis of its premier organ of sense, an analysis which implied that the eye was constructed on much the same lines that the scientific mind had devised for the optical lens.

It followed that the elaborate mythology of the eye, and its iconography, would have to undergo some revision. No longer could the eye be seen as the microcosmic sun, illuminator of the world which was its object, nor as the shaper and creator of the world as seen. The image on the retina revealed by Scheiner's scalpel, as shocking and intriguing as the camera obscura images with which Kepler regaled Sir Henry Wotton in 1620, and which Wotton reported to Francis Bacon with enthusiastic interest[4] – that image established beyond question that the eye 'saw' only what impinged on it from without. Further, it acted with hitherto unsuspected passivity in transmitting the image of the object from 'out there' to the back of the eye itself, and thence via the optic nerve to the chambers of the brain, which were still secure in the comfortable and familiar furnishings of faculty psychology. True, the understanding of what happened to the retinal image after it had been created momentarily on the curved back of the eyeball was long in coming, and is still not complete. But the very existence of the image resolved, once for all, the puzzling over how an object larger than the eye itself could get 'into' the eye; and it narrowed the uncertainty over the way the eye selected among the emanations of light which the visual object gave off in all directions. Above all, Scheiner's display created a new dimension within the doctrine of man as universal microcosm; at least one kind of correspondence between the created world and the conscious creature was shown to be an actual mirroring. Not a metaphor, it was a smaller cosmos that was also an exact material imitation of the greater cosmos, albeit a translation into two dimensions of the spherical world-in-depth that we see daily. The retinal image thus shared both the convincing clarity and the mysterious deceptiveness of Brunelleschi's famous lost perspective painting of the Baptistry in Florence, completed precisely two centuries earlier than Scheiner's anatomy lesson.[5] That is, the retinal image was at once a clear representation of the thing that called it into being and a distortion of that thing; and the discrepancy between its two modes of being could be bridged only by the brain – if one were to follow the empiricists – or by the rational soul – if one were a traditional natural philosopher. Brunelleschi, in attempting to reproduce in two dimensions the effects of the visual laws of perspective, if not to analyse and define them, had copied his painting from the mirrored image of the building, and had painted that image itself on a mirrored surface, as if deliberately to evoke confusion between the intended aesthetic image and the reflective powers of lighted surfaces.[6] In short, the perspective painting, which in itself relies upon our consent to use illusions the better to reproduce an impression of reality, in Brunelleschi's work was also a comment on the links between the properties of mirrors and the intentions of the artist. Implicit in that comment was the speculative possibility that the truths of created nature could be discovered, embodied, and conveyed through the senses to the understanding only by drawing heavily on the technique of mathematically precise deceptions. Thus while Brunelleschi, Masaccio, Donatello and their successors were quite consciously modifying the way in which the Western mind saw the world, they nevertheless remained thoroughly committed to the artist's traditional goal of revealing and communicating the truths of nature.

The empiricism of Leonardo issued a challenge from within that tradition to some of its fundamental assumptions; even his sketchbook procedures, his insistence on rapidly evolving, sometimes superimposed, forms rather than variations of pattern-book examples, argue for his commitment to observation and the particulars of existence, as Professor Gombrich has taught us.[7] But for the most part the theories of art that developed in the Renaissance followed the direction intimated by Brunelleschi's demonstration. What has been called, properly, the Renaissance rediscovery of perspective laws was curiously consonant with the progress of the

Copernican revolution in cosmology – and equally subject to apparently anomalous fits of superstition, denial of the obvious, internal contradictions of the developing principles of empirical science, and an ineluctable idealism which led Galileo, for example, to reject Kepler's mathematical proofs of elliptical planetary orbits,[8] in all probability because it remained unthinkable to him that heavenly bodies should move in any but the circular paths required by their exalted status – this despite the fact that Galileo himself had deployed the instrument supremely fitted to the task of bringing such presuppositions into question. When Brunelleschi imitated what he knew of the facts of perception he achieved a degree of detachment from his own mental and visual acts that presages the mathematical analysis of nature, or rather the universal success of that form of science, whose struggles for supremacy go back to Pythagorean number theory. The triumph of mathematics, itself a language of symbols, in the life of the intellect from Descartes to Newton, is symbolic of a cardinal and irreversible shift of world views, a shift which has been described by a plethora of intellectual and cultural historians, and which has often served as a secular version of the myth of the Fall of Man. But here I would like only to observe that in the case of the theory of vision this shift to the mathematical occurred not without complications and internal divisions. As an example, we may revert once more to Father Scheiner's dissection of the eyeball, and note that the end of that demonstration was to confirm hypotheses about the lens functions of the eye that had been advanced by Kepler twenty years earlier, purely on the basis of geometrical analysis and constructions. Thus Scheiner was yoking experiment to theory, showing that the truths of experience fulfilled the predictions of conceptual science. In discovering and displaying the retinal image, Scheiner also minted new symbols for the relationships between the subjective and the objective, the knower and the known, inside and outside, and primarily for that between the visual object and the faculty of sight.

In discussing this part of the history of modern optics it is nearly impossible to avoid using terms and concepts that one encounters repeatedly in reading Marvell; and the reasons for that are numerous and fairly clear. With the casual generosity typical of her, the late Rosalie Colie reminded us, in a passing phrase, in her book on Renaissance paradoxes, that 'Marvell internalized the functions of optical instruments as the functions of the human mind'.[9] Indeed, fascination with the recently developed and improved forms of the telescope and microscope was widespread, to the extent that the telescope became a popular and expensive toy, and the figure of the amateur astronomer began to appear frequently in satires and parodies.[10] But for more thoughtful natural philosophers, besides the giddiness of watching new universes emerge from behind a lens – what Robert Hooke in *Micrographia* described as a 'new visible world discovered to the understanding'[11] – there was also the realization that ancient metaphors of sight seemed to be both true and tantalizingly incomplete at the same time. For example, Nathaniel Culverwell, writing his aptly titled *Spiritual Opticks* at about the same time that Marvell was serving as tutor to Mary Fairfax and, we presume, composing his major lyrics, grounded his universal analogy between vision and spiritual understanding in a variety of specific images and metaphors implicitly asserting that identity: thus St Paul's 'piercing eye' is equated with his 'clear . . . insight into the mysteries of salvation'; the reflection of Jesus in the Gospels is compared to the image of a human face that has somehow become fixed in a mirror; and Adam's legendary and intuitive ability to name the animals as they passed before him in Eden is explained as the direct consequence of his having a 'soul full of light' and 'sparkling eyes' which enabled him to 'read the smallest print, the least jot and tittle in the book of Nature'.[12] By a reverse token, one of Robert Boyle's *Occasional Reflections*, a few years later, finds the explanation of the learned preacher's power to 'inflame his Hearers' in the behaviour of sunbeams, which though they 'do but illustrate not heat' the burning-glass, manage to 'kindle subjects' by virtue of its index of refraction.[13] The argument may be compared to that of George Herbert's 'The Windows', except that Boyle's emblem is a colourless but precisely ground piece of optical glass rather than a window in which is annealed Christ's story.

In that difference, of course, lies the potential for much troubling of spirit. As many as there were to welcome the new powers that optical instruments had given to the human eye, there were others who were dismayed either by the effect of these instruments on cherished beliefs or by their penchant for shaking the stable world of social and psychological convention. Thus, theologians pondered the significance of the obvious superiority of the microscope and telescope to Adam's powers of sense and intellection, whose perfection had always been central to the doctrine of the Fall, and whose restoration was the goal of man's moral and spiritual endeavours in his life on earth, as Milton insisted in his tract on education. From a slightly different perspective, the revelations of microscope and telescope in many cases clearly surpassed or contradicted the testimony of the senses, and thereby rendered normal dioptric 'seeing' problematic. Prior to their invention all theories of vision needed merely to correspond to the facts of commonplace sense experience; accordingly, the scientist, the artist, and *l'homme moyen sensuel* saw the same world and saw it similarly.[14] To demonstrate that man could see beyond the capacity of his organ of sight was to bring all his relationships with the visible external world into question. And even those difficulties were compounded by the fact that the disruptive agent itself, the optical lens, had been devised according to mathematical laws drawn up by the mind, and in replication of the structure of the human eye whose powers it transcended.

The presence, then, of optical instruments and images and metaphors alluding to them and to their operations in Marvell's poems is not surprising, given his almost preternatural alertness to ideas, styles, gestures, and objects which expressed the civilization in which he was immersed with the greatest exactness and economy. But, typically of Marvell, his consistent and pointed use of this fairly new metaphoric convention is firmly grounded in an ancient and richer convention, the multifarious identification of the faculty of sight with intellection and spiritual enlightenment, and the exaltation of sight over the other bodily senses. This view of the nature of vision – notice how inevitably one must resort to the language of optics in order to talk about concepts, generalizations, or abstractions of any kind – and the analogies and linguistic devices it generates, is of course endemic in Western thought, while most prominent in all the historical forms of Platonism and Neoplatonism. And it might be as well to remember that this profoundly appealing idea of correspondence is based at least in part on some plain and irreducible elements in our sensuous experience. As an example of the way metaphor can shade into pragmatic observation in conventional praises of vision, let me quote William Sanderson, whose *Graphice* first appeared in 1658:

> The excellency of *Sight*, is especially, in four things / 1. Variety of *objects*, which it presents to the *Soul*. / 2. It's meanes of *Operation*; altogether Spirituall. / 3. In respect of its particular *object, Light*: the most *Noble* / *Quality* that *God* hath created. / 4. In respect of the *certainty*, *of his Action* / (In a worde, all things, under the first *Moveable Orbe*, are / subject to the *power* of *sight*.) / For the first, all *Naturall* Bodies, are *Visible*; but all are not / *Effectuall*, to other *Senses*. *Heaven*, (the World's Ornament) / is not to be touched; *Harmony* of the Spheres is not to be *Heard*; / No *taste* in the *Earth*, or *Fire*; *All* these May be seen.[15]

In short, sight commands the objects of other senses, while their powers are more limited. This ascendancy of vision is to be found as well in the processes by which we attempt to explain mental operations. As Father Ong points out, we have no choice but to use the terminology of the senses,[16] and of those only the language of vision serves to clarify, literally to explain by ordering and displaying; here too, seemingly in the nature of language itself, the other senses prove themselves to be further from naming and revealing truth than are the eyes and the processes of seeing.

It is not in the least surprising, then, to notice that Marvell uses in his poetry the language of sight and seeing more often than he refers to the other senses or their objects; the same might be said of almost all poets writing in English. It may be slightly less predictable, however, that he uses that language in the imperative mood more often than any of the poets with whom he invites comparison. As the concordances of Renaissance poets have congregated on our shelves in recent years, it has become easier for all of us to confirm our intuitive (or auditory) certainty about a poet's linguistic habits of mind; and probably as often to find that what we thought was true was not the case, but possibly something more interesting. In any event, it can be said that, as compared with Sidney, Donne, Herbert, Milton, and Vaughan in *Silex Scintillans*, Marvell *commands* or *invites* his reader to see or to look at his poetic subjects much more frequently than they do; it may be somewhat more surprising that his exhortations to vision occur more often in his lyrics than in the satires or even in the painter poems. What remains to be considered is what Marvell means when he asks us to see, what he thinks that act to be, what he expects us to do, and what we may finally understand as the purpose or consequences of our seeing.

We will notice almost immediately that Marvell's notorious elusiveness, his penchant for miming the characteristic voice of a poetic genre without embodying it in a stable, identifiable poetic personality, finds its parallel in the way he treats his coercive invitation to look at and into his poems. Especially in the lyrics, Marvell denies himself the venerable resources of ethos to win our assent either to his logic or to his suasions. Similarly, in the poems that approach the reader by turning his attention to the artist's display rather than toward the speaking figure, we find that what at first seems a simple enough set of instructions is in fact an involuted and self-contradicting exercise. The gesture that appears merely to ask us to look at the poet's speaking picture barely manages to conceal the impulse to challenge our preconceptions about what we do when we see, and thus our ways of understanding the very subject presented to us by the poet. That impulse is indulged and even elaborated in 'On a Drop of Dew', where Marvell enlists syntax and emblematic form to deepen and complicate his meditation on the phenomena of catoptrics. The two long passages that describe the dew drop and the soul reflect each other as the dew drop reflects the heaven from which it has been exuded, and as the soul reflects the light of its source, the greater heaven. Even Marvell's poetic numbers reinforce the effect of mirroring in the poem: a major portion of each stanza is cast into triplets or quatrains, while the lines that announce the decisive moral stance in favour of life 'above', fall almost inevitably into couplets, whose rhyme is an aural reflection of the concept of union.

The outward form, then, of the poem and the generously shaped analogy which serves as its structure combine to reassure us that a comparison between earthly and heavenly things is going to move toward an act that chooses high perfection and rejects the base. But we should be alert to the fact that Marvell has asked us not only to see the drop of orient dew, but to see *how* it behaves; to notice that it frames its native element by a mirror reflection, but also to try to understand *how* it accomplishes that end as it 'Round in itself incloses'. The line itself invokes a clear, if complex, visual image, even as its syntactic ambiguity discovers itself and blurs that image by superimposing another. A cursory glance at any selection of annotated editions of Marvell will show the nature of the debate over what constitutes a subject and an object in the first long clause of 'On a Drop of Dew'; and I am sure Marvell would have enjoyed the fact that the grammatical terms at issue themselves reflect the problem he is exploring. To put it perhaps too crudely, the question is whether the dew drop is said to enclose within itself the 'clear region where 'twas born', or whether it displays its careless contempt for 'its mansion new' because of its preference for its native region by closing in upon itself. What is clear, at all events, is that the phrase 'Round in itself incloses' becomes, paradoxically, a clear puzzle only when we come to the punctuation that concludes it, because until that moment we are led to expect that the verb 'incloses' will govern a direct object. Instead, as in the shift of the eye that decides to perceive the rabbit after having identified the duck, we realize that somehow or other we have already encountered the direct object without recognizing it. That realization is like the simultaneous confusion and illumination we experience when, in the first invocation in *Paradise Lost*, Milton calls upon the Spirit who simply *knows*, without telling us *what* he knows that the poet needs to learn. In contrast to Milton's, Marvell's lines achieve what we might call a metaleptic effect; the verb turns back upon itself as we discover that what has been enclosed has already been specified, and it is the encloser itself. But even this precarious state of assuredness is shaken directly, when the lines that follow, 'And in its little globe's extent, / Frames as it can its native element', leave us uncertain whether they are in addition to the act of enclosing, an expansion of it, or purely an apposition to it.

What I have been describing is essentially a syntactic structure, shaped by a master of nuances and manipulated by a mind as sensitive to the responses and guesses of his imagined reader as he is to the rays of possible meaning that spread out in every direction from the luminous core of the single word through the medium of visual and aural awareness. But such a description is to the larger purpose of the poem as the geometrical hypothesis of the retinal image is to the full consciousness of human vision. What Marvell appears to be pursuing, by virtue of his syntactic ambiguities and his skill at *trompe-l'oreille*, is a way to think about the moral effort that goes into maintaining one's sense of self as distinguished from the world around. And he seems to suggest that psychic energy for that effort must be drawn from the connection with, the reminiscence of, perhaps merely the belief in another world which defines itself by its separation from the environment of the self. Those connections of essence or faith are figured in the poem as mirrorings, and the act of reflecting is spoken of as a deliberate and difficult choice. The problem that Marvell focuses his and our attention on is that the crucial reflection is made possible and sustained only by an equally demanding act of withdrawal into the self, a protective and shape-giving movement of ingathering. The paradox, then, concerns how one – one person, one soul, one dew drop, one sphere of any description – maintains its link with the source of its being by rolling in upon itself. Marvell gives the paradox substance, glitter, wit and interest by directing our eyes and our mind's eye to the surface phenomena of reflected images; and as we come to see the full scope of what was meant in the first line by his asking us to see *how* the drop encloses 'Round in itself', we also realize that we have been reflecting upon the poem as its lines, rhymes, images reflect themselves and upon themselves.[17]

The first strophe of the poem ends on a note of resolved hope, as the 'warm sun', source of light and heat at once, responds to the emotions of the dew drop – figured as optical reflections and deliberate gestures, gazing, shining, rolling, and trembling. The sun expresses its pity for the dew drop's pain and brings it home again by acting through the physical metamorphosis of evaporation; its imputed warmth of feeling is translated directly into vapourizing heat energy. The entire trope serves as a prediction of that miniature *commiato*, the poem's concluding couplets, by allowing the comparative 'So' which begins the strophe on the soul to suggest a reference both to the soul's behaviour and to its ultimate destiny. The momentary blur of confusion between the two possible comparisons allows Marvell also to introduce his governing analogy, between the soul and the drop, without immediately acknowledging its tenuousness, in that it pretends to compare the visible to the invisible by inviting us to see both. Thus, by the time the appropriate conditional phrasing appears in line 21, 'Could it within the humane flow'r be seen', he has established a perspective which makes it equally plausible that the soul's retiring modesty and fastidiousness account for its not being seen within the fleshly rose of the body as does its metaphysical status. The technique is reminiscent of Milton's tactic of opening *Paradise Lost* in an intensely material and vividly imaged hell, so that when the bard's blind eye shifts to heaven in Book III we sustain the impression of visual reality, although the landscape of Heaven receives no truly direct description but exists, by negation, as an after-image on the retina of the mind. Just so Marvell's soul acquires a visionary solidity from our experience of having contemplated the dew drop; in the movement from strophe to strophe, and even while the verbs of action continue their work of persuading us that the soul behaves as the dew drop did, we are taught how to shift from looking at an object to seeing it even when it is invisible. In other words, the analogical frame of the poem is a lesson in moving, or more properly rising, from sight to vision, from perception to recognition, from sense to understanding, and, a little more tentatively, from the created world to the incorporeal.

Within each strophe one major focal point is an act of reflection, which is of course itself reflected in the mirroring of the two strophes. But Marvell is as scrupulous as he is inventive in working his theme, and reminds us twice that, as in catoptric surfaces, reflection also involves reduction. Thus the dew drop 'Frames' only 'as it can its native Element' 'in its little Globes Extent', and the soul expresses 'The greater Heaven in an Heaven less'. But the compelling symmetry of Marvell's figure must also accommodate within the circle of reflection some sign of distinction between the mirror image and the imaged object; some device in the poem that will help us to see differences as well as identities, as we manage to reconcile perceptually the mirror's reduced image and our knowledge of the actual size of the thing it is reflecting. The discrepancy in Marvell's poem – the distance that corresponds to the real and theoretical line between the eye and the perspective vanishing point in the mirror – is the ontological abyss between the dew drop and the soul. Marvell bridges that gap, or ignores it, or diverts our attention from it with his sleight-of-hand involving images of reflection and the implications of words of comparison and identification like 'So'. But he also provides enough evidence of the distance at the heart of his analogy for us to correct our vision of the poem's structure. For example, the soul is introduced together with its definition, 'that Drop, that Ray / Of the clear Fountain of Eternal Day'; like the dew drop, it is a liquid sphere, but born of a fountain and therefore substantially like its originator rather than exuded from the morning sky. Moreover, it comes from a fountain of light, and thus holds within itself the power which alone is able to enfranchise the dew drop at the end of its restless sojourn in the blowing rose. The dew drop, as it gazes back at the skies from which it came, 'Shines with a mournful Light'; the implication seems clear that this is reflected light, made lesser and mournful by reduction. In contrast, the soul, as it remembers 'its former height', recollects 'its own Light'; *pace* Pierre Legouis,[18] the soul differs from the dew drop in that its mental acts have the force of effective gestures, to remember is to recollect in the sense of amassing light, Marvell treating excellence as if it were actual corpuscular illumination.[19] More to the point, the soul recollects *its own* light under the stimulus of remembering what and where it has been. As in Pythagorean and Platonic optical theory, the soul itself gives off light, as the eye was believed to emit a beam that rendered its object visible. Moreover, the soul expresses 'the greater Heaven' in its 'pure and circling thoughts', disembodied and abstract spheres whose epithets suggest the ways in which the dew drop's reflections are merely imitative, lesser forms of the intimacy between the soul's 'thoughts' and the transcendent ideas of which, however abstract and refined they may seem to the worldly view, they are only a crude reflection.

We have all learned, to our delight and enlightenment, and sometimes to our embarrassment, that Marvell conducts a poetic argument so that we may feel ourselves free to consider it as in itself it appears to be, with intellectual detachment, as in a sort of conceptual paraphrase, without attending to the formal structures of logic and prosody in which it is embodied. Thus, once he has said that the soul expresses 'The greater Heaven in an Heaven less', and set resonating in our minds the trope of comparing great things with small,[20] he does not pause an instant before remarking confidingly to us on the figure in which the soul is wound. The figure, of course, is of his own creation, and its most obvious surface appearance is that of a mirror. But the rhetorical figure finds *its* mirror image in what we might call the posture of the soul as a moral figure; and here our attention is turned to the involutions, the actual turnings into and away from, that shape the spherical integrity of the heaven-homesick soul. I think that what Marvell is suggesting here is a way to express the interplay between the ambivalence of evaluation and feeling and the task of defining the self, which necessitates resolving ambivalence. 'Every way it turns away', he says of the soul, and we can see the illogic beneath the emotive gesture; to turn away every way is to turn in no specific direction, but at the same time to describe all the arcs of a circle, and thus to mime perfection. Similarly, in 'So the World excluding round,' roundness attaches itself with roughly equal pertinence to the shape of the world being excluded and to the protective circle from within which the soul excludes the world. Where the dew drop had enclosed 'the clear Region where 'twas born' 'Round in itself', and left us richly unsure whether the roundness was the drop's or the region's, or an adverbial note on the nature of enclosing – and all this to Marvell's purpose – the soul creates its shape by casting out, thrusting back, excluding round. To be sure, it yearns toward and opens itself to the day, its former height, 'above'; but Marvell is almost importunate in keeping before us the toll of these defences, the effort that goes into rejection. He envisions the predicament of the soul, exiled in the 'humane flow'r', by envisaging it as a reflective sphere illuminated from above, and translates what he observes in imagination into descriptive terms that move as easily from the visual surface to the inward consciousness as his metaphors move from the visible to the invisible. The soul is:

> Dark beneath, but bright above:
> Here disdaining, there in Love.
> (ll. 31–2)

That the darkness is not altogether an optical phenomenon is suggested by its parallel in 'disdaining'; like the false ladies in *The Faerie Queene*, or all the ladies in romance and Petrarchan traditions whose chilling champion is the Giant Disdain, this emotion draws its power from its status as the reverse image of love, negating it but tied to it in meaning by that very fact. To disdain, in Marvell's lines, is also to 'dis-stain' the natural brightness of the soul and plunge it into darkness beneath.

It is thus not the case that the poem is concerned primarily to vary and elaborate its chosen themes of bright and dark, up and down, greater and lesser. It rests as uneasily on those stable oppositions as do its subjects on their temporary common places. Rather, Marvell allows the figures that form naturally around his dualistic theme, flocking like denizens of Hades, to reveal the antecedent decisions and values that are involved in the clear alternatives they seem to present. In a way, Marvell is asking us to see that the mirror image comments on what it reflects, and to toy with the idea that moral mirrors, so to speak, can distort an image for particular, self-serving, or self-justifying purposes. Notice, for example, how the description of the soul, 'loose and easie hence to go: / . . . girt and ready to ascend', plays on the qualities of relaxation and rigour, yoked in parallel but not married, in the soul's attitude. Oddly enough, its reaction to the world, its eagerness to leave what it has shunned and disdained so avidly, is now characterized as loose and easy; while its loving and receptive loyalty to the greater heaven has become the cinched-in, tightly girt state of preparedness we associate with warriors, martyrs, heroes of dedication and sacrificial effort. 'Moving but on a point below, / It all about does upwards bend' describes in comparable language the combination of precariousness and strain, equipoise and muscular striving that makes the soul's situation something more than a simple homiletic example.

The difficulty with a mirror poem like 'On a Drop of Dew' is in finding a place from which to view the reflections in a perspective that will encompass and clarify the viewer's relation to what he is seeing. Marvell adjusts the telescope merely by saying 'Such', a word that places not only the dew drop we have been watching and the soul we have been imagining, but also the experiences that have been attributed to both. The perspective he establishes is of another kind altogether, one that depends on our looking through the lens of memory into the distance of history. And there we see that the dilemma represented in the reflecting structure of the poem has been resolved in the type of the descent of manna to the wandering Israelites. Even here Marvell orders his retelling to point to interrelationships of images and the concepts that give them value, just as they both necessitate *and* depend on them for expression. The phrase, the 'Manna's sacred Dew', glances at the fact that the manna appeared with the morning dew,[21] perhaps enclosed within it, and disappeared as the dew evaporated each day, as part of God's test of the Jews' faith and obedience. But is the natural dew 'sacred', or is manna God's figure for the sanctification of the natural and therefore the sacred dew itself, expressed in the lesser heaven of the diurnal dew drop? Marvell's language will not tell us, because it is subject to the same limits as is the perspective from which we view the speaking picture he is painting for us. One can 'see' only surfaces;

the question is how to achieve vision rather than sight. The problem is put before us once more in 'White, and intire, though congeal'd and chill'; surely that which is sent down from heaven, away from its source of heat and light, is white and entire *because* it is congealed and chill? The poem has shown us, or reminded us, that whiteness and integrity are among the words we use to direct the orientation of worldly exiles toward their heavenly home; they are, in short, synonyms for 'the good'. [22] But, using the same device that inanimates 'A Dialogue between the Soul and Body' – the interchange between the languages of fleshly and spiritual experience – Marvell shows us that whiteness is the mark of icy cold, as entireness is the result of self-sufficiency, isolation, and rejection. That which is white is colourless; but colours are of the earth. That which is entire is whole; but the Ark was filled in twos. Every achievement entails a loss; every image reflects an object, and diminishes it; to realize that light is above one must know that dark is below. In the modes of our thought, as in the ways of our seeing, we are limited by our inability to reconcile the oppositions within them.

Except that Marvell at last releases us into the knowledge that this is true on earth; as the warmth of the sun evaporates the dew, 'exhaling' back to the sky, as its light obliterates lesser reflections by absorbing them back into the point they have imaged, our desire to resolve the balancings, the doublenesses, the ambivalences and mirror images in the poem is transcended by the sun's power to dissolve what has congealed here into images of spherical, white purity. As they go back to their origins even the shape which our eyes tell us repeats the spherical form of the greater heaven is rendered shapeless; all of our attempts to capture meaning in form are rendered inappropriate by the 'Glories of th' Almight sun'. This is true both in the visual sense that the sun overgoes weaker kinds of illumination, and in the figural sense that the antitype of all embodiments of meaning is the Incarnation.

Marvell's consistently vigorous interest in genres, in styles, in types of language, in all stylized and conventional means of expression, leads naturally to his larger fascination with the way one kind of thing can be made to fit into another that is both like and unlike it; thus we have his redoubtable ability to invent dialogues between soul and body, to cast love poems in the language of geometric proofs, above all to forge metaphors that test the capacity of language to express the abstract in the concrete, what Rosalie Colie described, in a different context, as his habit of naturalizing the artificial or artificializing the natural.[23] One would think that having joined Donne and Herbert and Crashaw in the company of those poets who speculate on the poetic act in the shadow of theological doctrines of creation and incarnation, Marvell might have found a field fertile enough even for his procreative mind. But many readers have noticed that, as intrigued as he may be by the yoking of unlikes, he is even more unusually attracted to the idea and the image of things immersed in their own qualities, reflections so perfect that their individual essences are lost or merged.[24] Perhaps the most Marvellian way to put it is to point to the Janus-like nature of the word that expresses the problem that attracts Marvell – 'identity'. One's identity is that which establishes one's difference from all other comparable beings; to be identical is to be exactly the same as another being. Both in nature and in the literary conventions which Marvell inherited, the most freely accessible and versatile images for these paradoxical notions were, of course, spheres of all kinds, and more particularly the common figures of astronomy, and human eyes and tears.

Nothing could be more conventional in the mid-seventeenth century than a poem on tears; perhaps it is sadly ironic that Marvell's poem was reprinted, most unusually, ten years after his death, and that it is one of the very few lyrics by him to be mentioned during the eighteenth century.[25] But despite the fact that it includes a reference to the Magdalen, 'Eyes and Tears' is very different from Crashaw's 'The Weeper' and all the other poems that constitute the genre to which we must nevertheless assign it. And if the poem strikes us as typically Marvellian in its relation to its model – a lesser form that both reflects and distorts a greater – it is so in the way it treats its subject as well. Marvell begins by praising nature's wisdom in giving eyes a double function, and ends by surpassing nature's economy, finding a way for the two functions to interchange themselves and so make the dependent tear identical with the eye that produces it. The wit resides in the poet's presumption in perceiving and then perfecting nature's design; but the ingenious point would be blunted without the poignant realization on which it is based – that to view the world is inevitably to grieve over it.

The mock-encomium that opens the poem,

How wisely Nature did decree,
With the same Eyes to weep and see!
(ll. 1–2)

strikes the same note as Donne's 'How witty's ruin!',[26] wry and knowing appreciation of the care with which the universe has been designed so as to assure man's fall into sober reality. It is clear immediately that Marvell's plan is not to accumulate emblematic instances to suggest how many things a tear can resemble in meaning, but to assume that the mirroring of eye and tear has a meaning in itself, and to follow the implications of that hypothesis, as if they constituted the kind of regression one sees in a mirror image of a mirror. He proposes at first that we have but one organ 'to weep and see' only so that we need waste no time in beginning to cry once we have looked at the world. But Marvell's pose of sophisticated disenchantment is only an initial pose, as we might suspect from the unstable adjective in the phrase 'having viewed the object vain'. The essential problem in distinguishing between perception and vision is to specify who it is that sees what we think we see. If you recall Father Scheiner's experiment with the eyeball, you will realize that the discovery of the physical actuality of the retinal image involved optical philosophers in the kind of infinite regress I just figured as a house of mirrors. That is, if the eye 'sees' that image by incorporating it and displaying it on the retinal screen as in the manner of a camera obscura, who or what is it in the brain that 'sees' the image coming from the eye? Is there another eye in the brain, the intellect, the rational soul? Traditional metaphors had always insisted that there is; but physiological optics shook the cogency of those metaphors, ironically enough, by showing that they might be literally true.

That Marvell is sensitive to such implication is suggested by the second stanza, which offers another explanation for the link between seeing and crying:

And, since the Self-deluding Sight,
In a false Angle takes each hight;
These Tears which better measure all,
Like wat'ry Lines and Plummets fall.
(ll. 5–8)

It would be enough, in a conventional poem about the fallibility of the senses and the wisdom of humility, to note that the faculty of sight is easily deceived and often mistaken. But for Marvell the object seen is as vain as is the effort to see it truly; thus the eye is not only deluded by fallen nature but deludes the self because of its intrinsic nature. It is typical, I think, that Marvell is utterly even-handed in allowing the angle to be false because of its emblematically corrupt shape, or the eye to choose a false angle because it is essentially self-deluding; and perhaps we can find in Marvell's political attitudes, as reflected in the poems of his Nun Appleton residence, some explanation of why the eye spends all of its time estimating heights, taking them in false angles. In any case, tears are shown to be better surveyors, better moral geometricians, because they fall in straight lines. As in 'The Definition of Love', truth runs straight in parallel lines, while falsehood, like 'Loves oblique', greets itself 'in every Angle'. As the poem proceeds, the division between what is seen and what is felt and understood grows, greater wisdom residing with grief, the intuitive response to life in the world. The paradox expands so that Marvell can advise us sagely:

> Yet happy they whom Grief doth bless,
> That weep the more, and see the less:
> And to preserve their Sight more true,
> Bath still their Eyes in their own Dew.
>
> (ll. 25–8)

In the invocation to Book III of *Paradise Lost* Milton will identify the belief in a 'sight more true' with his inner irradiation by a divine power; Marvell's only access to true sight is his understanding of the causes of sorrow. As he says, 'others too can see, or sleep, / But only human eyes can weep'. He began with a sardonic compliment to nature for saving us effort, but ends by discovering within the human condition the solace for the pain of its double, deluded, and often self-deluding state of being. Milton prays that his actual blindness will be compensated for by an implantation of transcendent light; Marvell urges, ironically and paradoxically, that we blind ourselves by weeping, so as to protect our powers of moral perception. Like the dew drop and the soul, the eye in 'Eyes and Tears' maintains its integrity, its purity, its invulnerability to deceit and false allures, by cutting itself off from the world around it, by overwhelming and even maiming its proper sensuous function; the ideal is now an eye that does not see at all but weeps because it knows what is true without looking at it. The double function with which the poem opened, an exemplum of *concors discordia*, is transmuted in the concluding stanza to an assertion of identity in which the two subjects interchange attributes and become 'These weeping eyes, those seeing tears'. The correct view of the matter, then, is *discors concordia*, a distinction of like things, so that eyes will see truly only by weeping, while tears will become the spherical lens through which vision is finally possible. To put it another way, the conventional mirror image of eye and tear reflecting each other – which we do find in Crashaw, in Donne, and even elsewhere in Marvell, as in 'Mourning' – is here revised by inversion: the transparent, lens-like organ which is designed to see is now blinded and opaque, while the liquid sphere that can but reflect what is outside it inherits the function of sight. Once again, Marvell's interest in differences and likenesses, enclosures and exclusions, reflection and identity, finds expression in the vocabulary and figures of optical theory.

I have been thus self-indulgent in treating at such length 'On a Drop of Dew' and 'Eyes and Tears', poems usually and perhaps rightly regarded as less imposing than the glittering anthology prizes, for a number of reasons. Among them are the thorough and imaginative discussions which in recent years have been devoted to the importance of visions, viewpoints, and optical phenomena of many kinds in particular in *Upon Appleton House*;[27] and my certainty that to engage that poem in the way I have looked at the other two would keep us here until 'the dark Hemisphere' threatens to overtake us like the salmon fishers looming so strangely out of the river below to Marvell's 'shining Eye'. But, not entirely daunted, I want to take just a few moments to remark on one focal image in that poem, and then to offer one or two final comments, a perspective on perspective, if you will permit me.

That the act of seeing will be crucial to assessing the extended experience rendered in *Upon Appleton House* is made clear immediately; of the four parts of the estate Marvell specifies in stanza 10, 'fragrant Gardens, shady Woods, / Deep Meadows, and transparent Floods', we notice that only the garden's epithet draws upon a sense other than sight, and that only in traversing the garden does the poet master the scene entirely with witty conceits. By contrast, he finds the woods, meadows, and the flooded river problematic and even mysterious, though not uncongenial. The gardens are the Lord Fairfax's, but the deep, shady, and transparent outer landscape is preeminently the precinct of the poet's moving eye. Or, as he calls it, his 'slow eye', which moves and measures while his 'footstep', with oddly transferred epithets, stays pleasantly where it is. Marvell enacts, and enjoys, that momentary stasis in stanza 46, directly before the descent into the fascinating and somehow menacing world of the meadows and the flood; or at least 'the sight' imitates Fairfacian heroism by playing at being a battery of guns firing at the walls of Cawood Castle. But it finds its true object in playing upon the meadows below, or gazing in apparent innocence on the abyss into which the mind and eye will now descend. The disorientation that overtakes Marvell, which he seems both to fear and to delight in, as with a child's shiver of pleasure at being frightened in known and anticipated ways, is characterized by comparing walking in deep grass to immersion in water; the point, of course, is that location – identity perhaps – depends on scale and comparison. The world below the gardens of Nun Appleton is very like the world of perception we have observed in 'On a Drop of Dew' and 'Eyes and Tears'; it proves repeatedly, through metamorphosis and anamorphosis, that shifts in perspective, or the absence of familiar visual reference points, can have the effect of effacing one's sense of stable identity. Contemporary optical science says much the same thing, as do the earliest authorities of the Italian school of perspective painting. Marvell, as is his wont, uses explanatory scientific data to vivify our sense of the dilemmas of consciousness. More specifically, the deliberate disruption of visual convention is the key to the poem's drive to encompass political, literary, historical, and theological motifs without insisting on a single vantage point from which to view or understand them.

I regard the famous fifty-eighth stanza as a species of free fantasia on a minor theme sounded by the mention of Davenant's 'Universal *Heard*'.[28] Marvell plays with the shapes and sizes of the cattle as a child plays with a telescope, and invites us to do the same, almost as if to force upon us the sensation of rapidly inverting reversing scales which is so important to his explorations in meaning. That it is the sensation rather than the exotic images themselves that is central is shown, I believe, by the quick succession of the Denton's flood, by which the meadow becomes what it truly is rather than what it 'but seem'd before, a Sea', and in which the cattle, our momentary cynosure, are less interesting than the spectacle of the river drowned in itself. And even when the waters recede, the river remains a centring image, a possible source of illusions and visual error, as in stanza 79, where the danger is that 'it self you will mistake'. Beyond that, it both folds in the meadow now and at the same time covers it with a reflecting surface, so that, in Rosalie Colie's words, the 'river presents a picture of the world to the world, a picture so perfect that the things reflected in the river seem to lose their identity in their reflections, or in the reflections of themselves.'[29] Gazing at themselves, 'all things' 'doubt / If they be in or without'. The mind in 'The Garden' acted out that poem's metaphysics by including all the kinds within itself, but here being both in and out is not a sign of universal order but an instance of the universal experience of change and uncertainty.

Upon Appleton House, of course, is a poem of compliment and is governed by different generic conventions from those of 'The Garden'; and so it is Mary Fairfax who orders, reconciles, and dissolves the apparent parallax of the visual world. The 'viscous Air' takes colour from the emblematic halcyon, the stream jellies and becomes crystalline, and Maria vitrifies all of nature. Stasis is the reply to the metamorphic riot of the sojourn in the woods and meadows; there is a counterbalance to the dissolution of the congealed whiteness of the manna's sacred dew. Each poem has its own optic, and its own way to reconcile opposites; but what is quite clear in *Upon Appleton House* is Marvell's insistence on the revolutionary nature of moving perspectives. To organize a poem about a consciousness in motion is not unusual; but to treat that concept with scientific exactness is. Marvell asks us to recognize that the laws of perspective, as Alberti knew, both recreate our perception of reality and create an illusion that does not correspond to what we know to be reality.

Throughout its long history in antiquity and the Middle Ages, *perspectiva* had been the term for the entire science of optics itself; it was only with the experiments and innovations of the fifteenth century that the word came to mean the mathematical and psychological ways of determining the viewpoint from which a thing is seen. In the excitement over this wonderful new method to reproduce the illusion of visual reality and to understand the natural laws that governed the process, it was not so clearly realized that perspective also brought with it limitations and distortions.[30] While it put the eye and mind in comprehensible relationships with the outside world, it also restricted the consciousness to a static point, and placed it at a remove from the object of contemplation. More to the point, it rendered the act of understanding at once simpler and more difficult; from a given perspective, the object appeared clear and conformed to known laws of optical behaviour; but were the observer to move and thus change the perspective viewpoint, all the problems of distance, identification, and relative scale had to be solved again *ab initio*. The world of perspective, then, insisted on a kind of ordering that was rigid but evanescent, and that depended very heavily on the viewer rather than on the pattern of relationships inherent in the objects observed, saving always the laws of perspective themselves.

Modern optical theory and modern philosophy beginning with Berkeley's theories of vision have provided at least two prescriptions for easing the dilemma. The succession of perspective views we establish and recognize as we move through the world, distinct though they may be, are placed in relationship to each other by the mind, which establishes a continuity between discrete moments of vision which we call 'the world' or our experience of it. In James J. Gibson's explanation,[31] this continuity is the 'visual world', in which our visual experience is supplemented by knowledge accrued through all the senses and all kinds of experience. In the visual world we may see an ellipse, but we know that the dinner plate is 'really' round. In the visual field, by contrast, we perceive what we see; and it is this limited vision that we carry with us when we focus on particular parts of the visual world. It is the visual world we believe in, which we know to be the reality lying beneath and supporting the separate acts of the eye that convey external nature to us. And yet this world cannot be 'seen' in the way we see things at each moment.

Similarly, Berkeley first argued, and Professor Gombrich has continued to try to get us to see, that visual perception itself works much like a language, in which arbitrary signs and customary ways of interpreting them play a much more important role than the conscious optical apprehension of 'the thing itself'. In short, neither classical nor Newtonian optics, while explaining the way the eye works by innate geometrical principles, can touch upon the way we perceive and interpret as we see. The dependence of vision on the interpreting consciousness is, of course, among Marvell's interests in *Upon Appleton House*, as we can tell merely by his reminding us constantly that the things we are asked to look at change, both as we move through the imagined landscape and as we try to decide what they are in essence. We shall, for instance, see that he 'was but an inverted Tree', but only if we turn him upside down; the cattle will look big or small depending on how we interpret the image we focus on in the specular glass; and we are included in the category of 'all things' that, gazing upon the reflecting river, doubt whether 'they be in it or without'.

There is no more inventive nor comprehensive treatment in Marvell of the delights and dilemmas of perspective views than *Upon Appleton House*, as we might have suspected from the sheer variety of explanations that have been offered over the years for the poem's peculiar structure. If it is not truly epic in design, surely it is in the scope of investigation of Marvell's commanding theme, the life of mind and spirit in the world – a theme that deserves our speculation and reflection.

In this poem Marvell plays upon the division within our visual and mental functions, a division which is nevertheless underpinned by the connections and similarities between seeing and knowing, connections honoured in the metaphors Marvell inherited and to whose richly evocative store he added uniquely.

Notes

1 See Joseph Priestley, *History and Present State of Discoveries Relating to Vision, Light, and Colours*, London, 1772, I, p. 112. Priestley found the story in Caspar Schott, *Magia Universalis Naturae et Artis*, Frankfurt, 1657, p. 87.

2 See David C. Lindberg, *Theories of Vision from Al-Kindi to Kepler*, University of Chicago Press, 1976, pp. 178–208. Kepler's theory appeared in *Ad Vitellionem paralipomena* in 1604.

3 *Paradise Lost*, III, l. 59.
4 *Life and Letters of Sir Henry Wotton*, ed. Logan Pearsall Smith, Oxford, Clarendon Press, 1907, II, pp. 205–6.
5 See Samuel Y. Edgerton, Jr, *Renaissance Discovery of Linear Perspective*, New York, Basic Books, 1975, pp. 124–52; and John White, *Birth and Rebirth of Pictorial Space*, New York, Thomas Yoseloff, 1958, pp. 113–21.
6 Marvell seems to have had something similar in mind when he described the cattle, in stanza 58 of *Upon Appleton House*: 'They seem within the polisht Grass / A Landskip drawen in Looking-Glass'.
7 E. H. Gombrich, 'Leonardo's Method for Working out Compositions', in his *Norm and Form*, London, Phaidon Press, 1966, p. 58.
8 James S. Ackerman develops this point in 'Science and Visual Art', in *Seventeenth Century Science and the Arts*, ed. Hedley Howell Rhys, Princeton University Press, 1961, pp. 80–1, and refers to Erwin Panofsky's remarks in *Galileo as a Critic of the Arts*, The Hague, 1954.
9 Rosalie Colie, *Paradoxia Epidemica*, Princeton University Press, 1966, p. 284.
10 John Wilkins, for example, was the butt of the remark, 'Oxford scholars are good at two things, at diminishing a commonwealth and at multiplying a louse'. See Charles Webster, *Great Instauration*, London, Duckworth, 1975, p. 176.
11 *Micrographia*, London, 1665, sign. a2^{V}.
12 *Spiritual Opticks*, London, 1652, pp. 177, 188, 191.
13 *Occasional Reflections upon Several Subjects*, 2nd ed., London, 1669, pp. 399–401.
14 See Ackerman, as above (note 8), pp. 64–5.
15 *Graphice*, London, 1658, p. 3.
16 Walter Ong, S. J., 'System, Space, and Intellect in Renaissance Symbolism', *Bibliothèque d'Humanisme et Renaissance, Travaux et Documents*, XVII (Geneva, 1956), p. 231.
17 Cf. Colie, as above (note 9), p. 282.
18 Legouis regards similar notions as 'fancied ambiguities'; see his note to l.24, p. 244 of *Poems and Letters*, I.
19 Milton suggests the same ambivalence in Satan's 'recollecting' 'his wonted pride' (*Paradise Lost*, I, ll. 527–8).
20 See John S. Coolidge, 'Great Things and Small: the Virgilian Progression', *Comparative Literature*, XVII (1965), pp. 1–23.
21 Rashi and other Biblical commentators argued that first dew had fallen, then manna over the dew, and then dew again over the manna; thus the manna was enclosed between two layers of dew.
22 Compare Donne's 'Muse's white sincerity' (*La Corona*, I, 6).

23 '*My Ecchoing Song*', Princeton University Press, 1970, p. 97.
24 Elsie Duncan-Jones makes an interesting point in this regard about the portrait of Douglas in *Last Instructions to a Painter*; see her 'Marvell: a Great Master of Words', *Proceedings of the British Academy*, LXI (1976), p. 277. The theme is one of particular attraction to Herrick, too.
25 See Legouis's note in *Poems and Letters*, I, p. 245.
26 *The First Anniversary*, l. 99.
27 Part IV of Rosalie Colie's '*My Ecchoing Song*' is devoted entirely to the poem; M. J. K. O'Loughlin's 'This Sober Frame: a Reading of *Upon Appleton House*', in George deF. Lord, ed., *Andrew Marvell: A Collection of Essays*, Englewood Cliffs, Prentice-Hall, 1968, pp. 120–42, has received deserved praise; James Carscallen, 'Marvell's Infinite Parallels', *University of Toronto Quarterly*, XXXIX (1970), pp. 144–63, and Frederic H. Roth, Jr, 'Marvell's *Upon Appleton House*: A Study in Perspective', *Texas Studies in Language and Literature*, XIV (1972), pp. 269–81, are original and illuminating. Kitty W. Scoular's *Natural Magic*, Oxford, Clarendon Press, 1965, retains its powers to delight and inform.
28 *Gondibert* was published only recently, in 1650.
29 Colie, as above (note 23), p. 209.
30 See Erwin Panofsky, *Early Netherlandish Painting*, Cambridge, Mass., Harvard University Press, 1964, p. 6; Colie, as above (note 9), p. 288.
31 *The Perception of the Visual World*, Boston, Houghton Mifflin, 1950, pp. 3, 27, and *passim*.

15

Special contribution

'Loose Nature' and the 'Garden Square': the gardenist background for Marvell's poetry

John Dixon Hunt

'the Conceits of the mind are Pictures of things'
Ben Jonson[1]

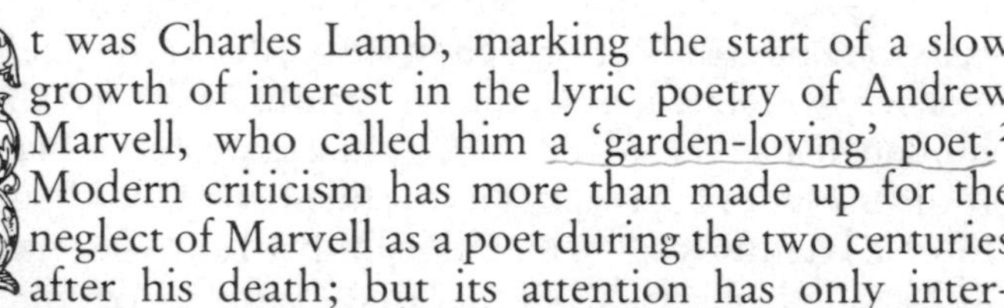

It was Charles Lamb, marking the start of a slow growth of interest in the lyric poetry of Andrew Marvell, who called him a 'garden-loving' poet.[2] Modern criticism has more than made up for the neglect of Marvell as a poet during the two centuries after his death; but its attention has only intermittently been focused upon the relationship of Marvell's garden poetry to its contemporary 'gardenist'[3] culture. And on such occasions literary perspectives necessarily impose their own demands upon architectural or horticultural history, which has been variously neglected or sketched very tendentiously.[4] It is the aim of this essay to provide a larger and more detailed map of seventeenth-century garden theory and practice. No attempt will be made to relate this to the poetry in any detail; rather, it is hoped to provide other Marvellians, intent – in Jonson's phrase – upon the literary 'Conceits of the mind', with fuller 'Pictures of things' that may have shaped or conditioned Marvell's thinking.[5]

I

The history of gardening, as far as it concerns England during the seventeenth century, is essentially the importation of European models to enlarge the scale and concept of the Tudor garden. It also involves the acquisition of fresh mental habits within these new gardens and the discovery that even gardens of the old style were hospitable to this new gardenist psychology.

The sixteenth-century English garden, examples of which inevitably survived into the following century, was generally small and unadventurous in scope or decoration. Not long since emancipated from the need to be fortified, the manor house simply extended its interior spaces into the out-of-doors (Plate 15.1):[6] painted rails divide these exterior 'corridors' and 'rooms', which may be, according to Gervase Markham, quartered and decorated by 'either a conduit of antic fashion, a standard of some unusual device, or else some dial or other pyramid that may grace and beautify the garden'.[7] Such decorations persisted throughout the seventeenth century (see Plate 15.2)[8] until they were absorbed and expanded into the more elaborate parterres of French-style gardens after the Restoration.

There were, of course, the exceptions of the 'prodigy' Elizabethan buildings like Holdenby (Northamptonshire), Theobalds (Hertfordshire), or Hardwick (Derbyshire), where the gardens were aptly more adventurous.[9] Some, indeed, provide what may be seen either as Elizabethan revivals of that first, abruptly curtailed, flowering of Renaissance culture under Henry VIII, when the gardens of Nonsuch were probably modelled, like the palace, upon the Italianate designs of Francis I's Fontainebleau, or as early examples of the Italianate/French creations under James I and Charles I. What distinguished these 'prodigy' gardens was mainly a more lavish display of ornament. A Continental visitor, Paul Hentzner, appreciated the 'many columns and pyramids of marble' in the Nonsuch gardens, as well as the Grove of Diana with Actaeon 'turned into a stag'; at Theobalds he similarly approved of a labyrinth, *jet d'eau*, columns, pyramids, and the cisterns to keep fish.[10] But, ornament apart, these grander gardens largely comprised repetitions of the simple square structure already noted. At Wimbledon House, for example, though the northern aspect had a distinct Italian air, with terraces descending by complex staircases,[11] the gardens, orchards and vineyards on the other sides (Plate 15.3) were simply variations of the square or rectangle, placed side by side. They held, doubtless, many delights,[12] but the designer's manipulation of space does not seem to draw a visitor from one section to the next nor to involve him mentally or psychologically in his explorations.

One has only to compare these basically sixteenth-century gardens with visions of a new kind that Inigo Jones sometimes offered his courtly audiences as settings in Jacobean or Caroline masques (Plate 15.4).[13] These images reveal a sophisticated repertoire of garden elements: fountains, statues, grottoes, casinos, terraces with divided staircases connecting different levels, or covered walks that offer ambiguous territory ('inside' outside) and suggest new interplay between man-made and natural environment. But above all Jones suggests a new excitement with spatial discovery: in the design for 'A Garden and a Princely Villa' we seem to have been drawn towards an opening and find ourselves at the top of stairs leading down into an area where our eyes will tempt our steps to explore further intricacies. This new garden experience – 'The idea of "regular" nature was now superceded by that of "capricious" nature, full of "inventions" and of the unpredictable'[14] – can only be guessed from Jones's flat designs. However, the written commentaries for these masques, since words are apter to convey sequential experience of discovery, confirm the visual illusion. In *Lord Hay's Masque* (1607) the 'broad descent' and 'two ascents' from the grove to the bower of Flora and to the House of Night[15] suggest the interplay of possibilities; in *Coelum Britannicum* (1634) a scene is described almost as if we were moving through a landscape:[16]

> the scene again is varied into a new and pleasant prospect clean differing from all the other, the nearest part showing a delicious garden with several walks and parterr as set round with low trees, and on the sides against these walks were fountains and grots, and in the furthest part a palace from whence went high walks upon arches, and above them open terraces planted with cypress trees. . . .

This description, the consciousness of something entirely new in the design of garden space and the resulting psychological behaviour in a garden, is essentially Italian. The Italian garden comes to England by, roughly, three distinct means, each of which suggests different kinds of evidence to invoke for such a survey as this: first, the direct experience of gardens and villas in Italy, such as Inigo Jones would have had or, later, John Evelyn; second, a direct experience, but mediated via visual and verbal descriptions – among the former would be engravings (Plate 15.6) or paintings (Plate

15.10), and published travel descriptions or private letters among the latter;[17] third, Italian designs 'edited' as they spread northwards through France and the Netherlands (Plate 15.5)[18] and known, in their turn, indirectly and at first hand. Drawing upon these materials, it is possible to establish the components of the gardenist experience for the travelled or well-informed Englishman of the seventeenth century.

Largely because of their location on classical ground, the Italian villa and garden were often thought of by visitors, and indeed had sometimes been envisaged by their architects, as modern realizations of Roman retreats. Since archaeology was in its infancy and few authentic sites of Roman villas were known (Hadrian's villa below the modern town of Tivoli was a crucial exception), the Renaissance relied almost exclusively upon literary accounts of classical gardens;[19] it was therefore relatively easy to convince oneself that a modern villa and its grounds had adequately revived the quintessential Roman mode. Reconstructions of classical sites, like those in Laurus' *Antiquae urbis splendor* (Plate 15.7), were tendentious extrapolations from literary texts of images current in Renaissance Rome, where it was also easy to establish new villas amongst the ruins of classical antiquity (Plate 15.8: note the ruins at top left and bottom right).[20] Such ruins even became an essential element in garden architecture for most English visitors: George Sandys delighted in the 'Duke of Telodos orchard' near Naples, a modern paradise to emulate the still visible ruins of 'Ciceroes Villa' and the 'Manor house of Servilius Vatia';[21] while in 1691 William Bromley recorded his approach to the Villa Ludovisia in Rome 'through a sweet Walk, where are the Ruins of Lucullus's Palace'.[22] Where gardens could not manage this deliberate juxtaposition of old and new, as the Villa d'Este did not at Tivoli, the Roman examples in the vicinity (Hadrian's and Horace's villas) were recalled by other devices such as sculptural models and inscriptions.[23] At Palladio's Villa Barbaro, Maser, in a countryside not abounding in Roman remains, Veronese and others painted on the interior walls landscapes redolent with imagined classical ruins.[24]

Gardens, then, performed a vital role in that recovery of the Roman past which was a central motive of any Italian visit. Coryate saw for the first time in the botanical gardens at Padua the plane trees that until then he had only read about in 'Vergil and other

PLATE 15.1 From Thomas Hill, *The Gardeners Labyrinth*, London, 1577

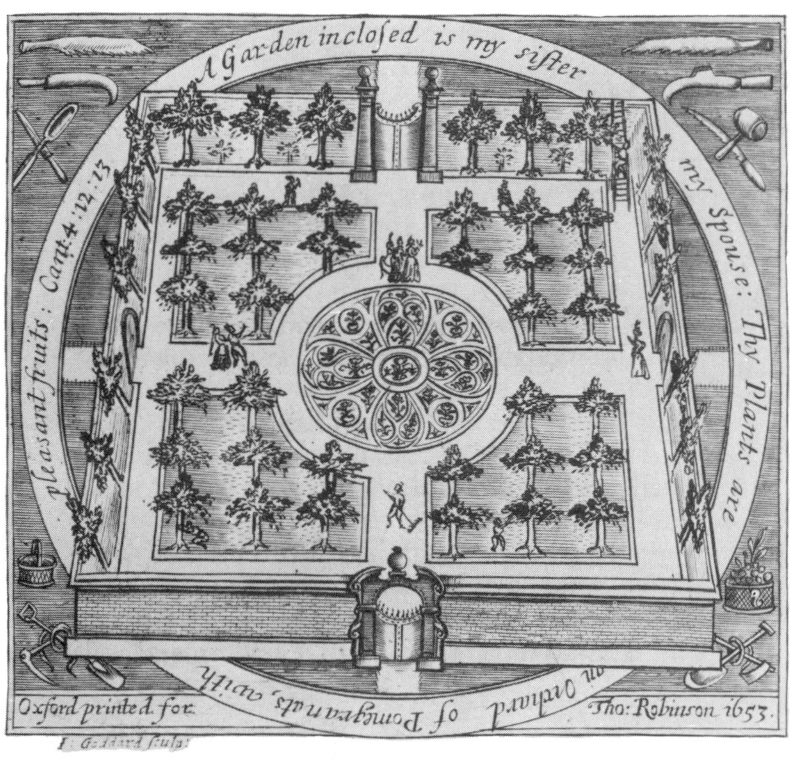

PLATE 15.2 From Ralph Austen, *A Treatise of Fruit Trees*, Oxford, 1653

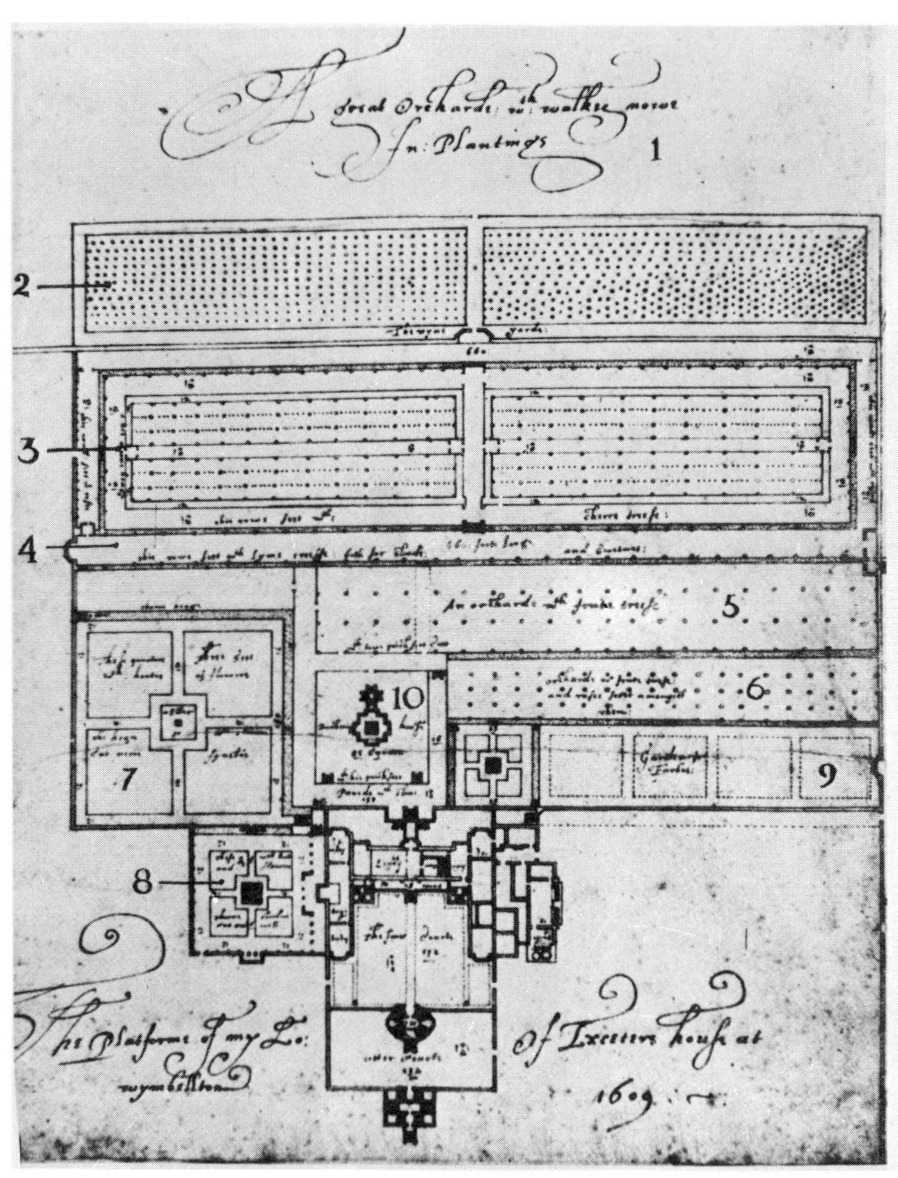

PLATE 15.3 John Smythson, plan of 'The Platforme of my Lord of Exeters house Wymbellton 1609'

PLATE 15.4 Inigo Jones, *A Garden and a Princely Villa*, 1634?

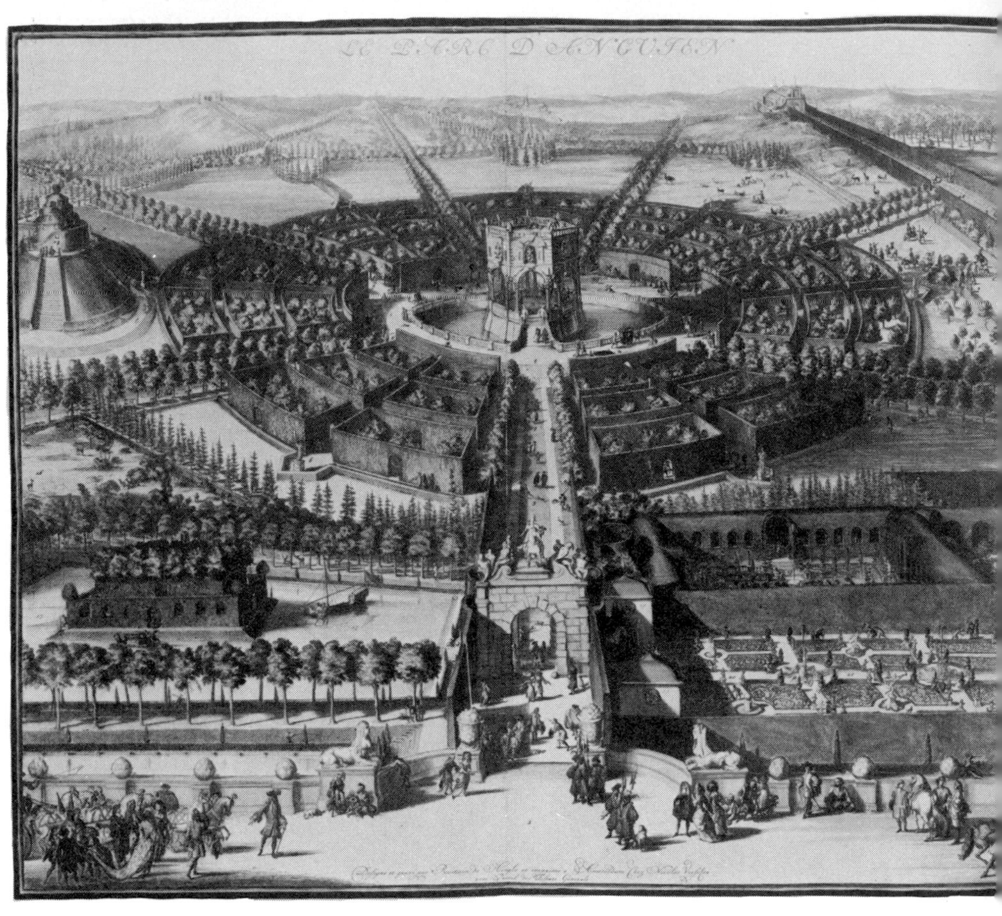

PLATE 15.5 Le Parc d'Angujen (garden of the Castle of Enghien), engraving by Romeyn de Hooghe, 1685

HET PERK VAN ANGUIEN

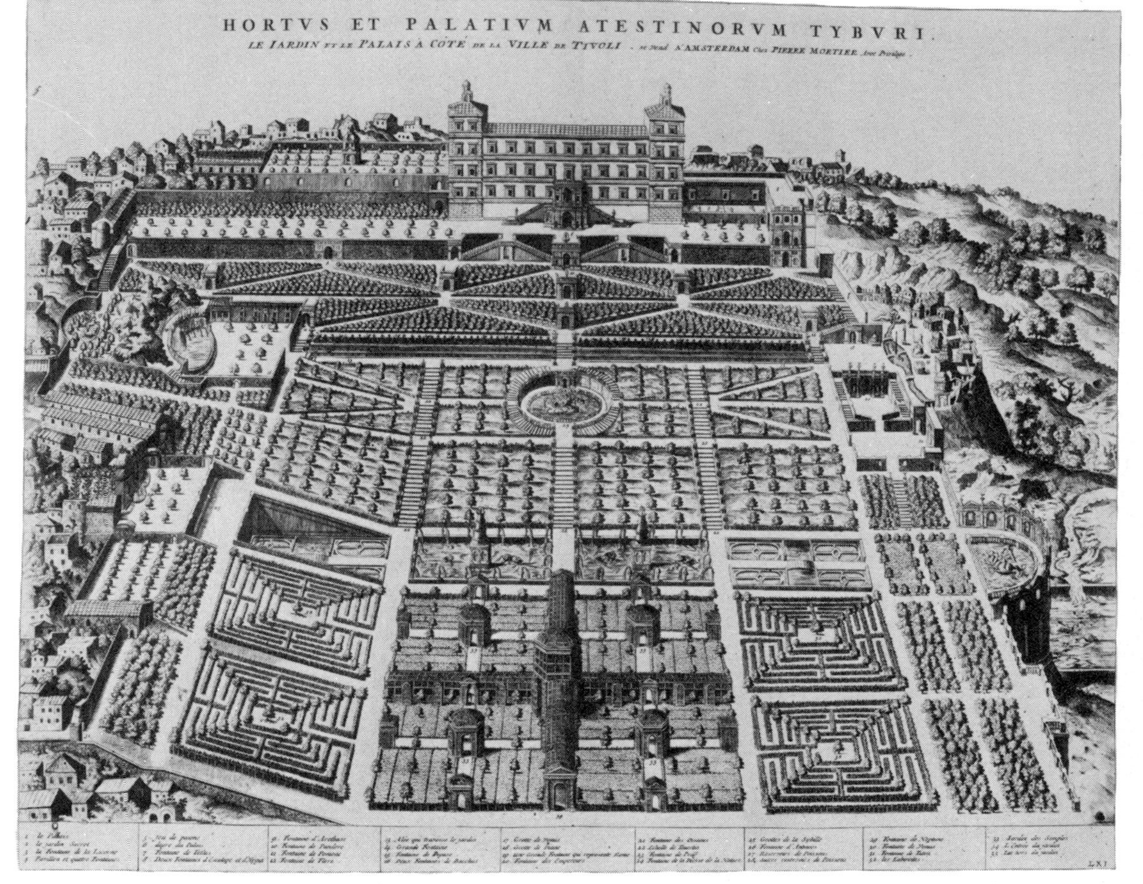

PLATE 15.6 Villa d'Este at Tivoli, engraving from Jean Blaeu, *Théâtre d'Italie,* Amsterdam, 1704

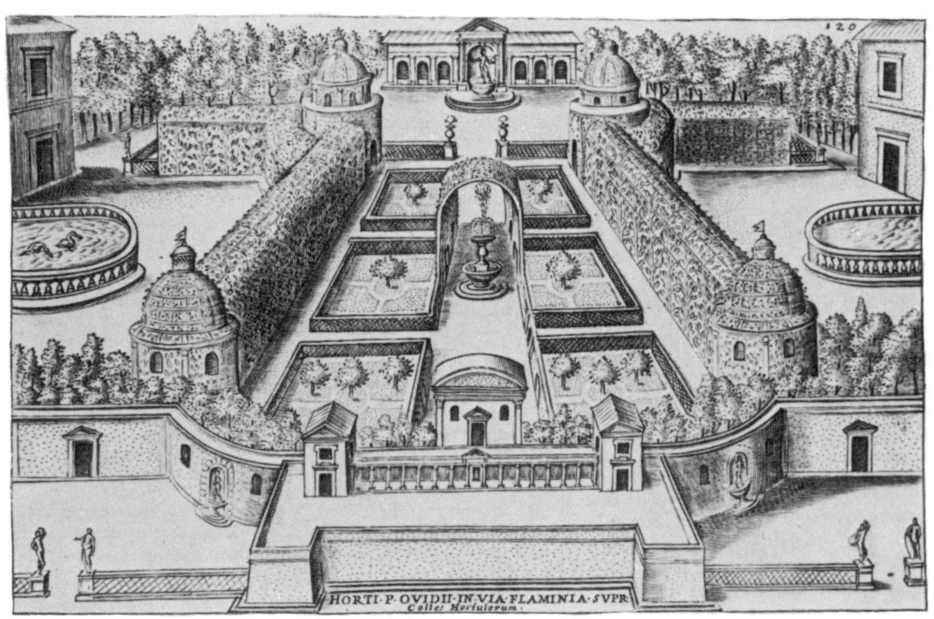

PLATE 15.7 Reconstruction of Ovid's gardens, engraving from Jacob Laurus, *Antiquae urbis splendor,* Rome, 1612

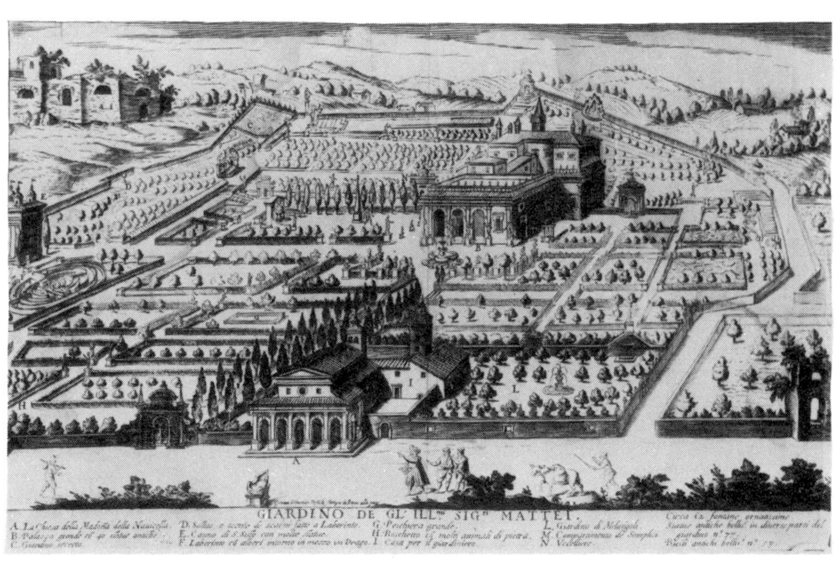

PLATE 15.8 Gardens of the Villa Mattei in Rome, engraving from *Nuova racolta di fontane,* Rome: G. J. Rossi, 1650

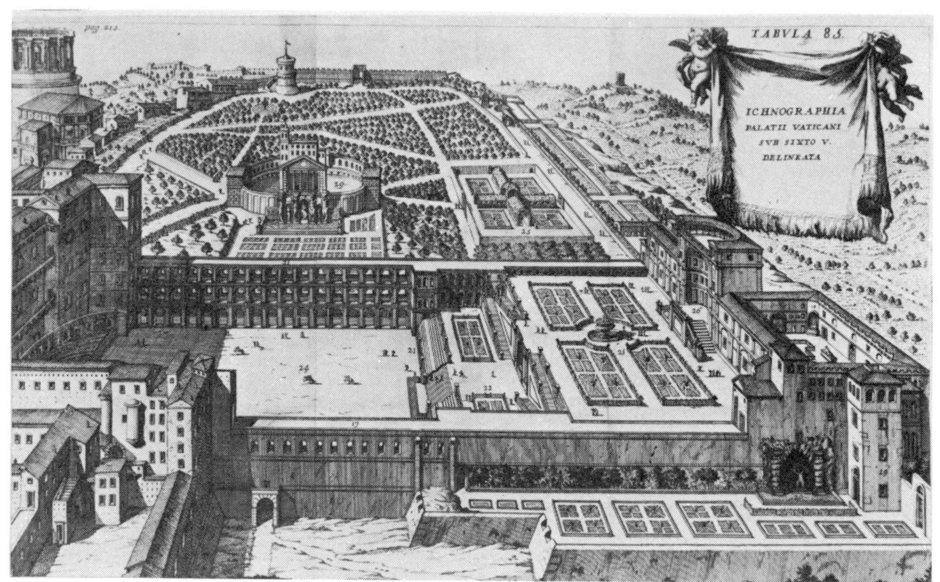

PLATE 15.9 Belvedere Courtyard and Vatican gardens, engraving from F. Bonanni, *Templi Vaticani fabricam,* Rome, 1696

PLATE 15.10 Henrick van Cleef III, *Cardinal Cesi's Antique Sculpture Garden,* 1584

PLATE 15.11 Artist unknown, painting of Villa Lante, Bagnaia, near Viterbo; seventeenth century

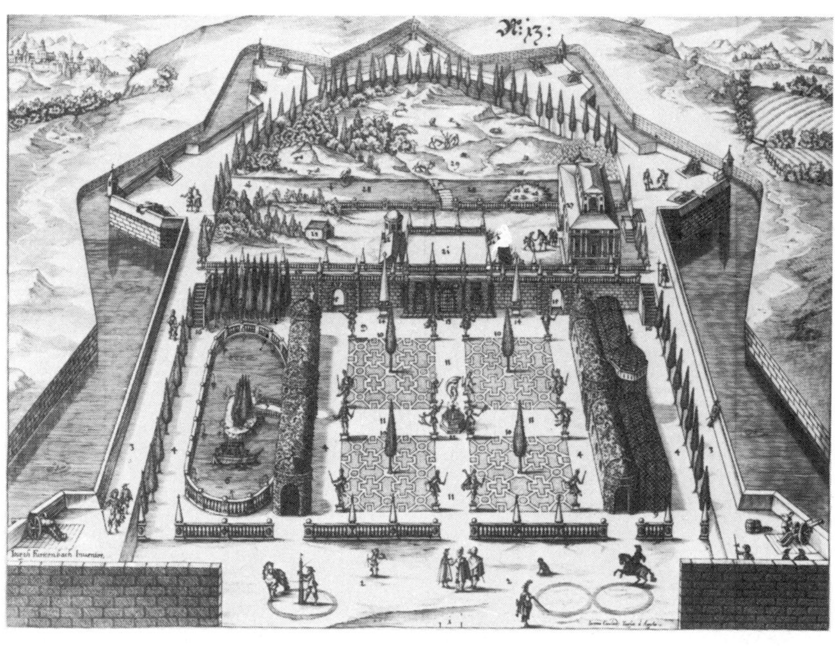

PLATE 15.12 Imaginary garden, engraving from Joseph Furttenbach, *Architectura civilis*, Ulm, 1628

PLATE 15.13 Dragon Fountain, Villa d'Este, Tivoli

PLATE 15.14 River god in the upper garden, Villa Farnese, Caprarola

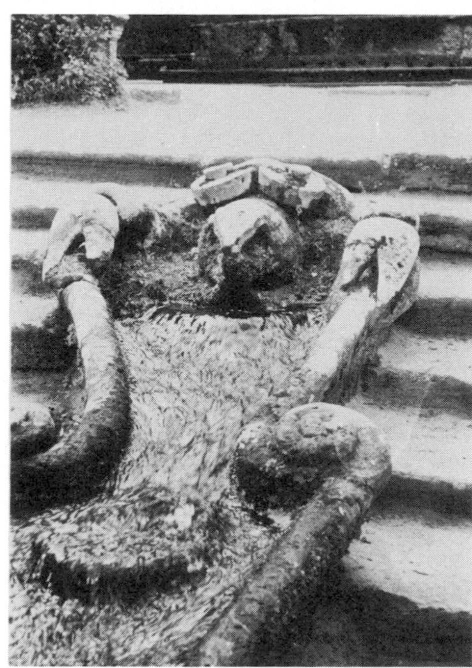

PLATE 15.15 The head of the 'catena d'acqua', Villa Lante, Bagnaia

PLATE 15.16 Theatre in the upper garden, Villa Farnese, Caprarola

PLATE 15.17 Paul Bril, *Month of March: Work in the Vineyard* (detail), pen and wash drawing, 1598

PLATE 15.18 Giusto Utens, *Castello*, painted lunette, 1599

PLATE 15.19 Design for a grotto in Salomon de Caus, *Les Raisons des forces mouvantes,* Frankfurt, 1615

PLATE 15.20 Giovanni Guerra, drawing of Grotto of Galatea at Pratolino, late sixteenth century

PLATE 15.21 C. Johnson, *The Capel Family,* 1640

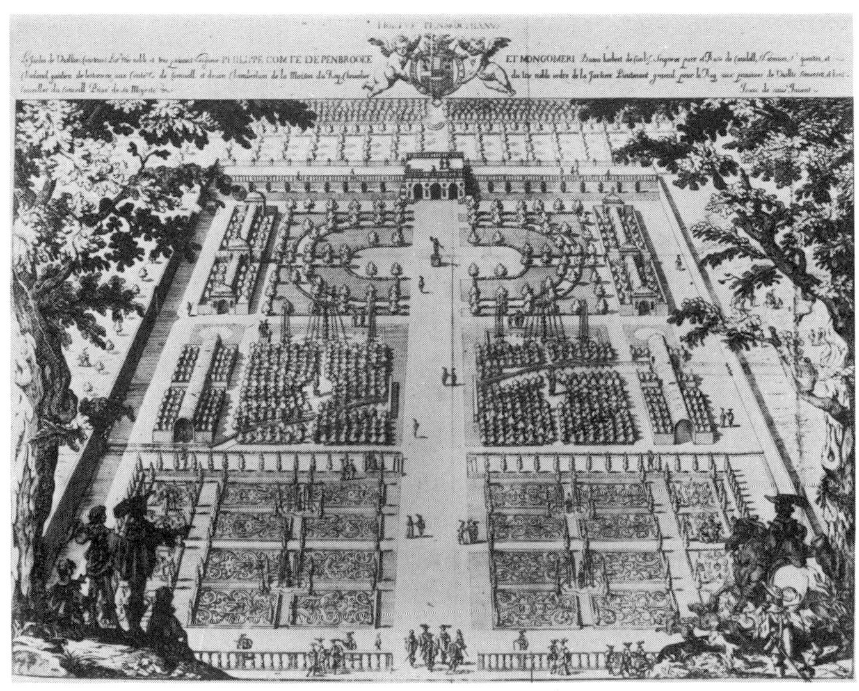

PLATE 15.22 Isaac de Caus, *Gardens at Wilton House,* engraving, 1645

PLATE 15.23 Water Theatre at the Villa Aldobrandini (Belvedere), Frascati, engraving from *Nuova racolta di fontane,* Rome, 1650

PLATE 15.24 Bas-reliefs of Ovidian subjects along the walk of the hundred fountains at the Villa d'Este, engraving from Falda and Venturini, *Le Fontane ne' palazzi e ne' giardini di Roma,* Rome, 1670s

PLATE 15.25 Jan Soens, *Rinaldo in the Enchanted Garden of Armida*, after 1581

Authours'.[25] Evelyn in Rome noted that 'We went to see Prince Ludovisio's Villa, where was formerly the Viridarium of the Poet Salust'.[26] Sometimes the *color romanus* was simply a matter of appropriate associations, as when Palladio, who had published his immensely successful little book, *L'antichità di Roma*, in 1554, explains in his *Quattro libri dell'architettura* (1570) that the owner of a villa

> being overlaboured by the fatigues of the city, will be singularly recruited and recreated . . . [like] those ancient Sages, who . . . used frequently to retire to . . . Pleasure-Houses, Gardens, Fountains, and such other objects of diversion. . . .[27]

But there were other, less impressionistic, means of contriving classical allusions in gardens. The fundamental structure of Italian gardens, so many of which are constructed on steeply sloping sites, derives from the Temple of Fortune at Praeneste (the modern Palestrina).[28] It inspired the hemispherical centre piece of Bramante's Cortile di Belvedere (Plate 15.9) as well as the whole theme of descending ramps, staircases that zigzag down the slope and lines of niches or alcoves. They in their turn became a prototype for gardens all over Italy. Bramante's pupil, Raphael, exploited this formal device for the Villa Madama, and Ligorio, who took over the Belvedere project after Bramante's death, contrived a dramatic version of it for the Villa d'Este (Plate 15.6). What seems to us today a self-explanatory structure to accommodate descending terraces down a hillside evidently announced distinct archaeological 'messages' to the Renaissance: Edward Warcupp's *Italy in Its Originall Glory, Ruine and Revivall* passes straight from reviewing classical writings on Rome to discuss the Belvedere courtyard, while John Raymond exclaims rather breathlessly how

> in Niches, shut up, are the best and most ancient statues of Rome, as that of Laoccoon and his two sonnes, all of one Marble, the Cleopatra, the Niobe, the Romulus and Remus sucking the Wolfe; the Nilus; the Tybre, all famous pieces. . . .[29]

The Belvedere sculpture garden was quickly imitated, among others by Cardinal Cesi (Plate 15.10).[30] These elaborate and beautiful showcases for sculpture – the Villa Montalto 'so beset with Statues,

Inscriptions, Relievos, and other Ancient Marbles', for example[31] – were a constant reminder, not only of the classical past and those collections of statuary that Cicero, among others, wrote of in his villas, but also of the modern skill at reviving those ancient arts. The collection of marbles made by and for the Earl of Arundel is perhaps the most famous English example of such Renaissance connoisseurship.[32]

II

Yet these classical allusions – either formal, structural elements or the decoration of sculpture, reliefs and inscriptions – would be less crucial to the gardenist experience had they not also contributed to larger patterns of psychological and intellectual response. We obtain an immediate glimpse of these from a passing reference to how Arundel chose to place the gift of a 'head of Jupiter' that he received from Sir Dudley Carleton, James I's ambassador at the Hague: it was sited 'in his *utmost* garden, so opposite to the Gallery dores, *as being open,* so soon as y^{u} enter into the front Garden y^{u} have the head *in yor eie all the way*'.[33] The sculpture at a distance captured the eye and ultimately led the feet to it (just as Marvell explained his response to the Nun Appleton estate). Visual exhibits, carefully arranged openings and vistas, terraces that end in double stairways where choices have to be made, inscriptions and deliberately allusive imagery – all involve the spectator and convey him, as Wotton put it, 'by several *mountings* and *valings*, to various entertainments of his *sent* and *sight*' and thence of his mind.[34]

The Villa d'Este at Tivoli may be taken as a prime example of this manipulation of the garden visitor. Designed to be approached from below, the upward routes offered a series of alternatives; depending upon which choice was made, the visitor encountered images of various mythic events which first presented or dramatized the choice of Hercules between vice and virtue. But Hercules gradually assumes even larger significance, as the villa itself is approached; the patron deity of the Este family and of Tivoli, Hercules overcame the dragon that guarded the golden apples in the garden of the Hesperides, as it still does at one mid-point of the garden (Plate 15.13); so

Hercules links the various choices in the garden with the owner and patron of the whole enterprise and with the geographical situation of the villa itself at Tivoli.[35]

As can be seen from contemporary views of the Villa d'Este, as well as from various English accounts of its gardens,[36] it is the design's immense *variety* that authorized and sustained visitors' involvement with its 'meanings'. Variety, in fact, was one of the essential attributes of the Italian garden, singled out by many visitors and gardenists.[37] One has only to look at various views (for example, Plates 15.6, 15.8–15.11 and 15.23) to register that whatever a ground-plan of such sites might suggest the actual exploration and discovery of these garden spaces would have been most involved. Modern architectural historians tend to equate 'formal' and 'predictable', retrospectively recalling the English landscape garden's rejection of both; but the almost stupefying anthology of gardenist structures offered to the visitor at the Parc d'Angujen (Plate 15.5) establishes the perfect compatibility in Italianate work of 'formal' (i.e. geometric) designs with variety and the element of surprise. Where such Dutch examples would necessarily differ from most examples in Italy itself – and the engraver has in fact tried to compensate for it – was in the absence of any slopes, which allowed, as Wotton again reminds us, 'a generall view of the whole *Plott* below but rather in a delightful confusion, then with any plaine distinction of the pieces' (*Elements of Architecture*). Even at the low-lying Nun Appleton this over-view was possible ('The sight does from these bastions ply') before the 'pieces' were encountered one by one.

One central aspect of this Italian garden variety is that it accommodated what today would be termed 'informal' areas. At Angujen there were examples of far less organized scenery on the far side of the huge circular labyrinth. At Bagnaia, near Viterbo, much of the elaborate fountain and sculpture work in the Villa Lante (Plate 15.11) is concentrated in the garden that descends the hillside between the two pavilions, but these devices and their iconography extend into the wooded areas, notably to the circular Fountain of Pegasus at the right of the main water terrace. To judge from a design of Joseph Furttenbach's (Plate 15.12),[38] 'formal' and 'informal' elements were designed to complement each other, there being as much versatility with 'natural' imagery in the first part of the garden – with its pond and island, grotto (inevitably) in the casino and covered walks – as the eye could find in gazing over the landscape contrived in the further section. This assumption that a 'garden' incorporated both highly structured elements and 'natural' (or indeed natural) scenes[39] is worth recalling when we consider Marvell's reactions to the meadows and woods beyond the immediate garden at Nun Appleton. The proximity of garden and estate in Italian villas is revealed clearly in Paul Brill's drawing of vineyard work, where the pergola and gazebo of the house abut upon the agricultural land (Plate 15.17). Yet another example, this, of the Renaissance maintaining the traditions of Roman villa life such as the younger Pliny recounts at his country estates at Tusculum and Laurentum.

III

As a garden visitor explored these intricately devised and connected spaces of an Italianate garden, his eye and mind would be involved in reading the ornaments and furniture. Most gardens would have been constructed after a specific literary programme – there was one at the Villa d'Este, as Professor Coffin has demonstrated (see note 35), and at least one other, that for the garden and grotto of the Medici villa of Castello, near Florence (Plate 15.18), has also been recovered and shown to have comprised a topographical allegory of Florence by Tribolo, complemented by Varchi's of the four seasons, the whole elaborated into a celebration of the Medici.[40] Even where no programme drew together and articulated all the items in a garden or when visitors, as must often have occurred, failed to read the garden aright (as perhaps at the Palazzo Giustiniano, 'well stor'd with statues, being so full that it seems a Ware-house of them'),[41] individual items would have announced their discrete 'message'. A river god (Plate 15.14) not only recalled the famous Roman examples discovered on the Quirinal but visualized, as *genius loci*, some locality related to the site or its owner. An obvious programme for any villa and garden would somehow be arranged around the celebration of its owner. At Tivoli the whole enterprise was largely dedicated to the Este family. At the Villa Aldobrandini (Frascati) a legend in vast Roman capitals, recalling those on Trajan's Column, proclaims the diplomacy of Cardinal Aldobrandini, nephew of Clement VIII.[42] Other such tributes were managed more modestly, even wittily, like the Montalto cluster of hills on the central fountain at the Villa Lante and the stone crabs (Plate 15.15), arms of the Gambara family who initiated the lovely garden; here, in addition, there is a visual-verbal pun on *gambero*, meaning crab.[43] These devices constitute the garden's mode of proclaiming its provenance and allegiance, analogous to the pervasive seventeenth-century painting that portrays a family in their own garden (Plate 15.21).[44] Marvell's reading of Fairfax history in the ruined nunnery and the modern Yorkshire estate seems to draw upon both the painterly and the gardenist modes as much as upon the traditions of 'estate' poems.

But it is equally evident from seventeenth-century accounts of garden visits that reading the emblematic and symbolic details was not the only form of response. In fact, we witness the beginning, inevitably mirrored in gardenist experience, of some radical adjustments to man's relationships with the natural world. Broadly, this entailed a gradual development of an expressive vision at the expense of the emblematic (or 'hieroglyphic', as Sir Thomas Browne has it),[45] of an empirical regard rather than the discovery of *a priori* ideas in nature. The constantly shifting, relativist world of an Italian garden experience necessarily put a premium upon personal reactions, encouraging simple, expressive delights:

> The gardens without the wals are so rarely delightfull, as I should thinke the Hesperides were not to be compared with them; and they are adorned with statues, laberinths, fountains . . . so as they seem an earthly Paradise.[46]

Such appreciation of the less specific, more emotional effects of a garden world meant less insistence upon using the garden as some system of mystic codes, which is how the Jesuit, Hawkins, still invokes a garden in *Partheneia Sacra* (1633). The actual images so used will often coincide with the gardens more empirically treated – as in Ralph Austen's title-page (Plate 15.2), which announces, in connection with a fairly traditional garden, both horticultural concerns in the tools around the edges, and, relying still upon a classic text in Canticles, his spiritual regimen.[47] As those tools on Austen's title-page imply, a large part of this shift away from a hieroglyphic vision coincided with an enormous increase in botany and horticulture,[48] in its turn a direct result of Continental ideas and practice. It seems apt that of the two Danvers brothers, Henry became the moving spirit and financial backer of the Oxford Physic Garden, opened in 1621, with fine Italianate doorways, and John, according to Aubrey, 'first taught us the way of Italian gardens'.[49] Botanical gardens became an essential ingredient of a Continental tour: Coryate's visit to the earliest of these at Padua, established in 1545, has already been cited; Evelyn visited them wherever he could, particularly enthralled by the Jardin des Plantes in Paris (*Diary*, II, p. 102); in 1634 William Brereton attended a class at Leyden University, held in the Physic Garden by Adolphus Vorstius, who instructed him in the botanical and medicinal properties of the herbs and simples rather than in their arcane and symbolic meanings.[50] Even the *library* at the Montalto villa in Rome seemed to Richard Lassels 'nothing but physick gardens for the mind'.[51]

IV

Scientific skill at cultivating, even manipulating, the natural world had its counterpart in the contrivances, mainly hydraulic, which decorated seventeenth-century gardens (cf. ''Tis all enforced, the fountain and the grot' with 'The pink grew then as double as his mind'). The Italian fascination with waterworks penetrated northwards perhaps more speedily than other gardenist elements:[52] at Brussels Evelyn discovered intriguing examples in 'a most sweete and delicious Garden' –

> another Grott, of more neate & costly materials, full of noble Statues, and entertaining us with artificial musique: But it was the hedge of Water, which in forme of Lattice-Worke the Fontaniere caused to ascend out of the earth by degrees exceedingly pleased & surprised me; for thus with a pervious Wall, or rather Palisad-hedge of Water, was the whole Parterr environd. (*Diary*, II, pp. 71–2)

Such devices were even carried indoors, as Evelyn and Brereton both reported of a house in Amsterdam with 'divers pretty Water workes rising 108 foote' into the air.[53] Evelyn's progress through France ensured him many encounters with both modest and grandiose waterworks. At St Germaine-en-Laye were

> six incomparable Tarraces built of brick & stone descending in Cascads towards the river, & cut out of the naturall hill, having under them goodly Gallerys vaulted, whereof 4 have subterranean Grotts & rocks, where is represented severall objects in manner of sceanes, & other motions by the force of Water, to be shown by the light of torches onely: Especialy that of Orpheus, with his musique, & the Animals which daunce after his harp [see Plate 15.19]: In the 2nd is the King and Dolphin; in the 3rd the Neptune sounding with his trumpet, his charriot drawne by sea-horses: In the 4th the story of Perseus & Andromeda; not to insist on the mills, the solitude of Eremits, men a fishing, birds chirping & the many other devices. (*Diary*, II, p. 111)

The previous day he had visited an equally magnificent water garden, created for Richelieu at Rueil (*Diary*, II, pp. 109–10); but he could be as readily impressed with the more modest contrivance in the garden of the *virtuoso*, Louis Hesselin, at Essones: here were 'Fountaines & Pooles of Fish . . . a noble Cascado, and Prety Bathes with all accommodations: Under a marble table is a fountain of Serpents twisting about a Globe' (*Diary*, II, p. 121).

These encounters in Holland and France were, as most travellers realized, but a foretaste of Italian delights. The literature and the visual evidence on this is huge, since every visitor seems to have made extensive records. But two places were particularly noted for their waterworks: the Medici villa at Pratolino, north of Florence, where Fynes Moryson reported how the figure of Syrinx had changed into a reed before his eyes while Pan played his pipes,[54] and the hillside villas around Rome, the Villa d'Este and a whole cluster of them at Frascati.[55] As Evelyn's version of St Germaine-en-Laye makes clear, water was used to animate extensive dramas, not readily captured in engravings – Plate 15.19 shows how popular the Orpheus subject was, if not its movements. But a Modenese draughtsman, Giovanni Guerra, actually tried to capture the changes hydraulically engineered at Pratolino (Plate 15.20), about which writers could enthuse more graphically:

> 'tis situate in a huge meadow like an amphitheater, ascending, having at the bottom a huge rock, with Water running in a small Chanell like a Cascade. . . . The Gardens delicious & full of fountaines; In the Grove sits Pan feeding his flock, the Water making a melodious sound through his pipe, & an Hercules whose Club yields a Showre of Water, which falling into a huge *Concha* has a Naked Woman riding on the backs of Dolphins; In another Grotto is Vulcan & his family, the walls richly composed of Coralls, Shells, Coper & Marble figures; with the huntings of Several beasts, moving by force of water.[56]

The Frascati villas were even organized around huge water theatres (Plate 15.23), in the separate rooms of which different inventions, lovingly catalogued on engravings, were installed for the admiration of all beholders.

Waterworks, and their facetious cousins, *giocchi d'acqua*, that sprayed visitors without warning, were only one, if the most pervasive, example of a garden's metamorphic delights. The manipulation of water into what W. H. Auden was to call 'gesticulating fountains' was of a piece with topiary (near the Hague Brereton discovered 'the postures of a soldier, and a captain on horseback . . . portraited to the life in box'),[57] with confusions of art and nature ('artificial rocks, shells, mosse, and tophas, seem to excell even that which they imitate'),[58] with confusions of elements, like the 'pervious Wall' of water at Brussels, or stone and water exchanging shapes and texture (Plate 15.15). In gardens where real trees let fall artificially piped rain (Villa Borghese, Rome) or artificial birds sang and flapped their wings alongside real ones (Villa d'Este), it is not surprising that Ovid cast his spell over designers and visitors alike.[59] The *Metamorphoses*, narrating chaos resolved into harmony, animals turning into stone, humans becoming trees or birds and gods taking whatever shape tickled their fancy, is ideally suited to garden art. Sometimes the poem was actually illustrated in a garden: at the Villa d'Este (Plate 15.24) Evelyn noted 'the whole *Ovidian* Metamorphosis in *mezzo Relievo* rarely sculptur'd (*Diary*, II, p. 396) – they still survive, though sadly overgrown; at Frascati the Stanza di Apollo of the Villa Aldobrandini was decorated by Domenichino and others with various moments of metamorphosis (most of these are now in the National Gallery, London).

V

Such 'theatrical' entertainments were ineluctably linked to gardens. Most Renaissance gardens in Italy were used for dramatic entertainments; some actually contained either amphitheatres, like the Boboli Gardens in Florence, or more intimate 'theatres' (Plate 15.16); others, as we have seen (Plate 15.23), were wholly shaped into theatres. At Buen Retiro in Spain, mentioned in *Upon Appleton House*, the back wall of an Italian-designed theatre could be removed to disclose a garden beyond which thus served as three-dimensional backdrop. The masque-like entertainments in the Nun Appleton water meadows, in short, were endemic to most Italianate gardens. The instructional motive of gardens, teaching their visitors through an elaborate system of images and inscriptions, together with the strongly metamorphic impulse of their designs, transformed whole gardens into magical peripatetic theatres, locations for a *commedia improvvisa* as the spectators strolled through their spaces. English visitors to Italian gardens even recorded their impressions in the language of masque – Wotton talked of being 'magically transported', while at Tivoli 'In the descent into the first garden shews itself the Colossus of Pegasus' or 'riseth an Island cut in the shape of a ship'.[60]

These dramas also recalled to some visitors the magic gardens of romance in Tasso, Ariosto or Spenser. Armida's enchanted garden was a favourite topic for painters and in Jan Soens's version (Plate 15.25) have been captured many of the psychological entertainments of such places as the Villa d'Este – the temptations of prospect and of rival routes, the sensual attractions of fountain, arbour or grove, the transformations, and the surprises of sudden discovery. It is a painter's very knowledgeable tribute to a garden's dramas and to a poem where they are celebrated.

When Evelyn called the Villa Mondragone at Frascati a 'Theater of Pastimes' (*Diary*, II, p. 393) he was at one level obviously employing a conventional noun to indicate a compendium or complete collection of pastimes. But there lurks in garden ideology, too, an extension of the notion that the world was itself a theatre: if the garden, with all its imagery, represented the *theatrum mundi*, then the garden was a theatre too. Whether we read the garden as theatrē in the Calvinesque mode – man as a fairly passive spectator 'placed in this very splendid Theatre' of God's work to admire – or whether it is the more problematical Platonic version, in which we do not quite know whether we are actor or spectator, active or passive, the garden surrounds us and involves us somehow in its dramas. To these versions of the garden as drama must be linked the whole notion of mnemotechnic theatre, such as Giulio Camillo advanced in the strange and elliptical book, *Idea del Teatro* (1550): the garden thus becomes a whole apparatus of devices to recall us to ideas and memories we have stored and maybe forgotten until we meet their images again among the green shades of a garden.[61]

Such are the basic ingredients of a seventeenth-century Englishman's gardenist experience. They are essentially Italian, hence the basic concentration of this essay. Italy was easily recognized as the source of most northern European designs and ideas ('built after the Italian manner', Evelyn noted in Holland – *Diary*, II, p. 35). Though the extent to which this new garden style penetrated England is not yet clear, and though the Civil Wars must effectively have interrupted elaborate garden work, it is the Italianate mode that, directly or indirectly, affected the English until the Restoration; then, with the importation of fresh Continental ideas, it was the French grand style of gardening under Le Nôtre – Italian-derived, but significantly different in spirit and intention – that found favour. There is evidence that throughout the later seventeenth century until the advent of the English landscape garden Italy continued to represent an ideal gardening ideology, notable above all for its flexibility and variety, that could be opposed to the French.[62]

But, *pace* Legouis who thought Marvell looked forward to William Kent,[63] the proper context for his garden poetry is undoubtedly the rich Italian-inspired gardens that spread across Europe to reach England during the first forty years of the century. Even if Marvell had not been able to spend four years abroad, as we gather from Milton that he did,[64] he might have had some opportunity to experience the new style at home. The gardens at Wilton House, for example (Plate 15.22), deploy most of the features canvassed here: fountains, statues, topiary, a grotto in the central pavilion, pergolas, covered walks and a general 'over-view'. Aubrey's designs for his own Easton Pierse[65] demonstrate his application of Italianate ideas on a modest scale. Danvers's house in Chelsea, the object of Aubrey's encomium already cited,[66] was an outstanding example of the new style: visitors enjoyed 'two delightfull Visto's' in different directions, garden stairs that 'turned on the right or left hand', spaces modulated into 'elevations & depressions', statues noted for their variety of expression as well as a grotto that 'affects one with a kind of Religious horrour'. By an apt coincidence this house and gardens in Chelsea were occupied from 1685, three years before Marvell's death, by Thomas, Lord Wharton, the son of his friend and correspondent.

Notes

1 Jonson, *Discoveries*, in *The Works*, ed. Herford and Simpson, Oxford, The Clarendon Press, 1947, VIII, p. 628.

2 *The Works of Charles and Mary Lamb*, ed. E. V. Lucas, London, Methuen, 1903, II, p. 155. Cf. Pierre Legouis, *Andrew Marvell*, Oxford, The Clarendon Press, 1965, p. 42: 'For many who do not know him otherwise Marvell is the poet of gardens'.

3 The useful term, 'gardenist', is borrowed anachronistically from Horace Walpole; see Isabel W. H. Chase, *Horace Walpole: Gardenist*, Princeton University Press, 1943, p. 184.

4 Among the main attempts to relate Marvell's work to contemporary gardens see especially Nicholas A. Salerno, 'Andrew Marvell and the Furor Hortensis', *Studies in English Literature*, VIII (1968), pp. 103–20, and A. E. Berthoff, *The Resolved Soul*, Princeton University Press, 1970, note 11 and *passim*; also items noted below by McClung (see note 6) and by Stewart (note 47).

5 Despite the invitations of Jonson's apophthegm I shall *not* be concerned with any painterly or pictorial contexts for Marvell's poetry. For one thing, they have been explored with much enterprise and imagination by Rosalie L. Colie, *'My Ecchoing Song': Andrew Marvell's Poetry of Criticism*, Princeton University Press, 1970, and by James G. Turner, 'Topographia and Topographical Poetry in English 1640–1660', Oxford University D.Phil. dissertation, 1976. For another, as this essay will argue, it became of some moment during the early seventeenth century that gardens provided *three*-dimensional experiences, totally different from those with the planar surfaces of painting.

6 For a garden still virtually excluded by the need for fortifications, see the engraving of Berkeley Castle reproduced in B. Sprague Allen, *Tides in English Taste*, Cambridge, Mass., Harvard University Press, 1937, p. 133. For a garden as extension of manor house see perhaps Haddon Hall (Derbyshire), which is discussed in a recent book by William A. McClung, *The Country House in English Renaissance Poetry*, Berkeley, University of California Press, 1977.

7 Markham, *The English Husbandman*, 1613, p. 112.

8 Other examples may be seen in Miles Hadfield, *Gardening in Britain*, London, Hutchinson, 1960, p. 103. The persistence of the tradition may be judged from the various 'dials' and layouts shown in J. Van der Groen, *Den Nederlandtsen Hovenier*, Amsterdam, 1669, of which there is a French edition (*Le Jardinier hollandois*) of the same date.

9 On these 'prodigy' buildings see John Summerson, *Architecture in Britain 1530–1830*, 5th rev. ed., Harmondsworth, Penguin Books, 1969, ch. IV, and Hadfield, as above (note 8), pp. 50–4, 63–5.

10 Hentzner, *Travels in England in the Reign of Elizabeth*, 1889, pp. 78, 52.

11 Illustrated in Summerson, as above (note 9), Plate 42; the terraces are shown on the bottom of Plate 15.3 here. *Pace* Summerson (p. 76), the terraces at Wimbledon seem less a direct debt to the Farnese Villa at Caprarola than simply the invocation of an Italianate terrace complex; see further, p. 335 below. On Caprarola, see note 38.

12 See the parliamentary survey of 1649 reprinted in *Archaeologia*, X (1792), pp. 412 ff.

13 Further illustrations may be consulted in Stephen Orgel and Roy Strong, *Inigo Jones: The Theatre of the Stuart Court*, Berkeley, University of California Press, 1973, II, pp. 484–5, 510, 514–15, 518–19, 654. Orgel and Strong argue that even if Jones had been in Italy before his visit there with Arundel in 1613–14, his designs show 'no significant Italian influence until after 1614' (I, p. 20n); but this perhaps ignores his obvious debts to garden art – an important part, obviously, of his inspiration.

14 Quoted by Christian Norberg-Schutz, *Meaning in Western Architecture*, London, Studio Vista, 1975, p. 260. See generally the author's important analyses of villa and garden space, pp. 257 ff.

15 Orgel and Strong, as above (note 13), I, p. 116.

16 Ibid., II, p. 579.

17 This is a vast reservoir of material, largely untapped for its evidence of English interest in Italian gardens. A survey of the scope of such writings is offered in my essay, 'English Mirrors of Italian Gardens', *Country Life*, 15 September 1977. A basic bibliography of studies of Italian

gardens would begin with the catalogue for the *Mostra del giardino italiano*, Palazzo Vecchio, Florence, 1931; Georgina Masson, *Italian Gardens*, London, Thames & Hudson, 1961; and *The Italian Garden*, ed. David R. Coffin, Dumbarton Oaks, Washington DC, 1972.

18 Here difficulties of interpretation tend to arise from the blending of Italianate ideas, as they moved northwards, with native traditions – as in the Netherlands – or from their being reshaped into styles that obscure the original inspiration – as in France. On this latter see F. H. Hazlehurst, *Jacques Boyceau and the French Formal Garden*, Athens, University of Georgia Press, 1966; catalogue for *L'Art des jardins classiques*, Musée de Lunéville, 1967; and *The French Formal Garden*, ed. Elizabeth A. MacDougall and F. H. Hazlehurst, Dumbarton Oaks, Washington DC, 1974.

19 The best analysis, using this literary material, is Pierre Grimal, *Les Jardins romains*, Paris, Presses Universitaires de France, 2nd ed., 1969. See also, for more general and archaeological accounts, A. G. McKay, *Houses, Villas and Palaces in the Roman World*, London, Thames & Hudson, 1975, and A. Boëthius and J. B. Ward-Perkins, *Etruscan and Roman Architecture*, Harmondsworth, Penguin Books, 1970.

20 For another garden established inside a classical ruin and for a discussion of its relevance to Marvell's treatment of the nunnery in *Upon Appleton House*, see my *Andrew Marvell: His Life and Writings*, London, Elek, 1978, Plate 18 and pp. 96–9. On other aspects of the relationship of Italian gardens to classical artefacts see Elizabeth MacDougall, '*Ars Hortulorum*: Sixteenth-Century Garden Iconography and Literary Theory in Italy', in Coffin, as above (note 17), and her 'The Sleeping Nymph: Origins of a Humanist Fountain Type', *Art Bulletin*, LVIII (1975), pp. 357–65.

21 George Sandys, *A Relation of a Journey begun An. Dom. 1610*, 3rd ed., 1632, pp. 272, 274–5, 288–9.

22 Bromley, *Remarks in [sic] the Grand Tour of France and Italy, performed by a person of quality in the year 1691*, London, 1705, p. 183.

23 See David R. Coffin, *The Villa d'Este at Tivoli*, Princeton University Press, 1960, Plates 21 and 23.

24 See A. Richard Turner, *The Vision of Landscape in Renaissance Italy*, Princeton University Press, 1966, pp. 205–11. Palladio apparently mistook ruins in Rome, such as those of the Temple of the Sun near the Arco di Portogallo, as part of 'gardens in ancient times' (see catalogue, *Andrea Palladio 1508–1580. The Portico and the farmyard*, London, Arts Council, 1975, pp. 178–9).

25 Coryate, *Crudities*, etc., Glasgow, Maclehose, 1905, I, p. 292.

26 *The Diary*, ed. E. S. de Beer, Oxford University Press, 1955, II, p. 234. Evelyn, the English gardenist *par excellence* of the seventeenth century, and incidentally abroad in the 1640s at exactly the time Marvell must have been travelling, is the foremost authority for this topic.

27 *The Architecture of A. Palladio . . . with Notes and Remarks of Inigo Jones*, 3rd ed., 1742, I, p. 55. In *L'antichità di Roma*, Venice, 1554, Palladio writes 'Hebbero li antichi Romani molti horti famosi' (p. 16v). Further north, classical associations were organized by statues, say, of the twelve Caesars and Aristotle, which Edward Browne found in a garden in Vianen belonging to Count Brederode (*Account of Several Travels*, 1677, pp. 21–2): Marvell, incidentally, dates a letter from Vianen in March 1663.

28 Pirro Ligorio's reconstruction of the temple, which makes evident that it must have been more visible in the sixteenth century than it is at present, is illustrated by Masson, as above (note 17), p. 123.

29 Edmund Warcupp, *Italy in Its Originall Glory, Ruine and Revivall*, 1660, Pt II, esp. pp. 177–9 (*N.B.* Warcupp's book is essentially a translation of F. Schotus, *Itinerario d'Italia*, 1600 *et seq.*), and Raymond, *II Mercurio Italico. An Itinerary containing a Voyage made through Italy in the year 1646, and 1647*, 1648, pp. 91–2. On the Belvedere see James S. Ackerman, 'The Belvedere as a Classical Villa', *Journal of the Warburg and Courtauld Institutes*, XIV (1951), pp. 70–91, and Hans Henrik Brummer, *The Statue Court in the Vatican Belvedere*, Stockholm, Almqvist & Wiksell, 1970. On the Villa Madama, see Norman Neuerburg, 'Raphael at Tivoli and the Villa Madama', in *Essays in Memory of Karl Lehmann*, ed. L. F. Sandter, New York University, 1964, pp. 227–31; Frances Huener, 'Raphael and the Villa Madama', *Essays in Honour of Walter Friedlaender*, ed. 'Marsyas', New York University, 1965, pp. 92–9; and David R. Coffin, 'The Plans of the Villa Madama', *Art Bulletin*, LIX (1967), pp. 111–22.

30 On this picture see the article by Marjon van der Meulen, *Burlington Magazine*, January 1974. For another famous sculpture garden see my *Andrew Marvell* (as above, note 20), Plate 21.

31 Evelyn, *Diary*, II, p. 240. Where original antique sculpture could not be obtained, modern imitations were used.

32 See D. E. L. Haynes, *The Arundel Marbles*, Oxford, Ashmolean Museum, 1975.

33 M. F. S. Hervey, *Thomas Howard, Earl of Arundel*, Cambridge University Press, 1921, pp. 101–2; my italics.

34 *Elements of Architecture*, London, 1624, pp. 109–10. Wotton is discussing an unnamed but 'incomparable' Italian garden. For further commentary on this crucial passage see *The Genius of the Place: The*

English Landscape Garden 1620–1820, ed. John Dixon Hunt and Peter Willis, London, Elek, 1975, pp. 8, 48, 70, and my *The Figure in the Landscape: Poetry, Painting and Gardening during the Eighteenth Century*, Baltimore, Md, The Johns Hopkins Press, 1976, pp. 24–5, 36.

35 The full details are available in the admirable monograph by Professor Coffin, cited in note 23; see especially ch. V.

36 See, for example, 'A true Description and Direction of what is most worthy to be seen in all Italy' (*c.* 1610) in *The Harleian Miscellany, VIII* (1811), pp. 109–10; Fynes Moryson, *An Itinerary*, Glasgow, Maclehose, 1907, I, p. 225; Evelyn, *Diary*, II, pp. 393–7; Raymond, as above (note 29), pp. 167–72; Warcupp (same note), pp. 309–11; and Richard Lassels, *The Voyage of Italy*, 1670, Pt II, pp. 314–16.

37 See Evelyn, *Diary, passim*; Henry Cogan, *A Direction For Such as Shall Travell unto Rome*, 1654, p. 263 (on the Borghese Gardens); and Raymond, as above (note 29), p. 37 (on the Boboli Gardens). The *variety* of Italian gardens became the hallmark by which they were differentiated from the French style after the Restoration: see my *The Figure in the Landscape* (as above, note 34), pp. 34–5.

38 There is an interesting parallel, too, between Furttenbach's design and the flower garden ('In the just figure of a fort') at Nun Appleton. A famous villa built as a fortress was that at Caprarola: see J. Coolidge *et al.*, *La vita e le opere di . . . Vignola*, Bologna, Casa di Risparmio di Vignola, 1974, Plate 37. See also Evelyn's delight in Dutch fortifications decorated with gardens (*Diary*, II, p. 67).

39 The point is well made by Elizabeth MacDougall in the article cited in note 20.

40 L. Chatelet-Lange, 'The Grotto of the Unicorn and the Gardens of the Villa di Castello', *Art Bulletin*, L (1968), pp. 51–8.

41 *A Tour in France and Italy, made by an English Gentleman 1675*, 1676, p. 74.

42 *Great Houses of Italy*, with a preface by Jean Giono, London, Weidenfeld & Nicolson, 1968, p. 200. Sometimes the themes announced or depicted were of more general application to their owners: for example, the paintings of active and contemplative life at Caprarola, see O. F. Bonvicini, *Caprarola: Il Palazzo e la Villa Farnese*, Rome, 1973; it was an obvious and frequent theme for country houses of famous men, as Marvell himself makes clear at Nun Appleton.

43 Angelo Cantoni, *La Villa di Bagnaia*, 2nd ed., Rome, 1964.

44 This is a particularly favourite topic of Dutch seventeenth-century paintings; some fine examples are illustrated in Mario Praz, *Conversation Pieces*, University Park, Pennsylvania State University Press, 1971.

45 *Works*, ed. Geoffrey Keynes, University of Chicago Press, 1964, I, p. 25.

46 Fynes Moryson, as above (note 36), I, p. 239. Some literary analogues are studied by A. Bartlett Giamatti, *The Earthly Paradise and the Renaissance Epic*, Princeton University Press, 1966.

47 See Stanley Stewart, *The Enclosed Garden: The Tradition and the Image in Seventeenth-Century Poetry*, Madison, University of Wisconsin Press, 1966, and, on some more practical implications for actual gardens, the first chapter of my *The Figure in the Landscape*, as above (note 34).

48 See Blanche Henrey, *British Botanical and Horticultural Literature before 1800*, Oxford University Press, 1976; the relevant sections of Charles Webster, *The Great Instauration. Science, Medicine and Reform 1626–1660*, London, Duckworth, 1975; and Hadfield, as above (note 8), pp. 78–82, 93–105.

49 Bodleian Library, MS. Aubrey 2, f. 53 (see also the last paragraph of this essay). For the Oxford Physic Garden see Jennifer Sherwood and Nikolaus Pevsner, *Oxfordshire*, Harmondsworth, Penguin Books, 1974, p. 266.

50 William Brereton, *Travels in Holland*, etc., 1844, p. 40.

51 Lassels, as above (note 36), p. 169.

52 See, besides the considerable publications on hydraulic engineering, culminating in England in Robert Boyle's *Experiments physico-mechanicall* (1660) and including that from which Plate 15.19 here is taken, Aubrey's own projections for fountains at Easton Pierse (Bodleian MS. Aubrey 17, ff. 18, 19), and the local examples discussed and illustrated by R. Plot, *The Natural History of Oxfordshire*, 2nd ed., 1705, pp. 240–4.

53 Brereton, as above (note 50), p. 56, and Evelyn, *Diary*, II, p. 47.

54 Moryson, as above (note 36), I, p. 329.

55 Most of the travellers already cited devote many pages and much enthusiasm to these latter, the extent of which can be seen from the modern study by C. L. Franck, *The Villas of Frascati*, New York, Transatlantic Arts, 1966.

56 Evelyn, *Diary*, II, p. 418. On Pratolino itself see articles by Detlief Heikamp in *L'OEil*, CLXXI (Mars 1969), pp. 16–27, and in *L'Antiquità viva,* VIII (1969), pp. 14–34, in both of which more Guerra drawings are reproduced. Also, Webster Smith, 'Pratolino', *Journal of the Society of Architectural Historians*, XX (1961), pp. 155–68.

57 Brereton, as above (note 50), p. 38.

58 Sandys, as above (note 21), p. 272.

59 Raymond, as above (note 29), pp. 94–5 for Villa Borghese and pp. 167 ff. for Villa d'Este.

60 Wotton, as above (note 34), pp. 109–10, and (for Tivoli references) Warcupp, as above (note 29), pp. 309–11.

61 On this intricate congeries of ideas see W. Tatarkiewicz, 'Theatrica, the Science of Entertainment', *Journal of the History of Ideas*, XXVI (1965), pp. 263–72; Richard Bernheimer, 'Theatrum Mundi', *Art Bulletin*, XXXVIII (1956), pp. 225–47; and Herbert Weisinger, *The Agony and the Triumph*, East Lansing, Michigan State University Press, 1964, pp. 58–70.

62 See above, note 37. With gardens it was, as Milton wrote in a different context, 'above all, Italy' (Milton, *Complete Prose Works*, New Haven, Conn., Yale University Press, 1966, IV, p. 553).

63 Legouis, as above (note 2), p. 44.

64 *The Life Records of John Milton*, ed. J. Milton French, New Brunswick, NJ, Rutgers University Press, 1949–58, III, pp. 322–3.

65 Bodleian Aubrey MS. 17, 'Designatio de Easton-Piers in Com: Wilts', dated 1669.

66 Bodleian Aubrey MS. 2, ff. 53r–57r. Part of Aubrey's account of Danvers's Chelsea house and gardens is quoted by Walter H. Godfrey, 'New Light on Old Subjects', *The Architectural Review* (May 1911), pp. 274–5. I am grateful to Mrs Bess Stein for drawing this article to my attention.

Index to Marvell's Poems